KT-509-485

financing gender equality

Commonwealth perspectives

2007

Published for the Commonwealth Secretariat
by Nexus Strategic Partnerships

Financing Gender Equality; Commonwealth Perspectives 2007

Launched at the 8th Commonwealth Women's Affairs Ministers Meeting (8WAMM), June 2007, Kampala, Uganda.

The various Commonwealth declarations and statements are copyright-free, although the Commonwealth Secretariat should be appropriately acknowledged.

Text © Commonwealth Secretariat 2007 or as otherwise credited

Volume © Nexus Strategic Partnerships Limited 2007

Country maps © Oxford Cartographers

All rights reserved. No part of this publication may be reproduced, stored in a retrieval system, or transmitted in any form or by any means, electronic, mechanical, photocopying, recording or otherwise without the permission of the publisher.

Applications for reproduction should be made in writing to Nexus Strategic Partnerships Limited, St John's Innovation Centre, Cowley Road, Cambridge CB4 0WS, UK.

The information in this publication is believed to be correct at the time of manufacture. Whilst care has been taken to ensure that the information is accurate, the publisher can accept no responsibility for any errors or omissions or for changes to the details given. Views expressed in this publication are not necessarily those of the Commonwealth Secretariat or the publisher.

A CIP catalogue record of this book is available from the British Library.

A Library of Congress CIP catalogue record has been applied for.

First published 2007

ISBN 978-0-9549629-6-8

Nexus

Published by Nexus Strategic Partnerships and available from:

Online: **www.nexuspartnerships.com**
             www.commonwealth-of-nations.org
Telephone: +44 (0) 1223 353131
Fax: +44 (0) 1223 353130
E-mail: orders@nexuspartnerships.com
Mail: Nexus Strategic Partnerships
             St John's Innovation Centre
             Cowley Road
             Cambridge CB4 0WS
             UK

and through good booksellers

For the Commonwealth Secretariat

Marlborough House
Pall Mall
London SW1Y 5HX
UK

www.thecommonwealth.org

Printed at Nutech Photolithographers, New Delhi, India

Contents

Part 4

Promoting peace and democracy

Part 5

The role of the public sector

Part 6

Gender profiles of member countries

Part 7

References

Foreword

Rt Hon Don McKinnon, Commonwealth Secretary-General

Why a Commonwealth Women's Affairs Ministers Meeting and not a Men's? In essence, because half of the people on this planet bear considerably more than half of its problems.

Worldwide, two-thirds of those below the poverty line are women, as are two-thirds of those who cannot read or write. Girls account for nearly two-thirds of the 115 million children who are out of school. Half a million women die every year in pregnancy or childbirth. The face of HIV/AIDS is now that of a young African woman.

In the first decade of the 21st century women are still dying of discrimination – in our Commonwealth and beyond.

The 'gender agenda' goes further. It asks, for instance, why only four of the 53 Commonwealth countries have met our agreed target of 30% female representation in Parliament.

The issue of gender equality impinges upon everything we do. This is why we have developed a comprehensive *Commonwealth Plan of Action for Gender Equality 2005–2015*, which was approved by our Heads of Government at their last meeting in Malta in November 2005.

The *Plan of Action* sets out what we will do to ensure that gender equality is an intrinsic part of our work on democracy, peace and conflict, on human rights and the law, on poverty eradication and economic empowerment, and on HIV/AIDS.

In Kampala in June 2007, our Commonwealth Women's Affairs Ministers meet for the eighth time since they met in Nairobi in July 1985. At their last meeting, in Suva, Fiji in 2004, they approved the current ten-year workplan. Perhaps most famously, at their Fifth Meeting in Trinidad in 1996, they launched the whole concept of Gender Responsive National Budgets, which has now been adopted by 30 Commonwealth countries and 30 more beyond. The first task of these budgets is simply to qualify and quantify the impacts of different elements of national expenditure on both men and women. We now require that Commonwealth Finance Ministers report to us on this. The second task is to reallocate resources where necessary to benefit both men and women. In pilot projects (for instance alongside the United Nations Development Programme in Sindh, Pakistan) we are developing practical guidance on this allocation.

In Kampala, Women's Affairs Ministers will reaffirm that gender equality is one of the fundamental principles of the Commonwealth – both as an 'end' and a 'means' for democracy and development.

But they will then ask themselves a very difficult question. Why, if we believe this, are we not allocating sufficient financial resources to make it happen?

Because while the plight of women worsens, the money with which we can meet some of the challenges melts away. A 2006 research paper commissioned by the World Bank estimates a shortfall of no less than $30 billion for the year in the funds needed to meet Millennium Development Goal 3 on gender equality. On current projections, that figure will rise to $70 billion by 2015.

The irony, of course, is that all the tools are at the ready: our challenge is merely to mobilise them.

The Commonwealth and its member countries have already done the policy work to ensure that gender is recognised as a component of all government policy – on health and education, on business and on political representation. They have already produced the training manuals and capacity-building programmes to turn policy into practice; they have already developed the systems to monitor and evaluate progress.

So 8WAMM faces the fact that one of the biggest impediments to gender equality is lack of money. It will discuss national budgets as the primary way to deal with this. Further, it will share ways of making aid more effective and encouraging women to start their own business activities.

This collection of articles addresses 8WAMM's theme of *Financing Gender Equality for Development and Democracy*. It discusses the key areas highlighted in the 2005–2015 *Commonwealth Plan of Action*. I commend it to all Commonwealth Ministers responsible for Women's Affairs, and to all those who work with and for you. I believe it can inspire you all to bring political, financial and practical commitment to making a reality of gender equality.

At stake is the overarching issue, that men and women are born equal and must live as equals.

Nexus | Strategic Partnerships Ltd

Nexus Strategic Partnerships is an innovative force in contract publishing, event management and membership services.

With over 40 years experience of international commercial publishing and partnership marketing between them, the directors of Nexus Strategic Partnerships share a passionate belief that:

- Clients need cost-effective and high-quality vehicles that engage with the right stakeholders in the right way
- Commercial partners need opportunities to contribute best practices & thought leadership and drive global agendas

Furthermore, we believe that these key drivers are complementary, rather than conflicting, and our unique Partnership Marketing Model ensures that our projects exceed the expectations of both our clients and partners.

Contact us for more information on our unique approach

Email   info@nexuspartnerships.com
Tel   +44 (0)1223 353131
Fax   +44 (0)1223 353130
Web   www.nexuspartnerships.com
         www.commonwealth-of-nations.org
         www.cedol.org

Nexus Strategic Partnerships is proud to be associated with the **Commonwealth Secretariat.**

As well as publishing COMSEC's flagship annual publication – the *Commonwealth Yearbook* – we have also produced:

- The official publication for the 16th Conference of Commonwealth Education Ministers – 2007 *Commonwealth Education Partnerships*

- The official publication for the 8th Women's Affairs Ministers Meeting – *Financing Gender Equality Commonwealth Perspectives*

- The first officially supported web portal dedicated to promoting Commonwealth member states – Commonwealth of Nations

- An online community of education stakeholders across the Commonwealth, to share best practices and experiences, encourage debate and collaboration – Commonwealth Education Online

Introduction

Ann Keeling

At the end of 2006, the UN High-Level Panel on System-Wide Coherence recommended that the UN establish a new, independent agency for women. That landmark decision signalled a growing trend: the recognition that insufficient attention has been paid to gender equality and women's rights with very detrimental consequences for social, economic and political development.

Over the last couple of years several multilateral and bilateral development organisations, including the Commonwealth Secretariat, have reviewed their approach to promoting gender equality and asked whether gender mainstreaming inevitably means that gender equality and women's rights become invisible and slip off the policy agenda. Many of these organisations have concluded that this has been the case and some have shifted to a more explicit focus on realising women's rights. At the same time, the relatively new aid delivery mechanisms such as Budget Support and Poverty Reduction Strategy Papers are being closely examined to see whether the move from development projects to channelling development aid through these new modalities has further marginalised the views and the priorities of women. There is clear evidence that funding to women's rights NGOs has fallen dramatically in the last decade, diminishing their ability to engage with aid and other processes, advocate for gender equality and women's rights, and call governments to account when they fail to meet their obligations. We feel that the creation of a new UN women's agency demonstrates that the tide is finally turning and that the international community has recognised that there can be no development or aid effectiveness without gender equality.

The 'theme' of the 8th Commonwealth Women's Affairs Ministers Meeting (8WAMM) due to take place in Kampala, Uganda 11–14 June this year, *Financing Gender Equality for Development and Democracy*, is therefore very timely.

All these questions will be discussed both by Ministers at their meeting and at the preceding Partners Forum by representatives of civil society, the private sector, parliamentarians and young people. Ministers will also consider the effectiveness of the structures set up at national level to advance gender equality and women's rights. These National Women's Machineries now take quite different forms across the Commonwealth, from women's ministries to high level units attached to the offices of presidents or prime ministers, independent national commissions, and ombudspersons. 8WAMM will consider how gender equality is being financed (or not, as the case may be) and what structures and processes are most effective

in turning commitments made in conventions like the Convention on the Elimination of All Forms of Discrimination Against Women (CEDAW) and our own Commonwealth *Plan of Action for Gender Equality 2005–2015* (PoA), into real change and better lives for women. 8WAMM will give us an opportunity to share Ministers' conclusions with Commonwealth heads of government who will meet at the Commonwealth Heads of Government Meeting in November 2007, also in Kampala.

I hope you will enjoy the articles contained in this publication and that you will be with us (in spirit if not physically) at 8WAMM in Kampala.

Education – a lethal blow to AIDS

Today in Africa, it is vital for us to answer the call for a solution to the rising tide of HIV infections especially among the most vulnerable: girls and young women. With 75% of HIV positive Africans being women aged between 15-25 and with the rate of infection of young women and girls rising faster than that of any other group, we must address the root causes of women's vulnerability in a way that will not alienate women or their communities, but rather tap into their existing strengths.

It is no coincidence that women suffer disproportionately from HIV/AIDS. AIDS thrives among the poor and the powerless, and it is women who, too often, are the poorest. As the primary carers, women's own sickness and death is traumatic, but its consequences for their families and communities are even more so. Women in sub-Saharan Africa speak of their terror of leaving their children orphaned. They also say that they are frustrated of being told to change their sexual behaviour – change requires choice and they have none. As Mary Robinson, former UN High Commissioner for Human Rights, has said, 'Economically vulnerable women cannot successfully challenge male sexual coercion, violence or infidelity. They may have little choice but to transact sex with multiple partners for basic necessities, such as food, school fees or help with the harvest.' (Speech in Gaborone, Botswana, September 2003).

Initiatives that address the impact of AIDS in Africa must begin by recognising the causes of women's disempowerment and their roles at the core of the communities' social fabric. The education of girls is critical to winning the battle against HIV/AIDS. It is their right and it can open a 'window of opportunity' (Education and HIV/AIDS, World Bank, 2002). Education gives girls the tools and the power to resist sexual pressure, to delay sex in relationships and protects them from early marriage – all factors in the spread of AIDS.

CAMFED's programmes do precisely this and are the proof of the success of this approach. Our holistic programme for girls and women in Africa ensures that girls complete school and that as young educated women they become agents of change in their communities. We work with men and women, traditional chiefs, national and local government officials, national and international organisations, and young women from poor rural areas.

The ultimate proof of success is that those young women who have completed their education are now at the vanguard of change. CAMFED trains these young women in leadership, health and business and offers them the necessary tools and financial backing (through business start-up funds) to succeed. These young women, working in their own communities, are breaking the silence around stigmatised issues of AIDS-related

deaths and illnesses, sex, rape, incest and women's economic and social empowerment.

Simply put, the work of these young women is effective because they have the respect and trust of men and women who know them and who are desperate for real solutions to AIDS.

With the support of donors including the Commonwealth Foundation and Commonwealth Secretariat, CAMFED reaches hundreds of thousands of people in rural communities across Zimbabwe, Zambia, Ghana and Tanzania, and attitudes are changing. In 2006, we worked in partnership with over 20,612 community activists to solve problems that prevent girls from attending school; we have openly discussed harmful cultural practices such as early marriage, virginity testing and female genital mutilation with traditional leaders and those leaders now speak from their own platforms about the need for change; and we have successfully lobbied Ministries of Education to revise policy with regard to reporting and punishing teachers who abuse their students.

There is one clear lesson from CAMFED's work: education and empowerment of women are lethal to the progress of AIDS. If we are going to win against AIDS – and we must – we have to commit ourselves to the women of Africa today.

Ann Cotton, Executive Director
CAMFED International
22 Millers Yard, Mill Lane
Cambridge CB2 1RQ
United Kingdom

Tel: +44 (0) 1223 362648
Fax: +44 (0) 1223 366859
Email: info@camfed.org

www.camfed.org

CAMFED INTERNATIONAL

Setting the scene for 8WAMM

Sarojini Ganju Thakur and Auxilia Ponga

The rationale

The Millennium Development Goals define the development agenda of the 21st century. Apart from Goal 3, which directly refers to 'gender equality and women's empowerment', there are five other goals – relating to poverty reduction, educational achievement, maternal mortality, infant mortality and combating AIDS, malaria and TB which cannot be achieved without ensuring gender equality. Gender equality is also a human rights issue and has intrinsic value in the context of social justice. This is the background to the choice of this year's theme for the 8th Commonwealth Women's Affairs Ministers Meeting (8WAMM), *Financing Gender Equality for Development and Democracy*.

The meeting will address the theme from four perspectives. The economic aspect will be considered first. There is compelling evidence to indicate that gender equality can lead to poverty reduction and that it can be linked to economic growth. Numerous studies highlight the links between investment in education and health and economic growth and improved well-being. However, issues are interlinked and cannot be divorced from each other. While, on the one hand there is 'feminisation of poverty', on the other it is equally true that countries with high poverty levels often have a high degree of conflict, and experience demonstrates the centrality of gender equality for peace and security.

The *Beijing Platform for Action* and the Convention on the Elimination of All Forms of Discrimination Against Women (CEDAW) broadly map out the road towards gender equality and women's empowerment and recognise that gender mainstreaming is a means to this end. Most Commonwealth countries have committed themselves to achieve gender equality and this has resulted in the development of national policies for women and plans of action. However, national and state budgets and overall development plans have not reflected the same priorities. In other words, inadequate resource allocation has meant that these plans have not been implemented.

The context

The report *Gender Responsive Budgets in the Commonwealth: Progress and Challenges*, which was presented to the Commonwealth Finance Ministers Meeting in 2005, painted a mixed picture. On the positive side was the fact that in recent years some of the best practice and progress in gender responsive budgets (GRBs) has been in Commonwealth countries such as Tanzania, Uganda and India. But the other side of the picture showed that out of 53 countries in the Commonwealth only 30 reported any progress on GRBs, and that for the majority progress was extremely slow. Most countries were in an environment-building and awareness-raising phase and had not yet moved to the stage where they actually understood the impacts of budgets on gender equality and the importance of influencing them. Budgets are political documents and reflect spending priorities. Since achieving development goals depends on gender equality, it is clear that we need budgets to provide funding for attempts to move towards it. In 2005, Commonwealth Finance Ministers made a commitment to report biennially on progress made on GRBs, and the Commonwealth Secretariat's Gender Section is now compiling a report which will assess the progress made since 2005.

The 8WAMM theme derives even greater significance in the current context for aid. Aid commitments since 2005 have been scaled up significantly and there are attempts to improve the process and quality of aid. The 2005 Paris Declaration on Aid Effectiveness focused on the principles of country ownership, harmonisation, alignment and mutual accountability. But while a mention of gender equality is tucked away in one of the sections (paragraph 42), the challenge in the context of the new aid modalities – joint assistance strategies, direct budgetary support, sector-wide approaches and poverty reduction strategy papers – is to ensure that more resources are allocated for gender equality.

Reviews of gender mainstreaming in bilateral and multilateral organisations have also indicated the extent to which some of these agendas have become ghettoised within these agencies, or where there has been 'policy evaporation'.

This renewed focus on the importance of gender equality has led all major funding agencies to re-examine their strategies and devise new action plans. The World Bank has developed its *Gender Equality as Smart Economics* programme and the UK Department for International Development has finalised its *Gender Equality Action Plan*. The UN system has also recognised the critical importance of enhancing resources for gender equality and its high-level panel has recommended the creation of a single UN agency for women. With all these changes, 8WAMM provides Commonwealth countries with a strategic opportunity to focus on the critical subject of how to finance gender equality.

Programme for 8WAMM

8WAMM will focus on various aspects of financing gender equality. One session will focus on making the funding more visible and accessible through improved aid and fiscal processes. It will also look at the impact of the new multilateral trade regime on women, the need to enhance women's capacities to deal with the changing context, improved access to finance and the role of the private sector. It is hoped that considerations of these subjects will take into account the important recognition that has been given to equality between women and men for sustainable people-centred development.

The discussions in this session will focus on analysing economic policies and strategies with a view to encouraging more explicit attention to the promotion of gender equality in order to improve progress towards overall economic goals. This approach reflects the view of an increasing number of economists who have highlighted the fact that macroeconomic policies that do not take gender perspectives into account not only impact negatively on women relative to men, but also makes the macroeconomic goals more difficult to achieve.

The second session of the meeting will deal with the cost benefit analysis of mainstreaming gender in the public sector and the role of national women's machineries in achieving gender equality. The role that governments and the public sector can play in mainstreaming gender will be central to this session. Governments must ensure that the process of resource mobilisation and allocation is in line with overall development goals, including social goals, political participation and gender equality. The session will address the fact that it is not sufficient to plan, implement and monitor the various options from a purely economic standpoint. Social development and governance issues must be taken into account and questions of equality and equity should be high on the agendas of governments in order to achieve sustainable development from all perspectives. The cost benefit analysis of mainstreaming gender will be presented to showcase the way in which a gender equality perspective makes economic sense in development planning.

The meeting will also deal with the causes and effects of conflict; the gender and budgetary implications of these issues, particularly as they relate to democracy, will be discussed in detail and there will be a presentation of case studies that illustrate the costs of conflict. The disparity between the roles of women and men in decision-making and women's lack of participation in governance structures contributes to loss of finances; lopsided responses to conflict and peace-building processes continue to deprive countries of financial resources that could go into development efforts.

Because of their subordinate position in many parts of the world, women suffer more than men in situations of war and conflict. On the other hand, there can be significant gains for countries when women play a major role in conflict resolution. For this to become possible, equality and equity issues need to be central to all the processes in the political arena.

The final aspect that the meeting will address is the critical issue of HIV/AIDS and its cost implications, and the impact of these on gender equality. Are HIV/AIDS interventions cost effective and are they exacerbating the gender inequalities that already exist? Given both the social and economic implications of the HIV/AIDS pandemic, social protection schemes, particularly in developing countries, highlight the fact that more women than men are carers of people with AIDS. This means that they not only carry the burden of care, but also have financial responsibility for their family's survival. The implications of the important roles played by women in securing the continued livelihoods of families in contexts of considerable economic and social stress need be identified and addressed.

All these themes are central to development, democracy and the promotion of human rights. If they can be addressed in the context of how gender equality should be financed there is hope of achieving sustainable development through which both women and men will benefit. This meeting will therefore lay bare the consequences of failing to finance gender equality and will send a powerful message to the next Commonwealth Heads of Government Meeting that will be a turning point in financing gender equality in the Commonwealth.

tracking
the money

Financing gender for development

Debbie Budlender

Introduction

This article begins by outlining what have been described as 'landmark' developments in the area of financing for development. It goes on to discuss the implications of these developments for those interested in promoting gender equality. It considers, in particular, how gender-responsive budgeting (GRB) can be used to take advantage of some of the opportunities offered.

'Landmark' developments

Thakur (2006) labels 2005 as a 'landmark year' in respect of financing for development. The events that she sees as significant include the signing of the Paris Declaration on Aid Effectiveness in March 2005, the G8 meeting at Gleneagles in June 2005, the Commission for Africa report and the Millennium Summit outcome document. Thakur points out, however, that 2005 was also the year in which the target for the Millennium Development Goal (MDG) 3, to eliminate gender disparities in primary and secondary education, was missed.

The Monterrey Consensus of the International Conference on Financing for Development was reached in March 2002, with achievement of the MDGs as its core focus. The Monterrey document is very wide ranging. In paragraph 8 it refers to the need for 'a holistic approach to the interconnected national, international and systemic challenges of financing for development – sustainable, *gender-sensitive*, people-centred development' (emphasis added). The Monterrey document, alongside its many other calls, explicitly names the area of 'social and gender budget policies' in paragraph 19. Paragraph 64 calls for mainstreaming of a gender perspective 'into development policies at all levels and in all sectors'.

The challenge of the Monterrey document is that it promises too much. Thus it is important to monitor which elements of Monterrey are followed through and which are not.

The Paris Declaration on Aid Effectiveness was developed as a follow-up to the Monterrey Consensus and other international agreements. The Declaration focuses more narrowly on aid than the much wider-ranging Monterrey agreement. In particular, it emphasises management of aid, national ownership, alignment with national plans and objectives, harmonisation between donors, managing for results, and mutual accountability of donors and recipient countries. The Declaration mentions gender only once. In paragraph 42 it states, somewhat vaguely, that '[s]imilar harmonisation efforts [as those in environment] are also needed on other cross-cutting issues, such as gender equality and other thematic issues including those financed by dedicated funds'.

Gaynor (2006) notes that the focus of the Paris Declaration in the first period was on the technocratic and efficiency aspects of aid delivery. She nevertheless suggests the following areas of 'considerable congruence' between the Declaration and gender equality objectives.

- The focus on *ownership* means that the voices of local women as well as men must be heard and incorporated in plans and processes.

- The focus on *alignment with national plans and objectives* means that recipient country commitments in respect of gender equality must be reflected in donor funding.

- The focus on *managing for results* implies that results in respect of gender equality must be included in performance assessment frameworks.

- The focus on *mutual accountability* mechanisms must include accountability to women. In addition, monitoring and reporting should be done using gender-responsive indicators.

Implications of these developments

National development plans and national leadership

The concern over national ownership suggests that aid should be provided for implementation of nationally developed plans rather than of plans and objectives perceived to be imposed by donors. The high level and lack of detail of the national development plans nevertheless allows significant leeway to governments (and donors) as to what is done and which aspects of the broad objectives they focus on. This is an area where focused monitoring, awareness raising and advocacy by gender advocates could be important.

Many countries have provided for special initiatives to ensure that gender is addressed in their national development and sector plans, but mentioning 'gender' and 'women' is not in itself enough to ensure effective actions to promote gender equality. Some national development plans consider gender, or women, as one among a range of 'vulnerable groups' or 'cross-cutting' issues that should be addressed. The danger, where documents adopt these approaches, is that insufficient attention is paid to the differences in the situation and needs of the different groups. A further challenge is that where there are many such groups or issues to be addressed, it can easily become overwhelming for implementers.

Gaynor (2006: 11) quotes a DFID Commission gender audit in Malawi, which distinguished three different ways in which gender could disappear from the agenda, even when it is incorporated in policy documents. These are:

- evaporation, where commitments disappear at the time of implementation

- invisibilisation, where there are weaknesses in monitoring and reporting

- resistance, where those responsible see gender as too time-consuming or not particularly important.

GRB can assist in tackling all three of these. Evaporation and invisibilisation are at the heart of what GRB is set up to prevent in that GRB asks that gender be explicitly discussed and reported on in budgets and related implementation. Resistance can be addressed if GRB can be presented as an approach that is in line with, and adds value to, the new public finance management methods which are being introduced in many developing countries (see below).

There is also need for more thinking as to how national gender action plans relate to the other national development documents. UNIFEM (2006) notes that more than 120 countries have national action plans for the advancement of women, but that these plans are usually not properly integrated into national development plans and adequate budgets are not allocated for implementing them.

Schematically, two options are possible in respect of national action plans. The first would see gender advocates arguing for a separate budget to implement the national action plan. The second would see gender advocates ensuring that the activities envisaged in the national action plan are included in the country's sectoral and overall national development plans. The first approach might seem attractive to gender advocates who want a simple way to monitor what is being done in respect of gender, a clear focus for advocacy and the ability to claim credit for specific actions. Ultimately, however, the second approach may be wiser in terms of sustainability.

New aid modalities

Many see the core of the Paris Declaration as lying in its promotion of 'new' aid modalities. The most common forms of these new modalities include:

- a sector-wide approach (SWAp) where government and donors together develop a policy for a particular sector, and donors subsequently contribute to a single fund that is used to implement the policy

- direct budget support, which typically goes beyond a specific sector to provide funding in support of a national development programme such as a Poverty Reduction Strategy Paper (PRSP).

UNFEM (2006) warns that if an increasing proportion of aid financing takes the form of direct budget and sector support, there will be less opportunity for the special donor-funded 'gender projects' that have been used to address at least some parts of the

national action plans. The new aid modalities could, in this sense, worsen the situation in respect of gender equality.

Holvoet (2006) is more optimistic. She points out that programme-based funding should have a greater impact than isolated projects if one can ensure that the underlying programme is gender sensitive. She notes further that many of the principles and reforms underlying programme-based funding increase the potential for gender sensitivity and, specifically, for GRB. She points, in particular, to the attention paid in these reforms to the process of policy-making, implementation, monitoring and evaluation and 'inclusiveness'. The 'results orientation' and emphasis on evidence-based policy making also provide openings, in that GRB offers more concrete and differentiated evidence. Holvoet nevertheless notes the need for active and deliberate engagement by gender advocates and others to ensure that these opportunities are used.

Despite their signing of the Paris Declaration, most donors are likely to retain some portion of their funding outside gender budget support. On the one hand this provides the potential for gender-targeted financing. On the other hand, it also allows the possibility for donors (and governments) to 'do' gender in the form of such targeted activities, and then to feel that there is no need for serious gender mainstreaming in activities supported through general budget support.

More positively, non-general budget support funding can be used to support piloting of approaches (such as GRB) that will, after refinement, become mainstream.

Budget reform

Several elements of the Paris Declaration focus on the extent to which the recipient country has 'reliable country systems' in respect of financial management and procurement. This focus is clearly driven by the desire of donors that their money should be well spent, as well as concerns around corruption. These concerns can be used to good effect by gender advocates. First, reliable and honest systems of reporting, if they include gender-sensitive elements and provide for disaggregation, will give a good record of what is being done and achieved and thus indicate potential gaps. Second, reduction in corruption should leave more money available for gendered development purposes.

GRB initiatives have also, over recent years, increasingly engaged with the budget reforms that are ongoing in many developing countries. Typically these involve the introduction of a medium-term expenditure/budget framework (MTEF/MTBF) and some form of performance-oriented budgeting.

The MTBF element requires budgets to be planned over more than one year. This reform presents opportunities for gender advocates in allowing more time for lobbying and advocacy.

The performance-oriented approach is intended to ensure that budgets follow policy rather than vice versa. It requires that budget reporting includes not only the financial numbers, but also an indication of what was bought and delivered with the money. As a first step, budgets should reflect outputs, such as how many people were reached through various types of service delivery. Ideally, budgets should also reflect outcomes – the changes in the situation of the country's people achieved through the expenditure.

This aspect of the reforms also holds significant potential from a gender perspective if those responsible can be convinced that the output and outcome indicators should be gender-responsive, i.e. sex-disaggregated where they relate to individuals, and include gender-relevant indicators.

Monitoring, indicators and statistics

UNIFEM notes that the tracking of results-based aid at the country level is envisaged as being achieved through country performance assessment frameworks made up of a set of indicators based on national development strategies and programmes. The extent to which this is good news from a gender perspective depends on the extent to which gender has been integrated in the standard set of indicators.

In some cases the MDG indicators are used to track national development plans. This raises at least two problems. The first is that the MDGs are a generic set of goals with generic indicators. Unless these are adapted for a particular country, they are unlikely adequately to reflect the particular situation of that country. The second problem is the lack of integration of gender in the standard indicators for all but the third MDG and the goal relating to maternal mortality.

In order to have useful gender-sensitive indicators, there is a need to focus on both survey data (to describe the situation of women and men, and girls and boys in the country) and administrative data (to monitor what services government and others are providing). Administrative data are particularly important when engaging with budgets in countries where some form of results-oriented budgeting has been introduced, as these data are, or should be, the main source for the output indicators that are central to such systems. Some countries have now introduced specific requirements in their budget call circulars for line agencies to report on delivery in sex-disaggregated form. Agencies in these countries will need administrative management information systems that produce sex-disaggregated data.

Civil society

In most mainstream discussions about the new aid modalities relatively little thought has been given to the implications for the funding of the activities of civil society organisations (CSOs). Yet to the extent that civil society is often one of the strongest sources of support for gender equality, including providing gender expertise, the question of the impact of new aid modalities on civil society seems relevant. In addition, CSOs are often seen by government as parallel service delivery agents in areas such as reproductive health, gender-based violence and others. Yet the shift to programme-based funding combined with a focus on gender mainstreaming has tended, over time, to channel funding away from gender-oriented CSOs (Clark et al., 2005).

In some cases governments argue that all funding for CSOs in their country should be channelled through them, as the CSOs should be contributing to the national development effort and this should be coordinated by government. This approach can, however, constrain the independence of civil society actors as they will be wary of being effective watchdogs if by so doing they could starve themselves of funds. From a gender perspective, the experience in

GRB work is that the work is seldom sustainable without the active support and engagement of civil society.

Conclusion

Among donors there is much talk of the Paris and other declarations and new aid modalities. Such talk is probably far less common inside most recipient countries, except in very restricted circles.

This chapter suggests that gender advocates should, nevertheless, take an interest in these developments and learn what they are about and what opportunities and challenges they pose. For some countries, these investigations may show that the developments have little meaning and impact. For others, they may reveal important developments which gender advocates ignore at their peril.

In these countries, gender advocates need to acknowledge both the opportunities and challenges. The challenges must be recognised not so that we can bemoan how the cards are stacked against us, but rather so that we can plan how to circumvent the difficulties. The opportunities must be understood so that we can take full advantage of them. In particular, GRB and related initiatives can play a role in taking advantage of some of the opportunities and ensuring that the 'reforms' have a better outcome in respect of gender equality.

REFERENCES

Clark, E., Sprenger, E., Veneklasen, L., Duran, L.A. and Kerr, J. (2005). *Where is the Money for Women's Rights? Assessing Resources and the Role of Donors in the Promotion of Women's Rights and the Support of Women's Rights Organizations*, Association for Women's Rights in Development, Toronto.

Gaynor, C. (2006). 'Paris Declaration Commitments and Implications for Gender Equality and Women's Empowerment', DAC Network on Gender Equality, paper for consideration by the OECD-DAC Network on Gender Equality and the OECD-DAC Working Party on Aid Effectiveness, 6–7 July 2006, OECD, Paris.

Holvoet, N. (2006). 'Briefing Note: Gender budgeting: its usefulness in programme-based approaches to aid', EC Gender Help Desk, Antwerp.

Thakur, S.G. (2006). 'Putting development first: mainstreaming gender for aid effectiveness', Commonwealth Finance Ministers Meeting 2006: 84–86, Commonwealth Secretariat, London.

UNIFEM (2006). *Promoting Gender Equality In New Aid Modalities and Partnerships*, United Nations Development Fund for Women, New York.

DEBBIE BUDLENDER is a specialist researcher with the Community Agency for Social Enquiry (CASE), a non-governmental organisation working in the area of social policy research. She was the overall coordinator of South Africa's Women's Budget Initiative from its inception in 1995. She has served as consultant to NGOs, governments, parliamentarians and donors in countries in Africa, Asia, Europe, the Middle East and Latin America. Debbie has a BA Hons degree in Economics, an MA in Industrial Sociology and a BSc in Computer Science and Mathematics.

Development, aid effectiveness and gender equality

Sarojini Ganju Thakur

The Millennium Development Goals (MDGs) are accepted as the international framework for development until 2015. While all eight of the MDGs have gender-equality dimensions, it is clear that at least six of them cannot be achieved without integrating a gender perspective. Issues of gender equality, therefore, are central to the aid effectiveness agenda.

In March 2005, 35 donor countries, 26 multilateral agencies, 56 countries that receive aid and 14 civil society organisations signed up to the Paris Declaration on Aid Effectiveness. The Declaration focuses on improving the quality, management and effectiveness of aid and on improving its impact on development. It defines principles and processes – country ownership, alignment, harmonisation, managing for results and mutual accountability – to ensure that aid benefits those for whom it is meant. Its targets and indicators are also related to these aspects. The Declaration makes only a passing reference to gender equality (paragraph 42), and this is mainly in the context of harmonisation. Nevertheless, it offers a real opportunity, through its implementation and monitoring and evaluation processes, to bring gender centre stage.

It is, therefore, of particular importance at this stage to assess the manner in which gender equality is being brought into the implementation of the Paris Declaration agenda. This is both from the perspective of a continuous assessment of the way in which gender equality is being addressed, and also in preparation for the Accra High Level Forum on Aid Effectiveness, 'Assessing Progress and Deepening Implementation', which will take place in September 2008. This forum will assess how the principles of the Paris Declaration have been operationalised, identify good practices and problem areas, and chart the way for the remaining years of the Declaration's programme; in fact, it is a mid-term review of its implementation. It will also examine issues related to broadening participation, mutual accountability and the choice of aid instruments.

The focus of this article is twofold. First, it examines the extent to which gender equality has been promoted in the implementation of the aid agenda; second, it proposes actions that can be taken by various stakeholders to ensure that gender moves from the margins to the centre of this agenda.

The story so far

The last ten years have seen major changes in the way in which aid is disbursed. Project approaches found to be non-sustainable, donor driven and non-strategic have given way to other aid instruments This section, based on existing reviews and evaluations, focuses on the manner in which the new aid modalities and country-led planning processes promote or impact on gender equality and related development outcomes.

Direct budget support (DBS): In theory, DBS offers an opportunity to enhance policy dialogue between donors, civil society and actors, and the harmonisation aspects can increase institutional capacity for results-oriented planning and budgeting. In practice, reviews have indicated that equity issues are not automatically addressed. A joint evaluation of general budget support 1994–2004 undertaken through the Development Assistance Committee network indicated that gender was 'boxed in' rather than mainstreamed.[1] The first-hand experience of DFID advisers also emphasises that for DBS the principal interlocutors are usually the Ministry of Finance and Planning and that not only do the issues of social exclusion and gender take a back seat, but also the organisations that represent these issues barely have a voice in determining priorities.[2]

Sector-wide approaches (SWAps): The experience of SWAps is better, but the positive experiences mainly relate to education, health and agriculture. Initiatives like the Fast Track Initiative for girls' education also illustrate the nature of progress that is possible when donors come together to harmonise their work and align it with country initiatives. In other sectors, such as water, transport and rural infrastructure, gender perspectives are rarely integrated.

Poverty reduction strategies: Analytical reviews of Poverty Reduction Strategy Papers (PRSPs) highlight the gender blindness of the first generation strategies. A study of 13 PRSPs completed in 2002[3] indicated that while three were gender sensitive, eight dealt with gender primarily in a limited context, reproductive health and education, and two did not address gender issues at all. The joint staff assessments for funding were found to have only superficial gender analysis.

However, there are several examples where in second-generation PRSPs special efforts have resulted in gender being taken into account. In Uganda, as a result of a process driven by the Ministry of Gender, Labour and Social Development, a Poverty Eradication Action Plan (PEAP) gender action team has been established with membership from civil society organisations. In Pakistan, a special paper on gender was commissioned with a view to integrating its findings into the new poverty reduction strategy. However, it should be pointed out that the lapse between the original strategy and the introduction of gender has taken seven years.

Joint Assistance Strategies (JAS): JAS make it easier for countries to coordinate donor interventions and align them with national priorities, and to mainstream gender equality. In Tanzania, Zambia, Kenya and Ghana, government JAS are being or have been developed. While it is too early to assess their impact on implementation, resource allocation and prioritisation, it is clear that in these countries 'gender' is more visible that in the earlier aid modalities.

In Zambia, a pilot country for the aid harmonisation and alignment agenda, donor partners have supported the government in the development of the Fifth National Development Plan. Gender has been identified as a cross-cutting issue, but also recognised as a sector within the plan. The impact of this on implementation has yet to be seen. In Kenya, a Harmonisation Alignment and Coordination Group has been formed to draft a JAS. UNIFEM is working on engendering the process through the recruitment of a gender adviser.

In Ghana, various mechanisms are in place such as the Aid Harmonisation and Effectiveness Action Plan and a partnership strategy in preparation for the plan to draw up a JAS for 2007–2010. A Gender Equality Standing Team has been formed to harmonise an approach to gender equality and women's rights. Although policies are in place, resource allocations to the Ministry of Women's Affairs and Children are insufficient for it to influence the process. The ministry was not invited to take part in the JAS consultation processes and had to fight for observer status.[4]

Gender audits of donors: A recent review of the approach of DAC members to gender equality presented to the OECD Gender Network[5] summarised the progress thus:

> *Almost all DAC members have gender equality policies and many members have strengthened these policies since 1999. But almost none of them have the staff, budgets and management practices needed to implement these policies. Lip service looms large, practice remains weak.*

The review concluded that while on the one hand the MDGs had helped to focus attention on gender equality, the move to country ownership and programme-based approaches had made the promotion of gender equality far more dependent on country views. However, 'what partner countries emphasise often reflects the incentives that donors provide'.

The majority of agencies perceived the lack of concern of some partner governments as a constraint to official development assistance being used to promote gender equality. Issues identified ranged from poor participation of civil society organisations in consultation to the problems of conducting a dialogue on gender equality in a country where the issue is not a priority. However, at country level this is viewed differently. In Zambia, for instance, the UN is the lead cooperating partner for gender. This highlights two issues: first, the very important point made by a Zambian official about the 'low levels of interest exhibited by most cooperating partners in being selected to the gender cross cutting issue';[6] and second, that the UN will be dependent on other bilaterals to support this agenda.

National action plans for gender equality and women's empowerment

Since 1995 many countries have developed national action plans to promote gender equality and promote the implementation of the *Beijing Platform for Action*. This process has invariably been led by the national women's machineries (NWMs), which have inadequate resources and usually are not strategically located where they can have a significant influence on other departments and ministries.

From the above it is clear that from the mid-1990s onwards several factors have combined to lead to greater awareness, both in countries and partner agencies, of the need to promote gender equality for development. These include events like the International Conferences on Women and Development, Health and Population, commitments to the *Beijing Platform for Action* and CEDAW, and the adoption of the MDGs as the international development framework. Countries have developed policies for gender equality and women's empowerment, but this has not always translated into the necessary prioritisation and mainstreaming of gender into the planning process or the allocation of resources. In fact, most of the first generation PRSPs were completely gender blind. There have been more successes in specific sectors, such as education and health, but little effort has been made to track the impact on women of expenditure in other sectors, such as transport, water and sanitation. Among donors in the survey cited, only three (out of 27) reported that 'most' of their programmes take gender into account[7] – in other words that they have successfully mainstreamed gender into all their activities. The recent experience of Zambia and Ghana in the formulation of joint assistance strategies indicates that 'gender' does not appear to be a priority concern for external partners. The MDGs have created greater awareness of the need for gender equality, but they do not always translate into country-led processes. However, the neglect of gender mainstreaming can seriously jeopardise the achievement of development outcomes. For development, aid has to be linked to these.

Gender equality and development outcomes: strategies and opportunities

In the context of the transformation of the aid environment and the very significant scaling up of aid, the central issue, especially given past experience and the critical role of gender equality, is how to take advantage of opportunities and influence current strategies to promote and impact on gender equality for development effectiveness.

The next section sets out some of the strategies, priorities and opportunities on which it is important to focus in order to effect change within the framework of country-led harmonised processes for administering development assistance.

At country level

Participation of and consultation with organisations representing women's interests in all planning processes

In order to ensure that national plans and strategies reflect women's needs and interests, the systematic and regular participation of national women's machineries and civil society organisations in the planning processes (including PRSPs) and consultations is essential.

'Ownership' must include men's and women's voices. Women's civil society organisations have made a big contribution through analysis of the existing situation and have influenced policy changes. Examples are the Tanzania Gender Networking Programme in Tanzania, the Women's Budget Group in the UK and the Self-Employed Women Association (SEWA) in India.

While many countries include women, quite often the association is limited to specific sectors, especially education, health and welfare. But many other sectors impact on the lives of women, including transport, rural and urban infrastructure, and legal reforms, where there is a need for their interests to be represented. There should be participation at all stages – planning, policy formulation, programme implementation, and monitoring and evaluation.

Gender-responsive budgets

As increasing amounts of aid will be passing through the budgetary process it is important to be able to track the gender impacts of expenditure and revenue-raising measures. Analysis and tracking of the resources allocated for women's needs and interests, and assessment of their impact on gender equality, are critical for achieving development outcomes. In a way the importance of this has been recognised – almost 60 countries worldwide have adopted gender-responsive budgeting, and Commonwealth Finance Ministers at their meeting in 2005 made a commitment to report every two years on the progress made in their countries. Many countries are still at an initial stage of awareness raising and capacity building, but some countries, such as Tanzania, Uganda and India, have gone beyond this, so that the budgetary processes, called circulars, take gender into account. In some cases, analysis of the impact of user fees and land registration systems have resulted in policy changes that are friendly to women.

Capacity building of NWMs and other organisations

NWMs and civil society organisations that represent women's interests are not always well equipped to deal with issues related to macroeconomic processes. In order to participate meaningfully in some of the consultations it is important to enhance their capacities to enter into dialogue. For example, the Commonwealth Secretariat has launched a series of regional workshops on gender, trade policy and export promotion with a view to integrating gender analysis into trade policy formulation, implementation and planning. The participants include NWMs, trade ministries, Export Promotion Boards and civil society organisations, as well as multilateral and bilateral organisations.

Capacities also need to be strengthened for gender audit and monitoring so the capacity exists to contribute to monitoring and evaluation processes effectively.

Monitoring and evaluation of processes

- Improving statistical systems for generating sex-disaggregated data

The lack of information and availability of data on access to resources by women and men, and girls and boys often limits the design and understanding of various developmental issues. In the case of the Zambian Joint Assistance Strategy, strengthening the Central Statistical Office has been given priority. This is an area where development partners can often help to share good practice across the world so that time is not lost in re-inventing the wheel.

For instance, countries such as Australia, India and New Zealand could share some of their experiences of time-use studies.

- Impact assessment and evaluations

As in the case of the environment, systems need to be adopted that ensure there is a gender audit or impact assessment of all new proposals. In New Zealand, all cabinet proposals are accompanied by a statement setting out their gender implications. Indicators in national planning processing and PRSPs need to be able to measure progress against gender equality objectives to strengthen accountability. Joint evaluations and monitoring should build in gender assessments.

Public sector performance

In many countries, there has been tremendous progress since the 1990s. 'Gender' has entered the development jargon, but this has not been accompanied by the necessary attitudinal changes, mainstreaming and prioritisation in the public sector as a whole. The adoption of gender-responsive budgets and gender-impact assessments of all proposals would bring about some change in the public sector, but this needs to be accompanied by gender sensitisation across departments. In order to deal with much of the resistance that exists in this area and enhance accountability for gender equality performance appraisal it is important to make the promotion of and impact on gender equality a key parameter. Needless to say, this will depend on the political will.

For development partners

Influencing the Paris Declaration agenda

Multiple ways have been identified[8] to influence the Paris Declaration agenda. The GenderNet of OECD-DAC has been working very systematically on 'engendering' the Paris Declaration. It has pioneered and disseminated papers, and is working closely with other DAC networks and the working party on aid effectiveness, whose main remit is to facilitate and monitor the implementation of the Paris Declaration. A recent example of this was a workshop on 'Development effectiveness in practice, applying the Paris Declaration to advancing gender equality, environmental sustainability and human rights', jointly organised by these networks in Dublin in April 2007. The purpose of this workshop was to assess what lessons had been learnt so far from the field about the implementation of the Declaration, and to identify what needs to be done to improve its implementation for cross-cutting issues. There was a strong view that indicators need to be developed under the five principles of the Declaration to reflect progress on gender equality.

Peer review

The impact of peer review of policy and practice within donor agencies on the implementation of gender mainstreaming has been cited as one of the most useful mechanisms for assessing the progress and commitment of various agencies to gender equality in the aid effectiveness agenda. At the Dublin meeting it was felt that these should be systematic and frequent.

Mainstreaming gender within agencies

Donors need to work towards mainstreaming gender in their own internal processes. This means consciously working towards enhancing capacity across the organisation for gender mainstreaming, greater accountability for meeting gender equality objectives and increasing the number of gender specialists and financial resources committed to this. While gender responsive budgets measure commitment within countries, donors can apply the same principles to their own budgets.

Strengthening country processes and mutual accountability

Donors need to consciously support all interventions that will strengthen the commitments of countries to gender mainstreaming. It is also important to work together with the countries to meet broader international commitments and to ensure that gender equality forms part of performance assessment frameworks. The observation cited above in the case of Zambia suggests that mainstreaming gender as an approach in JAS has been problematic when it comes to implementation. In the case of Ghana too it was observed that:

> [A]lthough development partners in Ghana have adopted gender policies there is limited policy alignment among them due to differing political agendas. As a result there is an uneven level of commitment and accountability for gender-responsive development outcomes.[9]

It is clear from other cases that it is often easier to support gender as a sector rather than mainstream it.

Aid instruments

There is evidence, especially in education and health, of the effectiveness of SWAps and a harmonised approach, resulting in significant progress. Before the Accra High Level Forum in September 2008 it is important to evaluate the impact of different aid instruments on the promotion of gender equality. This will help in reviewing the manner in which resources are allocated for gender equality, and in understanding the importance of looking beyond the public sector to the financing of civil society organisations that work on gender equality and women's rights.

While the struggle to promote gender equality and empower women in development assistance continues and the approach to gender equality tends to be dominated by functional and instrumental arguments about how gender equality impacts on development, it is important to remember that gender equality is not a means of development. It is actually the end and goal of development. There can be no development without gender equality.

ENDNOTES

1 Gaynor, C. (2006). 'Paris Declaration Commitments and Implications for Gender Equality and Women's Empowerment', Paper presented to OECD-DAC Network on Gender Equality and OECD-EDAC Working Party on Aid Effectiveness, 6–7 July 2006, OECD, Paris.

2 'Aid Instruments: Social Exclusion and Gender', Background paper for DFID internal guidance on aid instruments, March 2006, Social Development Direct.

3 Zuckerman, E. and Garrett, A. (2003). *Do Poverty Reduction Strategy Papers Address Gender?* A Gender Audit of 2002 PRSPs, Gender Action, Washington, DC.

4 *Promoting Gender Equality in New Aid Modalities and Partnerships: Experiences from Africa – Burundi Consultation Outcome Report*, July 2006, UNIFEM.

5 *The Approach of DAC Members to Gender Equality in Development Cooperation – Changes since 1999*, Report presented at DAV Network on Gender Equality, 5–7 July 2006.

6 Written statement by Paul Lupunga, Ministry of Finance and National Planning, Zambia at 51st session of the Commission on the Status of Women, New York, February 2007.

7 Gaynor, C. (2006), op. cit.

8 Gaynor, C. (2006), op. cit.

9 UNIFEM (2006), op. cit.

SAROJINI GANJU THAKUR is acting head of the Gender Section of the Commonwealth Secretariat, and adviser, Poverty Eradication and Economic Empowerment. She is on secondment from the Indian Administrative Service (Himachal Cadre), which she joined in 1977. Her latest postings in the Government of India were as joint secretary, Department of Women and Child Development, and deputy director, LBS National Academy of Administration, where she worked primarily on mainstreaming gender training for civil servants.

Challenges to financing gender equality: a macroeconomic view

Mariama Williams

The theme of 'financing gender equality for development and democracy', which will dominate this year's Commonwealth Women's Affairs Ministerial Meeting, raises the stakes on gender mainstreaming and gender policy to a new level. It is asking governments to 'put their money where their mouth is'. This poses many challenges for governmental economic decision-makers: it will involve re-thinking and re-examining a wide range of decisions about economic management and governance.

The issue of financing gender equality brings to the fore at least seven underlying systemic challenges.

1. The need for a deeper examination of both the content and processes of the macroeconomic, financial and trade policies which shape the environment in which spending and financing decisions are made.

2. How to track money intended for economic development and poverty reduction projects and programmes, including opening up frameworks such as poverty reduction strategy papers (PRSPs) and raising the social and equity considerations involved in issues of debt sustainability; and the transfer burden of debt servicing, including how to distribute the burden more equitably.

3. The issue of gender and domestic resource mobilisation, including the generation and retention of national and domestic saving.

4. The domestic regulation and operation of financial markets and monetary policy.

5. The issue of remittances and private capital flows, and the issue of regulation of the capital account.

6. Official aid flows and the adequacy, responsibility and accountability of development cooperation.

7. The social content of trade reform, aid for trade and trade-related capacity building.

These are all issues that must be explored if there is any serious intention of financing gender equality adequately and successfully in the context of development and democracy. In this brief article there is space to elaborate only on some of the issues highlighted above.

The macroeconomic policy environment

Macroeconomic policy is often designed and implemented in a void without much consideration of the linkages and reinforcing effect of policy instruments on the primary and secondary incomes of citizens, especially those who have few economic and social resources. There seems to be a general lack of awareness of the critical role of social reproduction in the formal and informal economy. Macro policy designers at the World Bank, International Monetary Fund (IMF) and national ministries of finance often view their domain as a technically neutral, ultra-scientific space where they design instruments that have the precision of guided missile systems. For example, the public expenditure design of the medium-term expenditure framework which underlies PRSPs focuses on the links between 'inputs' and 'outputs', apparently shuttling towards politically neutral predetermined outcomes. But what constitutes the 'inputs' and 'outputs'? What are these outcomes, who or what determines them, and how do they take into account gender and other social dimensions?

In prioritising the objectives and targets of economic policy less attention is paid to how policy variables will impact on social infrastructure such as childcare and housing, and to the kinds of subsidies that could help to compensate for the structural and other changes generated by policy shifts that impact on the livelihood and adaptability of individuals and households in the care economy, and that may also have implications for micro-, small- and medium-sized domestic enterprises.

Fiscal policy has been shown to have asymmetric effects on women. Typically it focuses on ensuring the proper rate of growth of the capital stock. The general prescription of fiscal policy reforms is to offer tax relief to capital (either in the form of tax credits on structures and equipment or tax cuts on corporate income). In either case, this imposes an increase in the tax burden on the poor in terms of loss of benefits and earnings as governments reduce expenditure by laying off workers or cutting social expenditure. The reduction in social expenditure, which tends to increase the burden of social care in households and communities, tends to have a disproportionately negative impact on women, due to the unequal burden of responsibilities that women shoulder.

Women's primary responsibility for the household means that they must try to protect household budgets and ensure stable food management by increasing food preparation at home or seeking additional income to maintain family living standards. In addition, women are more likely than men to attend to sick family members who no longer have access to care. Women themselves are likely to be more vulnerable to declining health and rising morbidity because they have less food and more restricted access to medicines.

The burden of home-based care rests heavily on the female members of families. Research by UNAIDS has shown that HIV/AIDS increases women's unpaid work as women are forced to carry more responsibility for sick relatives as well as compensate for loss of income from parents, spouses or siblings who are affected by the disease. Yet fiscal policy does not attempt to take into account the externalities of such unpaid care work. A gender-sensitive approach to fiscal policy would seek to ensure the supply and quality of goods and services that would impact positively on home-based care activities (UNDP, 2004).

In general, the prioritising of the objectives and targets of fiscal policies leaves much to be desired. First, priorities are rarely open to discussion. Second, less attention is paid to how policy variables impact on social infrastructure such as childcare and housing. As a result, reform of fiscal policy has typically focused on measures to address budget deficits and tax reform in favour of business and capital. Nevertheless, there is a direct and reinforcing link between the budget and social policy. Restrictive fiscal policy measures such as the imposition of value added taxes or a rise in sales taxes on consumer items have a pronouncedly negative effect on social equity because these instruments impact directly on household budgets. World Bank research confirms that 'indirect taxes increase poverty due to their regressive nature' (World Bank, 2001: 70). It is also well known that higher taxes on consumer goods increase the relative price of such goods. What is less frequently acknowledged is that given increases in the relative price of consumer goods in the context of static incomes, women will seek to produce these goods themselves in order to protect their family's consumption patterns rather than purchase them in the market (UNDP, 2004).

Monetary policy has differential impacts on women and men in terms of access to credit for consumer durables, housing and investment funds. In the context of gender bias in the loan market, which may be coupled with gender inequality in terms of ownership of land and other collateral, high interest rates and tightened credit conditions that squeeze domestic investment are likely to crowd out women's demand for investment finance more than men's. Even in fairly stable and unconstrained credit markets women are at a disadvantage to men due to existing gender biases, low income (given a gendered segmented labour market and women's predominance in temporary and casualised jobs) and lack of access to conventional collateral items, such as land titles. The latter problem has historically shunted poor women into informal and micro lending. But a credit-constrained environment will impact on even middle- and upper-class women as tightened credit requirements, loan eligibility and higher borrowing costs come more into play.

Bakker (1994) has detailed the asymmetric impact of both fiscal and monetary policy instruments on women. The use of gender-sensitive budget analyses can further elaborate how the welfare burden is shifted from the capital budget to the social sector, and from the formal economy to the informal and household economies, with implications for women's labour, productivity and access to productive resources.

Debt management[1]

Conventional thinking on debt analysis assumes that the welfare burden of debt servicing affects men and women equally. However, it is now widely recognised that the adjustment burden of debt payment has disproportionately negative impacts on women, especially the poorest.

These gender-differentiated impacts stem from several factors.

- Societal and gender bias that ensures that women shoulder the primary role in social and community reproduction. Thus women are responsible for most unpaid work.

- Existing gender inequalities, such as access to land, credit, training and social capital, work to the disadvantage of women. This raises the issue of women's and men's different constraints in terms of opportunities, capability, security and empowerment.

- Gender bias in macroeconomic, labour market and social policies privileges men and male heads of households. This affects women's employment opportunities, their efforts to earn decent wages and gain access to adequate social protection such as unemployment compensation, sick leave, and disability and old age pensions. Women receive significantly lower wages than men for comparable work and are more likely than their male counterparts to work in lower-paid jobs or the informal sector and have less access to credit.

Research shows that in many countries women and children shoulder the main responsibility for collecting, storing and distributing essential goods such as water and fuel within the family and community. The PRSPs of Ethiopia, Malawi and Zambia made specific reference to women's 'water bearing burden', while others made linkages between 'reproductive health and women's water carrying burden' (Zuckerman and Garrett, 2003). Lack of easy access to water and fuel imposes a tremendous burden on women's time and their health, as they are often required to expend substantial amounts of time and energy in meeting these responsibilities. Contrary to conventional expectations, the privatisation of essential services, as implemented under structural adjustment programmes and continued within the PRSP and trade liberalisation agendas, has not improved women's access to health care and other necessities.

Trade policy, trade reform and aid for trade

Current approach to trade policy-making in Commonwealth countries is driven by trade agreements, negotiated multilaterally in the WTO and increasingly in regional or plurilateral fora. In general, most trade policy targets and policy instruments are focused on market access, with the presumption that this will generate the necessary employment. However, less attention is paid to the after effects of import liberalisation on the livelihoods of poor women and men. This includes the potential negative effects of liberalisation-induced fiscal and monetary policy on income and asset distribution. For example, monetary policy may support trade liberalisation by shifting credit towards the export sector at the disadvantage of the domestically oriented sector. This has implications for employment, business development and housing construction. Additionally, tight money policy has implications for liquidity for other sectors of the economy such as small and medium-sized businesses and the housing sector.

Likewise, the fiscal budget is expected to support different aspects of the trade reform agenda such as customs reform and trade facilitation efforts, producing a trade-off between different items and areas of the fiscal budget. As with general tax policies, discussed above, the fiscal effects of tariff reduction and the elimination of licensing fees have particularly negative consequences for social sector aspects of the budget.

The adjustment costs of trade liberalisation, whether under the Agreement on Agriculture (AOA), Trade-Related Aspects of Intellectual Property Rights (TRIPS), the General Agreement on Trade in Services (GATS) or other WTO provisions, have been a source of considerable tension in multilateral trade negotiations. The resulting impacts of these costs on development, as well as on social and gender equity, have also been a source of concern for those working on poverty eradication, women's economic empowerment and gender equality. As a result, over the last ten years increasing attention has been paid to the need for additional financing for trade and trade-related development.

To this end, in the Doha Round greater attention has been paid to aid for trade as a potential mechanism for redistribution and compensation. However, there remains some debate around this issue.

Aid for trade is relevant to the discussion of women's economic empowerment and gender and trade because of its wide scope, which ranges from the issue of trade policy and regulation, trade development and trade-related infrastructure to trade-related

adjustment.[2] In the area of trade policy and regulation, women, in their multiple roles as workers, community and household caretakers and business actors, are impacted by reforms of trade policy and trade regulation arising from trade-offs, trade disputes and the institutional and technical support that aims to facilitate the implementation of trade agreements. Women business owners, who are usually under-capitalised and have less access to finance and credit than their male counterparts, must grapple with complying with rules and standards emanating from changing trade policy and trade regulation. Likewise, women and men workers in the import-competing sectors are also differently impacted by trade rules that liberalise these sectors.

Ultimately, the macroeconomic, trade and debt management policy instruments and policy targets that are currently in vogue in Commonwealth countries tend towards regressive income and asset distribution, as signalled by persistent and growing poverty and inequality. This not only reinforces a false choice between efficiency and equity, but engenders commitment by governments to a limiting anti-poverty framework, which in turns muddies the water for gender equality, women's empowerment and community development.

Currently, there is very little interaction between macro-level planning, macro phenomena (fiscal policy, trade liberalisation, financial liberalisation and privatisation) and gender mainstreaming at the level of policy analysis and application. Thus at the level of the economy there has been less rapid movement in transforming bargaining power to determine or define the use of resources, resource ownership rights and control between men as a group and women as a group. Yet the public and private infrastructure available to individuals, households and businesses is critical in enabling individual functioning and capabilities. To the extent that there are adequate social (childcare and early childhood support) services and physical infrastructure such as water, electricity, land and housing, individuals and families have a good base from which to undertake the process of securing sustainable livelihoods.

Thus any economic framework for women's and community empowerment must focus attention on housing, sanitation, health care, education and skills training, with particular attention to unpaid work, the care economy, basic schooling, employment and enterprise development, and the development of public infrastructure within communities.

Likewise, the simplistic appeal to (micro-credit driven) community development must be replaced by a comprehensive and structural plan to eliminate public poverty and at the same time create the dynamics for generating sustainable livelihoods for men and women based on their strategic gender needs and interests. This is especially important for communities where the structural effects of a long history of neglect and abuse are pervasive.

Thus, there is a need to move the discussion and action agendas beyond poverty reduction to look at structural issues of inequality and economic injustice that reinforce old forms of poverty, as well as creating new types of poverty and inequalities. Gender equality must be reaffirmed as an end in itself and not simply a means to an end.

This will require a shift in perspective from seeing and treating the national budget as only a device for debt and debt services payment to re-integrating the social function of the budget. The focus of economic decision-makers must shift from the current over-emphasis on generating the primary surplus as the main target of fiscal policy towards more people- and gender-sensitive budgets. The targeting of the primary surplus has led to over-emphasis on fiscal restraint and decreased or stagnant growth. This has occurred even in the context of structural unemployment and low interest rates growth (Celasun et al., 2005; Marano, 1999). Tight fiscal policy has had significantly negative outcomes for policy options to generate employment and for the growth and competitiveness of the domestic economy. This means that more balanced attention needs to be paid to alternative options such as increasing public investment and lowering interest rates. This may mean reducing the primary surplus in order to create real resources for the economy.[3] Increasingly, research shows that a reduction in the primary surplus can co-exist with a reduction in debt (especially when there is a rise in GDP due to the relaunching of economic growth). This can also be consistent with debt sustainability.

In conclusion, shifts in macro-policy impact on the provision of care in households and communities. Caring for men and women in their various life cycles and in preparation for life in the labour market and as citizens who contribute to society is critical to overall economic development, growth and performance. Social reproduction, which has primarily been the work of women, is the life blood of the economy. Therefore, economic decision-makers should work to better orient economic policy to support social reproduction. This can be achieved partly by promoting access to

basic social services and the reduction of public poverty, and partly by directing shifts in the financing of social spending in a more balanced way in the allocation between different sources of revenue. In addition, in order to meet the needs of, and to prioritise, social reproduction, macroeconomic policy must have broader goals and an extended time horizon. Greater attention must be paid to the distributional impact and the high cost of pro-cyclical macroeconomic management. Thus, in order to be more effective for social reproduction needs, macroeconomic management should be designed to counter the business cycle's swings in economic activities.

It is only through such thoughtful approaches to the management of the economy that sustainable financing for promoting gender equality can be undertaken.

REFERENCES

Bakker, I. (1994). *The Strategic Silence*, Zed Books, London.

Celasun, O., Debrun, X. and Ostry, J.D. (2005). 'Primary Surplus Behavior and Risks to Fiscal Sustainability in Emerging Market Countries: A "Fan-Chart" Approach', IMF, 18 October 2005.

Marano, A. (1999). 'The Road to Sound Public Finance: Economic Growth vs. Primary Surplus', http://www.memo-europe.uni-remen.de/downloads/Marano_Papier.PDF

UNDP (2004). 'Costing the Care Economy', December 2004.

World Bank (2001). *Global Development Finance*, World Bank, Washington, DC.

Zuckerman, E. and Garrett, A. (2003). 'Do Poverty Reduction Strategy Papers Address Gender? A Gender Audit of 2002 PRSPs', Gender Action, http://www.genderaction.org

ENDNOTES

1   For a more in-depth discussion, see Williams (2003), 'Engendering African Governments, participation in the reform of PRSPs – how effective can this be in the service of gender equality?', http://www.bridg.ids.ac.uk/reports/CEP-Trade-OR.doc

2   Aid for trade is a controversial and highly political issue. The gains for women will depend on where the weight of the discussion and funding lands between the tug of war over whether aid for trade should be more adjustment oriented (dealing with balance of payment problems and revenue loss from trade liberalisation) or trade enhancing (dealing with demand- and supply-side issues).

3   Some models suggest that a 1% reduction in the primary surplus can yield as much as a 0.5% increase in structural GDP, in some cases higher. See simulations for Italy, Belgium and Turkey.

MARIAMA WILLIAMS PhD is an international economics and trade consultant and an Adjunct Associate at the Center of Concern, Washington, DC. She is a research associate with the International Gender and Trade Network, co-research coordinator, Political Economy of Globalisation (Trade), Development Alternatives with Women for a New Era (DAWN), and a director of the Institute of Law and Economics (ILE-Jamaica). She is the author of *Gender Issues in the Multilateral Trading System*, and a consultant adviser on gender and international trade to the Commonwealth Secretariat, London.

Strengthening the connection between gender and growth

Growth Team, Policy and Research Division, DFID

Following recent evaluations across the development community it has been established that a 'step change' is required in promoting gender equality. As the UK Department for International Development (DFID) puts it, gender equality is 'at the heart of development'. Such a move is necessary as gender mainstreaming initiatives often fall foul of 'policy evaporation', where good policy intentions fail to be followed through in practice.

This article, based on a recent briefing note,[1] sets out recent evidence linking gender equality and growth and looks at emerging issues for development agencies, including DfID policies and programmes.

Reducing poverty through economic growth

The UK 2006 White Paper *Eliminating World Poverty: Making Governance Work for the Poor* emphasises that economic development and growth are the single most important means by which poverty can be reduced worldwide. The most impressive examples of poverty reduction have been driven by economic development in countries such as Vietnam and China. While performance is less strong in Africa, it is still economic growth that is driving poverty reduction in many countries, such as Tanzania and Rwanda.

Evidence now points to the fact that gender equality is key to improving governance, environmental sustainability and education and health objectives.

Gender equality is both a cause and a consequence of economic growth. Yet many of our developing country partners often prioritise growth and economic development, seeing these goals in opposition or as alternatives to investment in issues such as gender equity. This article sets out how pursuing gender equality is linked to accelerating growth.

Key linkages

The evidence is clear that gender equality affects growth.[2] The following are the key links between gender and growth.

Gender equality improves overall growth: It has been estimated that between 0.9 and 1.7% of the regional growth difference between the East Asia/Pacific region and the Middle East/North Africa region can be accounted for by gender gaps in education and employment.[3] Is this sufficient to worry about? Put into dollars

lost it would seem that it is. If the countries of the Middle East and North Africa had the same level of gender equality in education as East Asia, their GDP would be between US$5.8–7.4 billion (1996 prices) higher and their per capita GDP would be between US$16–20 higher: for many of the poorer African countries this would be a considerable increase.

Investment in human capital and future generations increases: Improved gender equality significantly changes the welfare of the whole of society. There is good evidence that greater gender equality improves children's lives, which in turn improves economic prospects. Higher female earnings and bargaining power translate into greater investment in children's education, heath and nutrition, which leads to economic growth in the long term.[4] Investment in children's health, nutrition and education affects their future income-earning capacity. An increase in women's bargaining power in their households, their economic and social status, and the proportion of household assets and income that are under their control are all positive determinants of the human capital outcomes of their children,[5] and thus of future economic growth.

Education of women and girls reduces fertility rates: Less education of women and girls results in lower growth and is associated with low-income status. A number of factors are at work here which are difficult to separate, as the conditions which limit equality in education are often the same as those that that affect labour markets and women's economic participation.

Labour market participation increases growth: In many countries there are significant barriers to women's access to paid work. Labour market institutions – both formal, such as employment protection regulation and informal, such as job information networks – often operate to limit and reduce female labour market participation. This has significant costs to economic development.

First, unequal participation has a *direct* labour market effect on overall growth. Research found that in 2003 between 0.9 and 1.7% of the regional growth difference between the East Asia/Pacific region and the Middle East/North Africa region could be accounted for by gender gaps in employment in addition to education. The effects on growth were considerably larger when employment was taken into account.[6]

Second, limited labour market participation of women seems to have an *indirect* effect through reduced productivity of firms and businesses.

Wage equality is good for savings, efficiency and productivity: Micro evidence shows that more equal wages are associated with higher levels of household savings. In developed countries there is evidence that higher women's incomes translate into high growth from domestic investment, but there are few studies on this in developing countries.[7]

Business and enterprise need women's involvement: Barriers to women's role in business are costly to overall economic performance and are considerable in many countries. Often women-run businesses are unable to respond to emerging economic opportunities as regulations concerning the right of women to own assets and operate businesses in their own name prevent them from doing so.

Rural productivity improves: Greater gender equality is associated with higher agricultural productivity. Two mechanisms seem to be at work here. First, unequal access to the basic resources for production limits the productivity of farm units. Second, greater bargaining power of women within rural households improves productivity and decision-making on the farm.

Moving on: programmes, policies and interventions

This evidence points in a number of policy and programme directions. These areas are briefly outlined below. A key element in tackling gender and growth issues effectively is to understand the complex interactions between formal and informal institutions, market processes, social norms and culture. In general, successful interventions have approached combinations of issues and barriers to increased women's economic empowerment as opposed to single sector interventions. However, much of the evidence on policy effectiveness is at present impressionistic or based on small-scale programmes and limited data.

Closing the gender gap in human capital, providing incentives and opportunities for paid female work outside the household and reducing the time burden of female domestic activities should be pursued simultaneously. Knowing which incentives to provide and which public investments to promote requires an understanding of which *domestic* activities are responsible for women's time constraints, as well as both the informal and formal barriers to women's employment and entrepreneurship in the wider economy.

If development policy and practice are to respond to linking gender inequality and growth, an obvious first step is *gendered growth analysis*. But such analysis is dependent on *appropriate information being available*, and data availability and analytic coverage remain problematic in country level policy analysis and engagement.

Getting the best information and analysis possible considerably increases the chance of effective interventions – and this does not just imply quantitative data analysis. Linked to appropriate data is the need to *combine statistics with the views of men and women, as well as taking into account their interpretation of causal relations and solutions*.

A key part of the story, as we have seen from the evidence, is women's and girls' education. Progress has been impressive in this area and DFID is heavily engaged in girls' education around the world. Emerging lessons are that success in girls' education is linked to approaching enrolment and quality from a number of perspectives, including access, incentives, family politics and culture. While there has been considerable progress, there are signs that higher enrolment is not translating into marketable human capital and labour market participation to as high a degree as expected. Success in expanding universal primary education is putting pressure on secondary education, where educational attainment is actually falling. Drop-out rates in secondary education are rising, especially among girls.

Reducing the *time burden of non-paid or domestic labour* is key for economic empowerment in a number of settings. Reducing the time burden frees up women's time to engage in paid employment, improve the productivity of farm labour or increase entrepreneurial activity. Key interventions in these areas are likely to be:

- targeted infrastructure such as wells, energy (stoves, lighting, etc.) that improve access, reduce time burdens and increase ease of use of domestic services

- reducing the cost of existing infrastructure and domestic services to increase usage

- childcare schemes, which are often essential for labour market participation by reducing time burdens.

A number of countries have taken advantage of the link between *greater gender equality and its impact on fertility and growth*. Counties usually achieve this by:

- raising educational attainment for women

- free and easy access to reproductive health services

- removing incentives to have large families by way of credits or social schemes

- reducing cultural barriers to family planning.

Establishing *balanced labour market regulation and incentives to support growth, higher productivity, labour market expansion and increasing gender equality* is difficult, particularly as many women work in the informal sector which is hard to reach with labour regulation.

Experience seems to suggest that combinations of measures are needed to improve prospects for women's employment and greater equality in the labour market. Successful interventions aimed at reducing gender inequality in the labour market have been focused on:

- promoting women's education

- promoting export growth and foreign direct investment

- recognition of new, informal sector, workers' movements

- minimum pay legislation.

Changes in the welfare regime focused on directly encouraging women to engage in wage labour and market economies can be important. If social protection and other schemes become more common in developing countries, this area will be increasingly important. The connection between welfare regimes and employment in Europe has been studied extensively. For developing countries, this is less well-developed as yet.

In terms of reducing pay disparities there is also limited evidence. Legislation has had some effect in developed countries but the pay gap still ranges from 15 to 20% in Europe.

To support women's businesses and entrepreneurship both formal rules and informal governance must be conducive. Getting the legal and regulatory structure right is critical, but state enforcement is often undermined by long-standing social norms and behaviours. Actions taken to address land titling bias in some countries have taken the form of the removal of regulatory impediments to women's land ownership, awareness raising among both men and women of women's right to own and register land, and the removal of administrative obstacles to women's land ownership.

Another key barrier to the expansion of women-owned businesses has been lack of finance. Access to financial services and credit is still very unequal and is a major issue for women's economic empowerment and development. It is widely argued that micro finance schemes, frequently targeted at groups of poor women, can bring them out of poverty and enable women who would not otherwise be able to do so to start their own small enterprises. However, more recent analysis and evaluation has indicated that micro-finance has limited long-term impact on many of the barriers to women's empowerment; deeper financial sector reform to extend the reach of banking to women and poor clients may be a more appropriate and sustainable intervention.

Moving forward

DFID's policy agenda for 2007/08 consists of a mixture of gathering more evidence on the key linkages, testing core methodologies and approaches, and providing support to developing country governments and international partners to work on gender and growth. Specifically DFID will do the following:

- Take forward its programme of gender and growth assessments with the International Finance Corporation (IFC), the World Bank and others. DFID is currently undertaking work in India and Nigeria, and will be expanding into new regions this year.

- Support the development and refinement of new tools and methods for gender and growth analysis. This will include work with the International Poverty Center (IPC), the World Bank, IFC and others, looking at more effective and appropriate methodology to analyse gender and growth linkages.

- Examine further evidence of how social policy, including gender issues, affects growth prospects, and specifically how appropriate social policy can help remove constraints on growth and economic development.

BIBLIOGRAPHY

Bhorat, H. (2000). 'Are wage adjustments an effective mechanism for poverty?', Trade and Industrial Policy Secretariat (TIPS), 2000 Annual Forum, Development Policy Research Unit, University of Cape Town, Cape Town.

Blackden, M., Canagarajah, S., Klasen, S. and Lawson, D. (2006). 'Gender and Growth in Sub-Saharan Africa: Issues and Evidence', UNU-WIDER Research Paper No. 2006/37, UNU-WIDER, Helsinki.

Ellis, A., Manuel, C. and Blackden, M. (2006). *Gender and Economic Growth in Uganda. Unleashing the Power of Women*, World Bank, Washington, DC.

Esteve-Volart, B. (2004). 'Gender discrimination and growth: theory and evidence from India', Development Economics Discussion Paper No. 42, STICERD, LSE, London.

Klasen, S. and Lamanna, F. (2003). 'The impact of gender inequality in education and employment on economic growth in the Middle East and North Africa', Background paper for World Bank Study: Women in the Public Sphere, World Bank, Washington, DC.

Mazumdar, I. (2006). 'Impact of Globalization on Women Workers in Garment Exports – the Indian Experience', in Jha, V. (ed.), *Trade, Globalization and Gender Evidence from South Asia*, UNIFEM South Asia Regional Office, New Delhi, India.

Quisumbing, A.R. and De la Brière, B. (2000). 'Women's assets and intrahousehold allocation in rural Bangladesh: Testing measures of bargaining power', FCND Discussion Paper 86, International Food Policy Research Institute, Washington, DC.

Quisumbing, A.R. and Maluccio, J.A. (2000). 'Intrahousehold allocation and gender relations: New empirical evidence from four developing countries', FCND Discussion Paper 84, International Food Policy Research Institute, Washington, DC.

Schultz, T.P. (2002). 'Why Governments Should Invest More to Educate Girls', *World Development* 30 (2): 207–25.

Seguino, S. and Sagrario Floro, M. (2003). 'Does gender have any effect on aggregate saving? An Empirical Analysis', *International Review of Applied Economics* 17: 147–66.

Smith, L.C., Ramakrishnan, U., Ndiaye, A., Haddad, L.J. and Martorell, R. (2003). 'The importance of women's status for child nutrition in developing countries', in Quisumbing, A.R. (ed.), *Household Decisions, Gender and Development*, International Food Policy Research Institute, Washington, DC.

Thomas, D. (2002). 'Health, nutrition and prosperity: A microeconomic perspective', *Bulletin of the World Health Organization* 80 (2).

Thomas, D. and Chen, C.-L. (1994). 'Income shares and shares of income: Empirical tests of models of household resource allocation', Labor and Population Working Paper 94-08, RAND Corporation, Santa Monica, CA.

Tzannatos, Z. (1999). 'Women and labor market changes in the global economy: growth helps, inequalities hurt and public policy matters', *World Development* 27 (3): 551–69

Verschoor, A, Covarrubias, A. and Locke, C. (2006). *Women's Economic Empowerment: Gender and Growth: Literature Review and Synthesis*, Report to GIG, DfID, Overseas Development Group, University of East Anglia, UK.

World Bank (2006). *Kenya: Gender and Economic Growth Assessments*, World Bank, Washington, DC.

Zveglich, J.E. and Rodgers, Y. (2003). 'The Impact of Protective Measures for Female Workers', *Journal of Labour Economics* 21 (3).

ENDNOTES

1   DFID Briefing Note: Gender and Growth Practice Paper, March 2007.

2   Verschoor et al. (2006). This section of the paper draws heavily on this review, commissioned by the Growth Team in DFID as part of its gender and growth work programme.

3   Klasen and Lamanna (2003).

4   Thomas (2002); Schultz (2002).

5   See Thomas and Chen (1994) for evidence for Taiwan; Quisumbing and De la Brière (2000) for Bangladesh; Quisumbing and Maluccio (2000) for Ethiopia, Indonesia, Bangladesh and South Africa; and Smith et al. (2003) for a comparative study of the regions South Asia, Sub-Saharan Africa and Latin America and the Caribbean.

6   Klasen and Lamanna (2003).

7   Seguino and Sagrario Floro (2003).

Financing for gender equality: the challenge for micro finance

Ramesh S. Arunachalam

Background

Micro finance has long been considered as having its roots in the gender movement. While this is true of the evolution and development of micro finance in many countries, it is also time that we recognise a basic fact – micro finance, as it exists today, has more finance and less gender in its overall make-up.

If there is a single major recent trend in micro finance, it is the greater emphasis on enhancing sustainability and expanding outreach. Without question, the sector has come a long way – from a focus on implementing individual projects to a desire for the sustainability of micro finance institutions. As micro finance traverses this largely uncharted terrain, it becomes important to professionalise it so as to optimise its performance and achieve the objectives of sustainability, inclusive outreach and an impact on livelihoods and gender inequality.

This article attempts to provide a brief overview of recent developments in micro finance; discuss specific issues that need greater understanding from a gender perspective; highlight the gender challenges of micro finance; and outline some basic strategies and actions to meet them.

The origins of micro finance: a tool for women's empowerment

From the early 1970s, women's movements in a number of countries became increasingly interested in the degree to which women were able to access poverty-focused credit programmes and cooperatives. In India, several organisations,[1] with their roots in the Indian women's and labour movements, viewed enhancing access to credit as the key to their work with women workers in the informal sector. Micro finance came to be seen as the magic wand that would eradicate poverty and overnight empower women economically by giving them access to credit and then to financial services.[2]

Micro finance programmes that targeted women became a major plank of donor poverty alleviation and gender strategies in the late 1980s and early 1990s. With increasing evidence of the centrality of gender equality to poverty reduction, combined with the higher credit repayment rates achieved by women, a general consensus emerged on the desirability of targeting women. Not only 'reaching' but also 'empowering' women became the second official goal of the Micro-credit Summit Campaign. (See Box 1.)

BOX 1 **Characteristics of early micro finance programmes**

Several characteristics made the early micro finance programmes an attractive alternative in serving poor women.

- They provided services for marginalised and vulnerable people – their typical clients were poor women who needed access to collective bargaining through group mechanisms, did not have savings bank accounts, were often illiterate, belonged mainly to the most economically backward communities and were generally daily wage earners, piece rate workers, etc.
- They were perceived to be less intimidating and more accessible than formal financial institutions.
- They provided doorstep delivery of loans in many cases and doorstep recovery in most cases. This was convenient for the poor and for women, who were confined to their homes by household chores. It also meant lower travel and related expenses, all of which reduced transaction costs.
- Typically they did not ask for collateral, margin money or loan security: social collateral was substituted for physical collateral.
- Documentation was simple and informal, with loans being speedily agreed and disbursed. While it took many visits by poor women to formal institutions to obtain a loan and there was no guarantee that they would get one, just one or two visits were required to get a loan from a micro finance programme.
- Micro finance programmes provided loans with shorter lead times and could be easily accessed at all times, including emergencies.
- They offered credit at affordable interest rates, compared to local money lenders or formal institutions.

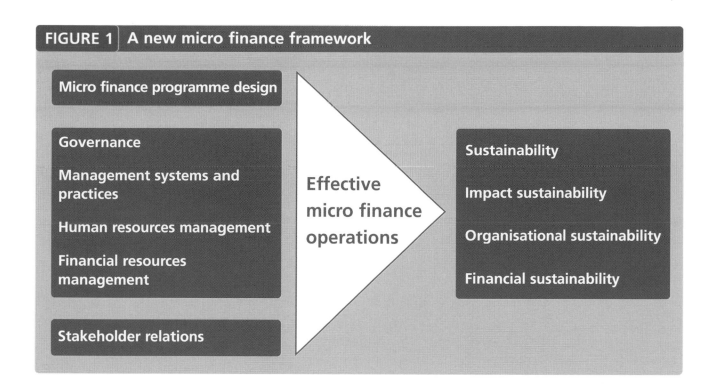

FIGURE 1 A new micro finance framework

Micro finance programme design

Governance

Management systems and practices

Human resources management

Financial resources management

Stakeholder relations

Effective micro finance operations

Sustainability

Impact sustainability

Organisational sustainability

Financial sustainability

Micro finance today is very different, as institutions are now being created to meet the twin objectives of expanding outreach to more poor people and enhancing the sustainability of micro finance institutions (MFIs). As micro finance goes to scale, institutions and programmes are trying to put adequate mechanisms in place with regard to various components – governance, management practices, human resources management, financial resources management, programme design and stakeholder relations, so as to professionalise the delivery of micro finance (see Figure 1).

This concern for a professional approach is the biggest focus of institutions and programmes, which see competence in the above areas as essential for scaling-up micro finance activities.

Growth trends, scaling-up and performance

Worldwide, micro finance programmes and MFIs have burgeoned over the last few years. As Figure 2 shows, they have enhanced their outreach over the period 2001–2004 in every region. This growth is visible not only in terms of the number of active borrowers but also in gross loan portfolio and total assets.

Government-sponsored programmes have also tried to enhance their outreach. The role of India's National Bank for Agricultural and Rural Development (NABARD) in multiplying women's self-help groups is a classic case of how a state-led mainstreaming strategy of linking women to banks has worked. Self-help groups in India are now a household word – many stakeholders recognise them as an effective distribution mechanism for the delivery of financial services to low-income people. (See Box 2.)

While performance in terms of outreach has indeed been spectacular, the financial performance of micro finance programmes and MFIs measured by their operational sustainability, portfolio at risk and return on assets has been equally phenomenal. Figure 2 summarises recent trends from the global mix market database.

The number of low-income clients who have gained access to financial services has risen; but two aspects require qualification. The first is the fact that there is still a paucity of accurate data on the absolute number of women clients and poor women served – both in the mix market and micro-credit summit databases. Second, databases use largely self-reported data and hence there are issues of double counting across levels of analysis and lack of confidence in the data provided by individual micro finance programmes/MFIs. Notwithstanding these data limitations, it can still be argued that micro finance has enhanced its outreach over the last few years and that its largest client 'segment' is women. Figure 3 shows that women form a large proportion of micro finance clients. This varies from MFIs with almost 100% of women clients in Asia to MFIs with about 59% in Latin America and the Caribbean. (See Box 3.)

Second, while micro finance has done well in terms of extending access to financial services to low-income women, its focus has largely been in terms of delivery of credit. Within credit delivery the focus, at least over the last few years, has tended to be on consumption loans and very small production loans. In reality,

BOX 2 NABARD

NABARD: the world's largest micro finance programme

As at March 2006, more than 33 million women have been linked to banks which provide them with financial services through 2.2 million self-help groups. Growth has been spectacular in the past few years: approximately 620,000 groups were set up in 2006 with more than 9 million women members. NABARD expects to have formed more than 10 million self-help groups by 2012.

Source: NABARD website

FIGURE 2 | Portfolio quality of micro finance programmes/MFIs across years[3]

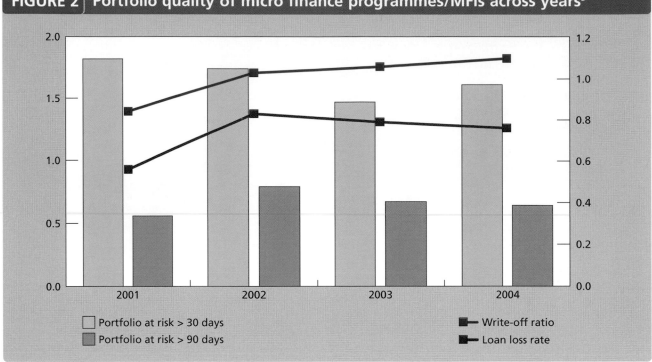

Legend:
- ☐ Portfolio at risk > 30 days
- ▨ Portfolio at risk > 90 days
- ■— Write-off ratio
- ■— Loan loss rate

several critical financial needs have yet to be satisfied. Hence, the gender gap in terms of access to other financial services, such as formal/flexible voluntary savings, health, asset, accident and life insurance, and larger production and livelihood credit, remains to be addressed.[4] (See Box 4.)

Thus, low-income women have a range of evolving needs as shown in Figure 4. They need access to a wide range of financial services, especially to counter the risks and vulnerability that they and their families face in their daily struggle for survival. Micro finance has a great business opportunity and social obligation in facilitating ongoing delivery of risk-mitigating financial services for low-income women on the required scale.

BOX 3 | Micro finance focus

Why does micro finance focus on women?

- Women have proved to be good clients and borrowers, at least from a micro finance perspective.
- They are considered as less of a credit risk: as a client segment, they have tended not to willfully default.
- They are perceived as an easy client group to handle.
- They are said to have immense savings potential.
- Working with women is seen as a great entry point to work with the household.
- Governments and other stakeholders, including donors, have specified working with women as an important agenda item and have incentivised some parts of this process.

Women's access to and control of resources

Large numbers of women have gained access to financial services such as credit, but the key question is whether they are of any real use. It is critical to look at what access to a basic credit or savings product has done for low-income women. Micro finance has four discernible broad level impacts.

1. It has enabled women to have a collective bargaining mechanism at local level.

2. It has enabled them to move out of their households and build relationships with various stakeholders.

3. It has given them a means of combating various forms of social oppression.

4. At a very basic level, the self-management that it has fostered has perhaps led to greater empowerment for some women.

Thus, while micro finance has brought women together and empowered them at a basic level, very little[5] is known about what it has achieved in terms of closing the gender gap in areas such as the ownership of and control over assets, control of income, access to domestic and community resources or women's indebtedness. Nor is it clear how it has affected women's productive as opposed to their reproductive role.

The picture that emerges almost three decades after the beginnings of micro finance may not be quite as good at a deeper level at it appears on the surface. While success stories are touted round every conference or seminar on micro finance, and very attractive statistics are reeled off, certain critical questions remain. Do women have adequate access to resources and finance? Do they have any real control? These are critical issues for true empowerment of women, as well as for sustained poverty alleviation.

FIGURE 3 | Outreach by gender

Outreach by gender of micro finance programmes/MFIs across regions and years[6]

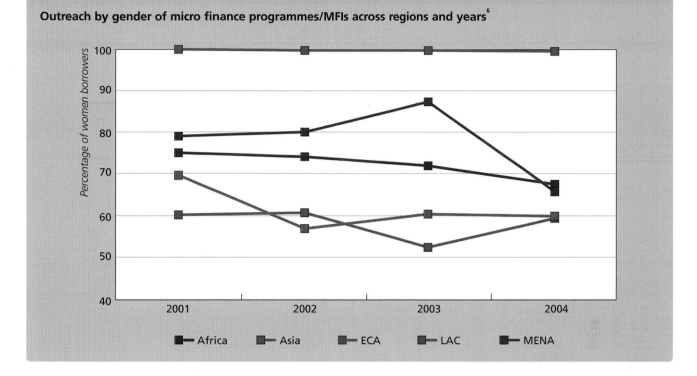

FIGURE 4 | Evolving needs of low-income women

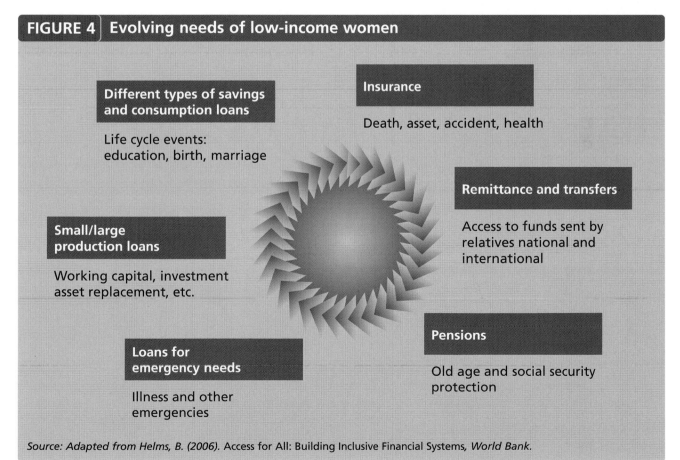

Different types of savings and consumption loans

Life cycle events: education, birth, marriage

Insurance

Death, asset, accident, health

Remittance and transfers

Access to funds sent by relatives national and international

Small/large production loans

Working capital, investment asset replacement, etc.

Loans for emergency needs

Illness and other emergencies

Pensions

Old age and social security protection

Source: Adapted from Helms, B. (2006). Access for All: Building Inclusive Financial Systems, World Bank.

Undoubtedly, poverty has a large gender dimension and any serious attempt to reduce poverty must be holistic and address its gender aspects. Mere provision of credit cannot tackle poverty unless it means that women have control over the income that they earn. There are too many instances of women earning the money and men using it to buy alcohol and for other indulgent purchases.

Consequently, while women have been extremely good clients for MFIs and micro finance providers as clients, borrowers and members, it is unclear whether micro finance has really been good for women in terms of financial, social and personal empowerment. Some of these aspects are mapped in Box 5.

Box 5 suggests that important questions remain unanswered, even in relation to women's access to credit. Have micro finance programmes truly guaranteed access to credit and financial services for all of their target clientele? While it cannot be denied that the micro finance sector has achieved some success in providing access to a considerable number of women, including those living in remote areas, it has only made a start. The number of poor people, particularly women, who are yet to be covered by micro finance is still large. This will continue to be a question for debate as long as credible gender and poverty disaggregated data on micro finance remain unavailable.

Likewise, the issue of control also requires serious attention. Are micro finance programmes ensuring women's empowerment merely by enabling access to credit and financial services? What checks are in place to ensure that the women who obtain credit actually have control over the use of the funds? There are many incidents where the end users of credit are men and the women are proxy recipients. Unless there is a significant change in perception, in the minds of the women themselves, of their rights and privileges vis-à-vis the men in their households, providing credit and financial services will only provide a veneer of empowerment and not power in the true sense of the word.

As Susan Feiner Drucilla Barker has observed:

The evidence on micro credit and women's empowerment is ambiguous. Access to credit is not the sole determinant of women's power and autonomy. Credit may, for example, increase women's dual burden of market and household labor. It may also increase conflict within the household if men, rather than women, control how loan moneys are used. Moreover, the group pressure over repayment in Grameen's loan circles can just as easily create conflict among women as build solidarity.[7]

This leads us to the question of what specific gender challenges exist for micro finance: this is discussed in the next section.

BOX 4 | The generic financial products demanded by poor women

Savings: Savings mobilisation contributes to an institution's sources of funds for on-lending, and is also a financial service that is equally, if not more, important to poor women than lending. In the absence of formal savings opportunities, poor women often pay depositors or store money in insecure places. The micro finance sector is still in its infancy in this area because of regulation in many countries, and simple/effective savings mechanisms are still in great demand.

Short-term finance: This is finance for working capital, such as inventories or (agricultural) inputs. Such short-term finance needs to be properly linked to crop and business cycles. The micro finance sector needs to provide flexible cash flow-based financing suited to needs of low-income women.

Term finance: Term finance, defined as loans with terms of around or over one year, may be used for equipment, improvements, livestock and tree crops. Term finance does not only involve loans, but also can include leasing. Term finance tends to be more costly and risky than short-term finance, since it ties up larger amounts of money for longer periods and requires the mobilisation of long-term funds. Again, these are required to meet the long-terms needs of low-income women as producers and owners.

Leasing: In a lease agreement, the leaseholder makes a regular payment for the use of the equipment, while the legal property remains in the hands of the institution. Due to the ready availability of collateral (the leased equipment), it may be an easier product to provide by financial

intermediaries than other finance, but its viability clearly depends on appropriate tax, legal and other incentives. Micro-leasing is now a legitimate product and it needs to be more generally available; it has great value in Islamic countries for low-income women and governments should create an enabling environment.

Money transfer for remittances: Income from national or international remittances is important in many developing economies and may sometimes be the principal source of income. Remittance monies can make an important contribution to consumption smoothing. Thus, efficient mechanisms for money transfers are widely demanded by the poor, and especially by women. However, care needs to be taken to ensure that access to remittance services will not be misused for money-laundering purposes. The micro finance sector has yet to make a significant response to this need. The product is also in demand for the transfer of money from urban to rural areas. Remittances are important in sectors where there is large-scale migration and low-income women need access to remittances as a survival strategy.

Insurance: Insurance products are in demand among low-income women. They include credit life loan insurance, health, accident, asset and other forms of general insurance, crop and life insurance. Experience with the performance of these products has been mixed. More importantly, they are not available on the required scale. Recently micro-pensions have also been launched. Such risk mitigation products need to be further refined and scaled up to meet the needs of low-income women.

BOX 5 | The gender impact of MFIs/micro finance programmes

Areas where strong evidence is available about the impact of micro finance on women

- Women in micro finance support other women – for example, by paying for missed loan instalments or compulsory savings
- Increased personal savings
- Increased confidence and assertiveness of poor women
- Greater respect at home
- Greater access to basic savings or credit at an affordable interest
- Experience in dealing with local government officials
- Enhanced self-confidence
- Better understanding and dealings with markets
- Improved knowledge of banking procedures
- Enhanced ability to understand accounts, interest rates, etc.
- Emergency coping mechanisms for women and families
- Pressure on banking institutions to improve services for poor women

It is unclear whether the following are the results of micro finance:

- Enhanced role for women in the community decision-making
- Freedom from tied and exclusive transactions with landlords, moneylenders, brokers and traders
- Improved food security
- Increased attendance at school for girls and children
- Investment in education by and for women and their families
- Investment in housing by and for women and their families
- Reduced alcoholism and violence against women
- Wider access to new resources and arenas

Areas where partial evidence is available about the impact of micro finance on women

- Women participate in community action on various social issues like tackling dowry problems or alcoholism
- Women learn how to deal with banks and the outside world
- Repayment of old loans by women and families
- Release from indebtedness
- Reduced abuse and injustice
- Pledged articles can be redeemed by women and their families
- Political participation of low-income women in local government bodies
- More interaction with local or other government officials
- More interaction with formal financial institutions and banks
- Increased access to timely and affordable credit in sufficient quantities
- Greater respect and support from women's husbands
- Confidence to participate in local politics
- Family members are happy because of the new support system of micro finance
- Enhanced incomes
- Enhanced ability to cope with emergencies at individual and household level
- Changes in men's attitudes to women

No serious evidence is available with regard to following as impacts of micro finance:

- Reduced workloads for women
- Women have greater control over their income and assets
- Greater control over spending patterns
- Increased leisure time
- Less time spent on monotonous work
- Increased ownership of other assets such as jewellery
- Increased role and influence in financial decision-making
- Enhanced women's influence on issues such as marriage and education
- Reduction in dowry-related problems and incidents

Gender challenges and micro finance

The first issue facing providers of micro finance is how to provide greater access to the vast majority of women who they are still not reaching. Even in countries like India, which have supportive policy frameworks, a large number of women are still excluded from access to a wide range of financial services.

A second serious challenge is that micro finance primarily targets women who already have very few assets. So from a financial standpoint micro finance, which increases *debts* for women, may, as Box 6 shows, be contributing to making their net worth *negative*, at least at a basic level.

A third challenge is that micro finance puts the debt and poverty burden almost exclusively on women, as it considers women to be less of a credit risk. In addition, micro finance has traditionally supported women in group settings – self-help groups, joint liability groups, solidarity groups, etc. – and has done very little to enhance women's access to the larger individual loans required for establishing and running SMEs.

There is also the issue of gender oppression. Most MFIs deliver financial services through field workers or loan officers, who are generally men. When male field officers deliver loans to woman clients issues arise which require urgent attention from a *consumer* protection and gender standpoint.

Most micro finance programmes work through group-based delivery mechanisms. These mechanisms place an extra burden on women in terms of attendance at weekly meetings, record-keeping and compliance on all aspects required by the self-help group/NGO/MFI. The net result is a significant increase in transaction costs. The question here is how women really feel about these activities. There is also an *instrumentalist approach* to micro finance delivery in the group setting. The women in groups, especially self-help groups, are used for routeing a wide range of

BOX 6 | Assets and liabilities, post-micro finance

Assets

- Post-micro finance, not much change in asset ownership for women within the household
- Cash obtained as loans is used for consumption and/or production
- Some automatic empowerment in terms of being a part of the micro finance platform – self-help group, joint liability group, solidarity group, etc.

Liabilities

- Increased liabilities
- Post-micro finance, increased debt burden for women
- Increased financial pressure for repayment, including onus and responsibility
- Increased vulnerability

government-sponsored development messages and schemes, and women alone shoulder the burden of work, saving and repayment.

A further problem is that people who belong to marginalised groups like Dalits, tribal and Muslim communities and migrant workers, as well as women-headed households are often unable to save or repay regularly – a precondition of most micro finance programmes. As a result, the poorest may be excluded.

It is therefore critical that micro finance providers address these gender challenges as the sector moves forward in its journey of empowering the poor, especially women. The needs of women are unique and they often face the *double* drudgery of providing economic security for their families and physically looking after their households. Micro finance must therefore rediscover its original mandate of empowering women. This is possible only if the various stakeholders participate holistically and resolve to address these gender challenges. There is a real need for gender-sensitive micro finance. Providing it involves the following.

- Establishing gender-sensitive governance mechanisms, including greater and real representation for women as directors and senior managers in MFIs.

- Instituting gender-sensitive management systems and processes at MFIs, including real transfer of authority together with responsibility.

- Helping more women to become a part of the micro finance human resource pool and providing special incentives to institutions that support this.

- Allocating the financial resources required for gender sensitisation of various stakeholders, including MFIs, regulators, rating agencies and others.

- Designing, testing and rolling out special micro finance products and delivery mechanisms suited to the unique needs of women.

- Evaluating micro finance programmes not just on the basis of financial parameters but also using social performance indicators that focus on women's empowerment and their access to and control over resources, and making these as important as prudent financial management in evaluating, rating and supporting micro finance programmes.

- Ensuring that women, who form the largest client segment for micro finance, are protected by instituting appropriate 'client protection' and 'client literacy' measures and incorporating these in the legislation that governs micro finance.

All this calls for the micro finance industry to provide sound, responsive, affordable and market-oriented financial services that are tailored to special and unique needs of low-income women clients in ways that are advantageous to both the women, as clients, and MFIs, as institutions. Only this will help micro finance rediscover its original and laudable mission of truly empowering women, the most vulnerable among the poor.

ENDNOTES

1   Among the pioneers were the Self-Employed Women's Association (SEWA) and Working Women's Forum (WWF) in India.

2   A large number of specialised institutions that catered for women's need for financial access were set up in the 1980s and 1990s, such as the Grameen Bank, Accion and Finca.

3   Compiled from Mix Market Data (2007).

4   While innovative micro finance/MFI programmes have delivered the same to selected clients, the larger and wider penetration of these services is still minimal.

5   While there have been some studies at local and country levels, these aspects need to be consistently explored and measured over time and analysed. There is a clear need to integrate GENDER and IMPACT data in management information systems of micro finance programmes/MFIs. This is currently lacking.

6   Compiled from Mix Market Data (2007).

7   Susan Feiner Drucilla Barker (2007). Microcredit and Women's Poverty – Granting this year's Nobel Peace Prize to microcredit guru Muhammad Yunus affirms neoliberalism. Website: http://www.dominionpaper.ca/articles/935

RAMESH S. ARUNACHALAM is a specialist in the financial services sector, rural finance, management information systems, micro, small and medium enterprises, and development. He has 21 years of direct implementation and field experience. The primary focus of his work has always been to provide pragmatic and innovative solutions that foster the delivery of a wide range of competitive, gender-responsive and sustainable market-based financial and business development services to low-income clients and women. He has worked in south Asia, Africa, Europe and North America (in about 200 assignments) with a large number of stakeholders.

Gender equality as smart economics

A World Bank Group Gender Action Plan

World Bank

In January 2007 the World Bank Group (WBG) launched 'Gender Equality as Smart Economics: A WBG Gender Action Plan' (GAP). The GAP is a four-year effort that seeks to implement the Bank's gender mainstreaming strategy (approved in 2001) in the economic sectors, where the Bank's performance in terms of gender mainstreaming has been weakest. This article gives the rationale and background for the GAP; briefly describes the principles behind and contents of the plan; and gives some examples of initial work under the GAP, highlighting work in sub-Saharan Africa, a priority region for the Bank. Since the GAP only covers the Bank's gender work in the economic sectors, the article also illustrates gender work in the Africa region in related sectors. Implementation of the GAP and, more generally, implementation of gender equality agendas internationally and nationally is not cost-free. This article ends with some estimates, based on preliminary data, on the financial requirements for implementing the gender equality and women's empowerment agenda.

Rationale

The business case

Gender equality does not necessarily mean equality of outcomes for males and females. Rather, it means equal access to the opportunities that allow people to pursue a life of their own choosing (World Bank, 2001). Ensuring this equal access to opportunities for women is intrinsically important – it responds to the principle of fairness and improves women's absolute well-being. But gender equality is also instrumental in reducing poverty and promoting shared growth.

A growing body of evidence shows that gender equality helps to reduce poverty and promote shared growth through two major pathways: (a) women's increased labour force participation, productivity and earnings as a result of better access to markets and more economic opportunities; and (b) the improved well-being of children as a result of women having better health and education and greater control over household decision-making and expenditure (see Figure 1).

While in the short run there are budgetary and other economic as well as political costs of promoting gender equality, in the long run greater gender equality can lead to more efficient economic outcomes, with benefits for poverty reduction and growth –

the major driving forces for the work of the WBG. Thus the conclusion that gender equality is 'smart economics' and the instrumental rationale for the GAP.

The gap in opportunities

The last decades have witnessed substantial progress in women's capabilities – that is, in reducing gender gaps in schooling and improving women's education and health status. Progress in expanding women's opportunities in the economy and in society has been more modest and is uneven. The share of girls enrolled in primary and secondary schooling has improved substantially in the last decade and is significantly greater than the share of women in non-agricultural employment and in parliaments.

The WBG's track record in mainstreaming gender in its lending portfolio and analytical work mirrors, perhaps not surprisingly, the comparatively slower progress in gender equality in economic and societal opportunities. The Bank has had considerably more success in mainstreaming gender issues in its social sector than in its economic sector operations. For instance, in the period 2003/5, 88% of Bank lending in the social sectors and only 69% of lending in the economic and financial sectors integrated gender issues in their design (World Bank, 2007a). Instrumental rationales and gender expertise have backed progress in the social sectors and are largely lacking in the productive sectors that underpin economic growth. In addition, the Bank's record is much better in mainstreaming gender issues in the design of operations than in their implementation; and it is weak in monitoring and measuring the development results of gender mainstreaming.

The GAP was, therefore, developed based on the business case of gender equality for the Bank's work and as an appropriate response to the gaps in progress in gender equality and the Bank's own performance.

Background[1]

Gender inequalities in the economy and markets are pervasive and constrain women's economic opportunities. In particular, women experience constraints to increasing their productivity and income in the labour, land, financial and agricultural product markets.

In terms of labour markets women face many constraints at home and in the marketplace when they seek paid employment.

FIGURE 1 | The pathways

Women's earnings, children's well-being, and aggregate poverty reduction and economic growth – the pathways

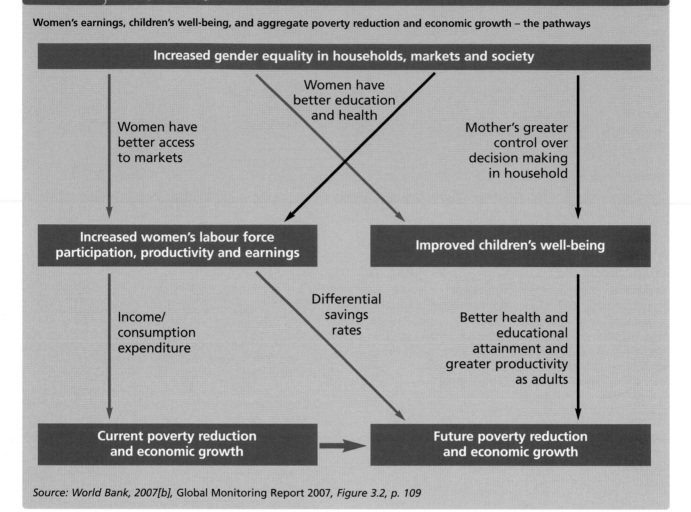

Source: World Bank, 2007[b], Global Monitoring Report 2007, Figure 3.2, p. 109

Numerous studies point to women's reproductive role affecting female labour force participation in general, and work for pay in particular. Besides childcare, women also face the time burden of domestic tasks, especially collecting water and firewood. In rural areas of Burkina Faso, Uganda and Zambia, the potential time savings from locating a potable water source within 400 metres of all households ranges from 125 hours per household per year to 664 (Barwell, 1996) – time that could be used to work for pay.

Wage gaps and discrimination against women in labour markets may lower labour force participation, both contemporaneously and for future generations. The contemporaneous effect occurs as the wage loss due to discrimination persuades some women to stay at home rather than engage in paid work. The wage loss due to discrimination will also cause parents to systematically under-invest in the education of girls relative to boys (see Anderson et al. (2003) for evidence on Malaysia).

With regard to land markets, the available evidence indicates that the distribution of land ownership is heavily skewed towards men. For example, in a set of Latin American countries, roughly 70–90% of formal owners of farmland are men (Deere and Leon, 2003). When women do own farmland, their holdings are typically smaller than men's. Similar evidence is found for sub-Saharan Africa (Doss, 2005; Udry, 1996; Quisumbing et al., 2004).

In much of the developing world, women's land rights are significantly circumscribed, if not in principle then in practice. For example, under customary law in much of sub-Saharan Africa, permanent land rights are held by men, typically male household heads. In contrast, women traditionally held (strong) usufruct rights to individual plots offered by men. These rights, however, are typically lost on divorce, widowhood or physical relocation.

In terms of financial markets, most studies find that women are not more likely to be rejected for loans or be subject to higher interest rates by lenders, but they are often less likely to apply for loans than men, partly because they do not have what it takes to apply (Baydas et al., 1994; Storey, 2004). Non-participation in credit markets can arise for two reasons: women may want a loan but fail to satisfy the loan eligibility criteria (for example, they may lack the appropriate physical collateral for obtaining a loan); or they may meet the loan eligibility criteria but have no need for a loan, so they voluntarily opt out. The former group is likely to be credit-constrained.

Agricultural product markets are heavily affected by technological innovation and adoption. Most of the evidence suggests that many of the barriers to adoption are not related to the characteristics of the technology, but originate in other markets relevant for the adoption decision, such as land, labour, credit and information. For example, Croppenstedt et al. (2003) find that female-headed households in Ethiopia have significantly lower endowments of land, and that land size is a significant positive determinant of fertiliser use.

Agricultural extension services also often fail to reach female farmers, in particular female-headed farming households, even though female farmers often indicate a strong demand for such services (Saito et al., 1994). Summarising evidence from six studies in sub-Saharan Africa in the 1980s, Quisumbing (1994) reports that male-headed households were roughly 30–220% more likely to have ever had contact with an extension agent than female-headed households.

Objectives and principles

In response to the above constraints, the GAP's main objective is to empower women economically by increasing their opportunities in four markets – labour, land, financial and agricultural product – and in their access to infrastructure. It seeks to 'make markets work for women' by identifying policy level interventions that will level the playing field, and to 'empower women to compete in markets' on an equal basis with men by investing in agency level interventions that enhance their access to infrastructure and these markets.

The World Bank's Africa Action Plan (AAP), initially developed in response to the G8 Summit in 2005, reiterates the central contribution of women to African economies, and now includes women's economic empowerment as one of eight flagship areas for increased focus. The GAP is a critical instrument to support the implementation of this flagship.

The GAP is founded on three key principles. First, it is based on financial incentives to staff rather than mandates to engender Bank operations, by providing leveraged up-front financial support. It requires matching contributions in cash or kind. The four-year GAP has a US$24.5 million budget to do this – half of which is expected to be financed by the WBG and half by donor agencies.

Second, the GAP is results oriented. It will devote resources to measure development outcomes and impacts. Third, it seeks to raise the visibility of women's economic empowerment for development globally and build international partnerships. In a meeting in Berlin earlier this year, German Chancellor Angela Merkel gave her full support to the GAP and promised to take the issue of women's economic empowerment to the G8 Summit, which Germany is hosting in Heiligendamm in June 2007.

Activities

The GAP funds activities in four categories: (1) activities to engender WBG operations in infrastructure, agriculture, financial sector and private sector development; (2) results-based initiatives – a set of policy and project pilot initiatives to increase women's economic opportunities in the short run that are accompanied by rigorous evaluation; (3) policy research on constraints to women's access to key markets, along with impact evaluation research and statistics; and (4) communications and capacity building.

In its first current year of implementation, most activities under the first category are concentrated in infrastructure and in financial and technical services for women entrepreneurs. Infrastructure activities span work in energy, transport, urban development, water, extractive industries, and agriculture and rural development. Activities in transport include analytical work in two regions to demonstrate how to design transport projects that involve women in road construction and to measure the links between infrastructure and women's labour force participation, and the design of a toolkit to scale up gender mainstreaming in transport operations.

Under the second category, three results-based initiatives are currently underway – in Egypt, Liberia and Kenya. The initiative in Egypt will promote employment and career development for women in private sector firms through a voluntary training and certification programme. In Liberia, a country that is rebuilding after 14 years of war and where food insecurity persists, a results-based initiative (RBI) will improve women's food production and marketing. In Kenya, the initiative will promote production and intensive marketing of crafts products for Masai women. The main executing agency for these RBIs is UNIFEM, working in-country in collaboration with national ministries and local agencies.

The World Bank has partnered with the UN Economic Commission for Europe and Central Asia and the International Labour Organisation (ILO) Statistics Bureau in selected countries to build national capacity to obtain more and better sex-disaggregated statistics, under the plan's third category of activities. It will lead the development of an analytical work programme to develop tools, methodologies and country cases addressing linkages between gender and economic growth at both macro and micro levels.

Finally, under the communications category, the Bank and its partners are working to raise international awareness of the importance of women's economic empowerment for development and will support capacity-building activities in gender and economics, for example in West Africa.

The following are some examples of GAP activities in Africa under the different markets.

- In product markets, the GAP is contributing to an analysis of the gender dimensions of competitiveness, as part of the Africa Competitiveness Report. Investment Climate Assessments in Cameroon and Ethiopia are tackling gender gaps in the analysis. Transport projects in the region have addressed the different needs of women, including domestic transport tasks, and lessons learned from these cases will be applied to a new transport project in Mali.

- In financial markets, the GAP will support the International Finance Corporation's (IFC) Gender Entrepreneurship Markets (GEM) Access to Finance technical assistance programme in Tanzania and Ghana, which will build the capacity of both bankers and clients to use credit lines that have been established in commercial banks to benefit women entrepreneurs. This is an integral part of gender and growth assessments in these and other countries, which examine legal and regulatory obstacles to women's entrepreneurship in Africa.

- In land markets, a gender component will be added to an energy project at appraisal stage in Burkina Faso, focusing on land

BOX 1 | Uganda: engendering poverty reduction support credits (PRSCs)

The gender-focused agenda of PRSC6, scheduled for Board consideration in April 2007, consolidates and expands on the actions launched under PRSC4–5. The programme focuses on: (a) supporting the mainstreaming of gender and equity objectives in planning and budgeting through further work to implement the gender and equity budget guidelines issued in 2004; (b) deepening the work programme on gender and growth linkages for policy-making in Uganda, with increased focus on trade issues; (c) further

implementation of the women's land component of the Land Sector Strategic Plan (LSSP), with particular emphasis on developing mechanisms for tracking the implementation of the provisions of the Land Act concerning family security of occupancy; (d) strengthening gender-responsive law reform; and (e) continuing support to the formulation and implementation of the country's National Gender Policy.

Source: Uganda, PRSC6 Programme Document, March 2007

tenure issues. In Ethiopia, a study will explore the productivity impacts of land certification and rental among female-headed households.

- In labour markets, a study in Ethiopia will explore factors constraining the productivity and availability of skilled female labour and limiting the earning power of women, and a study in Niger will address the relationship of high fertility with the labour market participation of women as part of the Multi-Sectoral Demographic Project (PRODEM).

In related work, the Bank is supporting the integration of gender issues into the budget support operations (PRSCs) in Uganda (Box 1), and is continuing an active 'gender and law' programme which has mobilised nearly US$7 million in grant financing in 13 countries to strengthen government and civil society partnership in engendering law reform, in legal literacy and education, and in improving access of the poor to legal services. Work is ongoing in Burundi, Kenya, Mali and Mauritania.

Financial requirements for gender equality work

While the GAP's four-year budget is US$24.5 million, full implementation of the GAP will cost significantly more. This amount will be used to leverage substantial additional resources that the WBG has available through its lending, including its soft-loan IDA window. More generally, gender equality work – that which seeks to mainstream gender issues in the social and productive sectors as well as specific gender equality initiatives – is not cost free. There can be substantial administrative, economic and political costs. Unfortunately, there are no reliable estimates of these costs, while it is safe to say that they are usually considered marginal. While gender mainstreaming interventions may in fact entail only a marginal change in project design, the process of identifying this change will often require significant investment. The lack of acknowledgment that gender equality work entails costs has probably affected the performance of countries in reaching MDG3.

TABLE 1 | Financial requirements for gender equality

Projected average annual per capita (US$ 2007) financial requirements to achieve gender equality (2006–15)

	Gender-specific interventions	Gender mainstream interventions	Non-targeted gender share	Total gender costs*	Total MDG costs	% Specific and mainstream of total MDG costs	% total gender costs of total MDG costs
Dominican Republic	$2.09	$7.52	$120.31	$129.92	$296.21	3.24	43.86
Ethiopia**	$0.13	$0.26	$35.24	$35.63	$115.07	0.33	30.96
Gabon	$6.38	$14.90	$71.48	$92.76	$173.62	12.26	53.43
Kenya	$4.64	$4.06	$41.08	$49.78	$141.95	6.13	35.07
Mauritania	$2.38	$9.78	$38.61	$50.77	$114.21	10.65	44.45
Niger	$2.24	$3.36	$43.19	$48.80	$105.44	5.31	46.28
Senegal	$0.00	$2.87	$8.60	$11.47	$83.25	3.45	13.78
Tajikistan	$1.50	$43.38	$61.27	$106.15	$170.49	26.33	62.26
Togo	$2.70	$7.05	$85.52	$95.27	$204.40	4.77	46.61
Yemen	$0.06	$5.82	$79.73	$85.61	$195.94	3.00	43.69

* All costs are based on average projected costs for the duration of 2006–15, provided by individual country needs assessments listed, and per capita costs are based on the UN 2004 population projections.

** The mainstream interventions for Ethiopia are under-reported for the health sector (since the MDG needs assessment results are not disaggregated for Goals 4 and 5 on child and maternal health). Similarly, the mainstream interventions for Tajikistan are over-reported to the extent that they include interventions to strengthen the primary health care system under the costs for Goals 4 and 5.

Source: Bahadur and Ebbeler (2007)

This section explores the budgetary requirements for gender equality work at the country level, using preliminary information gathered for the World Bank following the costing methodology of the UN Millennium Project, and complements this information with data from the OECD/DAC.

Methodology

At the outset, it is important to underscore the difficulties in calculating the financial costs of reducing gender inequality, since this inequality is both multi-dimensional and multi-sectoral, and efforts to reduce it must necessarily flow through multiple channels, not only those focused on gender. In addition, there is an inherent problem in assessing the amount of resources required for or allocated to actions that are mainstreamed. The more fully gender issues are mainstreamed into a programme or project, the more financial resources are mingled and the more difficult it is to track budget resources assigned to gender issues.

The UN Millennium Project developed a list of interventions for each MDG sector (education, health, rural development, urban development and slum upgrading, water and sanitation, and energy) and estimated the per unit capital and recurrent costs of implementing them. The proportion of the cost of each intervention that can be attributed to promoting gender equality was identified and added across interventions to obtain total costs attributable to promoting gender equality.

Interventions that promoted gender equality were divided into MDG3-specific interventions and gender mainstreaming interventions. In practice, specific interventions were defined as those implemented by the Ministry of Women's Affairs or a non-MDG sector ministry (for instance, labour). Examples of these interventions include monies to increase telephone support lines for victims of domestic violence in Niger, to alleviate the burdens of female-headed households in Ethiopia and setting a minimum age of marriage in Mauritania. Interventions directed at women in all other MDG sectors were defined as gender mainstreamed interventions. Examples include increases in health budget allocations for free pre-natal care in Tajikistan, as well as resources to increase land access for women in Senegal and female literacy rates in Ethiopia. Annex 1 gives a list of gender-specific and gender mainstreamed interventions and their estimated total and per capita annual costs.

It is important to note, however, that this usage is slightly different from the common definition, where 'gender-specific' refers to a 'stand-alone' intervention and 'gender mainstreamed' to an action integrated into a larger project, independent of the nature of the executing agency. In addition, the costs of other MDG interventions which were neither gender specific nor gender mainstreamed, but could indirectly promote gender equality, such as monies for new wells or rural roads, were also estimated.

Estimates

Table 1 presents projected average annual per capita (US$ 2007) financial requirements to achieve gender equality in 2006–15 for ten countries, which were involved in the UN Millennium planning exercise (Bahadur and Ebbeler, 2007).

The variation in costs for individual countries may partly be a function of underestimating or overestimating costs because of reduced capacity to account for and disaggregate costs by gender. Nevertheless, excluding outlier values, overall planned costs for gender-specific and gender mainstreamed interventions vary annually between US$36–130 per capita (in US$ 2007) and between 3–26% of total MDG costs. When the share of MDG interventions indirectly benefiting women is added, annual costs increase to US$105–296 per capita and to 30–62% of all MDG costs. This exercise makes the obvious but often ignored point that achieving MDG3 costs money. It also shows that planned gender-specific and gender mainstreamed interventions are only a small proportion of all MDG costs.

A desk exercise using the same methodology for five countries came up with comparable numbers but within a lower range – values did not increase as much as those done by the countries themselves. This exercise estimated the financing low-income countries would need in order to implement gender-specific and gender mainstreamed interventions for 2006–15. This value varied between US$29.7 billion in 2006 and US$83.2 billion in 2015, with a yearly average of US$47.5 billion (in 2003 dollars) for all low-income countries (Grown et al., 2006).

To give a sense of how large the financing gap is, the OECD/DAC gender marker showed that average annual commitments of bilateral overseas development assistance (ODA) for gender equality were US$5 billion in 2001–2005 – or 20% of the total ODA disbursed. These numbers are based on only 60% of the total reported bilateral ODA that is allocable by sector. The financing gap of US$24.7 billion could be considerably reduced by adding the 40% remaining ODA, as well as resources from the multilateral system, national governments and private foundations, if they all contributed to MDG3 with a similar proportion of available funds.

In addition to the planned national cost estimates, follow-up preliminary information is available for three countries (Dominican Republic, Kenya and Yemen) on actual expenditures for gender interventions. Despite progress in incorporating gender needs into the budget process in these countries, only a small proportion of planned expenditures for gender-specific action has translated into actual identified disbursements (on average, less than 15%). This low proportion is partly the result of the inability of national systems to disaggregate budget resources by gender, and does not mean that these countries are doing only 15% of what they planned. It is also the result of countries' slow progress in implementing the gender equality agenda. Countries are making progress, but in small incremental steps, while the challenge of MDG3 is one of intensifying and scaling-up gender equality actions throughout.

Conclusion

By emphasising gender equality as smart economics, the WBG Gender Action Plan shifts the focus of gender work onto the economic sectors. It provides an impetus to address women's economic empowerment in four key markets as essential to implementing MDG3. By providing incentive-based funding, it aims to catalyse a strong response both in the Bank and in countries to engender operational work, to support results-based initiatives, to carry out pioneering research and analysis, and to establish mechanisms for monitoring progress and performance.

This article was prepared on behalf of the World Bank by Mayra Buvinic and Mark Blackden, with the assistance of Ursula Casabonne.

BIBLIOGRAPHY

Agarwal, B. (1994). 'Gender and command over property: A critical gap in economic analysis and policy in South Asia', *World Development* 22: 1455–78.

Anderson, K., King, E.M. and Wang, Y. (2003). 'Market returns, transfers and demand for schooling in Malaysia, 1976–89', *Journal of Development Studies* 39 (3): 1–28.

Bahadur, C. and Ebbeler, J. (2007). 'Scaling up interventions to achieve gender equity: The impact of gender interventions in Millennium Development Goals needs assessment on national budget allocations', Draft paper, World Bank, Washington, DC.

Barwell, I. (1996). 'Transport and the village: Fundings from African village-level travel and transport surveys and related studies', World Bank Discussion Paper No. 344, Africa Region Series, World Bank, Washington, DC.

Baydas, M.M., Meyer, R.L. and Aguilera-Alfred, N. (1994). 'Discrimination against women in formal credit markets: Reality or rhetoric', *World Development* 22: 1073–82.

Buvinic, M. and Berger, M. (1990). 'Sex differences in access to a small enterprise development fund in Peru', *World Development* 18: 695–705.

Croppenstedt, A., Demeke, M. and Meschi, M.M. (2003). 'Technology adoption in the presence of constraints: The case of fertilizer demand in Ethiopia', *Review of Development Economics* 7: 58–70.

Deere, C.D. and Leon, M. (2003). 'The gender asset gap: Land in Latin America', *World Development* 31: 925–47.

Doss, C. and Morris, M.L. (2001). 'How does gender affect the adoption of agricultural technologies? The case of improved maize technology in Ghana', *Agricultural Economics* 25: 27–39.

Doss, C. (2005). 'The effects of intrahousehold property ownership on expenditure patterns in Ghana', *Journal of African Economies* 15: 149–80.

Grown, C., Bahadur, C., Handbury, J. and Elson, D. (2006). *The Financial Requirements of Achieving Gender Equality and Women's Empowerment*, World Bank, Washington, DC.

Kevane, M. and Gray, L.C. (1999). 'A women's field is made at night: Gendered land rights and norms in Burkina Faso', *Feminist Economics* 5: 1–26.

Lastarria-Cornheil, S. (1997). 'Impact of privatization on gender and property rights in Africa', *World Development* 25 (8): 1317–33.

Morrison, A. and Lamana, F. (2006). 'Gender issues in the Kyrgyz labor market', background paper for Kyrgyz Poverty Assessment, World Bank, Washington, DC.

Morrison, A.D.R. Raju, D. and Sinha, N. (2007). 'Gender equality, poverty and economic growth', background paper for the World Bank's *Global Monitoring Report* 2007, World Bank, Washington, DC.

Quisumbing, A.R. (1994). 'Improving women's agricultural productivity as farmers and workers', World Bank Education and Social Policy Department Discussion Paper 37, World Bank, Washington, DC.

Quisumbing, A.R., Estudillo, J.P. and Otsuka, K. (2004). *Land and Schooling: Transferring Wealth Across Generations*, Johns Hopkins University Press, Baltimore, MD.

Raturi, M. and Swamy, A.V. (1999). 'Explaining ethnic differentials in credit market outcomes in Zimbabwe', *Economic Development and Cultural Change* 47: 585–604.

Saito, K.A., Mekonnen, H. and Spurling, D. (1994). 'Raising the productivity of women farmers in sub-Saharan Africa', World Bank Discussion Paper 230, World Bank, Washington, DC

Storey, D.J. (2004). 'Racial and gender discrimination in the micro firm credit market? Evidence from Trinidad and Tobago', *Small Business Economics* 23 (5): 401–22.

Udry, C. (1996). 'Gender, agricultural production, and the theory of the household', *Journal of Political Economy* 104: 1010–46.

World Bank (2001). *Engendering development: Through gender equality in rights, resources, and voice*, Oxford University Press, New York.

World Bank (2007a). *Implementing the Bank's Gender Mainstreaming Strategy: Annual Monitoring Report for FY06*, forthcoming, World Bank, Washington, DC.

World Bank (2007b). *Global Monitoring Report 2007*, Washington, DC.

ENDNOTE

1   This section is extracted from Morrison, Raju and Sinha (2007).

ANNEX 1 | Proposed budget allocations

Country examples of proposed budget allocations for scaling up gender specific and mainstream interventions

Intervention	Country	Average annual cost in 2007 US$ millions (2006–15)	Average annual cost per capita in 2007 US$ (2006–15)
Gender-specific			
Eliminate gender-based violence through raising awareness, abuse hotlines, temporary housing for victims, and sensitivity training for police and military	Dominican Republic	$12.98	$1.36
Strengthen institutions to mainstream gender, defend equal rights to property and inheritance, and promote equal employment opportunities	Dominican Republic	$4.29	$0.45
Fight HIV/AIDS among female sex workers	Gabon	$1.60	$1.04
Strengthen ministries and government agencies to handle gender issues and implement international agreements on ending gender discrimination	Kenya	$52.30	$1.32
Build coalitions and mobilise community to ensure women's participation in political and economic affairs and raise awareness on reproductive rights and violence	Kenya	$62.50	$1.58
Support set up of data systems and increase data collection of sex-disaggregated information to monitor progress towards the gender equality goal	Kenya	$26.10	$0.66
Promote awareness of women's rights to legal redress and state services and improve state responsiveness to incidence of violence and victim rehabilitation	Kenya	$24.10	$0.61
Transition of secondary school girl graduates to vocational training and work place	Niger	$35.70	$2.13
Gender mainstream			
Construct 30 new and rehabilitate 43 child daycare centres, and construct emergency and community care shelters	Dominican Republic	$1.56	$0.16
Provide subsidies to mothers with children in pre-primary, primary and secondary school	Dominican Republic	$17.05	$1.78
Provide emergency obstetric care, capacity-building for public health staff, and antenatal and newborn care to reduce maternal mortality by three-quarters	Dominican Republic	$10.06	$1.05
Provide energy subsidies to female-headed households to facilitate income generation through biomass and renewable energy, petroleum and electricity	Kenya	$95.42	$2.41
Decrease maternal mortality through family planning for women and teens, management of malaria and anaemia in pregnancy and emergency obstetrics	Senegal	$9.85	$0.74
Increase micro-credit programmes for small farmers targeted specifically at women	Tajikistan	$5.65	$0.81
Free school lunch targeted to girls of poor families in primary grades 1–4	Tajikistan	$14.55	$2.08
Re-enrollment of mothers in primary and secondary education, who could not previously continue their education due to marriage or birth	Togo	$10.30	$1.45
Increase female medical staff recruitment, upgrade clinics with comprehensive obstetric care, increase medical coverage of deliveries and provide family planning	Yemen	$75.50	$3.03

Source: Bahadur and Ebbeler (2007)

Female employment in agriculture: global challenges and global responses

Stephanie Barrientos

Introduction

What are the effects of globalisation on women workers in agriculture? In many countries the spread of commercial agriculture has provided new openings for female employment. Women have long worked in agriculture, but often as unpaid family labour. The rise of supermarket retailing is contributing to the transformation of agriculture. Initially concentrated in developed countries, supermarkets are now growing rapidly within Africa, Asia and Latin America. Production for supermarkets generates opportunities for female employment. Accessing this employment can bring many opportunities for women, but also new forms of vulnerability.

Paid work allows women to participate more actively in economic and social life, increases their contribution to household incomes and enhances women's empowerment. However, these benefits are not always easily realised. Women workers still face high levels of embedded discrimination and inequality, they are more likely to be found in casual and temporary work and they are often exposed to significant health risks. Where they lack employment security or social protection, women agricultural workers (and their dependents) continue to be vulnerable to poverty.

Achieving more equitable poverty reduction in a global economy requires access by women to decent work, in which their rights, protection and voice are respected. Governments have an important role to play in protecting workers through labour regulation and implementation of Conventions agreed under the International Labour Organisation (ILO). But governments are often constrained where global supermarkets dominate production and employment practices. Civil society organisations (CSOs) have sought new ways to leverage better employment conditions in supermarket supply chains. This has spawned a number of voluntary initiatives, including supermarket codes of labour practice, and ethical and fair trade. Enhancing synergy between regulatory and voluntary approaches can help to secure decent work for women employed in global agriculture.

Women's employment in global agriculture[1]

Global agriculture has undergone significant changes over the past two decades. There has been a relative decline in the share in exports of traditional agricultural crops (such as grains, coffee and tea) and a rapid increase in high value agriculture (HVA), particularly horticulture, floriculture, rich protein meats and processed food products, both for export and growing domestic consumption. Two factors have played an important role in the expansion of high value agriculture in global production. First, technological innovation has allowed the operation of cool chain and transportation that facilitate the export of more perishable goods. Trade liberalisation has stimulated developing countries to expand into high value agricultural exports. Countries such as South Africa, Kenya, Zambia, Uganda and India now produce high value agricultural goods as a growing source of agricultural export earnings (Jaffee, 1993). By 2000 high value agricultural exports were estimated to account for approximately two-thirds of total agricultural trade (Dolan and Sorby, 2003).

A second factor has been the growth of supermarkets as dominant buyers of high value agricultural products, sourcing globally, regionally and locally. Supermarket food chains operate differently from traditional markets. Supermarket buyers exert high levels of control within their value chains in order to meet consumer demand and maximise their market share. They aim to provide the same produce all year round, regardless of local seasons. They operate through global networks of preferred suppliers, using pre-programmed or computer-controlled orders that are directly channelled through to their centralised distribution systems. They set stringent specifications and standards for their suppliers, which include product specification, food hygiene and, increasingly, social and environmental standards (Dolan and Humphrey, 2004). In the UK, supermarkets control 80% of all food retailed. A similar trend is also taking place in parts of Asia and Africa. In South Africa, supermarkets now account for 50–60% of all food retailed and are rapidly expanding outlets in other African countries.[2] In Kenya, supermarkets have grown rapidly to capture more than 20% of urban food retailing (Neven and Reardon, 2004).

Historically, women have worked in agriculture as unpaid family labour (Boesrup, 1970). Female labour has less often been found in certain traditional agricultural crops (e.g. livestock and grains), but has been prevalent in crops such as tea and coffee, often on estates or through family labour in small-holder production. HVA production has, however, stimulated a high level of female employment across both developed and developing countries. Table 1 provides a summary for selected HVA producing countries.[3] The source and composition of female employment vary by country and product. In South African fruit production, for example, women are concentrated in temporary and seasonal employment, with their employment traditionally tied to that of male partners or relatives (Barrientos and Kritzinger, 2003).[4] In Kenyan flowers they are more often found in regular employment, and in Kenya they are usually migrant labour.

The use of workers hired by third party labour contractors is rising in some countries, but is particularly prevalent in South Africa and the UK. Over the past decade, 'gangmasters' have become an important source of labour provision in UK agriculture. They provide 37% of all temporary labour, 32.5% of which is migrant labour from non-EU countries (Frances et al., 2005). Early studies in South Africa and the UK indicate that the gender composition of contract gangs is more likely to be male (65% in the UK). Women form a larger proportion of directly recruited labour employed when seasonal production peaks. This appears to reflect a preference by contractors for male workers who can be more mobile than local seasonal labour, which is usually female. But this could change with the expansion of female migration.

An important aspect of casual female and contract labour is their 'flexibility'. Agricultural producers face natural risks of seasonal production, climatic variation and vulnerability of crops to pest and disease. Producers in supermarket value chains also face high commercial risks in terms of meeting stringent standards and changing demands and orders from supermarket buyers, and rarely have assured supply contracts. Flexible employment allows producers to vary their employment levels on a rapid basis, while keeping labour costs down. The workforce can be varied daily through (compulsory) overtime for casual workers, and/or the use of labour contractors. Some international non-governmental organisations (NGOs) and trade unions argue that the purchasing practices of large supermarkets play an important part in driving labour casualisation. Suppliers face a pincer movement of downward pressure on prices and increasingly volatile orders plus rising quality standards and costs. Casual and contract labour provide a buffer against the risks they face in supermarket value

chains, with vulnerable women workers ultimately baring the cost (Actionaid, 2006; Oxfam, 2004).

Opportunities and challenges for women[5]

The expansion of employment in HVA production provides important opportunities for women to enter paid employment. However, the extent to which women are able to access the benefits of working in HVA is limited by their predominantly casual work status, reflecting embedded gender discrimination in hiring and promotion. A number of studies indicate that (with some exceptions) permanent workers are predominantly male. Permanent workers more often have a legal contract of employment, with greater stability and security of work. Normally they receive better wages (with a year-round income that most casual and contract agricultural workers do not enjoy), and have access to related benefits such as health and social insurance. Non-wage benefits are sometimes available to permanent workers, especially where they live on the farm or estate, including housing, social provision and transport. Permanent workers are also more likely to enjoy the right to freedom of association, although generally rates of trade union membership in agriculture are low.

Women usually constitute the majority employed in pack houses in HVA. Pack house workers often receive relatively good wages compared to field workers, and are more likely to have access to pro rata employment benefits and rights to which they are entitled. Overtime, however, is a key issue in pack houses. It is often required at very short notice to meet variable orders from supermarket buyers, so that workers do not know in the morning what time they are likely to finish that evening. This can make childcare arrangements extremely difficult, particularly for women. Women pack house workers may therefore reap some benefits from working in HVA, but still struggle when they have to combine this with family responsibilities.

| TABLE 1 | Comparison by country of selected high value agricultural production |

Country	Main market	Estimated level of employment	Gender composition	Type of employment
Kenya, Flowers	EU (UK, Holland)	40,000 (+ 4,000–5,000 small-holders)	75% female	65% temporary
South Africa, Fruit	Europe	280,000	69% of women temporary/casual 26% of women permanent	75% temporary
UK, agriculture	UK	99,460 recruited direct, 224,713 via temporary labour providers (TLPs), seasonal agricultural workers (SAWs) and students.	TLPs: 35% female 65% male	Majority temporary (31% recruited direct, 37% via TLPs, 32% SAWs and students)
Zambia, vegetables and flowers	EU	8,000	65% female (veg. only)	60–75% temporary (veg. only)

Sources: Dolan and Sorby, 2003; Smith et al., 2004; Frances et al., 2005

The problems facing casual and contract farm workers, however, are legion. They often have no contracts of employment (even short term) and have little information about their rights or terms and conditions of employment. They face high levels of work insecurity, even if they work regularly for the same producer for years. Wages (often paid on a piece rate) can vary on a day-by-day or week-by-week basis, depending on seasonal demand. Employees often receive no pay when production stops because of the weather, even if they have presented themselves at work. They may be forced to work long overtime hours, often with no additional pay. Casual and contract agricultural workers rarely receive their pro rata legal entitlements, such as health or social insurance, and compensation for work-related injury is often avoided. Because of their insecurity, workers fear making any complaint or joining a union, in case they lose access to work. Women often fall prey to verbal abuse and sexual harassment by male supervisors, who are normally arbiters in whether or not they are re-employed. These workers are thus in a highly vulnerable position.[6]

In agriculture, an issue that affects many workers is health and safety. This especially arises from the use of pesticides and other chemicals in the production process. It is a particular problem for workers in confined spaces such as greenhouses, where exposure tends to be high and workers are often female. Evidence suggests that health and safety procedures in relation to the handling of pesticides and chemicals are often lax or violated. The effects of chemical exposure can include skin irritation, respiratory problems, nausea and dizziness. The longer-term effects can be even more serious, including a higher risk of serious illness and adverse effects on children.

Despite the problems that face female agricultural workers in global production, many still express a preference for this work compared to the alternatives. Paid agricultural work provides increased independence within the household, ability to contribute to household income and greater socialisation. It also provides access to government and community support programmes, which may otherwise be inaccessible. Therefore even where there are negative work attributes, there are also many positives, and women may still prefer this work to the alternatives.

Global responses

A key policy challenge is how to enhance decent work for women who are working in high value agriculture. Decent work, as defined by the ILO, is employment that takes place 'under conditions of freedom, equity, security and dignity, in which rights are protected and adequate remuneration and social coverage is provided'. It provides a framework for the analysis of employment in global production combining four dimensions: employment, rights, protection and voice (ILO, 2000). In principle, all ILO member states are supposed to implement its core conventions, including the principle of no discrimination. In reality, even where legislation itself is good, enforcement can be weak, especially in the context of high value agricultural production, where the demands of overseas supermarket buyers can affect employment practices and producers strive to compete for orders. However, a complementary avenue for intervention has been found through voluntary approaches.

CSOs have put increasing pressure on supermarkets over poor employment conditions in their global supply chains. This has

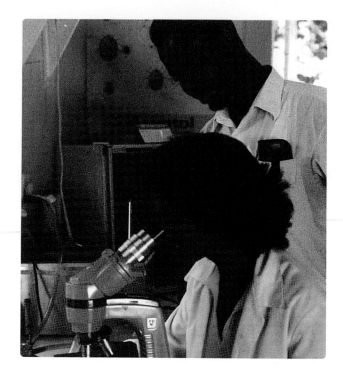

resulted in a number of supermarkets introducing codes of labour practice which lay out minimum labour standards for their suppliers. In some countries, voluntary approaches have led to the formation of multi-stakeholder initiatives involving companies, NGOs and trade unions. An example is the Ethical Trading Initiative (ETI) set up in 1997 in the UK, which includes the main UK supermarkets among its members.[7] Initially, the ETI focused on conditions in developing countries. But in 2002 the ETI set up the Temporary Labour Working Group, involving supermarket, NGO and union representatives, to establish minimum standards for UK 'gangmasters'. It played an important role in pressuring the government to support the Gangmasters (Licensing) Act, which was passed through parliament in 2004 and came into force in 2006 (Pollard, 2006). Under this Act, all labour contractors have to be registered and monitored by the Gangmasters Licensing Authority, and producers have been made jointly liable if they do not use registered contractors.

Similar moves have also been made in South Africa. It now has exemplary labour legislation, including the Employment Equity Act and Basic Conditions of Employment Act (BCEA), which also covers labour brokers. However enforcement remains a problem (Carr, 2004). The Wine Industry and Agriculture Ethical Trading Association (WIETA), was set up following an ETI wine pilot in the country to develop and monitor its own local code of labour practice based on ILO Conventions and legislation. WIETA members include trade unions, NGOs, producers, exporters, government and UK supermarkets. CSOs have played an important role in ensuring that the conditions of casual women workers are addressed in social audits. WIETA has also moved to include labour brokers in its membership, with the aim of monitoring their labour standards against its code of labour practice.

These examples highlight innovative ways in which voluntary and regulatory approaches can interact to address the employment conditions of workers in high value agriculture. Ultimately, however, the commercial environment in which this employment takes place also needs to be addressed. Civil society pressure on supermarkets to improve their purchasing practices is one dimension. The rise of ethical and fair trade highlights that many consumers seek assurance that producers and workers are treated fairly. Easing downward pressure on producer prices and volatility of orders could go some way to helping suppliers meet employment standards set out in supermarket codes of labour practice. It is also important that bilateral and multilateral trade negotiations, such as the EU's Economic Partnership Agreements, take the changing face of supermarket retailing and gendered nature of agricultural employment into account (Khan, 2006; Carr, 2004). Such trade agreements need to support moves by developing country suppliers and governments to upgrade within supermarket value chains, and to direct more of the benefits of participating in this high earning sector to women workers.

Globalisation has great potential to benefit women workers, which could play a significant role in lifting rural households out of poverty. But a proactive commitment is required by all actors – civil society, companies and government – to realise this potential.

REFERENCES

ActionAid (2006). *Impact of anti-dumping proceeding by EC on Vietnam footwear industry*, ActionAid, London.

Barrientos, A. and Ware Barrientos, S. (2002). 'Extending social protection to informal workers in the horticulture global value chain', Social Protection Discussion Paper No. 0216, World Bank, Washington, DC.

Barrientos, S., Dolan, C. and Tallontire, A. (2003). 'A Gendered Value Chain Approach to Codes of Conduct in African Horticulture', *World Development* 31 (9): 1511–26.

Barrientos, S. and Kritzinger, A. (2003). 'The poverty of work and social cohesion in global exports: the case of South African fruit', in Chidester, D. (ed.), *Beyond Solidarity? Globalisation and Social Cohesion in South Africa*, HSRC and NEDLAC, South Africa.

Boesrup (1970). *Women's Role in Economic Development*, St Martins Press, New York.

Carr, M. (ed.) (2004). *Chains of Fortune: Linking Women Producers and Workers with Global Markets*, Commonwealth Secretariat, London.

Dolan, C. and Humphrey, J. (2004). 'Changing Governance Patterns in the Trade in Fresh Vegetables between Africa and the United Kingdom', *Environment and Planning* 36 (3): 491–509.

Dolan, C. and Sorby, K. (2003). *Gender and Employment in High-Value Agriculture Industries*, World Bank, Washington, DC.

Du Toit, A. and Ally, F. (2001). *The Externalisation and Casualisation of Farm Labour in Western Cape Horticulture*, Centre for Rural Legal Studies, Stellenbosch, South Africa.

Frances, J., Barrientos, S. and Rogaly, B. (2005). *Temporary Workers in UK Agriculture and Horticulture*, Report by Precision Prospecting for Department of Environment and Rural Affairs, London.

ILO (2000). *Decent Work and Poverty Reduction in the Global Economy*, ILO, Geneva.

Jaffee, S. (1993). 'Exporting High-Value Food Commodities, Success Stories from Developing Countries', World Bank Discussion Paper 198, World Bank, Washington, DC.

Khan, Z. (2006). *Making Trade Work for Women: The likely impact of the Economic Partnership Agreements on Women's Rights and Gender Equality in Mozambique, Namibia and Zambia*, One World Action, London.

Neven, D. and Reardon, T. (2004). 'The Rise of Kenyan Supermarkets and the Evolution of their Horticulture Product Procurement Systems', *Development Policy Review* 22 (6): 669–99.

Oxfam (2004). *Trading Away Our Rights – Women Working in Global Supply Chains*, Oxfam International, Oxford, UK.

Pollard, D. (2006). 'The Gangmaster System in the UK – the perspective of a trade unionist', in Barrientos, S. and Dolan, C. (eds), *Ethical Sourcing in the Global Food System*, Earthscan, London.

Smith, S., Auret, D., Barrientos, S., Dolan, C., Kleinbooi, K., Njobvu, C., Opondo, M. and Tallontire, A. (2004). 'Ethical trade in African horticulture: gender, rights and participation', UK Workshop Report and IDS Working Paper 223, Institute of Development Studies at the University of Sussex, UK.

ENDNOTES

1 This section draws primarily on the following more detailed studies: Barrientos, Dolan and Tallontire (2003); Dolan and Sorby (2003); Smith, Auret, Barrientos, Dolan, Kleinbooi, Njobvu, Opondo and Tallontire (2004).

2 For example the South African supermarket Shoprite has 119 outlets in 16 African countries (Angola, Ghana, Egypt, Mauritius, Madagascar, Uganda, Zambia, Tanzania, Mozambique, Zimbabwe, Namibia, Lesotho, Swaziland, Botswana and Malawi), as well as India.

3 Official statistics for employment in HVA are very unreliable, and we have to depend on different estimates for country data.

4 Since 1994 there has been a process of rapid change in South African agriculture with the introduction of new labour legislation and rapid retrenchment of on-farm labour. There has also been increasing casualisation of agricultural labour, both male and female.

5 This section draws primarily on the following studies: Barrientos and Barrientos (2002); Dolan and Sorby (2003); Barrientos and Kritzinger (2003); Smith et al. (2004).

6 In the UK, media interest in the plight of gangmaster labour was most tragically bought to the fore by the death of 21 Chinese cockle pickers in Morecombe Bay in 2004. These were all undocumented migrant workers, controlled by unscrupulous gangmasters, who extracted long hours at low pay in hazardous and dangerous conditions (Pollard, 2006).

7 ETI company members include Tesco, ASDA, Sainsbury's, the Co-operative and Marks & Spencer. Morrisons is the largest supermarket that is not a member. See www.ethicaltrade.org

STEPHANIE BARRIENTOS is a Fellow at the Institute of Development Studies at the University of Sussex, UK. She has researched and published on gender and development in Africa and Latin America, globalisation and informal work, corporate accountability, fair trade, ethical trade and international labour standards. She coordinated a research project on Gender and Ethical Trade in African Horticulture and is now engaged in a research programme on the mainstreaming of fair trade. She has worked on projects relating to impact assessment and poverty monitoring and evaluation for the UN Industrial Development Organisation in India and the IFC South Asia Enterprise Development Facility in Bangladesh, and coordinated the UK Ethical Trading Initiative Impact Assessment (2003–2005). She has developed methodologies on 'Value Chain to Impact Mapping' and participatory social auditing, and is making a video entitled 'Participatory Social Auditing – A Gender-sensitive Approach'. She has advised and provided training for companies, NGOs and international organisations on various issues.

Spreading the gains of globalisation: linking women with global markets

Marilyn Carr

Introduction

In most developing countries, women producers and workers in the informal economy play a key role in providing the food and income which enable their families to exist. The impact of economic globalisation on these women has varied according to who they are, where they are, which sector they are involved in and how they are integrated in global production systems. While some women have lost markets and jobs or have seen a decline in working conditions, others have been able to find new markets for their products and new jobs on favourable terms. Recent literature has emphasised the growing casualisation of the labour force and the increased number of *women workers* who form the backbone of many global supply chains for garments, footwear and other consumer goods. However, this article focuses on *women producers* (who still form the vast majority of those earning an income in the informal economy) and seeks to show how they can take advantage of new economic opportunities arising from increased economic globalisation if they are enabled to do so.

Always marginal and vulnerable, women's informal enterprises and incomes have come increasingly under threat with the rapid spread of trade liberalisation and globalisation. In particular, their ability to grow food is decreasing as more land is devoted to commercial export crops, and women's traditional non-farm enterprises, such as basket weaving, oil processing and garment making, are disappearing as a result of the influx of cheaper and/or dumped goods from around the world.[1] While this is good for consumers, who benefit from lower prices, it is bad for women producers, who normally have neither the skills, credit nor information needed to diversify into alternative forms of production. Often, without adequate support, their only alternative is to move into less desirable sectors of the informal economy such as petty trading or open-cast mining, or to look for opportunities as outworkers or factory workers in subcontracting chains. The latter is especially common in east and south-east Asia, where the proportion of self-employed among non-agricultural women workers fell in recent years[2] as they were absorbed as outworkers or casual employees in factories and commercial farms supplying global subcontracting chains. In part, this has been the result of multinational corporations and foreign companies appropriating the land and other natural resources which used to provide a means of self-employment, thus forcing women and men to give up their independent status and to work for others in low-income and insecure jobs.[3]

Within this context, it is increasingly important for informal women producers to find ways to maintain their ability to earn a livelihood at the same time as retaining their sense of security. This will mainly involve: (a) upgrading quality and/or reducing prices so that they can compete with imports; (b) finding markets which are currently being filled by imported goods that could be supplied by local producers; and/or (c) diversifying into products that can find regional and global markets.

Experiences in spreading the gains of globalisation

There are several examples (although still too few) that demonstrate ways in which women producers can be assisted to link with global markets. While it is important to assess the likely impact of changes in trade policies from a gender perspective and to advocate for more gender-sensitive trade policies, it is also necessary to give attention to supporting national economic and social policies and legislation aimed at overcoming the constraints women face in benefiting from increased globalisation. Constraints include more restricted access than men to land, credit, improved technologies, skills and business training, and market and price information. These are both caused and compounded by women's reduced mobility and greater time poverty as a result of socio-cultural factors and family responsibilities; the constraints faced by women who wish to reach export markets are twice as severe as those for women who are supplying domestic markets.[4] The range of policy initiatives which have been successfully introduced to help women overcome these constraints include: financial policies, including guaranteed loans and provision of micro finance and meso-level finance for women;[5] education and training policies which widen women's access to the knowledge and skills important for integration in a globalised economy; and gender policies, including changes in women's rights to land which can provide collateral and also act as a base for economic activities. Most of these initiatives relate to women entrepreneurs in general and few of them help those women who are seeking to make links with global markets.

To assist women exporters in the most effective ways possible, there is a need to map existing global value chains carefully to see where women producers are currently located and identify where interventions can best be made in order to improve their position

within these chains. Current research reveals the importance of helping women producers to organise – in trade associations, producer/marketing cooperatives and community-owned businesses – so that they can bargain with middlemen more effectively and gain greater control over the marketing chain. They also need greater access to improved production/processing technologies which will enable them to add value locally and produce high quality goods which meet international standards.[6] At the same time, better access to new information and communications technologies will enable many women exporters to operate more effectively in global markets through:

- creating opportunities for them to bypass male-dominated and exploitative market structures

- providing a means to foster more efficient communication

- giving them a knowledge tool which will help to maximise their productivity and earnings.[7]

Such supportive measures can be complemented by specific interventions which aim at directly linking women with export markets. Some of the better known examples are fair trade, organic trade and gender mainstreaming national export strategies.

Fair trade

Fair trade is an alternative approach to conventional international trade which aims at sustainable development for excluded and disadvantaged producers through providing better trading conditions, awareness and campaigning. It is concerned with the welfare of the producer – especially women and indigenous people – and, through a range of fair trade organisations, offers easier entry, guarantees a minimum price to avoid risks from price fluctuations and pays a premium to be used in community development projects. In strict usage, 'Fairtrade' is a term used to describe the limited number of products, including coffee, cocoa, tea, bananas, honey and cotton, which are certified by the Fairtrade Labelling Organization (FLO). Although Fairtrade is growing rapidly with, for example, a 50% increase in sales in the UK from 2003 to £200 million in 2004, it is still relatively small, accounting for less than 1% of all goods traded and involving only 800,000 families worldwide. However, because it pays special attention to improving the incomes, access and decision-making roles of women, it has a special significance in strategies aimed at linking poor women producers with global markets.[8] The potential of Fairtrade to support women's empowerment can be seen in the Ghana cocoa cooperative (Box 1).

Fair trade (as opposed to Fairtrade) is a more general term referring to retailers and buyers who try to give poor producers a larger share of total costs. It relates to social responsibility, which is about large corporations trying to improve the returns to poor producers and workers in global value chains. Since women are the majority of the producers of fairly traded products (for example, they comprise 80% of the 100,000 producers involved in fairly traded handicrafts in Bangladesh), any gender-oriented export promotion strategies should incorporate fair trade.[9]

Organic trade

Organic trade overlaps to a certain extent with fair trade, but it is much larger in scale, with US sales up from US$1 billion in 1990 to US$20 billion in 2005 and with the European market growing at 200% per annum. Unlike Fairtrade, there is no guarantee against price fluctuations, and entry is difficult and costly.[10] In addition, with more multinational corporations becoming involved in production of organic produce, prices are beginning to fall, which is good for consumers but makes it difficult for small women producers to compete. For the moment, however, organic certification for expanding export markets seems to be a promising avenue which can enable small women producers to increase both sales and income. The example of women's coconut oil cooperatives in Samoa (Box 2) is a good example of this.

National export strategies

While fair trade and organic trade initiatives play an important role in linking women producers with global markets, the vast majority of trading activities take place in mainstream markets. The question is: can national export strategies work for poor women producers? Export promotion agencies, which tend to be fairly centralised, have a poor record in reaching out to poorer and more remote producers, so most are excluded from the services and technical assistance which these agencies seek to provide. One recent study reports that:

Although women are increasingly starting their own businesses and contributing more to national economies, the unique capabilities and assets of women entrepreneurs are not being harnessed and incorporated into national export strategies.[11]

Thus, even when trade barriers are lowered, the majority of small women producers lack the support they need to access export markets and to participate in the process of meeting export targets.

There are some (but still very few) examples of export promotion agencies and local government bodies which are involved in promoting exports – taking positive action to ensure that informal women and men producers are equally able to participate in and benefit from strategies aimed at expanding export output and revenues. One example of this is the Apiculture Export Strategy developed by the Uganda Export Promotion Board and the International Trade Centre (Box 3). Another is that of the Girijan Cooperative Corporation Ltd in Andhra Pradesh (Box 4).

Future directions

While successes in linking women producers with global markets have been achieved at local level, it is obviously important to assess the extent to which this can be replicated more widely and with what degree of sustainability.

It seems more than likely that the models outlined in the case studies referred to could be easily replicated if they were supported by governments, NGOs and donors. In Ghana, Kuapa Kokoo is helping to set up a sister cooperative so that even more farmers can benefit from its marketing system; it is also in touch with other West African cocoa-producing countries in an attempt to share its experience and offer assistance. In Samoa, the technology on which the village oil-processing enterprises are based came from Fiji and there is every indication that it could be transferred to other countries in the Pacific.[12] In Uganda, government funds are being used by both private companies and beekeepers' associations to reach out to other farmers, while in Andhra Pradesh, the hope of the GCC is that gum pickers in other Indian states will benefit from its successful model of increasing output and exports.

In general, the most common method of replicating these interventions is quantitative: scaling up is achieved by expanding

---

BOX 1 | Fairtrade and women producers in Ghana[13]

The Kuapa Kokoo cooperative in Ghana buys cocoa from its members for onward export and sale through the Ghana Cocoa Marketing Company. It has a membership of 45,000 smallholder farmers, of whom 30% are women. The cooperative was established in 1993 with the assistance of Twin Trading, UK in response to the partial liberalisation of the cocoa sector, and has grown rapidly from its original membership base of 2,000 farmers. A proportion of the cocoa output is tagged for the Fairtrade market, which guarantees a 'floor' and a 'premium' price, which between

1993–2001 resulted in US$1 million for investment in community projects such as hand-dug wells and corn mills which meet women's priority needs. Cooperative members own the Day Chocolate Company in the UK which moves them up the global value chain from production to more profitable retailing. The model has boosted women's morale, self-reliance and confidence, and has given them a voice at national and international levels, as well as within the decision-making bodies of the cooperative itself.

BOX 2 | Organic trade and women producers in Samoa[14]

A local non-governmental organisation (NGO) in Samoa, Women in Business Development Incorporated (WIBDI), has provided 13 family cooperatives headed by women with access to a new processing technology which enables them to export organic virgin coconut oil to Australia and New Zealand. Obtaining organic certification was a lengthy and difficult process, but proved to be a key factor in the success

of the project, with export sales increasing significantly following certification. While all family members are involved in the oil-processing businesses, it was the women who brought in the credit and enterprises through their involvement with WIBDI. Recognition of this has resulted in a significant increase in women's status within their communities.

BOX 3 | Apiculture export strategy and women producers in Uganda[15]

Uganda aims to increase honey production from the 2004 level of 3,000 tons to 13,000 tons in 2008 and to simultaneously improve quality with a view to breaking into rapidly expanding export markets. This will involve attracting an additional 200,000 farmers into beekeeping – a target which would be difficult to achieve without the full involvement of women. To achieve its targets, the government is following two approaches. First, it is assisting with the expansion and replication of the successful commercial company Bee Natural Products, which sources honey from more than 4,000 small farmers (of whom 25% are women) and turns it into a high quality product in its highly mechanised factory. This model should provide a relatively quick way of increasing the output of honey and achieving export standards, but although several measures are being incorporated to address specific training and other needs of women, it will not provide women farmers with any control over their participation in the production chain. In contrast, several community-based organisations (CBOs), many of them started by women, offer services to their beekeeping members. Although these are slower than private companies in reaching out to farmers and increasing supplies of good quality honey, once established they give members a great deal of control over their own enterprises. Government support is available to strengthen and build on these women's beekeeping associations and recent gender-oriented research has suggested that the formation of a national women beekeepers network would assist government to meet its twin targets of expanded output and exports and more equitable distribution of income and reduced levels of rural poverty.

BOX 4 | Gum exports and women producers in India[16]

The Girjijan Cooperative Corporation Ltd (GCC) was established in 1956 as an undertaking of the State Government of Andhra Pradesh to procure non-timber forest products, including Gum Karaya, from tribals and to market these to best advantage. When stocks accumulated because the poor quality of the gum meant that traders rejected it, the decision was taken to look for scientific and organisational solutions to increase quality, rather than reduce the procurement price. More than 10,000 gum pickers have been grouped in associations which have federated into a state-level trust. The trust employs scientists to work with young tribal boys and girls to transfer and monitor improved methods of gum collection and processing, and this has led to higher standards of output which meet export market criteria. To enhance women's economic empowerment in this initiative, UNIFEM has supported a project which helps to establish women as managers and sales people at procurement centres – thus shifting responsibilities in marketing from men to women.

size through increased membership, or extending schemes to other areas or countries.[17] While this is a useful approach, it is unlikely that the necessary numbers of informal women producers will be reached with appropriate support unless successful pilots can be used to advocate for a favourable policy environment. This type of *political* scaling up is evident in the case of the Ghana cocoa cooperative which, through its UK Chocolate Company, has played a role in advocating for more political support for fair trade in both the UK and the EU. The Andhra Pradesh cooperative has also shown how government bodies in other states can help women to increase exports.

Sustainability is a more difficult issue. While fairly traded chocolate (as well as coffee and tea) is now being mainstreamed in major retail stores, mainstream businesses demand a different approach to the Fairtrade niche: most buyers will not accept the late delivery, poor communications or changes in arrangements which are tolerated by Fairtrade organisations.[18] Organic virgin coconut oil targets a niche market which could easily be flooded if too many coconut-producing countries take advantage of new processing technologies. Markets for honey are large and growing, but as more and more women are drawn into the industry, competition will increase and prices will fall, making it necessary to diversify into more complex bee-products. And, as with most non-timber forest products, the increased harvesting of gum can lead to over-exploitation of natural resources with resulting loss of livelihoods unless – as has been done in Andhra Pradesh – sufficient care is taken to protect the resource and to train collectors in low-impact harvesting techniques.

There are now several examples of how women producers can be successfully linked to global markets on terms that are favourable to them. There is also an increasing number of examples of ways in which these models can be replicated on a sustainable basis. A concerted effort is now needed on behalf of all of the actors involved – governments, the private commercial sector, scientists and technologists, NGOs and women's associations, and consumer associations – to ensure that women are able to fully participate in and benefit from new economic opportunities arising from increased economic globalisation. Linking women producers with global markets offers a way to help with poverty reduction and achieve an equitable distribution of gains, while at the same time helping governments to meet their targets in terms of increased export earnings.

BIBLIOGRAPHY

Carr, M. (2004). 'Lessons Learned', in Carr, M. (ed.), *Chains of Fortune: Linking Women Producers and Workers with Global Markets*, Commonwealth Secretariat, London.

Carr, M. and Chen, M. (2004). 'Globalization, Social Exclusion and Gender', *International Labour Review* 142 (1/2), ILO Geneva.

Cretney, J. and Tafuna'i, A. (2004). 'Traditional, Trade and Technology: Virgin Coconut Oil in Samoa', in Carr, M. (ed.), *Chains of Fortune: Linking Producers and Workers with Global Markets*, Commonwealth Secretariat, London.

Ellis, A., Manuel, C., Blackden, C.M. (2005). *Gender and Economic Growth in Uganda: Unleashing the Power of Women*, World Bank, Washington, DC.

Guardian, 28 February 2004, London.

Hafkin, N. and Taggart, N. (2001). *Gender, Information Technology and Developing Countries*, Academy for Educational Development, Washington, DC.

Hooper, M., Jafry, R., Marolla, M. and Phan, J. (2004). *The Role of Community Scaling-up in Achieving the MDGs: Between the Lines, Equator Initiative*, UNDP, New York.

International Resources Group/KOVAL (2004). *Report of the Gum Karaya SubSector in Andhra Pradesh*, India, IRG, Washington, DC.

Kitukale, S., and Carden, C. with contributions from Naas, L. (2004). 'Enhancing Women Enterpreneurship Through Export Growth – Issues and Solutions', paper prepared for ITC Executive Forum on Competitiveness through Public-Private Partnership: Successes and Lessons Learned, Montreux, Switzerland.

Mehta, A.K. (1998). *Sustainable Interventions for Poverty Alleviation: A Best Practice of Gum Karaya in Andhra Pradesh*, India, UNIFEM, New Delhi.

Nadelman, R., Silliman, S. and Younge, D. (2005). *Women and Beekeeping: Challenges and Opportunities in Uganda*, New School/SEEDS, New York.

Redfern, A. and Snedker, P. (2002). 'Creating Market Opportunities for Small Enterprises: Experiences of the Fair Trade Movement', SEED Working Paper #30, ILO, Geneva.

Shiva, V. (2000). *Stolen Harvest*, Zed Press, London.

Tandon, N. (2003). 'Micro and Small Enterprise and ICTs: A Gender Analysis', unpublished paper prepared for the World Bank.

Tiffen, P., MacDonald, J., Maamah, H. and Osei-Opare, F. (2004). 'From tree-minders to Global Players: Cocoa farmers in Ghana', in Carr, M. (ed.), *Chains of Fortune: Linking Producers with Workers with Global Markets*, Commonwealth Secretariat, London.

Uganda Export Promotion Board, Apiculture Export Strategy, 2005–2009, UEPB, Kampala.

United Nations Statistical Division (2000). *The World's Women: Trends and Statistics*, UN, New York.

ENDNOTES

1 Carr, M. and Chen, M. (2004). 'Globalization, Social Exclusion and Gender', *International Labour Review* 143 (1/2), ILO, Geneva.

2 United Nations Statistical Division (2000). *The World's Women: Trends and Statistics*, United Nations, New York.

3 Carr, M. and Chen, M., op. cit.; Shiva, V. (2000). Stolen Harvest, Zed Press, London.

4 Tandon, N. (2003). 'Micro and Small Enterprise and ICT: A Gender Analysis', unpublished paper prepared for the World Bank.

5 In Africa in particular there is a missing middle in the area of women's credit. While very small and very large loans are on offer, the middle-level loans which are needed by women to graduate from very small enterprise activities into more technology-based industries are unlikely to be available. See, for example, Ellis, A. et al. 2005, *Gender and Economic Growth in Uganda: Unleashing the Power of Women*, World Bank, Washington, DC, 2006.

6 Ideally, interventions aimed at women entrepreneurs/exporters should seek to raise both income through increasing productivity and control over the marketing chain through organising and capacity building. All too often, interventions have concentrated only on the former, with the result that any progress made in

terms of increased income during a project's life is lost once the project comes to an end.

7 For examples of ITC-enabled women's enterprises, see N. Tandon, op. cit.; N. Hafkin and N. Taggart 2001, *Gender, Information Technology and Developing Countries: An Analytical Study*, Academy for Educational Development, Washington, DC, 2001.

8 Guardian, 28 February 2004.

9 Redfern, A. and Snedker, P. (2002). 'Creating Market Opportunities for Small Enterprise: Experiences of the Fair Trade Movement', SEED Working Paper #30, ILO, Geneva.

10 National Marketing Institute and the Organic Trade Association.

11 S. Kitukale et al. (2004). 'Enhancing Women Entrepreneurship through Export Growth – Issues and Solutions', paper prepared for ITC Executive Forum on Competitiveness Through Public-Private Partnership: Successes and Lessons Learned, Montreux.

12 Carr, M. (2004). 'Lessons Learned' in Carr, M. (ed.), *Chains of Fortune: Linking Women Producers and Workers with Global Markets*, Commonwealth Secretariat, London.

13 Tiffen, P. et al. (2004). 'Tree-minders to Global Players: Cocoa Farmers in Ghana', in Carr, M. (ed.), *Chains of Fortune: Linking Women Producers and Workers with Global Markets*, Commonwealth Secretariat, London.

14 Cretney, J. and Tafuna'i, A. (2004). 'Tradition, Trade and Technology: Virgin Coconut Oil in Samoa', in Carr, M. (ed.), *Chains of Fortune: Linking Women Producers and Workers with Global Markets*, Commonwealth Secretariat, London.

15 Uganda Export Promotion Board, Apiculture Export Strategy, 2005–2009, UEPB, Kampala; and Nadelman, R., Silliman, S. and Younge, D. (2005). *Women and Beekeeping: Opportunities and Challenges in Uganda*, New School/SEEDS, New York.

16 Mehta, A.K. (1998). *Sustainable Interventions for Poverty Alleviation: A Best Practice Case of Gum Karaya in Andhra Pradesh, India*, UNIFEM, New Delhi; International Resources Group/KOVAL (2004). Report of the Gum Karaya Sub-Sector in Andhra Pradesh, India, Washington, DC.

17 For a description of various types of scaling up, see Hooper, M. et al. (2004). *The Role of Community Scaling-up in Achieving the MDGs: Between the Lines, Equator Initiative*, UNDP, New York.

18 Redfern, A. and Snedker, P., op. cit.

MARILYN CARR is a development economist with more than 30 years' working experience in Africa and Asia. She has a D.Phil from the University of Sussex and an MsC (Econ) from the London School of Economics (UK). She has been director, Global Markets Programme, WIEGO; senior economic adviser, UNIFEM, New York; senior economist, Intermediate Technology Development Group, UK; and regional adviser on Village Technology at the Women's Centre of the Economic Commission for Africa in Addis Ababa. She specialises in gender and trade; gender, science and technology; and women in informal economy enterprises. She has written and edited several books on these subjects, including most recently the Commonwealth Secretariat publications *Chains of Fortune: Linking Women Producers and Workers with Global Markets* and *Mainstreaming Informal Employment and Gender in Poverty Reduction*.

Making financial markets work for small- and medium-sized enterprises

Anne Hilton and Andréas Antoniou

Introduction

Since 2003, the Commonwealth Secretariat has been engaged in a number of activities in support of the efforts of the New Partnership for Africa's Development (NEPAD). Meetings have been held with stakeholders in Africa, and especially South Africa as the host country, for most of these initiatives. The consultations have been held with the express purpose of identifying the obstacles to investment in small- and medium-sized enterprises (SMEs) and facilitating their access to affordable commercial long-term debt financing. A number of issues have been identified as key obstacles to the development of an emerging SME market in South Africa, and the aim is to share these findings with partners in other parts of Africa.

The South African small business environment is not short of capital, but it experiences the same difficulties as the SME market in many other economies. The market in South Africa faces the additional challenge of redressing the discrimination of the past. A primary driver, therefore, of SME development in South Africa is the need to redistribute wealth and opportunity and create jobs for those communities that were most under-resourced under apartheid. A structure, broad-based black economic empowerment is in place to address economic imbalances, but many barriers still face the emerging SME market. These include the following.

1. Lack of experience and skills in the workplace and in business due to the division of labour in the South African economy.

2. Inadequate financial and business management understanding and knowledge.

3. Lack of collateral and own equity due to a widespread inability to secure assets and equity in the emerging small business market.

4. Poor understanding of the types and sources of capital, and where to find it.

5. Particular problems for women, who find it even more difficult to acquire finance for small business: as in many developing economies, the bulk of women in business are in the micro-enterprise sector.

What constitutes an SME in SA is defined by the criteria in the National Small Business Act of 1996 (see Table 1).

Progress in addressing the key constraints in the SME finance market is slow, and many financial institutions still approach black economic empowerment and enterprise development within the paradigm of traditional asset-based lending. Few demonstrate any appetite for risk. Financial institutions have identified the high transactional costs of backing emerging SMEs as a key constraint, and have identified information asymmetry and poor business plan development as key factors in these costs. There is as yet very little innovation in the financial market to overcome the lack of collateral and assets faced by those sectors of the population that have historically been denied opportunities to accumulate assets,

TABLE 1	What constitutes a small- or medium-sized enterprise?			
Sector or sub-sectors in accordance with the Standard Industrial Classification	Size or class	Total full-time equivalent of paid employees Less than:	Total annual turnover Less than:	Total gross asset value (fixed property excluded) Less than:
Manufacturing	Very small	20	R4.00 m	R1.50 m
	Micro	5	R0.15 m	R0.10 m
Retail and motor trade and repair services	Very small	10	R3.00 m	R0.50 m
	Micro	5	R0.15 m	R0.10 m
Wholesale trade, commercial agents and allied services	Very small	10	R5.00 m	R0.50 m
	Micro	5	R0.15 m	R0.10 m

including women. In addition, insufficient risk funding is available for use in alternative and innovative risk management strategies in the absence of collateral.

Several other banking practices frustrate SMEs.

- Bank assessments are still largely based on the information provided by credit bureaux and this information is not yet comprehensive enough to support SME lending.

- Banks are reluctant to provide SME (business) related information. At present the only way of achieving this is if SMEs volunteer such information. Banks could benefit from economies of scale if the flow of SME information was more effectively managed internally and externally. The reluctance of banks would need to be overcome.

- Short-term and volume-driven lending are the order of the day, and banking tends to be fractured into silos with insufficient data sharing. The need to repeatedly provide information the banks already have is a burden for clients.

- Credit decisions are taken by credit managers who at best have an arm's length relationship with clients.

- Perceptions of risk are still based on gender and race.

- The lack of demand-side information means that many entrepreneurs simply do not bother to apply, as they assume they will be refused.

This frustrates efforts by the emerging SME sector to secure funding. The situation is exacerbated by a lack of experience, skills and resources on the part of aspirant business owners which would enable them to identify and assess business ideas, collate information and translate such information into bankable propositions. In addition, the emerging market has shown a lack of understanding of banks and their products and services. This puts inexperienced clients at a disadvantage.

At a meeting with stakeholders on 25 October 2006, several issues were identified as potential topics to be addressed through Commonwealth interventions.

1. Mechanisms to reduce transactional costs to credit granters.

2. Reducing the imbalances in information management between clients and institutions through providing professional and affordable pre- and post-loan support.

3. Mechanisms to manage risk which were not dependent on the traditional sources of security such as asset-based lending. One of these would be to put in place post-loan mentorship support to promote sustainability of borrowers and manage the flow of information to lenders.

4. Enhancing the availability of risk funds to augment the pool of capital available in the emerging market.

5. The enhancement of research and information on the SME market and the sectors and industries in which they operate. Such segmentation is not currently available to any adequate extent.

There is a need to bolster business development support from qualified and experienced business advisers in order to improve the quality and accessibility of pre-application support to the emerging SME market. This will have the effect of improving the information offered by clients, while also reducing the transactional costs to banks. At present many of the services available are not fulfilling this role. The banks and development finance institutions have expressed a need for this. Such a process must include the following.

- Viability assessments.

- Feasibility assessments of business ideas.

- Assistance to develop business ideas if they seem viable.

- Assistance to develop business plans.

- Ensuring that all the information needed for the bank of choice is available before the application is made.

One of the problems encountered in the South African business support arena is an over-emphasis on business plans without proper planning or consideration of their viability. This needs to change if access to funding is to be improved. Many inexperienced entrepreneurs fall into the trap of handing over these tasks to a third party; the latter often provides inadequate support and unbankable documents. Attention to these aspects of information asymmetry will have the potential to:

- improve the quality of business plans and information

- reduce the transactional costs to banks

- produce better prepared and more sustainable business ideas

- give start-up businesses greater access to available capital.

The result of information asymmetry is that banks rely on blunt instruments such as guarantee funds to offset their risk in the absence of other information, and on collateral to recover their losses in the event of business failure. While they protect the interests of the financial institutions, these interventions have no impact on the health of the business itself. Many financial institutions are still largely risk averse and are very selective in their loans to the emerging market, especially to start-up businesses.

In order to reduce the impact of information asymmetry, the burden of information collection and management needs to be enhanced in the interest of SME lending. This should include:

- more cooperative relationships between credit granters in terms of information sharing

- the integration of borrowings from micro-enterprise organisations, the clients of which have traditionally been unable to acquire any reputational equity for their repayment efforts, but who could be endorsed for larger loans as individuals

- the integration of the enterprise-lending environment to promote the sharing of credit histories from micro lending to formal lending in banks and development financial institutions. This should improve access to finance, especially for those locked into high interest-bearing credit due to a lack of collateral.

As the aim is to promote market efficiencies for the emerging SME market through the more efficient management of data and information, there is also a need to review the current practices of credit bureaux in South Africa. While credit bureaux are viewed very negatively by large sections of the population, they are nonetheless important sources of data, which could reduce the costs of banking transactions and information inequities.

Conclusion

SME information opaqueness could be overcome in several ways.

- By influencing and facilitating access to finance through the support of pre- and post-loan information management to the emerging SME market.

- By promoting better cooperation among different levels of lenders and facilitating the integration of financial information for all levels of lending in South Africa. This would imply the need to overcome resistance to information sharing in the SME lending environment.

- By enhancing the information available to financial institutions through further cooperation between selected data management companies and the Commonwealth Secretariat, for example through organising one-on-one workshops.

- By considering the information available to SMEs: if banks are reluctant to provide such detail in terms of perceived competitive constraints, financial literacy training for start-up and existing small business owners, would go some way to addressing the needs of SMEs to better understand funding and financial management.

For those financial institutions that are willing to take risks in this market, there is a need to augment the availability of risk funds to these institutions to address the lack of collateral in the target market. This will mean that more funding will be made available by institutions that are granting risk capital with the intention of graduating clients to commercial, asset-based funding.

ANDRÉAS ANTONIOU is deputy director and head of the International Finance and Capital Markets Department in the Economic Affairs Division of the Commonwealth Secretariat. Before joining the Secretariat he was Professor of Economics and Econometrics and Head of the Department of Business Studies at Philips College, Nicosia, Cyprus. Prior to that, he was Senior Lecturer at the Department of Economics at the University of the Witwatersrand, Johannesburg, and has taught at several universities in Quebec and Ontario. His research interests include international economics, game theory and economic development finance. He holds a Licence and a Maîtrise des Sciences Économiques-Econométrie from the Université de Paris 1 (Panthèon-Sorbonne), an MA from the University of Essex (UK) and a PhD from McGill University (Canada). He is currently Visiting Professor at the University of Stellenbosch Business School, South Africa.

ANNE HILTON is a South African-based consultant with experience in banking and specialises in entrepreneurship development.

Improving women's access to finance

Anne Hilton and Laureen Katiyo

In the Commonwealth, as in other parts of the world, women face significant challenges in terms of their sex and gender roles and their ability to run businesses and raise capital. One of the common threads, however, is the need for women to achieve greater recognition in terms of their economic contribution and their unequal access to financial services, which men in business often take for granted.

This article discusses the issues that impact on women's ability to raise capital and the gender-specific constraints they face, and makes recommendations to policy-makers and financial services which address these concerns.

For women who need funding for small- and medium scale businesses, issues such as limited access to assets for collateral and the requirements of financial institutions are still largely gender indifferent, and the institutions claim that gender neutrality is an effective tool which enables women to access their services. Entrenched inequalities, however, continue to deprive women of fair and equal financial options and opportunities in most economies.

We also need to understand the wider context of finance for small, medium and micro enterprise (SMME) development and women in business, together with the issues that impact on women's access to finance, the gender environment in which access is sought, the financial services available and their inadequacy. Governments must recognise that promoting gender equality and the empowerment of women brings significant economic gains that impact positively on poverty reduction and that this is the key to future economic growth and sustainable development.

Issues that impact on women's access to finance

Women are still likely to be employed in the least skilled, least influential and worst paid jobs in the economy, and this impacts negatively on their ability to accumulate assets and equity. This is still a reality in both developed and developing financial systems. Women have largely been excluded from decision-making both as the receivers and investors of capital in an environment where financial markets are still dominated by men. Men's predominance in financial institutions has fostered a culture which does not respect the needs of women clients and which may exclude them from opportunities, prospects and gender mainstreaming.

Further research and examples taken from several Commonwealth countries have shown that most women live in an environment in which they face serious obstacles and many of them are subjected to some or most of the following conditions.

Legal constraints: Traditional norms and values in many countries prevent women from acting as legal persons and accumulating assets such as property. Such constraints impact on women's ability to offer assets as collateral and obtaining finance is often therefore beyond the scope of a woman's available or limited assets. Examples drawn from countries such as Uganda show that ownership of registered land is gender biased with only 7% of women, but 93% of men, having access. Even so, in cases where legislation supports women owning assets in the form of land in their own right, very often the custom and practice within societies, communities and families prevents them from accessing funding.

Marital arrangements: Women are often in marital arrangements which put them in the position of legal minors and which largely prevent them from making independent decisions about their own finances. This leaves them without the relevant experience or credit histories on which to draw if they want to apply for funds, either as married or divorced women.

Lack of education: In cultures in which the education of women is regarded as a waste of financial resources, lack of literacy renders women incapable of reading about or understanding what financial resources are available to them or how credit systems work. This is a serious handicap when it comes to accessing finance.

Attitudes towards women: Negative attitudes to women based on their conflicting role demands and perceived time constraints are interrogated and held against women when they apply for funding.

Financial services

Financial institutions are largely unaware that women may face gender specific constraints when seeking funding. They tend to take a gender neutral position which assumes that men and women have the same access. When the institutions are not neutral, women are often discriminated against.

- Male decision-makers often consider the realities of women's lives as diverse and use the multiple roles women play as justification for refusing them business credit. This is despite statistics which prove otherwise. A good example is South Africa, where women have been identified as a better credit risk and credit bureaus recorded a 24% drop in adverse histories on women in 2005. However, experience shows that even where the risk is not high, funding does not necessarily follow.

- The size of the business is also a major factor affecting the likelihood of a loan being rejected. Since women's businesses tend to be start-ups, which are often initially operated from home, a majority of their credit applications are refused.

- The criteria for bank loans are usually asset-based and depend on an applicant's financial resources and ability to offer collateral, thus ruling out many women.

- For many women who are unexposed or underexposed to financial and legal matters the forms and processes presented by banks may be intimidating and daunting. This is compounded by the lack of clarity of information on how to apply for credit and on other bank services. Women generally lack sufficient information about financial services and products, and are largely unaware of how to access such information.

- Financial institutions often charge high fees for their services, which women cannot afford.

Financial options and possible models

Micro finance

Some progress has been made through the provision of micro finance. There are many micro-finance programmes which have had a positive impact on women in terms of improving income, household security, food security and educational levels. They work as a group mechanism for lending money to women. Some of the best models of micro finance are from India and Bangladesh, including the pioneering Grameen Bank where the sheer volume of women involved in micro finance has made these initiatives successful and popular. Despite their success, micro-finance programmes are not suitable for women who have been in business for some time and aspire to expand their operations. However, based on the emerging experience of such initiatives, questions have been raised about the role of micro finance in the economic transformation of women. There has been a shift in attitudes and analysts have begun to question the extent of the impact of micro credit on the lives of poor women. New recommendations are now being put forward for more gender-appropriate micro-credit programmes and the need to make it possible for women to graduate beyond the confines of micro loans and group credit.

In Africa and Asia, the expansion of the informal economy provides jobs for women as well as men but at the risk of their being unprotected and poorly paid. Blanket lending of money to a group of women for redistribution in small amounts means that women whose financial requirements are above the group's maximum are not able to benefit. There are no available statistics, even from the best examples of micro-finance programmes, to indicate that micro finance is the best path for continued future economic growth. There is no model for progressing micro-finance initiatives to the next logical stage of small to medium enterprises.

SMME finance

While there is an abundance of micro-finance programmes, the majority of women entrepreneurs struggle to access finance. At a certain point in women's business development funding becomes difficult to obtain, particularly in developing nations. In developed economies, considerable support and funding has been invested in women through agencies that represent small- and medium-scale enterprise. In Canada, women are involved in 70% of new business start-ups and hold majority ownership in 18% of these. In addition, women have harnessed their collective wisdom and power through well-organised associations, and have built workable and mutually beneficial relationships with some banks. Despite these efforts, they still experience disadvantages when they seek business capital. Even in Canada, the rejection rate of finance applications is 23.3% for the smallest businesses. The relationship between women's SMMEs and the banks in both developed and developing economies still has a long way to go to address inequalities which prevent women from accessing finance.

Venture capital

There are many features of venture capital which make it of limited use to business women.

- Venture capital resources are primarily aimed at men and by comparison women get a very small slice of the pie.

- In today's market, the most attractive venture capital candidates are those who have expertise in fields that traditionally have been dominated by males, such as engineering, bio-technology and physics.

- There is a substantial funding gap that limits women's opportunities to grow their ventures aggressively and to lead high value firms. For example, in the UK only 3% of venture capital goes to businesses owned by women.

- Pre-existing relationships (network connections) provide an important link between entrepreneurs and venture capitalists.

- Lacking connections to venture capitalists, women entrepreneurs have less chance of getting to the negotiating table.

- Women constitute a very small percentage of venture capital decision-makers and are less likely to be in senior positions.

Approaches to venture capital need careful consideration, particularly in developing economies.

Conclusions

Targeting women for access to financial services is a good start on the road to women's empowerment, enhancing opportunities for their individual growth, economic activity, decision-making in the household and in the community. Case studies give clear examples of this, although gender roles and opportunities tend to reflect socio-cultural (patriarchal) norms. Micro finance is predominately aimed at poor women and it is important not to transfer the burden of poverty and household security to women in the absence of sustainable support mechanisms and social interventions that improve the status of women in the economy and that encourage the participation of men in the welfare of households. There needs to be a balance of funding options available to women at various levels.

Further examination of the manner in which access to finance for women is managed in most countries has uncovered some fundamental weaknesses. Women are often not consulted about the problems they encounter by governments and financial institutions. As a result, governments overlook the need to establish appropriate interventions that link into other organisations at national, regional and international level. The relationship between governments and financial institutions regarding financing women in business is fragmented. Many financial institutions consider the provision of micro finance to be the responsibility of the government, thus dismissing the niche market for funding women's enterprises at micro finance and SME level. Significant opportunities exist for change if governments and financial institutions can form a cohesive approach to formulate joint policies and make funding for women entrepreneurs more accessible.

Recommendations

Recommendations to governments and policy-makers

Governments and policy-makers need to be vigilant in ensuring that changes in legislation or policy frameworks are gender inclusive and aim mainstream women into the economy. As a priority, governments need to pay more attention to support SMMEs as engines of growth together with the following changes.

- Legalisation and enforcement of women's property rights as a basis for collateral and access to finance.

- Monitoring the data management system for credit information with a view to promoting gender-positive practices.

- Implementation of regulations and policies for the financial services sector which are tested for gender appropriateness before being incorporated into law.

- Separation of micro-finance programmes from government-sponsored welfare.

- Creation of specific government-led SMME programmes with a focus on women entrepreneurs.

Recommendations to financial institutions

- Improve relations with women entrepreneurs in order to understand their financing needs, the real level of risk and the barriers they face in accessing finance.

- Assign trained staff to maintain consistent relationships in which women entrepreneurs are treated as individuals rather than subsumed under the preconceived generalisation that women entrepreneurs are a greater risk than male entrepreneurs.

- Simplify financial language in documentation and provide more accessible communication and customer service.

- Design specific finance packages aimed at women entrepreneurs.

- Review risk capital provisions to support and incubate businesses to entrance viability.

This article is a summary of a paper on access to finance written for the Commonwealth Business Women's Network (CBWN).

ANNE HILTON is a South African-based consultant with experience in banking and specialises in entrepreneurship development.

LAUREEN KATIYO is a consultant with the Commonwealth Business Council.

Making a difference for women entrepreneurs

Ram Venuprasad

Small- and medium-sized enterprises (SMEs) have great socio-economic relevance to the growth and progress of countries – big and small, developed and developing. In the Commonwealth, as in the rest of the world, the SME sector accounts for upwards of 90% of firms and employment.[1] An important, and striking, social feature of the SME sector across the world is the role of women, both as employers and employees. This article analyses the role of women in SME development and the work of the Commonwealth Secretariat in this area. It specifically highlights the role of a capacity building programme in engendering SME development work.

Over the last decade much work has been done to study the role of women in SME development. This has been for two reasons, economic and social. Women in SMEs have been seen as a source of untapped economic growth. As employees of small enterprises[2] women are important agents for savings, gainful economic activity and GDP growth. The same is true for women entrepreneurs, who have demonstrated innovative solutions to management, entrepreneurial opportunities and employment creation.

Women face several challenges in the area of SME development. In the case of women entrepreneurs these include lack of access to finance and unfavourable policies, including restricted access to training and development. For women working in SMEs, challenges include disparities in wage structures vis-à-vis men and lack of access to proper social facilities such as childcare.

The international development community, like national governments, is increasingly making gender a priority in its economic development agenda. Various development agencies, such as the Commonwealth Secretariat, now require gender to be considered an integral part of all their development programmes and projects.

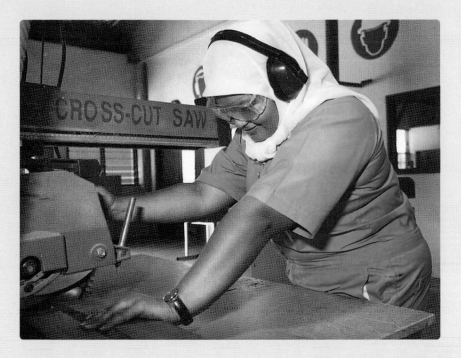

The Commonwealth Secretariat has more than three decades of experience in the area of SME development. Over the past five years its work has focused on providing front-end technical assistance, i.e. on the development of policies and strategies, and on institutional capacity building through training. Realising the importance and benefits of empowering women in SME development, the Secretariat makes a concerted effort to incorporate the gender dimension in the development of policies, strategies and training activities. This is done partly by working with the Secretariat's in-house gender experts.

The results of the Secretariat's gender mainstreaming strategy in SME development work have been positive, demonstrating tangible outcomes. The various programmes of the Secretariat's SME development work offer women entrepreneurs and policy-makers a platform to come together to share experiences, spread new ideas and network. This networking aspect, an often ignored resource, is extremely useful to women entrepreneurs and managers.

In recently concluded work in the Caribbean region, focusing on SME strategy development for three countries in the region, the Secretariat has incorporated a strong gender dimension in its SME strategies. This has included highlighting the financing needs of women, the development of support services, including training, the ability of women to participate in the labour force by ensuring the availability of affordable childcare and equal treatment at work. The Secretariat has achieved success in this project with all three participating governments accepting the recommendations of the SME strategies and allocating funding to implement various activities, including gender mainstreaming.

The Commonwealth-India Small Business Competitiveness Development Programme (CW-India Programme), a capacity-building training programme on SME development that the Secretariat has been hosting jointly with the Government of India since 2004, is a good example of this strategy. The programmes, six of which have been held between November 2004 and March 2007, have acted as a platform for women entrepreneurs and policy-makers from across the Commonwealth to come together and share their experiences and ideas on developing the SME sector to uplift women. Initially, 25% of those participating in the programme were women. But as a result of positive actions, which included encouraging greater women's participation and increasing the emphasis on gender issues, the proportion rose to 52% in the Sixth CW-India Programme, which concluded in March 2007.

From Selima Ahmed, who founded the Bangladesh Women's Chamber of Commerce and Industry, to Isobelle Gidley, who runs the Vanuatu Indigenous Development Alliance, the CW-India programme has brought together 125 other women from 39 Commonwealth countries to learn, share and network on SME development issues and opportunities. Tangible outcomes engendering SME development across Commonwealth countries have been a hallmark of the CW-India programme. The programme helped the Zambian Government to develop SME

initiatives with a strong gender focus for the country's Fifth National Development Plan. It has harnessed commercial opportunities by bringing together women entrepreneurs from India and the Caribbean islands. In addition, through the network that has been developed there is regular exchange of information on trade, business and investment opportunities for women entrepreneurs.

The CW-India programme has demonstrated to many of the smaller Commonwealth countries the various approaches and benefits of gender mainstreaming in SME development activities, including areas like creating women's self-help groups and financing mechanisms. This has been done through various field visits as well as experience-sharing presentations.

These are just some examples of the Secretariat's work in engendering SME development across the Commonwealth. The expected outcomes include unleashing economic growth and making progress towards gender equality and the empowerment of women through SME development. For the Commonwealth Secretariat, gender mainstreaming helps to maximise the development impact of its work as it ensures that benefits accrue to all sections of the population.

ENDNOTES

1 The unavailability of comparable and up-to-date data on SMEs from most countries, including Commonwealth countries, gives a patchy picture.

2 The terms 'SMEs' and 'small enterprises' have been used interchangeably in this article.

RAM VENUPRASAD is adviser, Enterprise Development, with the Commonwealth Fund for Technical Co-operation (CFTC), working in the Commonwealth Secretariat's Special Advisory Services Division's SME Development and Competitiveness projects. He has much experience in the development arena, backed by a good academic research background in SME and ICT, and was the Infobank/Izodia International Research Fellow at the Warwick Business School (UK).

financing
HIV/AIDS
interventions

Gender perspectives on HIV/AIDS from Jamaica

Nesha Haniff and Robert Carr

In 2006, Amnesty International in its report *Sexual Violence Against Women and Girls in Jamaica* highlighted the fact that:

> *The rate of sexual violence against women in Jamaica is very high and is accompanied by spiralling levels of community violence and homicide throughout the island. In 2005, the number of homicides in Jamaica, already high, increased to 1,669. At 0.55–0.62 per thousand people, this is one of the highest rates in the world. Sexual assault is the second most common cause of injury for women, after fights. Five per cent of all violent injuries seen in hospitals are caused by sexual assaults.*

Jamaica is symptomatic of the Caribbean and many parts of the world where entrenched discrimination against women means that many individuals fail to appreciate that forced sex carried out by an acquaintance or family member is a serious crime. This violence, which is a defining feature of masculinity, is meted out first of all against men, against gay men and against women. This is very clear when one looks at police records. What is often not recorded is the level of violence against gay men, because this falls under the general rubric of male violence. Ongoing research and the problematic of homophobic violence in Jamaica and the Caribbean is discussed in Carr (2003).

Gender and HIV

This context of violence and forced sex is central to the spread of HIV and the increasing infection rates of young women in Jamaica. The rates reflect international trends, where those most at risk are 15–29 years old. Statistics released by the Jamaican Ministry of Health in 2006 showed that in Jamaica the infection rate for girls in this age group is three times that of boys. The organisation Jamaica AIDS Support for Life (JASL), which works with the poorest and most marginalised people infected with HIV, now has a predominantly female client base, even though it originally provided services for gay men.

One index of the complexity of gender subjugation is the draconian response to gay men. This is immediately seen as a binary of male versus female. In the world of heteronormativity, to be gay is to abandon the power of patriarchy and be reduced to the category of female. This re-inscribes the entrenched low status of women as a category and so makes those who fall into it subject to human rights abuses, including abuses of sexual and reproductive rights.

Gendered violence is inextricably linked to the status of women since it ascribes to women minimal control over their sexual and reproductive health. Women's responsibility for child rearing, whether as grandmother, aunt or mother, and for keeping the household intact, locks the poorest women into a cycle of poverty. In the Caribbean, women represent a significant number of heads of households. Although the number of women now attending universities in the Caribbean is outstripping men, this is not true for the poorest women. Class divisions are therefore key to an understanding of the status of women in the Caribbean.

Although HIV does not discriminate, those who are the most vulnerable are the poorest, who have few resources for health care and no access to antiretroviral drugs if they become HIV-positive. Poverty in the Caribbean, like poverty elsewhere, is one of the important factors that drive women to transactional sex and high risk behaviour in order to keep their families and lives afloat. Even though women in the Caribbean may have a higher level of agency, as they can negotiate condom use, their ability to succeed in these negotiations is constantly met with resistance and accusations of infidelity. Haniff (2006) points out: 'Women who have economic choice and status are also in the same situation as poor women; they are also unable to negotiate condom use. It is the subjugation of women, regardless of marital status, income or privilege that makes women vulnerable to HIV.'

Martha's journey

In 2005, Nesha Haniff conducted a series of interviews documenting the life stories of women who were among the poorest section of the population and who were HIV-positive. The interviews were conducted through Jamaica AIDS Support for Life. Altogether 21 women were interviewed, over half of them in their 20s. The story of Martha is emblematic of the reality of very poor women who are HIV-positive. We see through her life on the frontline how the issues of gender subjugation, poverty, HIV and violence evolve in her everyday existence in Jamaica.

Martha was raised by her grandmother and did not know her mother. She left school at Grade 9. At the time of the interview she was 32 years old. She said:

> [W]*hen I am hungry, I cry eye-water and my friends will ask, 'Martha what happen to you?' And everybody will know that I am hungry because my grandmother doesn't*

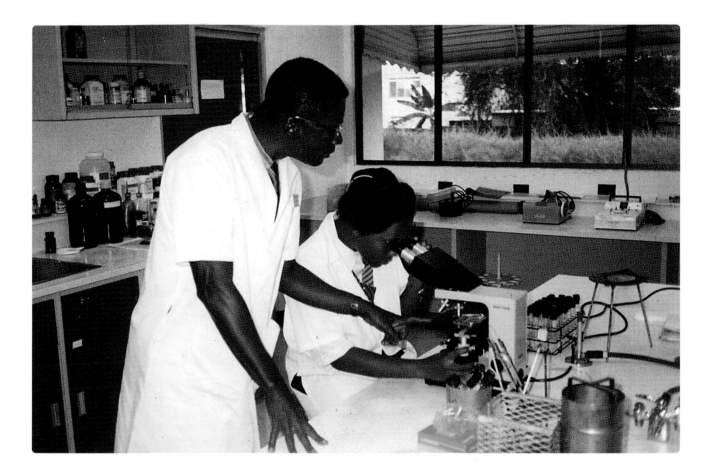

have it to give us. So one day during the time of Hurricane Gilbert I met this guy at a fête and he started coming to my house to call me. I told him not to come at my house because my grandmother will quarrel, until one night he sent and called me and he hold me down and have sex with me.

Asked if he raped her, she explained:

Not really. We were talking but I wasn't really ready for the relationship yet, because we were still young. He hold me down and took my virginity. So when I reached home I told my grandmother that I got rape. However, I didn't tell them who it was. She bathes me and took me to the hospital and to the station, yet I didn't tell who it was. In the other year I got pregnant for him.

This first encounter happened when Martha was 14 years old. She continued to see the man until she became pregnant even though she felt she was raped. She was pregnant at 15. Here we see that Martha has a contradictory reaction to forced sex. On the one hand she knows it is rape and on the other she accepts and continues the relationship. That she did not and could not exercise any control over her body illustrates her status as a victim. Entrenched discrimination against women means that many individuals fail to appreciate that forced sex carried out by an acquaintance or family member is a serious crime. She was hungry and became pregnant, which further exacerbated her poverty since she was unable to continue her education and so was ill-prepared for upward mobility.

Martha's life continued through many trials and tribulations. She had two more children, raising only one son herself. She had many relationships, but it was always her poverty that drove her to take many risks with her body and her life. She became a domestic helper and the man of the house constantly abused her. Here we see how class and male privilege are used to continue this woman's subjugation.

He always said that he likes my space teeth. I wasn't paying him no mind. However one day I was cleaning the fridge and he came inside the house and he started rubbing down my breast. I wanted to scream but his daughter was on the front verandah sleeping. She came in and said: 'Is what?' But because I didn't wanted his wife to cut him up, I don't bother say anything. Yes, I never tell anybody. He said he's sorry, but because I look neat. He offered me money not to talk and I took the money because I was desperate. His wife always locks me in the house.

Class divisions

Gender victimisation is not only a feature of men oppressing women, but also of the privileged class abusing their privilege over those who serve them. The mistresses also participate in the oppression of these domestic helpers, often violating their helper's dignity. Class divisions in Jamaica are very circumscribed and entrenched, but women's gendered oppression regardless of status is a feature of patriarchy where both the domestic helper and her mistress are caught up in relationships with male partners that undermine their agency.

As Martha continued down the path that was her life the inevitable happened. She became infected with HIV. At first she thought it was her boss, but it was not. It was someone else but she secretly hoped that she had infected her boss since he always refused to wear a condom. It was a man named Waggie.

Asked about the man who had AIDS and died, she said:

> *I don't really know him because I don't know if he was sick. … One night I never had anything to give the baby. The baby was crying from hunger. I was hungry. He was a security. He had the money. He invited me at his work place in New Kingston because he was cooking and he was planning on giving me money. We had sex, but the first time he was bleeding when he finished having sex. And I asked him, 'What happening?' He said he is sick, but he didn't tell me the kind of sickness. Then he gave me JA$200. I took it and buy 1lb corn meal, sugar and Lasco [powdered milk].*

Martha had sex with the man twice, and the second time he gave her JA$150.

> *When I got that I just get to know because people started to say my friend die from AIDS. Other said it's not AIDS. Other time, I started coming to workshop and somebody said it is contracted by blood. My mind runs on that. I was saying, him wicked. Because of money I allow myself to be infected.*

Martha's baby was hungry. The risk she took was not just for herself but for her child. She had no money and had sex with a man she did not know. Although Martha's case is extreme, it is one version of a major driver of HIV in women – transactional sex. This is particularly the case for young women like Martha who are unable to go to school and must find ways to pay for transport, lunches and school uniforms. But for women who must struggle, a transaction is always on the table.

Martha received JA$200 for her first encounter (approximately US$3), and JA$150 for the second (less than US$2.50). Martha became HIV-positive because she needed US$5. Whether it is US$5 or US$100, through staying in relationships in which they know they are at risk and failing in negotiations on the use of condoms, women are at a higher risk of HIV infection. In the Caribbean there is a population of women who do have agency, except in setting the terms of sexual relationships. Feminism has accomplished a great deal for middle-class women who can go to university and become professionals, but women continue the duality of being both professional and married woman, and are still unable to negotiate their sexual safety. They may have more than Martha, but they are still subjugated.

Martha's life remains a problem for societies that are unable to systematically lift such women out of the cycle of poverty. The solution is to begin again the great struggle for women's ownership of their bodies through the work of small feminist grassroots groups. Poverty and agency may seem contradictory, but they are not. Support systems need to be in place that can keep such women in school or enable them to learn a trade and to make them conscious that they have rights.

What did Martha risk her life for? She risked her life for JA$200. With this she bought 1lb corn meal, a packet of sugar and Lasco – food that was not for her, but for her baby.

REFERENCES

Amnesty International (2006). *Sexual Violence Against Women and Girls in Jamaica*, Amnesty.org/library

Carr, R. (2003). 'On Judgments, Poverty, Sexually Based Violence and Human Rights in 21st Century Jamaica', *Caribbean Journal of Social Work* 2, July 2003.

Haniff, N. (2006). *To Stand Up for Her Rights: Empowering Women to Protect Themselves from HIV Infection, A Manual for Community Activists*, Jamaica AIDS Support for Life, Kingston, Jamaica.

ROBERT CARR, PhD, MSW is a senior lecturer and director of the graduate programme at the Caribbean Institute of Media and Communication (CARIMAC) of the University of the West Indies in Mona, Jamaica. He also coordinates the Caribbean Centre of Communication for Development housed at CARIMAC. Trained in social work and management, he has worked as a counsellor, trainer and programme manager for numerous AIDS programmes and services in Jamaica, Trinidad and Tobago, and the wider Caribbean. Director of Jamaica AIDS Support from 2000–2002, he was a co-founder of the Caribbean Vulnerable Communities Coalition, a regional group representing populations especially vulnerable to HIV. In addition, he has served on the Board of Directors of the Canadian HIV/AIDS Legal Network since 2004 and on the Board of Directors of Jamaica AIDS Support for Life since 2006. He has been working on issues of gender and violence for more than a decade.

NESHA HANIFF is a senior programme adviser for Jamaica AIDS Support for Life and the Latin American and Caribbean AIDS Support Service Organization (LACASSO), and teaches at the University of Michigan. She has just completed her publication *To Stand Up for Her Rights: Empowering Women to Protect Themselves from HIV Infection, A Manual for Community Activists*.

Missing the women: policy responses to HIV/AIDS

O. Shisana

Introduction

Experiences in research, programming and policy in HIV/AIDS indicate that globally we are 'missing the women'. At the 2002 International AIDS Conference in Barcelona, a mere 9.6% of research presentations focused on women or the gender dimensions of the pandemic. In 2004 no substantial improvement was noted at the World AIDS Conference in Bangkok, with only 8.3% of the presentations addressing gender issues, despite increased awareness of the growing impact of HIV/AIDS on women and girls.

This article attempts to identify women who are consistently 'missing' in HIV/AIDS research and points to ways that could ensure that women's voices do not go unheard and that their perceptions and experience inform policy and programmes.

The impact of HIV/AIDS on women

When the epidemic began, it had the face of men, mainly gay men, but men empowered with resources and knowledge, who managed to advocate for action to contain the spread of HIV and to fast track the development of drugs to treat AIDS. The story of powerless women is different.

The epidemic is spreading at a faster rate among women than men. Globally, by 2005 50.8% or 17.3 million of the 34 million adults living with HIV/AIDS were women, up from 43% in 1998. In sub-Saharan Africa, where the majority of adults living with HIV/AIDS are to be found, 61.1% of them are women, with young women two to six times more likely to be HIV-positive than young men. The impact of AIDS on women has already changed life expectancy patterns in some countries such as Kenya, Malawi, Zambia and Zimbabwe, where the life expectancy of women is now below that of men.

The epidemic affects women not only in terms of morbidity and mortality, but also with respect to fertility. Women who are HIV-positive have reduced fertility rates, a reduction of between 25 and 40%. Women living with HIV/AIDS are often subjected to stigma and are made to feel ashamed of being infected; consequently they feel personally responsible for their HIV status, even when they have been infected by the only man with whom they have had sex.

The section opposite briefly examines certain categories of women who have been identified as especially vulnerable.

Ethnic minorities

There is a growing HIV/AIDS epidemic among women from ethnic minorities in high-income countries. For example, black and Hispanic women in the USA and First Nations women in Canada are experiencing increased AIDS prevalence, despite the availability of effective prevention techniques and treatment regimes. Blacks and Hispanics now account for 51% and 20% respectively of all AIDS cases in the USA. In Canada, First Nations women are over-represented in HIV/AIDS statistics. Common to these minority populations is a high prevalence of poverty, racism, sexism and lack of power to advocate for policies that would benefit them. All these create fertile ground for the development of social problems such as risky sexual behaviour, alcohol abuse, substance abuse and violence against women.

Sex workers

UNAIDS estimates that there are tens of millions of sex workers and hundreds of millions of clients. The majority are young and female, and the clients are mostly male. The prevalence of HIV among sex workers has been found to be as high as 73% in Ethiopia, 50% in Ghana and 68% in Zambia. Women sex workers are marginalised by political, legal and social exclusion, which leads to problems in reaching them through programmes aimed at changing sexual and other behaviour. There is a dominant moral disdain that leads to criminalisation of activities related to women's role in prostitution. Consequently, these women are less likely than men to seek help and protection from the law, and so become vulnerable to rape and other risky sexual behaviour forced on them by their clients.

Sex workers are arrested for soliciting and must constantly be on guard against arrest, especially if they are street prostitutes. A study conducted in Zambia showed how sex workers were vilified, labelled as the 'suppliers of AIDS' and ostracised.

HIV/AIDS among drug users

Women drug users are exposed to three major risks: use of unsterile needles; unprotected sex; and use of mind-altering substances, which affect decision-making and increase sexual risk-taking.

From the information presented it is clear that increasingly women are more affected by the epidemic than their male counterparts.

The impact is large whether they are part of the majority population in low- and middle-income countries or members of an ethnic minority in high-income countries. They become infected when having sex with their partners; sex workers are infected by their clients; and still other women are infected through a combination of sex work and drug use.

Certain regions that have borne the brunt of the epidemic such as sub-Saharan Africa have been able to respond to some of the measures required for HIV/AIDS prevention and treatment. More women are being reached. But some groups are still not covered. Which women, then, are 'missing'?

Missing the women

Despite the evidence showing that women constitute the majority of people living with HIV/AIDS, they are often missed in research, prevention and treatment programmes; however, specific groups are more affected than others. These are pregnant women, women living in some countries where the dominant mode of HIV transmission is not heterosexual, HIV-positive women who have sex with women (including those who do not identify themselves as lesbians or bisexual), non-drug using HIV-positive women in some high-income countries, non-sex workers or sexual violence survivors and domestic workers. Evidence suggests that these women have either been deliberately or inadvertently excluded from research, prevention or treatment actions.

Heterosexual women living in countries where the dominant mode of transmission is not heterosexual

In the USA, for many years those who classified AIDS cases inadvertently increased the focus on some groups to the exclusion of others. Pregnant women who could transmit HIV to their babies and drug users were at the top of the list, while non-pregnant heterosexual women were at the bottom. This led to underestimation of the HIV epidemic in the heterosexual population. It was no surprise that the incidence of AIDS among women in the USA increased by 1% and mortality declined by 12% at a time when AIDS morbidity among men decreased by 8% and AIDS mortality by 26%. These figures suggest that fewer women than men had access to prevention, treatment and care services.

Heterosexual women in south-east Asia are also likely to be missed. Women who are not pregnant are less likely to know their HIV status and hence are likely to delay in getting treatment. In Bangkok's two largest maternity hospitals, the overwhelming majority (73%) were diagnosed for the first time when they were pregnant. This clearly suggests that non-pregnant women, who constitute the majority of women, are seldom tested for HIV. Since most women undergo HIV testing during pregnancy, they are the ones who are likely to get access to voluntary counselling and testing which may lead to treatment. All other segments of the female population, including older women, are less likely to get access to these services, suggesting that they are likely to remain undiagnosed, perhaps until it is too late.

In high-income countries, heterosexual women who are not intravenous drug users (IDUs), sex workers or survivors of sexual violence are also less likely to be included in the statistics.

Older women

Few women over 50 receive any attention. It took African countries to conduct population-based surveys in which high rates of HIV were observed in this group. For example, in South Africa, the rate of HIV among women aged 50–54 is 7.5%, and among women aged 55–59 it is 3%. Grandmothers who take care of orphans and vulnerable children, in many cases using their meagre pension benefits, often do not receive state grants for the services they are providing. Few low-income countries have social security systems which support these women.

Disabled women

Although researchers have studied the disabling effects of HIV/AIDS on previously healthy people, little is known about HIV/AIDS and people with disability. Disabled people are incorrectly thought to be sexually inactive, unlikely to use drugs and at less risk of violence or rape. But despite the assumption that disabled people are sexually inactive, those with a disability, and in particular disabled women, are likely to have more sexual partners than their non-disabled peers. Extreme poverty and social sanctions against marrying a disabled person mean that they are likely to become involved in a series of unstable relationships. Awareness of HIV/AIDS and knowledge of HIV prevention is low in this group and sex education programmes are rare.

Women who have sex with other women

HIV-positive women who have sex with women (WSW) are seldom included in research or the advocacy efforts of AIDS service organisations, due to a lack of information. There is a belief that they are not at risk of contracting HIV, yet they are exposed to multiple risks such as drug use and sex work. They may very well engage in sex with partners whose serostatus they do not know. In high-income countries, studies have shown that a number of females who are IDUs are also WSW, and they exhibit increased HIV infections and risk behaviour. They are left out of research interventions because they do not fall neatly into the defined categories used in classifying risk groups.

Domestic workers

Women migrants who work as domestic workers are also often missing in HIV prevention and treatment programmes, despite having the highest risk of HIV. The risk is from their male partner, who often has other sexual partners because of the absence of his wife, or from his wife because she is away from her husband for long periods. She is also at risk because of forced sex by her employer.

Women caught up in armed conflict

Another group that is missed comprises women who are caught up in armed conflict, causing them to take refuge in or out of their own countries. Displaced women and men are often exposed to sexual assaults, and women and children make up 80% of refugees. A survey among Burundian refugees discovered that 26% of women had experienced sexual violence since becoming a refugee – a major risk factor for HIV.

From this brief review, it is apparent that researchers, policy-makers and programme implementers are missing specific categories of women.

Evidence-based interventions designed to benefit women

Research has been conducted to generate evidence to support HIV prevention and treatment interventions targeted at women. It covers prevention of transmission of HIV from mother to child, treatment of sexually transmitted diseases, antiretroviral therapy, condom use among sex workers and action to reduce risk factors that promote HIV infection among women. There is ample evidence to demonstrate what interventions work to prevent new infections and to treat those who have AIDS, as well as evidence about the determinants of HIV infection in women.

Recommendations

To ensure that specific categories of women are not missed in HIV prevention and AIDS treatment programmes, specific actions are recommended.

- Use conventions and laws to give women the right to reproductive health services.

- End harmful traditional practices – governments should pass legislation designed to end these practices and pass laws that prohibit and prosecute offenders.

- The causes that lead to infidelity by women should be addressed.

- Implement gender-based budgeting.

- Involve multiple key stakeholders in developing policies.

- Transform the nature of relationships between men and women so that women are empowered.

- End the stigma encountered by HIV-positive women.

- Introduce female-controlled methods of fighting the HIV/AIDS epidemic.

- Introduce legislation to protect the human rights of specific groups.

Finally, it is important to remember that gender inequity is a key obstacle to halting the spread of HIV. Therefore all of us must play our part to end gender inequity – starting with ourselves.

This article is based on a paper presented during the XVI International AIDS Conference held in Toronto, Canada in August 2006 at a panel convened by the Commonwealth Secretariat, Human Sciences Research Council, South Africa and Atlantic Center of Excellence for Women's Health, Canada.

DR OLIVE SHISANA is the first woman and black president and chief executive officer of the South African Human Sciences Research Council (HSRC). She served as executive director of the Social Aspects of HIV/AIDS at the HSRC, where she established and headed a national programme and Africa-wide network on the social aspects of HIV/AIDS and health. Prior to this she was professor and head of the department of Health Systems Management and Policy at the Medical University of South Africa. She has also served as Executive Director of the World Health Organization's Family and Community Health Unit, where she oversaw HIV/AIDS, reproductive health, women's health, and child and youth development programmes. She served as director-general of the South African Department of Health, the first woman to head national health services in South Africa.

Sonke gender justice and the 'one man can' campaign

Dean Peacock

In South Africa, as throughout the world, gender inequality continues to undermine democracy, impede development and compromise people's lives in dramatic ways.

Just 12 years into its hard-won democracy, South Africa is faced with the twin epidemics of HIV/AIDS and violence against women – each propelled in significant ways by prevailing gender norms that encourage men to equate manhood with dominance over women, sexual conquest, alcohol consumption and risk taking.

South Africa has among the highest levels of domestic violence and rape of any country. Research conducted by the Medical Research Council in 2004 shows that every six hours, a woman is killed by her intimate partner. This is the highest rate recorded anywhere in the world.[1]

Across the region, conviction rates for domestic and sexual violence are among the worst in the world. In South Africa only one in nine victims reports rape and fewer than 10% of reported rapes lead to conviction. Inadequate recording of statistics makes it impossible to determine conviction rates for domestic violence but a recent study of domestic violence homicides in South Africa showed conviction rates no higher than 37.3%.[2]

This violence and the unequal power it reflects between men and women is one of the root causes of the rapid spread of HIV in South Africa. Almost one-third of sexually experienced women (31%) reported that they did not want to have their first sexual encounter and that they were coerced into sex. As a result, young women in South Africa are much more likely to be infected than men and make up 77% of the 10% of South African youth between the ages of 15 and 24 who are infected with HIV/AIDS.[3]

These levels of violence are a threat to our new democracy and undermine our ability to enjoy the rights enshrined in our widely respected Constitution, especially Section 12, subsection 2 of the Bill of Rights, which makes clear that: 'Everyone has the right to bodily and psychological integrity, which includes the right (a) to make decisions concerning reproduction; and (b) to security in and control over their body.'[4]

While South Africa has alarming levels of gender-based violence, it is by no means unique. The recent WHO *Multi-Country Study on Women's Health and Domestic Violence* indicates that domestic violence is a grave problem the world over and represents a fundamental violation of women's rights.[5] Faced with this reality, efforts have been made to involve men in ending gender-based violence and in achieving gender equality. A number of international commitments have been made encouraging member states and signatories to implement strategies for engaging men and boys. (See Box 1.)

Sexual conquest and aggression

Men's violence against women does not occur because men lose their temper or because they have no impulse control. Men who use violence do so because they equate manhood with aggression, dominance over women and with sexual conquest. Often they are afraid that they will be viewed as less than a 'real' man if they apologise, compromise or share power. So instead of finding ways to resolve conflict, they resort to violence.

We have used the term 'men's violence against women' because it is men who commit the majority of all acts of domestic and sexual violence. However, research shows that South African men are not monolithic but instead hold a wide range of opinions about violence against women.

A number of studies have been conducted to determine men's attitudes and practices related to sexual violence.[6] For instance, a recent survey of 435 men in a Cape Town township revealed that: 'More than one in five men … reported that they had either threatened to use force or used force to gain sexual access to a woman in their lifetime.'[7] A 2006 Medical Research Council survey of 1,370 male volunteers recruited from 70 rural South African villages indicated that: '16.3% had raped a non-partner, or participated in a form of gang rape; 8.4% had been sexually violent towards an intimate partner; and 79.1% had done neither.' In addition, a 2006 Sonke Gender Justice (SGJ) survey of 1,000 men in the Greater Johannesburg area suggested that about equal numbers of men support and oppose government efforts to promote gender equality, with 41.4% of men surveyed saying that the government is doing too much to end violence against women and 38.4% saying that government is not doing enough. At the same time, 50.1% of all men surveyed felt that they should be doing more to end violence against women.[9]

This research shows that some men hold deeply alarming attitudes towards women, sex and gender equality. However, it also shows that a growing number of men and boys are strongly opposed to this violence and feel that it has no place in a new democratic South Africa. They recognise that it is a fundamental violation of women's human rights. These men give voice to the reality that many men are themselves negatively affected by domestic violence and rape. They remind us that boys who live in homes where their fathers abuse their mothers are often terrified by their fathers and the violence they commit and, as a result, can experience problems with depression, anxiety and aggression that interfere with their ability to pay attention at school. Similarly, they tell us that all men are affected when women they care about are raped or assaulted.

As a signatory to international commitments on engaging men and boys in ending gender-based issues and in recognition of these contradictory male attitudes, South Africa has made significant efforts to reach men and boys. Sonke

Gender Justice was commissioned by the National Office on the Status of Women to develop the South Africa country report submitted to the 51st session of the CSW. This report, available at www.genderjustice. org.za/sa-country-report-2007.html, chronicles the efforts of many government and civil society organisations. One such initiative described is the 'One Man Can' campaign developed and coordinated by Sonke Gender Justice.

Sonke Gender Justice Network and the Men as Partners approach

The South African NGO Sonke Gender Justice works within a human rights framework to promote gender equality and reduce the spread and impact of HIV and AIDS. To increase men's commitment to gender equality, Sonke Gender Justice is currently implementing Men as Partners (MAP) programmes in all of the country's nine provinces and in eight Southern African countries.

The MAP programme was established in South Africa in 1998 by the Planned Parenthood Association of South Africa (PPASA) with technical support from EngenderHealth, a US-based reproductive health organisation. Following joint training and technical assistance by PPASA and EngenderHealth to a number of organisations and government departments, including the South African National Defence Force, Western Cape tertiary institutions, Hope Worldwide, Congress of South African Trade Unions (COSATU), Federation of Unions of South Africa (FEDUSA), National Council of Trade Unions (NACTU), and the AIDS Consortium and its community-based organisation (CBO) affiliates, these organisations formed a Men as Partners network, which allowed each organisation to implement independent MAP programmes while learning from and building on each other's work.

The purpose of the MAP programme is twofold: to challenge the attitudes and behaviour of men that compromise their own health and safety, as well as the health and safety of women and children; and to encourage men to become actively involved in responding to gender-based violence and the HIV/AIDS epidemic.

Sonke Gender Justice currently implements MAP workshops with various groups of men in communities across South Africa. The process employed is participatory and non-directive, acknowledging the experiences that all participants bring with them. Central to any MAP workshop is a discussion of gender issues – reflecting on participant values about gender, examining traditional gender roles, understanding the power dynamics that exist based on gender, assessing gender stereotypes, and sharing male and female perspectives on gender.[10]

Sonke Gender Justice has provided training on MAP to a broad range of key stakeholders, including government departments at national and provincial level, as well as traditional healers, leaders of faith- based organisations, the police, organisations which serve youth, in and out of school youth, teachers and other CBOs and NGOs.

BOX 1 | International commitments to achieving gender equality

A review of international legislation and UN declarations presented at the 51st session of the Commission on the Status of Women (CSW) in 2007 reports that 'Equality between women and men is a fundamental principle of international law established in the United Nations Charter' and cites the following commitments.

The 1994 International Conference on Population and Development affirms the need to 'promote gender equality in all spheres of life, including family and community life, and to encourage and enable men to take responsibility for their sexual and reproductive behavior and their social and family roles'.[11]

The Programme of Action of the World Summit on Social Development (1995) and its 2000 review also addressed the role of men, in particular with regard to sharing family, household and employment responsibilities with women.[12]

The Beijing Platform for Action (1995) restated the principle of shared responsibility, and argued that

women's concerns could only be addressed 'in partnership with men'.[13]

The 26th special session of the General Assembly on HIV/AIDS (2001) recognised the need to challenge gender stereotypes and attitudes and gender inequalities In relation to HIV/AIDS through the active involvement of men and boys.[14]

An expert group meeting on the role of men and boys was convened in 2003 in Brasilia by the United Nations Division for the Advancement of Women (DAW/DESA), in cooperation with the International Labour Organisation (ILO) and UNAIDS to inform the CSW at its 48th session.[15]

At the 48th session, the CSW adopted agreed conclusions calling on governments, entities of the United Nations system and other stakeholders to, *inter alia*:

- promote reconciliation of work and family responsibilities
- encourage the active involvement of men and boys in eliminating gender stereotypes

- encourage men to participate in preventing and treating HIV/AIDS
- implement programmes to enable men to adopt safe and responsible sexual behaviour
- support men and boys to prevent gender-based violence
- implement programmes in schools to accelerate socio-cultural change towards gender equality.

In the ten-year review of the Beijing Platform for Action, member states emphasised that changing men's attitudes and behaviours required a range of strategies including legislative and policy reform, the implementation of programmes, the involvement of educational systems and the media, and partnerships with NGOs, the private sector and leaders from all segments of society, including religious leaders.

The review also encouraged member states to create opportunities for sharing experiences and good practices across regions and stressed that this offered important opportunities for cross-fertilisation.[16]

Evidence base for involving men and boys in achieving gender equality: As new programmes engaging men and boys have been implemented, a body of effective evidence-based programming has emerged and confirmed that men and boys are willing to change their attitudes and practices and, sometimes, to take a stand for greater gender equality.

In South Africa, research conducted by EngenderHealth and the MAP Network indicates that 71% of workshop participants in the study believed that women should have the same rights as men, whereas only 25% of men in the control group felt this way. Eighty-two per cent of the participants thought that it was not normal for men to sometimes beat their wives, whereas only 38% of the control group felt that way.

Similarly, the Medical Research Council's evaluation of the Stepping Stones initiative implemented in the Eastern Cape showed a significant reduction in partner violence by men at 12 and 24 months after the intervention.[17]

An ongoing literature review and analysis of 57 interventions with men by the WHO and Instituto Promundo reported that 24.5% were assessed as effective in leading to attitude or behaviour change using the definition previously cited; 38.5% were assessed as promising; and 36.8% were assessed as unclear. Those that addressed gender norms – within messages, staff training and educational sessions with men – were more likely to change attitudes and behaviour.[18]

Developing the 'One Man Can' campaign to strengthen the MAP approach

Sonke Gender Justice recognises that workshops alone will not promote sustained change in individuals. Given this, SGJ supports men who have been through MAP workshops to form Community Action Teams (CATs) which provide men with the support to take action at the local level and sustain their commitment to gender equality. Our experience implementing MAP CATs has indicated to us that men need materials and concrete strategies to sustain their commitment to activism.

With funding from the Western Cape Office of the Premier, SGJ conducted formative research and then, based on this, developed a campaign to encourage men to take action.

Called 'One Man Can', the campaign supports men and boys to take action to end domestic and sexual violence, to reduce the spread and impact of HIV/AIDS, and to promote healthy, equitable relationships that men and women can enjoy – passionately, respectfully and fully.

The campaign was created to promote the idea that all men have a role to play and that 'each one of us can create a better, more equitable and more just world. It encourages men to work together with other men and with women to take action, to build a movement, to demand justice, to claim our democratic rights, and to change the world.'

'One Man Can' partnerships: Recognising the importance of collaboration and the significant contribution made by many organisations across the world in developing the 'One Man Can' campaign, the initiative is a formal partnership with a wide range of South African and international organisations. These include the South African Office on the Status of Women; the National Department of Health, the National Department of Provincial and Local Government; the Treatment Action Campaign; People Opposed to Women Abuse; the South African Football Players Union; Targeted AIDS Interventions; the International Coalition for Women's Health; the Commonwealth Secretariat; the Family Violence Fund; and Instituto Promundo.

Formative research supporting the 'One Man Can' campaign: SGJ's research showed that many men and boys are concerned about widespread domestic and sexual violence and want it to stop. SGJ heard that men and boys do worry about the safety of women and girls – their partners, sisters, mothers, girlfriends, wives, co-workers, neighbours, classmates, and fellow congregants – and want to play a role in creating a safer and more just world.

To decide on the content of the various 'action sheets' containing suggestions for action men and boys can take, a youth research team conducted a survey of 945 men in Johannesburg to get their views on what role they see for themselves and the government. Literature reviews were also a useful tool to identify similar materials that had been developed elsewhere. Additionally, a formative research team conducted literature reviews to identify similar approaches used elsewhere and then ran many focus group discussions with survivors of violence, faith-based leaders, teachers, coaches and young and adult men.

The project team also carried out a number of street surveys, stopping men in shopping malls, restaurants, barber shops and bus stations to find out how they understood the problem of men's violence against women and what they would be willing to do about it.

For the campaign, SGJ developed a kit to provide men with resources to act on their concerns about domestic and sexual violence. This includes materials such as stickers, clothing, posters, music, video clips and fact sheets. In addition, the 'One Man Can' action kit provides specific information and strategies on how men can support a survivor of violence, use the law to demand justice, educate children early and often, challenge other men to take action, make schools safer for girls and boys, and raise awareness in churches, mosques and synagogues.

Following a number of TV, radio and print media interviews about the campaign, SGJ has received many requests for materials and assistance from other NGOs, private sector companies and individual men and women.

Following its launch at the end of 2006, SGJ has started to successfully implement the 'One Man Can' campaign and use the action toolkit in various parts of the country. In the Western Cape, SGJ has used the kits with men in Khayelitsha – including coaches, religious leaders, fathers, teachers, taverners, ward councillors and youth. Additionally the kits and workshop activities have been used with inmates and correctional staff in four prisons. The campaign and toolkit are also being carried forward by SGJ in rural areas in KwaZulu-Natal and the Eastern Cape in its project which develops the capacity of men to be advocates and activists in efforts to eliminate violence against women and children. In Limpopo province, the action kit and workshop activities have been adapted for use with commercial farm workers.

Other NGOs have also started to take the campaign forward – Hope Worldwide is making use of the CD and stickers in the Western Cape, raising awareness of the issues among taxi drivers and encouraging them to play the 'One Man Can' music CD on their routes and place campaign stickers on their vehicles. PPASA is in the process of printing a further 5,000 bumper stickers to use in their trucking and sex work projects.

South Africans have a rich tradition of working for social change and social justice and it seems that this campaign resonates with that history.

For more information on the 'One Man Can' campaign, visit www.genderjustice.org.za/onemancan or email dean@genderjustice.org.za

ENDNOTES

1   Mathews, S., Abrahams, N., Martin, L., Vetten, L., van der Merwe, L. and Jewkes, R. (2004). '"Every six hours a woman is killed by her intimate partner": A National Study of Female Homicide in South Africa', Gender and Health Research Group, Medical Research Council, Tygerberg, South Africa.

2   Ibid.

3   Pettifor, A., Rees, H. and Stevens, A. (2004). *HIV & Sexual Behaviour Among Young South Africans: A National Survey of 15–24 Year Olds*, University of the Witwatersrand, Johannesburg.

4   South African Constitution, 1996.

5   WHO multi-country study on women's health and domestic violence against women: summary report of initial results on prevalence, health outcomes and women's responses. Geneva, World Health Organization, 2005.

6   See the 'One Man Can' fact sheet for more data on masculinities, violence, HIV/AIDS and health at http://www.gender justice.org.za/onemancan/images/publicati ons/factsheet/factsheet_eng_lowres.pdf

7   Kalichman, S.C., Simbayi, L.C., Cain, D., Cherry, C., Henda, N. and Cloete, A.

(2007). 'Sexual assault, sexual risks and gender attitudes in a community sample of South African men', *AIDS Care* 19 (1): 20–27.

8   Jewkes, R., Dunkle, K., Koss, M.P., Levin, J.B., Nduna, M., Jama, N. and Sikweyiya, Y. (2006). 'Rape perpetration by young, rural South African men: Prevalence, patterns and risk factors', *Social Science & Medicine* 63: 2949–61.

9   Ambe, D. and Peacock, D. (2006). 'Understanding men's perceptions of their own and government's response to violence against women. Findings from a survey of 945 men in the greater Johannesburg area', Sonke Gender Justice Network, 11 December 2006; PlusNews Special, 'Closing the gap: Gender-Based Violence in South Africa: Men slowly turning away from gender-based violence'. Downloaded from http://www.plusnews.org/webspecials/PNG BV/6643.asp on 21 February 2007.

10 For more information on MAP, see Peacock, D. and Levack, A. (2004). 'The *Men as Partners* program in South Africa: Reaching men to end gender-based violence and promote sexual and reproductive health', *International Journal of Men's Health* 3 (3): 173–88.

11 See paragraphs 4.11, 4.24, 4.25, 4.26, 4.27, 4.28, 4.29, 5.4, 7.8, 7.37, 7.41, 8.22, 11.16, 12.10, 12.13 and 12.14 of the Cairo Programme of Action, and paragraphs 47,

50, 52, and 62 of the outcome of the 21st special session of the General Assembly on Population and Development.

12 See paragraphs 7, 47 and 56 of the Programme of Action of the World Summit for Social Development, and paragraphs 15, 49, 56 and 80 of the outcome of the 24th special session of the General Assembly on Further Initiatives for Social Development.

13 See paragraphs 1, 3, 40, 72, 83b, 107c, 108e, 120 and 179 of the Beijing Platform for Action.

14 See paragraph 47 of the Declaration of Commitment on HIV/AIDS: 'Global Crisis – Global Action'.

15 Report of the Expert Group Meeting on 'The role of men and boys in achieving gender equality', Brasilia, Brazil, 21–24 October 2003, http://www.un.org/women watch/daw/egm/men-boys2003/reports/ Finalreport.PDF

16 Paragrpah 669, ten-year review of the Beijing Platform for Action, UN, NY, 2005.

17 Personal correspondence with Rachel Jewkes, Principal Investigator, 17 November 2006.

18 Barker, G. (2006). Presentation on panel entitled 'Engaging Men in Gender Equity and HIV/AIDS', XVI International AIDS Conference, Toronto, Canada, 13 August 2006.

DEAN PEACOCK MSW is co-founder and co-director of Sonke Gender Justice, a South African NGO working across Southern Africa to promote gender equality, reduce the spread and impact of HIV and AIDS, and promote human rights. He was selected by the United Nations to attend the expert group meetings on 'reaching men and boys to achieve gender equality' held in Brasilia in 2003. In 2004 he gave a plenary address at the United Nations on the occasion of International Women's Day. He has contributed to many professional journals, including the *International Journal of Men's Health, Men and Masculinities* and *Agenda*. He is the author of *Gender Equality and Men: Learning from Practice, Defending Our Dreams: Global Feminist Voices for a New Generation, Baba? Men and Fatherhood in South Africa* and *From Moralizing to Preventive Action: HIV/AIDS and Human Security in South Africa*. In addition he is a member of the UCLA Program in Global Health and has worked as a consultant to many UN agencies, the London School of Hygiene and Tropical Medicine and, in South Africa, the Treatment Action Campaign, Soul City and the National Office on the Status of Women.

HIV/AIDS and Caribbean masculinities

David Plummer and Joel Simpson

Introduction

Gender roles drive the HIV epidemic. But because gender is so normalised in everyday life, the far-reaching impact of gender roles is easily overlooked and widely underestimated. Recently, however, a number of initiatives have attempted to address the role of gender in HIV, including those by the Commonwealth and by UNIFEM. These initiatives have identified a gap in addressing women's issues in relationship to HIV. We agree that adequate gender-specific initiatives have been lacking in this area. However, the problem runs deeper: so long as one half of a binary (in this case women) is overlooked, then the other half (men) need not be problematised either, despite it being the frame of reference or 'default' position. It is our contention that, apart from certain classic stereotypes (for example prostitute, unsuspecting victim), women have not been accommodated because they are powerless, while the role of men has been absent for the converse reason: that exposing the central role of male sexuality in driving the epidemic would put pressure on powerful socially sanctioned gender roles. This has been accentuated by the desire to avoid association with an epidemic that has homosexual connotations, and the exception to the avoidance of attention to men's role is, of course, the scapegoating of certain stereotypes, in particular gay men.

Gender plays a central role in all world cultures and the Caribbean is no exception. Masculinity is highly valued and male dominance is the norm. However, the last 25 years have witnessed important shifts in gender dynamics in the Caribbean, as elsewhere in the world. Women have made important advances in education and employment: there has never been a time in the English-speaking Caribbean when women were more likely to be the chief breadwinners and heads of household. Similarly, girls are succeeding at school and women at university in record numbers. Currently around 70% of graduates from the University of the West Indies are women.

These issues raise important questions for gender in the context of HIV in the Caribbean.

Men and sexual risk

Male gender roles have central significance for HIV control. Men are subject to comprehensive social pressures to conform to these roles. Those roles that relate to sexual risk-taking directly determine the epidemiology of HIV.

Boys learn very early about the complex codes of gender-based obligations and taboos to which they are subjected. In the words of Bailey et al. (1998: 53):

> *By the age of ten … boys began to realise that toughness, physical strength and sexual dominance, all features of traditional masculinity, were expected of them.*

Moreover, while it is commonly claimed that there are taboos against speaking about sexuality, this taboo does not extend to young people. On the contrary, their environment is saturated with sexual references and much of the information they acquire about sexuality comes from the age group just older than themselves (Bailey et al., 1998: 29). By way of contrast, parents and teachers are notable for their silence on these issues (Brown and Chevannes, 1998: 23). Clearly, young people are teaching themselves about sexual practice and the gender roles that should accompany that practice largely with inputs from older peers and popular culture.

All societies attach paramount importance to achieving an appropriately gendered identity. The combination of the absence of adults from sex education and of ceding sex education to young people has important implications for this achievement. Sexuality and gender are tightly intertwined, and accomplishing a masculine (gendered) reputation is tightly linked to adolescent discourses, peer group dynamics and sexual accomplishments. In the words of Brown and Chevannes (1998: 23):

> *Manhood is demonstrated by sexual prowess … it is usually measured … by the number of female sexual partners.*

Under these circumstances, where having multiple partners is integral to asserting one's masculine status, even being faithful to a single partner can be the source of scorn and loss of face. Bailey et al. (1998: 65–6) describe how:

> *… for males, multiple partnerships could become also a matter of status … The term 'one burner' applied to a faithful male in some Jamaican communities was a phrase of derision.*

Indeed, the importance to one's reputation of having multiple sexual relationships is tied to one of the deepest male social taboos, homophobia, as the following quotation from Crichlow (2004: 206) suggests:

Someone who did not have as many women as they did was 'sick', 'suspected as a buller'[1] or not 'the average young black male'.

The quality of men's relationships

The gendered youth cultures shared by Caribbean young people, at least in the English-speaking Caribbean, have consequences that go far beyond sexual practice: a combination of obligation and taboo imposed by gender codes profoundly configures the *quality* of young people's relationships – often adversely so.

The basis for this impact on relationships stems from equating successful masculinity with physical and emotional strength and social dominance: a consequence of this is the creation of taboos around weakness, tenderness and commitment. These taboos impact on relationships between men themselves and between men and women.

In the case of interpersonal relationships between males, gender taboos configure how men ought to interact. These taboos extend to how men express their feelings in acceptable ways. Contrary to popular opinion, boys do not become emotionless as they mature, but there are certainly some emotions that are taboo (typically those that denote weakness) and others that are actively cultivated (typically those that affirm strength – anger, glee in the face of triumph, etc. (Brown and Chevannes, 1998: 30):

Furthermore, as with all taboos, there are penalties for transgressing, as Parry quotes this respondent (2004: 176):

Boys have a real macho image to live up to. If a boy acts in an effeminate way he will be targeted and teased by the other students.

These penalties are aggressively policed and enforced by peer groups to the point that boys who are gentle and thoughtful or who prefer to abstain from sex can end up being severely bullied. Most boys want to avoid that fate and work hard to conform to the rigorous demands of hard masculinity.

In the previous and following quotations, deep misogynistic and homophobic taboos reveal themselves, as Bailey et al (2000: 8) demonstrates:

The culture demanded physical responses from boys and made toughness the hallmark of the real male. Young boys knew that if they performed outside the expected, traditional roles they would be ridiculed and labelled 'sissy' by boys and girls.

Although these taboos have their origins in misogynistic and homophobic prejudices, their influence underwrites a vast range of what is considered to be acceptable and unacceptable masculinity *for all men*. In the following example from Bailey et al. (1998: 82) we can see how these taboos can stunt the formation of relationships:

The inner-city youngsters felt that love was likely to make a person vulnerable in a relationship. If you loved someone and expressed it … it became a weakness which could be exploited.

The pressures to restrict one's emotions and signs of vulnerability and to project strength contribute significantly to valorising male physicality. Physicality is particularly important in contemporary life because it is an important way that men can differentiate themselves from the 'opposite' sex and is therefore central to modern gender identity formation. The emphasis on physicality also has consequences for relationships. For example, men are more likely to use physical means to resolve disputes. The converse is also true: that a man who backs away from a physical confrontation risks his reputation as a man. Risk-taking is integral to masculine identity in many modern cultures (Bailey et al., 1998: 17).

But it should be noted that the emphasis on physicality and risk-taking is a social construct of masculinity and is neither inevitable nor necessary. Providing the culture supports it, masculine identity can instead emphasise being responsible, considerate and gentle. As Parry (2000: 58) says:

[G]ender-related responses [in education] *have less to do with natural differences than they do with cultural expectations about how Caribbean males and females are supposed to respond.*

In contrast, deep social taboos on tenderness put pressure on men to embrace hard masculinities and these will supplant other styles of masculinity to become the dominant (hegemonic) standards against which all men are measured. This is the dilemma that modern-day Jamaica finds itself in, as Chevannes (1999: 29) describes:

The so-called inner-city don is a role model not only because of his ability to command and dispense largesse, but also because he is a living source of power – the power over life and death, the ultimate man ... Among the youth, a common word for penis was rifle.

Notice the sexualised gender allusion in the above quotation when power is physical and is literally held at the point of a gun. Note also the close linkage between male gender identity, sexuality and power.

Policing manhood

The question presents itself as to where these prevalent male gender codes arise from and how they are enforced. There is no doubt that the pressure for boys to embrace hard masculinities is widely present in Caribbean society and is reinforced by schooling and parenting. However, our research shows that perhaps the most influential social group to enforce and police male gender roles is the male peer group (Chevannes, 1999: 29). Indeed, Jamaican research has identified that young men are at the centre of a tug of war between the peer group and the influence of parents and teachers (Chevannes, 1999: 24):

[I]*t is often the case that the peer group or the wider community or society exert influences that are not only greater than the influence of parents, but which contradict those nurtured within the family.*

Further, it appears that there is a fine line between a peer group and a gang and in some cases the peer group takes on an organised and dangerous personality where hypermasculinity is refined to a dangerous extreme.

According to Bailey et al. (1998: 82), the influence of the peer group over a boy's behaviour ought not to be underestimated:

It appeared as if the younger teenaged boys had embraced, in the most uncompromising way, the [prevailing] male gender ideology.

The obligations on members to conform to peer group standards are potent and the penalties for transgressing the codes of group masculinity can be harsh. As we have seen, peer-based masculinities frequently entail the valorisation of risk and embrace sexual conquest as definitive of manhood. Loyalty to those codes is both policed and enforced as Chevannes (1999: 30) shows:

An adolescent boy's friends exact an affinity and a loyalty as sacred as the bond of kinship as strong as the sentiment of religion. They socialise one another, the older members of the group acting as the transmitters of what passes as knowledge, invent new values and meanings.

The preceding extract also alerts us to another important issue: peer groups have their own living culture – they are not simply passive victims of the American media. These cultures are actively created by the groups themselves. The codes are passed from older members to younger ones, often in the context of tension with the outside (adult) world. Boys' aspirations to achieving masculine identity are encoded into peer group cultures and those aspirations can override many of the expectations of wider society as Chevannes (1999: 11) graphically describes:

For many men, meeting the demands of a male identity is a far greater moral imperative than the virtues of honesty and respect for property and even life.

Masculinity and materialism

It is often said that HIV is related to poverty, but closer scrutiny reveals that this statement does not accord neatly with the facts. Around the globe it has been observed that HIV is typically concentrated along trucking routes, around military bases and in the vicinity of logging camps. In China, India and Eastern Europe, HIV has spread rapidly in tandem with greater economic freedom. Moreover, in the Caribbean, relatively rich countries like Trinidad are more severely affected by HIV than are many of the poorer neighbouring islands. Clearly the relationship between HIV and poverty is not a simple one.

So how do we make sense of these observations? When the same data are revisited with the aid of a gender lens another conclusion starts to emerge: that in the context of poverty, HIV is actually associated with economic activity. Thus, as in the case of the mines, the military bases and the logging camps, HIV is generally found at higher levels wherever there are *clusters of young males with significant disposable income*. What is particularly interesting when the data are viewed in this way is that the previously hidden gender dimensions start to emerge. It is in fact men and their economic power who are centre stage in driving the epidemic. Clearly we do not want to minimise the difficulties caused by poverty for women, in particular, but a richer picture emerges when men are written into the story too.

The emphasis on physicality also has implications for boys' education because academic achievement appears to have become increasingly taboo for Caribbean boys. Instead, physical power is pre-eminent above intellectual achievements in what defines a real man, at least in certain modern social settings. Of course, with an emphasis on material possessions as defining successful manhood, but a lack of education to provide the means of achieving material wealth, some men are increasingly resorting to crime as a way of enriching themselves, as Brown and Chevannes (1998: 33) report:

Education as a route to economic and personal achievement is devalued and new role models emerge from the DJ/Dancehall and donman/drug cultures where big money is highly visible.

This material emphasis has its impact on sexual risks and on the quality of relationships, as Bailey et al. (1998: 77) have shown:

Money was seen as an absolutely vital resource for a male in relationships. Much of his status was given in the equation where money was exchanged for respect, loyalty and sex.

Conclusions and policy implications

Given that gender roles drive HIV, and in order to prevent HIV and to manage the consequences of the epidemic, we have no choice but to engage with these roles at fundamental levels and in sophisticated ways. This paper finds that gender roles create a trap that disadvantages both men and women. Men are caught in a double bind: there are heavy social pressures that oblige them to embrace dominant masculinity (including hard, dangerous, risk-taking, anti-social hypermasculinities); while subordinate masculinities (including gentle, thoughtful, caring, faithful masculinities) are stigmatised and tabooed. The taboos that are most influential here are homophobia and misogyny; our research has shown that the male peer group is the principal means of policing and enforcing these codes. A key finding is that homophobia harms all men – not just gay men as is commonly assumed. Moreover, it emerges from this research that homophobia is very much a gender prejudice – more so than a sexual prejudice, which it is generally assumed to be. Through the twin mechanisms of obligation and taboo, a wide range of risks, including sexual risks, have become resiliently embedded in the social fabric and are therefore highly resistant to change.

But there is reason for optimism. Historians have shown that gender roles are in a constant state of flux and dominant masculinities have evolved radically over time and across cultures. Therefore, masculinities can and do change. To overcome HIV, it will be vital to achieve social change that remodels dominant masculinities to move them away from the harder risky versions that have become so valorised in popular culture in the 20th and 21st centuries.

All policies that affect HIV and AIDS must recognise that stereotypical gender roles drive the epidemic. Risk behaviours are deeply embedded and policy should address this or they will fail. Fortunately, standards of masculinity are fluid. Policies should therefore be geared towards reshaping prevailing standards of masculinity in order to reduce dangerous hyper-masculinities and risk-taking and to strengthen and valorise responsible masculinities. Taboos related to misogyny and homophobia will have to be unpacked and remodelled so that caring, kind, loving, considerate and cautious behaviours are no longer seen as the antithesis of masculinity. Paradoxically, homophobia emerges from our research to be a major gender issue, rather than primarily an issue of sexual identity. Policies need to reflect these findings and gender

programmes will have to address homophobia if they are ultimately to achieve their goals. It is clear that progress on HIV will not be optimal unless gender strategies address and reject homophobia – it is here that we have identified the deep and resilient source of stigma that haunts HIV and severely undermines effective interventions.

REFERENCES

Bailey, W. (ed.) (1998). *Gender and the Family in the Caribbean*, Institute of Social and Economic Research, Mona, Jamaica.

Bailey, W., Branche, C., McGarrity, G. and Stuart, S. (1998). *Family and the Quality of Gender Relations in the Caribbean*, Institute of Social and Economic Research, Mona, Jamaica.

Bailey, W., Branche, C. and Henry-Lee, A. (2002). *Gender, Contest and Conflict in the Caribbean*, SALISES, Mona, Jamaica.

Brown, J. and Chevannes, B. (1998). *Why man stay so – tie the Heifer and loose the bull: an examination of gender socialisation in the Caribbean*. University of the West Indies, Mona, Jamaica.

Chevannes, B. (1999). *What we sow and what we reap – problems in the cultivation of male identity in Jamaica*, Grace, Kennedy Foundation, Kingston, Jamaica.

Crichlow, W.E.A. (2004). 'History, (re)memory, testimony and biomythography: charting a buller man's Trinidadian past', in Reddock, R.E. (ed.), *Interrogating Caribbean Masculinities*, University of the West Indies Press, Mona, Jamaica.

Figueroa, M. (2004). 'Male privileging and male "academic underperformance" in Jamaica', in Reddock, R.E. (ed.), *Interrogating Caribbean Masculinities*, University of the West Indies Press, Mona, Jamaica.

Parry, O. (2000). *Male Underachievement in High School Education*, Canoe Press, Mona, Jamaica.

Parry, O. (2004). 'Masculinities, myths and educational underachievement: Jamaica, Barbados and St Vincent and the Grenadines', in Reddock, R.E. (ed.), *Interrogating Caribbean Masculinities*, University of the West Indies Press, Mona, Jamaica.

ENDNOTE

1   'Buller' is the term in the South-Eastern Caribbean for homosexual. The equivalent in the USA is 'faggot'.

DAVID PLUMMER is the Commonwealth/UNESCO regional professor in HIV Education for the Caribbean. He is based at the School of Education, University of the West Indies, St Augustine Campus, Trinidad. He is a physician and has a PhD in Sociology. His research is in gender, sexual health, marginalisation and health, and stigma and discrimination. He is a member of the UNAIDS Global Reference Group on HIV Prevention. He has worked on HIV in Australia, the Asia-Pacific region and the Caribbean.

JOEL SIMPSON is the UNESCO human rights researcher at the HIV Education Unit, University of the West Indies. He holds a Bachelor of Laws degree from the University of Guyana, where his areas of focus included Caribbean human rights law, family law and law in society. He has also served many regional institutions and projects as a human rights consultant, particularly in the field of HIV/AIDS and human rights.

Listening to HIV-positive women

Parliamentarians for Women's Health

The International Community of Women Living with HIV/AIDS (ICW), Centre for the Study of AIDS (CSA), International Center for Research on Women (ICRW) and Realizing Rights: the Ethical Globalisation Initiative (EGI) are working with parliamentarians as part of a consortium to improve women's access to health care in four countries: Botswana, Namibia, Kenya and Tanzania.[1] The aim of the Parliamentarians for Women's Health (PWH) project is to improve parliamentarians' understanding of the health issues that women, especially HIV-positive women, face, including barriers to accessing treatment and sexual and reproductive health facilities.

This article looks at the work that Parliamentarians for Women's Health project officer Jennifer Gatsi is carrying out in Namibia. Although the focus of the project is on women's health in general, this article deals with the health and rights of HIV-positive women.

Finding out what matters

An important first step in persuading parliamentarians to understand HIV-positive women's health issues and the barriers they face in trying to maintain their health is gathering evidence. The evidence-gathering component of the project served as a springboard to bring diverse groups together, such as HIV-positive women, health providers and government officials. This had several positive outcomes: the last two groups were helped to think critically about the impact of their actions on HIV-positive women, which provided a valuable opportunity to reduce the isolation faced by the women who were living with HIV and AIDS; and there was an opportunity to highlight issues that are often sidelined in work on HIV.

One important aspect of the evidence gathering was that it was largely conducted by the HIV-positive women themselves. This encouraged greater openness among participants, who were mistrustful of extractive research carried out by outsiders, where information is gathered but rarely fed back to the participants.

I introduced myself but I did not state my HIV status at the beginning of the meeting and this caused no openness from the group of their status either. During the discussions the group participants were saying they wanted to get this information so they can help positive women whom they knew in their community, but my observations were that they were not sure whether to state their HIV status but were comfortable to talk as if they wanted to help others rather than themselves. After realising this, I informed them that I was HIV positive and I felt the great relief from the group. They started to be open about their status and all participants started to participate openly without reservations. (Jennifer Gatsi, while she was conducting the treatment mapping described below)

Two information-gathering exercises led by Jennifer Gatsi are described below. The first focused on access to care, treatment and support. The gendered aspects of treatment access are rarely considered in treatment policy and programmes due to a lack of information and the erroneous conclusion that if, globally, women and men are accessing treatment in equal numbers, gender is not relevant. The project sought to address this information gap. The second exercise was a community-based assessment exploring women's health needs and available services. Fact-finding workshops were conducted with HIV-negative and HIV-positive women, health care providers and local leaders. The findings were presented to these groups, along with community members, parliamentarians, and public and private

service providers to ensure that the identified health needs and issues were addressed and improved on.

Following this work, Gatsi has helped to facilitate linkages between women with HIV/AIDS and parliamentarians.

Barriers to access for care, treatment and support[2]

Last year, Gatsi met with HIV-positive women's groups in four locations in the two regions of northern Namibia with the highest prevalence rates of HIV/AIDS (Caprivi and Kavango) to map the women's experiences of access to care and treatment.

They found that poverty is a major stumbling block in accessing care, treatment and support. A mother who had to take her sick HIV-positive child to hospital was refused medication for both herself and the child because she did not have money. Food shortages in general are a big problem. Most people do not have enough to eat, let alone sufficient nutritious options, and it is problematic to take some medications on an empty stomach.[3]

Gender inequalities also often constrain girls' and women's ability to access care, treatment and support. For instance, girls and women, including women living with HIV, were burdened by foregoing their own needs when caring for loved ones or the sick in the community. Their lack of decision-making power in the household makes it hard to access treatments for HIV and sexually transmitted infections (STIs), particularly if a woman has to ask a family member for money for medication or transport, and to use advice and treatment to maintain and improve their health. For example, women find it hard to negotiate condoms with partners and husbands. Yet condoms are one of the most effective ways of preventing STI transmission.

HIV-related stigma is a major obstacle to maintaining health, especially in urban areas and big towns where there is less community spirit and fewer family support networks. In the villages, where HIV prevalence is very high, stigma can be less acute due to a recognition that HIV is a community problem shared by all families, resulting in less stigma associated with accessing HIV-related services.

All the women complained about the lack of care, support and treatment from clinics and hospitals. They said the attitude of the health care workers is: 'You are going to die anyway, so why should we bother treating you?' Indeed, in some cases HIV-positive women were either denied services or pressured to access family planning services due to discriminatory attitudes regarding their sexual and reproductive lives. For example, Gatsi met with women who have been forced to go on injection contraception if they wanted access to antiretrovirals. Rejecting the contraceptive, in these cases, meant denial of access to life-saving medication. Lack of continuity of care for HIV-positive women meant that one woman who had been on a prevention of mother-to-child transmission (PMTCT) programme had to switch to breast-feeding her four-month old baby when she could not afford a milk substitute.[4] A lack of treatment monitoring equipment and of good quality medications also negatively impact on HIV-positive women's ability to maintain their health.

None of the groups and leaders of civil society organisations that Gatsi met had any knowledge of either women's right to sexual and reproductive health or of the international conventions that the Namibian Government has ratified. Fortunately, the PWH project staff have worked hard to identify and work with allies in the Ministry of Health and Ministry of Gender, and now there are a number of politicians who are working with HIV-positive women to understand what the issues are and how they can address them, through, for example, meeting with HIV-positive women and attending joint workshops.

ICW has used the results of these mappings in its international advocacy work for increased political support and resources for addressing the gendered barriers to care, treatment and support, and for an understanding that the connection between treatment and improved well-being cannot

simply be gauged by the numbers of women and men who are accessing antiretrovirals. Access to care, treatment and support is not just about getting medications. It is about quality support, advice and options obtainable for all. It is also about changing the conditions of women's lives so HIV-positive women can use those essential treatments successfully.

Participants' recommendations

Participants suggested that governments and donors should make medications free, provide food and impart skills which can help HIV-positive women avoid dependency. They also stressed that more information is needed on sexual and reproductive health (SRH) and HIV.

Assessing women's health needs[5]

The PWH project held three regional community assessments, led once again by Gatsi and her colleagues, to evaluate the availability and accessibility of HIV/AIDS health care services for women in three regions. The assessment results were used to raise awareness of women's health issues and rights, and build capacity among MPs for women's health teams. It is hoped that the information will be used to develop and design community-wide campaign and action plans to address shortcomings in women's access to health care services.

Separate workshops were held with HIV-positive women, negative and untested women, community leaders and service providers in three regions (Khomas, Caprivi and Kavango) to identify priority health issues and assess the availability and accessibility of related health care services. The assessments also took in site visits to a major hospital, community clinics and traditional health care providers.

HIV/AIDS, TB, high blood pressure, STIs and cancers were identified by all groups as priority health issues affecting women. Cancer is a concern because it is not detected in its early and treatable stages due to lack of preventative check-ups. Uterine cancer is a particular risk for HIV-positive women. High blood pressure was associated with stress and depression particularly resulting from HIV infection.

Mental health, rather than high blood pressure, was identified by the health service providers as a priority health issue. TB, the most common infectious disease, is prevalent among vulnerable populations, including those living with HIV. Other issues that impact on women's health included malaria and diarrhoea, and social issues such as alcoholism, violence against women, poverty, poor diets, unemployment and risky cultural practices such as polygamy.

Among the barriers to accessing health care services identified by women are: long distances to health facilities and lack of transport infrastructure; service and treatment fees; stigma and discrimination; lack of correct information about women's health; attitudes of health care staff, who are often rude and unfriendly; insensitive language and communication barriers (due to the fact that doctors are often from other African countries or Cuba); lack of understanding of the context in which women live their lives; and breaches in confidentiality. Confidentiality breaches occurring throughout the health system constitute a major barrier to accessing HIV treatment and care. These breaches can occur either because of the indiscretion of service providers or when a person inadvertently reveals his/her status by accessing segregated HIV services.

A lack of information about STIs combined with accompanying stigma also contributes to reluctance among women to seek treatment for sexual health problems. Women often find it difficult to talk about STIs and are unlikely to bring up sexual health concerns with anyone, including their husbands or partners. Reports from the workshops and site visits revealed that men are even less likely to seek treatment for sexual health problems. As long as sexual health issues remain taboo, the problems will be perpetuated, particularly as both partners need to be treated at the same time to maintain sexual health. Women can face harassment from clinic staff if they repeatedly present with the same symptoms of an STI, and often feel ashamed to return to the clinic for a repeat diagnosis and treatment.

While different services exist for health problems, people favoured going to hospital for treatment services as opposed to clinics, due to limited and poor quality, disrespectful staff and resource shortages

Linking HIV positive women and politicians

Two years ago, the majority of women (HIV-positive and HIV-negative) did not have any kind of information about their sexual and reproductive health and rights. Through our research work with women we have been able to highlight important aspects of sexual and reproductive health and rights. We have also been able to facilitate the bringing together of HIV-positive women and parliamentarians in order to ensure that true change happens. As Gatsi says:

A group of women whom I informed about the PAP smear and breast examination and on where to go and access these services took it upon themselves to approach the Ministry of Health together with the Director of the organisation this group was affiliated with. This led to the Ministry of Health collaborating with the Cancer Association, which is a private institution, to carry out PAP smears, breast examinations and provision of information on different kinds of cancer during their visits to regions and communities. There has been an increasing number of awareness campaigns in both the print media and on the radio.

Committees of HIV-positive women have been set up in each region by the project officers and other women with whom they have worked during the project. These committees help to build ongoing relationships with parliamentarians and HIV-positive women in their regions. The committees are developing lines of communications with each other so as to take all issues faced by HIV-positive women to the parliamentarians and to work together to address them. Gatsi continues:

I am excited as we are empowering our women to understand the mechanism of advocacy and encouraging them to be the voice of the voiceless.

Some of the women have also been involved in sexual and reproductive health and rights training, and more sessions are planned for the coming months.

Future plans

By training HIV-positive women to train other HIV-positive women, the project aims

(for example, of medications and medical equipment). Private clinics, community service organisations, churches and traditional healers provide a range of care and support services beyond what is available through the government health system. It was felt by a number of women that traditional healers provide greater holistic care than other kinds of health care. Services provided outside the government health system include home-based care, support for orphans and vulnerable children, voluntary counselling and testing, and family planning. Organisations tend not to link with each other, causing confusion, gaps, overlaps and poor coordination between services.

What the participants described as a good service consists of ethical staff who do not stigmatise and discriminate against women and girls seeking HIV and family planning services, and correct and consistent information on major women's health issues, especially HIV and AIDS, and on reproductive and sexual health. They also want adequate facilities providing women's health services within communities and improvement in health facilities such as cleanliness, comfortable waiting areas, more and accessible toilets, stretchers and ambulances. Access to clean water and nutrition are also an important part of being able to benefit from health care and medication.

The results of the project's assessment were shared by the project officers at a round

table discussion with parliamentarians and service providers at a women's health workshop held in October 2006. The Deputy Home Affairs Minister, Teopolina Mushelenga, who was present, backed the assessment findings by confirming that gender inequality and disparities, and socio-economic issues such as poverty, social exclusion, unemployment and poor housing are some of the problems having an impact on women's rights to health. This was an important demonstration of support for all women in Namibia.

'Women's health problems are further exacerbated by harmful cultural practices, domestic violence, prostitution, early marriage, rape and food insecurity. Considering the role that women play in the society as breadwinners, doing domestic chores and taking responsibility for the care of their children it becomes relevant that their health situation be addressed,' said Mushelenga.

The round table meeting made the following recommendations.

- An awareness campaign, particularly on HIV/AIDS and sexual and reproductive health that includes people living with HIV.

- Strengthening of dialogue between MPs and the Ministry of Gender Equality and Child Welfare on gender issues.

- Shelters, support and legal services for abused women and children.

to develop the capacity of positive women to ensure that they are meaningfully involved in making decisions, including national policies, that impact on their lives. Through training parliamentarians we hope to build the capacity of those in positions of power to engage with HIV-positive people in ways that are equitable, respectful and productive for all involved.

Gatsi and her colleagues plan to empower 13 women and girls and four female MPs through a series of training sessions which include sexual and reproductive health and rights. The aim is to train 13 women who will be linked with a committee of 26 women to be selected later in the year from the 13 regions (two women – one older and one young – from each region). Committee members will be trained by the 13 women so that they can spread information to women across Namibia, including to women in the villages. Gatsi also plans to engage the Namibia Institute of Democracy and the Legal Assistance Centre in giving further advanced training to HIV-positive women on advocacy and legal rights. As she says:

> We still have a long way but I am happy with the current turning of wheels.

ORGANISATIONAL NOTES

The International Community of Women Living With HIV/AIDS, a registered UK charity, is the only international network run for and by HIV-positive women. ICW was founded in response to the desperate lack of support, information and services available to women living with HIV worldwide and the need for these women to have input into policy development. ICW's vision is a world where all HIV positive-women:

- have a respected and meaningful involvement at all political levels where decisions that affect their lives are being made
- have full access to care and treatment
- enjoy full rights, particularly sexual, reproductive, legal, financial and general health rights, irrespective of their culture, age, religion, sexuality, social or economic status/class and race.

The International Center for Research on Women (ICRW) was founded in 1976. ICRW works with partner organisations and governments throughout the world to promote gender equitable development, reduce poverty, and change the lives of millions of women and girls and their communities. It undertakes focused, evidence-based, action-oriented research; provides technical assistance to partner organisations, donors and governments; and advocates for new or improved policies and programmes.

ENDNOTES

1   This is a three-year project funded by the Bill & Melinda Gates Foundation.

2   Gatsi Mallet, J. (2006). *Mapping of Experiences of Access to Care, Treatment and Support*, ICW, Windhoek, Namibia; ICW (2007). 'Charting a Journey Round Namibia', *ICW News*, 36.

3   Taking some medications on an empty stomach enhances their negative side-effects.

4   Switching between feeding methods for an infant increases the risk of mother-to-child transmission.

5   'Women Suffer a Host of Health Issues', Tuesday, 31 October 2006, by Wezi Tjaronda, featured in *New Era* and Namibia PWH Community Assessment Report, 2006.

Vamping it: women sex workers' efforts to protect themselves from HIV

Meena Shivdas

Introduction

Women sex workers are mainly portrayed and treated in public discourse and policies as vessels of moral hazard, vectors of disease and objects of pity. Their everyday lives are often beset by oppressive power relations and they tend to be socially excluded as their presence might trigger moral panic in communities. Consequently, they find themselves at the receiving end of instrumentalist interventions because they are perceived as a public health threat to be monitored. While women sex workers have been identified as active agents in HIV/AIDS prevention and are increasingly seen as partners in health interventions, their economic situations and socio-cultural realities largely shape their life conditions and determine their access to health information and services.

Despite sex workers becoming the focus of much bio-medical and social research and health programmes since the beginning of the HIV/AIDS pandemic, the stigma associated with sex work, and other barriers to self-organisation, often prevent the empowerment of sex workers.[1] However, the experience of women sex workers who are associated with an NGO, Sampada Grameen Mahila Sanstha (SANGRAM), based in Sangli in the Indian state of Maharashtra, reveals a different picture. These women, who operate out of certain areas in Maharashtra and Karnataka, have made considerable headway towards meeting some of the social and health threats in their lives.

The women formed a collective in 1996 and called it VAMP (Veshya Anyay Muqabla Parishad, or Women in Prostitution Confront Injustice) in an intentional reference to the social stigma they face and in an attempt to reclaim the term 'veshya' ('whore' in local parlance), by imputing meaning to it. The VAMP women's efforts to mobilise in order to speak out about HIV/AIDS and protect themselves from infection bring them into direct confrontation with ambiguous laws, policies and state agents who often subscribe to societal perceptions of women as either 'madonnas' or 'whores'.

Through their actions to prevent HIV/AIDS infection and help colleagues living with HIV/AIDS cope with their health and social problems, the VAMP women have questioned common perceptions of women sex workers, in particular the notion that women sex workers are vectors of infection and are therefore to be treated as significant threats to the social fabric. They have also drawn attention to the idea of risky behaviour in HIV/AIDS infection, as opposed to high-risk groups, and focused on responsibility in sexual relations. In so doing, they have shattered the culture of silence that surrounds sexual relations and HIV/AIDS in public discourse. Five thousand women sex workers from western Maharashtra and southern Karnataka are now members of the VAMP collective.

This brief article examines the efforts of VAMP and asks if the strategies employed to build awareness about women sex workers' rights to health and the steps taken towards the mobilisation of relatively powerless women are effective, given the gender discrimination and injustices that blight the everyday lives of sex workers.

VAMP(s) and rights

VAMP was set up with the aims of forging and consolidating a common identity among women sex workers and empowering them to assert their rights and protect themselves from HIV infection. By functioning as a loose collective, VAMP is able to attract members in the sex worker community. Membership is not formalised; any woman sex worker who makes use of VAMP's services or gets involved in the activities becomes a member. The board members of VAMP are peer educators who are in direct contact with the community. These women are community leaders who are effective in their condom distribution work and provide care and support to colleagues. These peer educators are called 'tais' ('sisters' in the local language, Marathi). Other categories of VAMP members are community workers and fieldworkers. Community workers assess condom requirements and monitor condom supply. They also help women to access medical services and offer informal counselling. Fieldworkers are the point people who collect condoms and arrange condom distribution to community workers. They also attend VAMP's weekly meetings and report back to their colleagues, who pass on the information to their constituents. Significantly, VAMP's board members are peer educators, women sex workers who know the pulse of the community. Each board member carries an identity card which often comes in useful when dealing with police harassment.

VAMP emphasises that a peer educator's portfolio spans the entire continuum of HIV: before, during and after infection. Their preventive work on HIV/AIDS is mainly through peer education, condom distribution and assisting sex worker colleagues who have sexually transmitted infections and other health problems to access

medical help. VAMP women have to play a supportive role when community members become HIV infected. Often peer educators become the *de facto* families and care givers of ill colleagues. Not only do they ferry these women back and forth from hospitals but they also organise food for them, look after the women's children, or even lovers who may be sick as well, and offer unconditional support. When a colleague succumbs to AIDS-related health complications they have to grapple with funeral arrangements and also deal with questions about their own vulnerability to HIV infection. Although relatives may sometimes come forward to perform the last rites according to traditional custom, in one particular district, when the men in the community refused to be the pall bearers, the women decided to carry their colleague on her last journey to the funeral site. Taking on hitherto male prescribed roles (according to Hindu custom, *only* men can be pall bearers) has made the women conscious of deep-seated discrimination and they realise that as women and as sex workers they have had to make compromises in their lives.

While HIV/AIDS forms a large part of the focus in VAMP women's initiatives to help themselves, considerable attention is also given to the socio-economic impact of women sex workers' health and well-being. VAMP plays a crucial role in promoting the interests of its constituents, the women sex workers, by mediating in community disputes, lobbying with the police, helping colleagues to access government systems and services, and facilitating leadership potential among its members. Women sex workers regularly face police harassment: not only are they routinely abused and beaten, they are also randomly picked up on charges of soliciting, which is deemed criminal under India's prostitution law. Brothel keeping is also criminalised and, more often than not, sex workers are implicated more than brothel keepers and pimps.[2]

Before the VAMP collective was formed, women sex workers could do little about routine police harassment. Now, they are treated with more respect when they approach police officers for help. In some cases, VAMP has successfully negotiated an end to police hostility and brothel raids. However, this does not mean that all VAMP members are able to confront and challenge police harassment. What has happened is that more women have become aware of their rights and recognise that they have the capacity to negotiate with others, including those in authority, to diffuse threatening situations. They are no longer in a position where they are told by others how to act, but are now empowered to decide for themselves what to do about problems and pursue conflict resolution. As well as the peer educator programme and advocacy initiatives that form the basis of its identity formation, and its leadership development and mobilisation efforts, VAMP has expanded its work to include specific clientele and members' children.

In 2000, an integrated project on STD and HIV/AIDS intervention among truckers was undertaken. Truckers who ply India's highways between Maharashtra and Karnataka are extremely mobile and have multiple sex partners. As they are also regular clients of VAMP members and form a large pool of the clientele, it was decided that the VAMP collective's experience with the peer educator intervention could be used as a model approach for the intervention with truckers. VAMP's emphasis on safe and responsible sex formed the core of the intervention, which was then combined with the women's knowledge of their clients' habits and behaviour patterns. The project succeeded in raising awareness about the need for protection during sexual encounters mainly because the truckers saw the VAMP women as their friends and lovers, and not as interventionists.

A VAMP initiative which is directed towards women sex workers' children is designed to help the children cope with the stigma of their mothers' involvement in sex work. Having a mother who is also a sex worker brings with it more than its share of stigma and marginalisation. VAMP members felt that their and their colleagues' children needed a safe space to explore and strengthen their ability to deal with the mainstream attitude towards them. Thus began the Supplementary Education for Kids scheme. VAMP uses tuition classes as an entry point to teach children core life skills. The children examine their identity and explore ways to reclaim spaces for respect, given the type of work and lives that are led by their mothers.

VAMP members' work and lives have also seen challenges and barriers to their HIV prevention and mobilisation efforts. While VAMP promotes the concept of 'responsible sex' rather than 'safe sex' to emphasise that women sex workers owe it to themselves to ensure that a condom is used every time they have penetrative sex, the collective is still grappling with how to impress this message further, because women sex workers tend not to insist on condom use for certain sexual encounters. During sex with pimps, male brothel owners and the police, women sex workers often find it difficult to demand that condoms be used, as these men have the power to refuse condoms. They are also not paying clients, so the women cannot simply turn down the business by refusing the money offered. At another level, *malaks*, or lovers, play important roles in the women's lives: they may have fathered their children, seen them through trying times and are usually emotional supports and good friends. As many women sex workers feel the need to differentiate between a client and a lover, the presence or absence of a condom helps to denote that difference. This is a complex issue and the women will continue to work at it to devise viable solutions.

VAMP members have started meeting other collectives of sex workers outside their home states and also at national and international meetings. For example, VAMP women actively participated in the World Social Form in Mumbai in January 2004 and at the XV International AIDS Conference in Bangkok in July 2004. As they network and share their experiences with other sex-worker activists, they will bring new perspectives to their mobilisation and advocacy efforts to prevent HIV/AIDS. VAMP is beginning to be an important player in lobbying efforts at district and state level. VAMP members' voices are also beginning to be heard at national and international level. They have emerged as people in their own right.

Conclusion

Through their actions to prevent HIV/AIDS infection and help colleagues living with HIV/AIDS cope with their health and social problems, the VAMP women have questioned common perceptions of women sex workers, in particular the notion that women sex workers are vectors of infection and therefore to be treated as a significant threat to the social fabric. They have also drawn attention to the idea of risky behaviour in HIV/AIDS infection, as opposed to high-risk groups, and focused on responsibility in sexual relations. In so doing, they have shattered the culture of silence that surrounds sexual relations and HIV/AIDS in public discussion.

The experiences of VAMP have key lessons for policy and practice. The following observations are a basis for further analysis and consideration.

- Any HIV/AIDS intervention with women sex workers that is initiated in collaboration with the sex worker community is more likely to succeed, as women in the 'business' know more than anyone else about what works and what does not.

- Any intervention that is based on needs assessment that captures women sex workers' perceptions, responses and interpretations of their lives and well-being is more likely to succeed, because it does not address HIV/AIDS in isolation.

- Identity formation, mobilisation efforts and empowerment from within are key factors for successful HIV/AIDS prevention strategies among women sex workers.

- Facilitating the realisation of rights entails giving marginalised women sex workers a 'voice' and the 'space' to realise their potential as agents of change in transforming unequal social situations.

This article is a summary of a case study prepared for the UN Economic and Social Commission for Asia and the Pacific (ESCAP).

ENDNOTES

1   Overs, C., Doezema, J. and Shivdas, M. (2002), 'Just lipservice? Sex worker participation in sexual and reproductive health interventions', in Cornwall, A. and Wellbourn, A. (eds), *Realising Rights: Transformational Approaches to Sexual and Reproductive Well Being*, Zed Press, London.

2   D'Cunha, J. (1992). 'Prostitution Laws – ideological dimensions and enforcement practices', *Economic and Political Weekly*, 25 April 1992, Sameeksha Trust, Mumbai; Gangoli, G. (1999). *The Regulation of Women's Sexuality through Law: Civil and Criminal Laws* in re/productions, Issue No. 2, April 1999, Harvard School of Public Health, Boston.

DR MEENA SHIVDAS is adviser on Gender, Human Rights and HIV for the Commonwealth Secretariat. She has worked on a range of women's rights issues with a focus on policy and action research, and on training modules and manuals. Her areas of interest and experience include sex trafficking, sex work, migration, violence against women, women's reproductive health, post-Beijing implementation and monitoring, women's human rights, CEDAW and HIV/AIDS. Before joining the Secretariat she worked in Asia, and has addressed gender and development issues in Nepal, Indonesia, Malaysia, India, Mongolia, Iran, Singapore and Thailand.

Removing glazed eyes with (S)expos

A new approach to education on gender and HIV/AIDS

Margaret O'Callaghan and Elizabeth Cox

Stereotyped gender roles in relation to sexuality may be the most important factor constraining both men and women from taking appropriate [HIV] *preventive measures.*[1]

Introduction

Much attention has been paid to the subject of HIV/AIDS over the past two decades, with a multiplicity of efforts to stem the epidemic. However, until recently little was done to recognise and address the gender implications of the spread of the disease, without which interventions will fail and scarce financial resources will not be used effectively. It has also been recognised by UNIFEM that there have been impediments to understanding both the subject of gender and its linkages with HIV/AIDS.

The UNIFEM Pacific Regional Office[2] recently made a breakthrough in addressing these constraints by developing an educational methodology which has become known as a (S)Expo learning experience. This article describes why the methodology was developed, how the concept works and why we think that this is a breakthrough which could be further adapted and replicated for a diverse range of groups. These could include senior policy-makers such as parliamentarians and heads of government departments, people in the private sector and NGOs, as well as young people and rural communities.

Background

The (S)Expo innovation developed as a response to our experience that the language used by development-oriented academics and other professionals is often alienating to others. In non-academic circles, concepts like 'discrimination', 'human rights', 'stereotype' and 'gender' are likely to fall into the category of mystifying jargon. This is so, even though these terms relate to the realities of everyday life and to forces that are very basic to every society, family and individual.

Many well-intentioned and passionate efforts have been made to educate people about the process and impact of gender. However, presenters have often failed to unpack the theoretical concept, and presentations come across as abstract and unsettling. Little understanding is conveyed and people's fundamental attitudes and behaviour remain unchanged.

A contributory factor is the unfamiliarity and 'foreignness' of terms like those above, which can be off-putting and therefore not conducive to effective learning about the important subjects of gender and HIV/AIDS. References to gender are often assumed to be one-sided, shaming and blaming men and sympathetic to women. We should not be surprised that when we want to address the very important issue of gender and HIV, we are confronted with glazed eyes or defensiveness, and that little learning and internalisation of the issues takes place.

The concepts of gendered inequality and the use of power, force and violence in relationships between women and men are not easily understood, let alone internalised. This is partly because they raise difficult questions about some very basic assumptions and social rules which often create discomfort. Consequently, the information is not fully understood, even if the basic facts of women's disadvantage are conceded.

In addition, the subject of men and HIV has, until recently, been largely neglected in gender and HIV/AIDS education and programmes, despite the fact that male and female are two sides of the same coin and the subject of gender encompasses both sexes. Worse, in discussions on gender, and in particular on gender and HIV, there has been a tendency to zero in on a stereotyped image of powerful men who offend and powerless women who suffer. Men also are made vulnerable by their socialisation and require support to address their needs, which in turn should have a positive impact for women, including making them less at risk of infection. A further challenge occurs when the subject of gender is meshed with the sensitive and poorly enunciated topic of sexuality and HIV/AIDS, which is often obscured by veils of prudery, taboo and guilt.

Sex and sexuality are fascinating subjects for most human beings, but despite this interest, people find it difficult to confront something so private and personal, especially in a public arena. The bottom line is that transmission of the virus is primarily sexual, so solutions must ultimately focus on the subject of male–female relationships, and especially on the stereotypes which are constantly promoted in all societies. Such stereotyping is at the root of the problems. In addition, because of its very personal nature, the subject of gender and HIV is not one that can be easily or effectively addressed in large groups with a whiteboard, glossy and colourful posters, or slick PowerPoint presentations.

The story is further complicated by the fact that education about the facts of HIV/AIDS has often been presented as a sort of cure-all, as if assuming that such knowledge will 'immunise' people. But in fact, behaviour often bears little or no relationship with levels of knowledge, to what people say they will do and their promises to change their behaviour. Education about facts is easy: it is much more difficult and time-consuming to look below the surface of people's behaviour, behind the denial, the platitudes and piousness. But if interventions are to be effective, this is what is needed.

Governments, as well as some development agencies, also find it difficult to go beyond

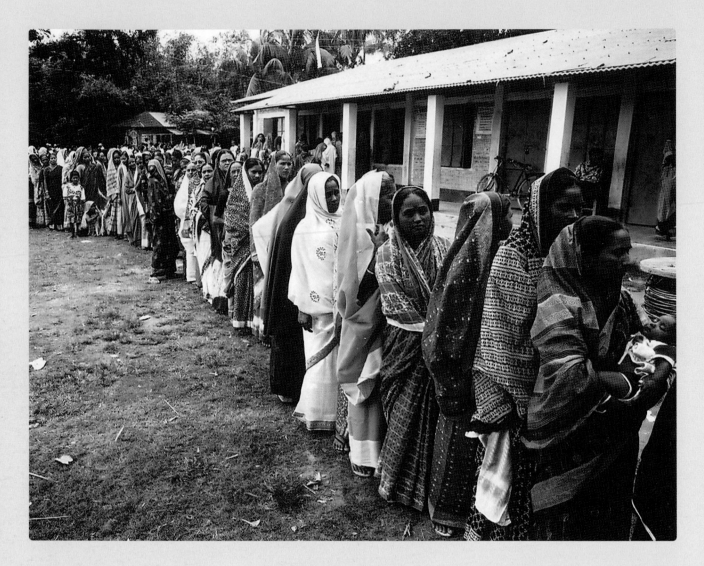

the dissemination of information because this implies trespassing onto very personal aspects of people's lives. It also means that people must critically examine the social and political structures of society that influence how people behave.

The spread of HIV will not be reduced unless the underlying gender, social and political issues are openly dealt with. However, we need to be smarter and more objective in getting the issues across. The key question is how to do so in ways that neither cause people's eyes to glaze over nor make them close their minds because of embarrassment, shame or guilt about the forces that are really driving the epidemic.

The (S)Expo concept

The Pacific Regional Office of UNIFEM, with the assistance of staff from other UN agencies based in Fiji, recently planned and organised a (S)Expo as a sensitisation/training activity aimed at addressing these issues. It aimed to show that, while the prevalence rate of HIV/AIDS in the Pacific is still very low, the region has many characteristics which make it fertile ground for a fully fledged epidemic.[3]

The concept was based on an expo-type experience which in the course of the inter-agency preparations became known as the (S)Expo. This play on words was the first step in turning the project into a novel and fun exercise. The name fitted and stuck because of its focus on the main mode of HIV transmission and the critical role played by gendered power relationships between the sexes. The name helped to reduce resistance to a programme of information and education that might otherwise have been perceived as 'yet another' gender training session.

The venue and layout helped to set the scene. Eight Pacific themed booths were set up around the edge of a very large hall. A plenary site, simulating a *bose* (council), was set up at the end of the room, with chairs arranged in a circle around traditional woven pandanus mats and a centrally located kava bowl. From the moment the participants entered, they could see that the (S)Expo was going to break away from the 'same old, same old ...' workshop mode and mentality.

Content and format

The day-long (S)Expo was based on a multi-sectoral approach with the scene set by outlining the broad social context in which HIV is spreading. The complex inter-sectionality of issues was broken down into key factors and participants were helped to gain an overview of the many influences that cause a particular society or setting to become fertile terrain for the spread of the HIV virus.

The themed booths afforded an opportunity to work on a selection of the intersecting issues one by one, as building blocks of the bigger and more complex context of what constitutes fertile terrain for the spread of the virus, looking through a gender lens. Areas covered were media and the arts, socialisation, biology, economics, psycho-social issues, political and legal issues, sexuality, violence and data. The effects of socialisation on male and female behaviour and attitudes as they relate to HIV risk and vulnerability connected all the focus areas.

A variety of short learning assignments were given to participants. Some were quite novel, intended to stimulate interest, such as analysing a family tree to better understand the effect of HIV on a family's income and other social protection and survival issues, and looking at the dates on tombstones in cemeteries in different countries. The analysis of health and demographic data, the Bible, images in magazines and the lyrics of pop songs also stimulated interest and tested analytical skills. Some of the subjects discussed, such as sexuality, were very personal and the necessary degree of intimacy and openness was made possible by the privacy of the small booths, and enhanced by the smallness of the groups and the partially enclosed spaces.

Groups of between six to eight participants rotated from one booth to another, spending an hour in most of them. Open discussion was facilitated by the small size of the groups and the interactive discussion-based formats. Facilitators, who were mainly non-experts, came from UN agencies and a partner project. Plenary sessions were held at the beginning and end of the day. These helped draw together the various threads and highlighted the rationale for the exercise and the all-pervasiveness of gender issues.

In order to provide an added cultural dimension, two young artists (one male and one female) from the University of the South Pacific were present all day. As the participants moved from booth to booth, each artist worked on their own oil painting on the theme of 'Gender and HIV/AIDS'. In addition, a local education group, Women's Action for Change (WAC), performed an interactive drama, *War of Words not Swords*, which addressed aspects of gender-based violence.

To complete the exercise, participants were given a short questionnaire to guide a gender analysis of a popular movie of their choice. An incentive was offered – participants who completed this task and submitted it to their UN agency's gender focal point would have their ticket refunded. They were also encouraged to involve family and friends in the gender analysis/film review homework. This was another engaging activity which helped to reinforce the day's learning. Staff were amused by the idea of their UN employer funding them to attend a movie. This novel learning mode further stimulated interest and a positive attitude to the subject.

Discussion

The (S)Expo process and content were both stimulating and educational. They stimulated participants to think about areas they had not previously considered and opened eyes and minds. This was in contrast to the learning outcomes of earlier, more conventional training on gender and HIV. In particular, participants gained an appreciation of the intersectionality of the key issues and a clear appreciation of how covert and pervasive stereotypes can be, and how socialisation can affect risks and vulnerability to HIV infection.

Part of the justification for the small group and non-expert facilitator approach was that the subject of sexuality and socialisation impacts both on our professional work and our personal experience. The use of 'non-expert' peer facilitators also encouraged the sharing of responsibility across UN agencies and promoted additional learning. Spontaneously, the process followed Paulo Freire's pedagogic theory – that popular education is a reciprocal exchange of learning. This is a far cry from traditional educational processes, which focus on lectures and do not encourage participation or value the knowledge and experience of the participants.

One unexpected outcome was that one of the facilitators who works in both the UN and the mainstream media was so impressed by the media and arts booth that he immediately talked about it with his colleagues at the local TV station. Plans are now underway to conduct training for them and their advertisers. Given the influence that the popular media, including

advertising, has on shaping stereotypes and attitudes towards masculinity and femininity, this is expected to be a potentially high impact entry point. In addition, it will involve the private sector, an area often neglected by development agencies.

UNIFEM Pacific, as part of its mandate to provide guidance to countries on how to address gender and HIV/AIDS issues, intends to further refine this learning approach to meet the needs of other groups such as parliamentarians, church leaders, men's sporting groups and students.

This new model and method of learning about gender and HIV does not have to be complex or involve high technology. In fact, the simpler it is the better, especially if the facilitators and examples are drawn from local cultures and organisations, be they sophisticated and urban or traditional rural communities. The effort required is in spending a little time on researching the local situation to identify examples familiar to the participants and to train local facilitators. Then it is a matter of obtaining simple visual and audio props, and helpful relevant quotes, together with flair and fun in setting up and convening activities in the learning spaces. The cost is no more than for a traditional teaching methodology.

Conclusions

The (S)Expo approach is innovative because it does more than teach and because it stimulates both professional and personal interest. It provokes an awakening and real interest in the subject of gender and HIV/AIDS and inspires participants to continue to read and share new insights and information with colleagues, family, friends and peers. The innovative process and content opens eyes and minds and avoids the glazed looks common to conventional training activities.

In-depth analysis of gender and HIV/AIDS issues inevitably provides surprising discoveries as the layers of secrecy, shame and taboo are lifted and the reality underneath is revealed. Suddenly the potential impact of these previously silenced and submerged subjects on people's vulnerability and risks of HIV infection are discovered. This knowledge uniquely informs understanding of the real nature of the spread of the infection. Such insights will help to inform programme planning and interventions and so enable far more meaningful and cost-effective interventions than the mere provision of knowledge. This is a methodology which has the power to enable understanding of how gendered attitudes and behaviours, and the resulting inequalities and power relations, are core drivers in the transmission of HIV, and how these factors are expressed in multi-sectoral ways.

The (S)Expo concept is a work in progress which is currently being refined and developed into a 'How to run a (S)Expo' kit by the UNIFEM Pacific Regional Office. There are convincing signs that the methodology is a breakthrough in effective gender and HIV/AIDS education. We look forward to finalising the kit so that it can be used by UNIFEM and other development partners in other countries and situations, thereby contributing to addressing HIV/AIDS much more strategically and effectively than in the past.

ENDNOTES

1   UNIFEM (2001). *Turning the Tide, CEDAW and the Gender Dimensions of the HIV/AIDS Epidemic*, UNIFEM, New York.

2   The UNIFEM Pacific Regional Office is based in Fiji and covers 15 countries.

3   For example, only 236 cases of HIV had been identified in Fiji by early 2007, the largest number in any island country in the region, apart from Papua New Guinea which has more than 13,000 cases.

MARGARET O'CALLAGHAN, who is now 'retired', worked for 12 years as United Nations Population Fund representative in Papua New Guinea and Zambia. Before she joined the UN she worked for AusAID, largely in the health sector. She first worked as a teacher and later trained as a health educator, working in NGOs. She is currently a consultant for the UNIFEM Pacific Regional Office, utilising her creative flair in developing the (S)Expo concept.

ELIZABETH COX is currently Regional Programme Director of the UNIFEM Pacific Regional Office. A citizen of Papua New Guinea, she recently worked on PNG's national HIV/AIDS programme as well as on extensive gender and HIV training and education across the country. She has worked for 20 years on Pacific regional advocacy and training programmes to end violence against women, and is involved at community and local level with popular, participatory approaches to education on key development and social justice issues.

using
human rights
approaches

Women's rights and development: addressing the preconditions

Andrea Cornwall

'Gender equality' may have made it into the language of mainstream development. But in most parts of the world, inequalities between women and men in the workplace, in political institutions and in the home have proven exasperatingly persistent. For all the valiant efforts that have been made, gender mainstreaming has largely failed to live up to its promises. The dilution and depoliticisation of the 'gender agenda' as it has been taken up by development institutions calls for more attention to be paid to what it really takes to make a difference to women's lives.

The human rights framework offers an invaluable analytical tool with which to think about what can be done to advance the realisation of women's rights. Its emphasis on the indivisibility and interdependence of human rights draws attention to the interconnections between different spheres of women's lives. This article highlights two 'entry-level' rights, women's rights over their bodies and the right to participate in decisions that affect their lives: these are, it is argued, fundamental to all other rights. It follows that greater attention needs to be given to measures that enable women to realise these rights as preconditions for equitable development.

Women, rights and development

There is virtually unanimous support among governments and international agencies for the idea that getting more women into work and addressing the gendered inequities in political representation is good for development. Women, it is argued, are more likely than men to devote their earnings to the well-being of their families, more inclined to get involved in activities that support their communities, less likely to resort to corrupt practices when in government, and are better champions of improved health and education in local governance. Some agencies go so far as to suggest that women are the motor for the kind of changes needed to lift families, communities and nations out of poverty.

Yet amidst this declared support for increasing the number of women workers and representatives, there is no agreement on the importance of promoting and protecting the basic rights that are needed to enable women to go to work, participate as citizens and take up demanding roles as politicians. The opening up of the global marketplace has brought with it increasingly fragile access to social rights. In some countries, economic reforms have further imperilled women's abilities to combine productive work with the demands that continue to be placed on them as carers. While innovative initiatives appear to be beginning to change the risky and violent behaviour of some men, issues such as unequal pay, unequal access to political representation and the grossly unfair domestic burdens placed on women remain largely unaddressed by efforts to 'involve men' and are sorely neglected by those men who have become involved in gender work.

Revitalising the 'gender agenda' in development calls for renewed attention to be paid both to what can bring about positive change in women's lives and to what is holding women back. Women cannot go to work if they are unable to secure decent childcare and have no control over the number of children they have. Nor can they survive and thrive in the workplace if they are expected to maintain their homes unaided by male partners and kin. Without access to the means to regulate their fertility, there is little chance that women will have the time and energy to participate in community affairs or politics until their children are grown up – unless they are of sufficiently elite status to be able to employ others to take care of their children and households for them. Women cannot get involved in politics, at whatever level, without access to the opportunities for political apprenticeship, connections and resources enjoyed by many men. Nor will they want to go into politics if they are subjected to sexual and moral harassment from men in the political arena.

Women's civil and political rights, then, are placed in jeopardy when women lack social and economic rights. And women's social and economic rights depend on their having greater and more effective representation in the political institutions which make the decisions that affect women's lives. Yet in order for women to enjoy their social, economic, cultural, civil and political rights, they need first to be able to enjoy two basic rights: rights over their bodies and the right to participate in decisions that affect their lives. These 'entry-level' rights are fundamental to the enjoyment of any other rights.

Sexual and reproductive rights

Sexual and reproductive rights have become a battleground on which questions of religious morality take precedence over concerns about what the denial of these rights really means to women's lives, well-being and opportunities. These rights are deeply entwined with rights that have been the source of less controversy, such as rights to health and education. Girls cannot go to or remain at school if they are subjected to sexual harassment. Restrictions on the provision of sexual and reproductive health services to non-married women, especially adolescent girls, place their lives and well-being at risk. The incidence of HIV infection in women and rates of maternal mortality are powerful indicators of the consequences of denying women sexual and reproductive rights.

Many countries continue to deny women the right to choose when and whether to have children, a key demand of the Beijing Platform for Action. In many of these countries, women's right to a sexuality of their own choosing is also denied them. Women who depart from the norm of heterosexual marriage face discrimination in their communities and workplaces, which can extend to an outright denial of their right to exist. The failure of many states to guarantee women their sexual and reproductive rights has far-reaching economic and political consequences. As Nicole Bidegain of the Latin American and Caribbean Youth Network for Sexual and Reproductive Rights (REDLAC) puts it:

Sexual and reproductive rights are part of citizenship, because if you can't decide for your own body, you can't decide for the destiny of your country, for the UN, for anything.[1]

The failure to address the inextricable connections between rights over the body and other fundamental human rights costs lives and jeopardises development. One of the most powerful examples of these interconnections arises in respect of abortion. An estimated 20 million women are forced to have clandestine and unsafe abortions every year. Tens of thousands of these women die as a result, the vast majority of whom have been marginalised by their poverty. For the estimated six million women who every year survive unsafe abortions but suffer often life-threatening complications, the costs of the denial of this right have broader economic and social dimensions.

A recent workshop at the Institute of Development Studies, at the University of Sussex, explored the global economic costs of unsafe abortion-related morbidity and mortality, and found them to be substantial.[2] In many countries where abortion is illegal, post-abortion complications are not only a leading cause of maternal death, but also of maternal morbidity, stretching scarce resources for maternity care and removing productive members of the family from income-generating and care-giving activities that are vital for household survival.

There is little prospect of meeting Millennium Development Goal 5 unless governments take up the challenge of reducing the incidence of maternal deaths that arise as a direct consequence of a lack of access to safe abortion and aftercare. Punitive measures against those seeking or providing abortion leave women ever more vulnerable to the risk of death and impaired fertility. Many of those who die or suffer permanent impairment to their fertility are teenagers, who are often denied even the most basic sex education and sexual and reproductive service provision.

The incidence of abortion-related maternal morbidity and mortality in countries where abortion remains illegal is sufficient proof that proscription simply does not work.[3] And there is mounting evidence of the ineffectiveness of abstinence-only programmes, which suggests that measures that seek to encourage young people to avoid sex rather than teach them about their bodies and about how to prevent pregnancy are no answer.[4]

What these and other studies demonstrate is the need for greater commitment on the part of governments to providing both comprehensive sex education and the essential services needed to help women of all ages to secure sexual and reproductive well-being. If progress is to be made towards realising human rights for all, it is critical that the real costs of the denial of women's sexual and reproductive rights are frankly acknowledged. In the face of so much needless death and suffering, there is a strong economic as well as moral and political case to be made for greater realism about how significant a threat the denial of these rights poses to women's abilities to enjoy any other rights.

The right to participate

In the case of women's rights to participate, far more needs to be done to go beyond measures to increase the *formal* representation of women to enhancing their *substantive* participation in decision-making at all levels.

More and more women are entering the political arena. But in most countries, there is a long way to go before women are equitably represented in political office. While measures such as quotas or reservations may be necessary, they are far from sufficient to address the considerable barriers that women face in claiming their right to participate.[5] And it is now generally acknowledged that increasing the numbers of women in politics is no guarantee that those women who enter the political arena will promote and defend women's rights.

Initiatives such as Brazil's *Mulher e Democracia* programme, which runs 'feminist schools' for women representatives in the legislative and executive branches of government, recognise that for women to be effective in advocating women's rights, they need not only enhanced political skills, but also new connections and new knowledge on the basis of which to make the case for women's rights.[6] Such 'schools' provide a learning environment that can foster new leaders, as well as increase the effectiveness of those who are already in politics.

Women's political participation is now recognised as so important for development. Governments have a vital role to play in supporting and enabling women to exercise their rights to participate, at all levels. Changing the culture of politics, which presents such a formidable barrier to women's political engagement in many countries, is a slow, difficult process: there are no quick-fix solutions. Yet there are practical measures that governments can take. One is to reform political institutions to make them more accessible for women who have children by providing crèche facilities and holding meetings at times and in places that permit women with domestic responsibilities to take part. Another is to provide financial, political and institutional support to scaling up initiatives like the Brazilian feminist schools and the training courses that have been used to such effect by feminist NGOs in countries like India to equip women with the knowledge, confidence and skills to enter and be effective in the political arena.

Yet a note of caution also needs to be sounded: a focus on increasing women's agency within existing constraints does not do enough to tackle the root causes of women's political exclusion. If women are to realise their rights to participate as *citizens*, rather than as tokens or proxies, far more needs to be done to reform the very basis of politics. This calls for broadening and deepening opportunities for political engagement at all levels, *democratising democracy* to open up politics and decision-making to a greater diversity of people. It calls for coalition building among progressive social and political actors who may at present have little to say to each other, so that they can harness their common interest in creating a fairer world to the pursuit of greater justice and equality for *all*. And it calls for building constituencies who will vote for and demand from their governments a commitment to women's rights as *human* rights.

Realising women's rights

The rights that are defined in international human rights conventions, notably the Convention on the Elimination of All Forms of Discrimination Against Women (CEDAW), offer the promise of greater equality for women. But to turn rights on paper into substantive opportunities for women to enjoy those rights requires renewed attention to be paid to the entry-level rights identified here.

Champions of women's rights in high political office, men as well as women, have a vital role to play in the realisation of women's rights. They can do much to pressurise their governments to address the contradictions between procedures, practices and funding mechanisms and what actually needs to be done to advance women's rights. Those in aid-giving as well as aid-receiving countries can make much of the human rights framework as a lens through which to analyse and monitor the effects of changing aid funding frameworks, and to hold to account those governments which promote policies and priorities that do little to promote, respect or protect women's rights.

Equally, there is much that aid-giving countries can do to support the realisation of women's rights through development financing. There is a perverse disjuncture between talk about the importance of promoting gender equality and women's empowerment and the current architecture of aid. A recent workshop organised by the Association of Women in Development highlighted the effects of the shifts in the funding environment for women's rights. Its findings need to be taken very seriously indeed. They indicate that far more support is needed for programmes that can make a difference to the realisation of women's rights.[7] These include leadership training for would-be female politicians, capacity building for women representatives at all levels so that they can acquire and exercise the skills that are needed to make effective arguments for women's rights, and support for the institutionalisation of sex education programmes and provision of basic sexual and reproductive health services that not only guarantee women's rights, but also save women's lives.

The progressive realisation of human rights depends on identifying priorities for change that can support and accelerate progress in other areas. Used as an analytical framework that can help to identify entry points for change, the human rights framework is a powerful instrument for assessing where governments can make the most difference to advancing greater equality and justice for all. The human rights principles of indivisibility and integrality offer advocates of women's rights and empowerment tools for thought and action that can help move beyond piecemeal interventions. These principles show the importance of addressing the entry-level rights identified here as an urgent priority for action.

ENDNOTES

1 www.iwhc.org/resources/nb011105.cfm

2 'Economic Costs of Abortion Related Morbidity and Mortality', Workshop held at the Institute of Development Studies, at the University of Sussex, UK, 17–18 April 2007.

3 See,for example, www.guttmacher.org/pubs/2006/08/08/Nigeria-UP-IA.pdf

4 www.mathematica-mpr.com/publications/PDFs/impactabstinence.pdf

5 www.ids.ac.uk/ids/news/Archive2005/AnneMarieBeijing.huml

6 www.cmnmulheredemocracia.org.br

7 See www.awid.org/moneyandmovements

ANDREA CORNWALL is a research fellow based at the Institute of Development Studies at the University of Sussex, UK, where she directs a multi-country DFID-funded Research Programme Consortium *Pathways of Women's Empowerment* (www.pathways-of-empowerment.org). Recent publications include the co-edited volumes *Feminisms and Development: Contradictions, Contestations and Challenges* (with Elizabeth Harrison and Ann Whitehead, Zed, 2007) and *Realizing Rights: Transforming Approaches to Sexual and Reproductive Wellbeing* (with Alice Welbourn, Zed, 2002).

Good practices in CEDAW implementation: an NGO perspective

Introduction

International Women's Rights Action Watch Asia Pacific (IWRAW) is an international organisation based in the south working nationally, regionally and internationally for women's human rights. It works to fill the gap between the promise of women's human rights set out in human rights treaties and their realisation at national level. It mobilises women's groups at all levels to pressure governments to put in place domestic measures to enforce human rights standards. IWRAW Asia Pacific was founded in 1993 and now works in 14 countries in south and south-east Asia and in more than 100 countries globally.

This article sets out IWRAW's approach to the implementation of the Convention on the Elimination of All Forms of Discrimination Against Women (CEDAW). What are good practices in the implementation of CEDAW? Within government, attempts to promote good practices usually focus on mainstreaming gender into national development planning, with an especial focus on the Millennium Development Goals (MDGs) as time-bound and measurable benchmarks of success.[1] There is no doubt that for governments to address policies that impact on women's equality and to monitor their own methods is a step in the right direction. CEDAW aids governments in this work of self and peer review by making them take a comprehensive look at the obligations they have entered into; it also sets standards which governments must meet to eliminate discrimination and promote equal treatment for women.

From the perspective of NGOs, good practice relates to the role they can play in making inputs into the development of standard setting by international or country-level mechanisms. It is defined by the interplay of forces involved in the promotion and protection of equality for women, the state, citizens and the global community.

IWRAW Asia Pacific's perspective

IWRAW Asia Pacific believes that its programme represents an overall 'good practice' in actualising the rights, guarantees and protections set out in the Convention. Over the last ten years, it has built up a significant presence in 12 south and south-east Asian countries, as well as working in east and central Asia and the Pacific. It has focused on building the capacity of women's groups to make use of the CEDAW Convention and its norms as a tool for establishing the fact of discrimination against women through research-based advocacy; for gaining recognition of their right to equality at the national level; for making the state fulfil its obligations under CEDAW; and for participating in the review process in New York. The IWRAW has also worked with governments in the region, enhancing their capacity to fulfil their obligations through advocacy and building capacity and skills.

For example, IWRAW Asia Pacific's annual programme 'From Global to Local' engages with the periodic review conducted by the state CEDAW committee to provide an opportunity for national civil society, especially groups that focus on women's human rights, to submit alternative information and enter into dialogue with the committee. This process represents the constructive dialogue envisioned in the Convention and advantages all three parties involved in the process – the CEDAW committee, the state party concerned and NGOs. The NGOs are able to raise critical issues with the committee, which in turn enables the committee to provide realistic guidance to the government. As a result, the government receives guidance that it can use to create enabling conditions within which its citizens can access and enjoy their human rights. This process is a political expression of IWRAW's programme, as it brings together women from different reporting countries to seek accountability – reminding governments that they must account to women globally for ensuring human rights to women nationally.

Through this programme IWRAW Asia Pacific has obtained interesting examples of how states have put the Convention and the concluding comments into effect at national level and of how NGOs have used the concluding comments to mobilise public opinion to promote calls for state accountability. On their return from the Global to Local programme, many groups have arranged press briefings and events to share the concluding comments of the CEDAW committee and used the opportunity to illustrate their state's duty to effect change. Occasionally, the mere presence of women at the review process can facilitate change, besides the advantage of hearing the explicit positions of their governments and the understanding of larger processes that women can take away from such an experience. One such example was the role played by four 'Global to Local' participants from Zimbabwe; they were able to highlight the contradictory action of the state in seeking to reinstate a discriminatory law,[2] and eventually the government was pressured into withdrawing the legislation.

Since its inception in 1993, IWRAW Asia Pacific has played a significant role in bridging the gap between the promise of women's rights and their actual realisation by setting up systems of NGO CEDAW monitoring networks in Asian countries and creating tools for assessing whether or not governments have carried out their obligations. The work of the CEDAW committee will only be fruitful if it can draw on well-researched information from those who work directly with women on women's issues. In most cases, state women's machineries have a small budget and too little political power in the general hierarchy to play a big role in public policy, or even provide information to the CEDAW committee. NGOs can make up for this by providing alternative information to the committee. This work has been carried out through a project called Facilitating the Fulfilment of State Obligation to Women's Equality. Through the project, IWRAW Asia Pacific and its national partners have initiated the following examples of good practice in CEDAW implementation at the domestic level (though, obviously, this is not an exhaustive list).

Good practice in CEDAW implementation

India

Through IWRAW Asia Pacific's monitoring and research framework, a women's group in India[3] initiated a study under Article 16 of the Convention to analyse rights in marriage, specifically in relation to forced marriage and matrimonial rights. In the course of using the Convention framework to analyse and monitor these issues, they were able to unpack the entire gamut of inequalities and discriminations faced by women throughout their life cycle. This led them to research the intersectional nature of discrimination against women arising from ethnic, systemic or cultural factors, giving rise to the related issues of crimes of honour against women, domestic violence, sexuality rights, reproductive rights and the right to work. The group moved to a more fruitful engagement with CEDAW and was able to relate what was superficially a violation of an individual right to choice to the larger human rights framework. Informed by a new understanding of the Convention that was substantiated by research findings, the group used effective media strategies to lobby for changes in law and policy. Another major strand was the development of a casework strategy to provide individual relief, while keeping a eye on reform at a higher level by filing public interest litigation for the reform of the way marriages are solemnised under the Special Marriages Act, 1954.[4] Litigation strategies such as these serve several functions besides the obvious one of obtaining justice for the victim; they also enable NGOs to raise the level of argument in existing national level case law on women's rights, ideally using CEDAW principles and standards and hence contributing to the evolution of progressive interpretations of CEDAW and human rights law.

Elsewhere, the Gender Unit of the National Institute for Advanced Studies (NIAS)[5] successfully lobbied for the removal of a discriminatory rule that was an obstacle to many women who were seeking to participate in politics at a local level. On 23 March 2000, an amendment to the Karnataka Panchayati Raj Act was passed by the Legislative Assembly deleting the clause on the 'toilet rule'. According to this rule, it was mandatory for an aspiring Panchayat (local self-government) member to have a toilet in order to qualify as a candidate in the Panchayat elections. Although this was part of an effort to increase health and hygiene in the rural areas and was gender neutral, in effect it discriminated against women as they did not have the same economic resources as men.

Malaysia

Women's Aid Organisation, our national level partner, and other women's groups have led initiatives in law and policy reform utilising CEDAW to engage the government with the international rights framework. Working on the rights of women in marriage and divorce through the facilitating project they translated their research findings and suggested strategies to bring about positive general changes such as the amendment of the Constitution of Malaysia to include 'gender' as prohibited grounds of discrimination in August 2001; the granting of equal guardianship rights to mothers[6] through the amendment of the Guardianship Act; and influencing a cabinet directive in September 2000, whereby rules permitting foreign husbands to work in Malaysia were relaxed and foreign wives who may be divorced were given entitlement to permanent residence status. The use that women's groups made of CEDAW also aided in the development of a shadow report to the CEDAW committee in 2006, allowing it to engage the state further on issues raised by Articles 5 and 16 and the connection with Shariah law as an obstacle to achieving equality for women.

Conclusion

The implementation of CEDAW at national level has clearly been informed by the interaction between NGOs, the state and its implementing agencies, and the CEDAW committee; through this interaction we can derive best practice in law reform, policy change, advocacy and awareness raising. Most of the examples described here incorporate more gender responsive legislation and constitutional guarantees to provide the legal framework for equality at the national level, informed by international standards. But this is only one step towards realising equality for women. Important conditions must be fulfilled before equality can be achieved.[7] These include standard setting at the international level; a culture of compliance with gender-sensitive human rights norms at the national level; women's ability to claim their rights; the necessary political will that can only be created if women form a constituency with its own strong voice; capacity building and gender sensitisation both among women and the bodies responsible for putting institutional changes in place, for example judges, lawyers, bureaucrats and parliamentarians; gender-sensitised enforcement mechanisms; and mechanisms for monitoring the fulfilment of state obligations under CEDAW. All these conditions imply a challenge to the bastions of male privilege and to the social and cultural constructs of sex roles and gender, and need ongoing efforts from NGOs and governments alike.

ENDNOTES

1 An example of this perspective is the ASEAN High-Level Meeting on Gender Mainstreaming in the Context of CEDAW, BPFA and MDGs, http://www.unifem-eseasia.org/newsroom/ASEAN%20ministers%20061115.htm

2 The Legal Age of Majority Act, 1982.

3 'Choosing a life ... crimes of honour in India: the right to, if, when and whom to marry', A report on Rajasthan and UP by the Association for Advocacy and Legal Initiatives (AALI) and CIMEL (a project of Interrights and the School of Oriental and African Studies, London), 2004.

4 Ibid, p. 61.

5 Gender Unit of the National Institute for Advanced Studies, India.

6 Initially this ruling only benefited non-Muslim women, as Malaysia practises a dual legal system and Muslim women came under Shariah law. However, on further lobbying by local groups, the Cabinet issued an administrative directive in August 2000 to expedite the process, rather than wait for state religious laws to be amended.

7 'List of Conditions for the Realisation of Women's Human Rights', IWRAW Asia Pacific Philosophical Framework.

Gender, human rights, culture and the law in African Commonwealth countries

Betty Mould-Iddrisu

International human rights

The legal obligation to eliminate discrimination against women is a fundamental tenet of international human rights law. The Convention on the Elimination of All Forms of Discrimination Against Women (CEDAW) was one of the earliest attempts to develop global legal norms on non-discrimination from a woman's perspective. In Africa, Commonwealth member states which have ratified CEDAW (some with reservations) are additionally bound by regional human rights instruments. The African Union (AU) has also created institutions to address specific regional problems which impede the progress of women in attaining the goals set out in CEDAW and in other international instruments. Furthermore, experts have posited that for human rights to be effective, they have to become a respected part of the culture and traditions of a given society. This brief synopsis attempts to highlight the context within which legal norms have to operate against a backdrop of the culture and human rights standards in Commonwealth member states in Africa.

Regional human rights instruments and bodies

In Africa the prevailing regional instruments that provide the normative framework for gender equality and non-discrimination are:

- the African Charter on Human and Peoples' Rights

- the Additional Protocol on Women's Rights

- the African Commission on Human and Peoples' Rights

- the African Court on Human and Peoples' Rights.

The African Charter on Human and Peoples' Rights entered into force in 1986 and has been ratified by every member of the AU. Even though the Charter attempted to address the rights of women, its preamble reflects the prevailing concerns at that time in Africa, which focused more on ensuring that it was free from colonialism and discrimination than on advancing women's rights.

After intensive lobbying by groups working on gender and law issues, an additional protocol to the African Charter was approved by the AU in 2003 and entered into force in 2005. The protocol provides a holistic conceptual framework within which women's rights are to be addressed in Africa. It is the most comprehensive instrument addressing issues relating to culture, and *inter alia* proscribes gender-based violence in all its forms and the elimination of harmful traditional practices.

The African Commission, which was established in 1987 under the African Charter, has a mandate to formulate principles and rules concerning human rights and to monitor the level of compliance by member states. It is not specifically mandated to examine breaches of gender rights and indeed until recently it was considered not sufficiently engendered. The Commission primarily receives complaints from individuals on alleged breaches of human rights by state authorities.

The African Court on Human and Peoples' Rights is a new institution established to look into complaints involving human rights violations in member states. The Court is only seized of jurisdiction after individuals have exhausted their own domestic remedies for redress and was effectively operationalised in 2006.

Constitutionalism

Most constitutions in Africa do not formally discriminate against women. However, the constitutions of several countries deliberately omit sex as grounds on which discrimination is prohibited. The constitution, being the supreme law of the state, should be the obvious reference point in the recognition of gender equality and equity. There is much that still needs to be done in Commonwealth Africa to inculcate a culture of constitutionalism within which the fundamental rights of women are expressly stated and enforced. This lack of a culture of constitutionalism in many African countries is a hindrance to the implementation of constitutional rights.

Conformity between national constitutional, regional and international standards of human rights relating to the rights of women is vital. Commonwealth member states are required to pass domestic legislation to give effect to the provisions of international treaties which they have ratified, but which are non-self-executing. Thus, domestic courts should interpret domestic legislation in a way that is consistent with regional and international human rights obligations.

Plural legal systems

Paragraph 3.18 of the 2005–2015 *Commonwealth Plan of Action for Gender Equality (PoA)* sets out the context within which

international human rights operate in Africa's plural legal systems. In such legal systems, statute law, common law and principles of equity and customary law co-exist within a single legal system.

Primary research in Africa shows that the system of legal pluralism has posed significant challenges to the achievement of gender equity in almost all areas of participation for vulnerable groups in some member states. Significantly, it appears that the operation of plural legal systems has resulted in the unequal and inequitable participation of women and the rural poor in accessing their legal rights.

In the wider context of globalisation, and international and transnational legal rules and conventions, plural legal systems create formidable challenges to the attainment of the rights of women, especially in the areas of land rights and family relations, which are vital for the progress of women.

The judiciary

The judiciary is the state structure responsible for enforcing human rights laws and international legal obligations. In Africa, it is recognised that it has been a big challenge for women to access statutory law and the justice system. Alternative dispute resolution systems are increasingly being advocated to address the systemic inequities women face when they attempt to access the judicial system. The theme of the eighth Women's Affairs Ministerial Meeting (WAMM), 'Financing for Gender Equality', is significant in the context of African judiciaries. Problems fettering women's full access to the judicial system must be addressed by investing in resources to enable the judiciary to enhance its capacity, improve its infrastructure and facilitate the speedy resolution of disputes. Most rural-based women have easier access to traditional courts to settle their disputes than to mainstream courts. However, the traditional

institutions are in the main male dominated and reflect outmoded traditional norms, thereby effectively denying women effective access to justice. Paragraph 3.24 of the *PoA* advocates legislative and constitutional reform, the strengthening of judicial capacity building and mechanisms for implementation, monitoring and accountability of gender equality commitments.

Cultural and traditional norms

No examination of the status of women in Africa is complete unless it takes into account cultural and traditional norms. The conceptual obstruction to the acknowledgement of women's rights, which is still pervasive across Africa, lies in stereotypical notions of what constitutes human rights, which are largely fashioned by the virtues of tradition and the values of African civilization. Unfortunately, these traditions have been interpreted in a manner which all too often places women in a position of practical inferiority, despite the intent behind the legislation. In addition to contributing to the retrogression of the rights of women, this also cheapens the value of culture, since historically culture contains both positive and negative values. These values, however, become negative when they infringe fundamental human rights and perpetrate inequality between the sexes.

The greatest single damage done by the persistence of outmoded customary norms is their impact on the rights of women, children and the poor. The extent to which this has been a bar to Africa's achievement of the Millennium Development Goals – particularly Goal 2, the achievement of universal primary education; Goal 3, the promotion of gender equality and empowerment of women; and Goal 5, the promotion of maternal health – remains a matter for concern for a continent which has the world's highest maternal mortality rates.

A rights-based approach towards advancing the agenda is implicit in the *PoA*, which addresses the fact that it is critical to promote active dialogue and engagement among those involved in the justice system, and among representatives of religious, cultural, traditional and civil institutions and communities, in order to address women's human rights in all cultures.

Property rights of spouses

It is widely recognised that the regulation of the rights of succession and ownership of property play a crucial role in gender relations and have critical implications for the productivity and empowerment of women. These rules are usually governed by customary law. Paragraph 3.25 of the *PoA* asks governments to ensure that women's rights to land, housing, property and inheritance are promoted and protected within the international and national context. However, in practice the impact of the customary law rules of succession, especially in the matrilineal communities of Commonwealth Africa, has been inequitable and militates against women's empowerment. In some African communities these rules preclude either spouse from inheriting from the other, but this has in practice created far more destitute widows than widowers. Additionally, Africa has suffered an extremely high incidence of war, ethnic violence and genocide, which, combined with the AIDS pandemic, has ravaged the continent and created a disproportionate number of widows and orphans. With the growing emphasis in modern times on the nuclear family, a critical burden falls on the wife or widow as primary care giver for the children – making it imperative for women to be accorded an equitable share of the matrimonial property on the death of their spouse.

Women in Africa are also faced with problems in regard to rights to their self-acquired property within marriage upon the dissolution of the marriage. Past practices indicated that a woman was regarded as merely assisting her spouse to acquire property: landed property was usually registered in his name alone. It is only recently that the courts have recognised a woman's contribution to matrimonial property or property acquired within a marriage.

Outmoded customary practices

Human rights instruments and, more recently, national constitutions have outlawed the perpetration of cruel and outmoded traditional practices which include the following.

- Female genital mutilation (FMG) – practised across some parts of west and north Africa. It is estimated that hundreds of thousands of Africa's girls and women are affected by this practice. Several African countries have enacted legislation proscribing FMG, but they are unable to enforce criminal prosecutions and thus the practice has been driven underground. However, with an increasingly enabling environment against gender-based violence and education about the harmful effects of the practice, it is slowly dying out.

- Customary servitude (*trokosi*) – practised mainly across the southern part of west Africa in Ghana, Togo and Benin. This is the customary practice whereby young girls (virgins) are sent to fetish priests in atonement for the perceived wrong/offence committed by a family member; this has also been outlawed and shrines are being closed down and the women freed. However,

the women find it extremely difficult to become reintegrated into society when they are released.

- Objectional marriage practices – such as childhood betrothal and forced abductions, which are practised across most of Africa.

- Cruelty to the aged – across Africa elderly women are accused of witchcraft and in some parts of west Africa are banished into camps where they live in isolation from the community.

- Trafficking in women and children is a global phenomenon, but is a complex reality that goes beyond the abuses involved in traditional labour deployment practices in west and central Africa. It has affected millions of African women and children who are trafficked for labour, for the sex trade and forced prostitution. The *PoA* advocates for anti-trafficking legislation.

Conclusion

The legal obligation to eliminate discrimination against women is a fundamental tenet of international human rights law. Various international and African regional instruments stress the important role that women play in democracy and development, and state that the principle of equality and the full participation of women in decision-making processes are essential to development.

International law and its practical implementation in Africa need to be examined against the dynamics of the tensions between human rights, law and culture in Commonwealth member states in Africa. The *PoA* is a tool and framework for stakeholders to take forward the agenda for the advancement of African women and seeks, in the words of the Commonwealth Secretary General, 'to close persistent gaps' in the advancement of gender equality. The inclusion of gender, human rights and law in the critical areas for action between 2005–2015 should be emphasised, and steps leading to gender equality and equity should be implemented by member states.

This article is based on the keynote address delivered at a conference on 'Gender, Human Rights, Culture and the Law in West and Central Africa', held in Yaoundé, Cameroon, 24–25 May 2006.

BETTY MOULD-IDDRISU is Director of the Legal and Constitutional Affairs Division of the Commonwealth Secretariat. She is a Ghanaian lawyer with a LMM degree from the LSE, University of London and a BL from the Ghana Law School. She worked at Ghana's Ministry of Justice from 1978–2003 in several capacities, rising to the rank of Chief State Attorney. She headed the administration of Intellectual Property Rights (Copyright) in Ghana and the administration of authors' rights at African regional level, 1990–2000. From 2000–2003 she was in charge of the Ghana Ministry of Justice's International Law Division where she spearheaded several cutting edge legal initiatives. She is widely known in Anglophone African countries for her work on international law, human rights and gender.

Advancing human rights in the Commonwealth

The work of the Commonwealth Secretariat's Human Rights Unit

Introduction

We believe in the liberty of the individual under the law, in equal rights for all citizens regardless of gender, race, colour, creed or political belief, and in the individual's inalienable right to participate by means of free and democratic political processes in framing the society in which he or she lives.

(Harare Commonwealth Declaration, 1991)

Commonwealth member countries have pledged their commitment to the principles of human rights, democracy and the rule of law under the *Harare Declaration*, as reaffirmed by successive Commonwealth Heads of Government Meetings (CHOGMs). In fulfilment of these principles, the Human Rights Unit (HRU) of the Commonwealth Secretariat engages with national human rights institutions and other national and regional actors. The HRU also works with the UN human rights machinery. Within the Commonwealth as a whole, strengthening democracy and respect for human rights is of key importance and the programme activities of the HRU support this strategic goal.

The HRU became a free-standing unit within the Commonwealth Secretariat in 2002, addressing all Secretariat programme areas. Its mandate focuses on the following thematic areas.

- Determining and developing Commonwealth-wide 'best practice' and standard setting in a common law context of existing international human rights standards, including assisting wider and improved adherence to international human rights conventions.

- Strengthening national and regional human rights mechanisms, thus developing and empowering Commonwealth human rights

institutions, including through training and technical assistance programmes and network building.

- Increasing knowledge and awareness of, and respect for, human rights throughout the Commonwealth, especially among key actors and agencies, and on key issues, including women's rights.

- Publication and dissemination of human rights information.

- Mainstreaming human rights in the Secretariat's programmes and policies, including working closely with the Gender Section.

The Secretary General of the Commonwealth, Rt. Hon. Don McKinnon, in a speech before the UN Human Rights Council on 14 March 2007, emphasised the importance of human rights in the work of the modern Commonwealth in its entirety – branding it a 'human rights organisation'. The Secretary General located the HRU as the key mechanism through which human rights protections are applied, strengthened and defended.

Thematic areas of activity

Standard setting and developing best practice

The development of best practice is underpinned by a focus on the implementation of major international human rights instruments. While Commonwealth members have expressed a clear commitment to human rights, some have yet to ratify human rights instruments in order to bring national legislation and local conditions into conformity with international norms, including those prohibiting discrimination against women. In many cases, this is due to a lack of capacity. The Commonwealth Secretariat seeks to achieve the universalisation of the two core international human rights

instruments, the International Covenant of Civil and Political Rights (ICCPR) and the International Covenant of Economic, Social and Cultural Rights (ICESCR) that underpin fundamental human rights. Some members have yet to ratify the UN Covenants as well as those prohibiting discrimination against women (CEDAW), racial discrimination (CERD) and torture (CAT). All Commonwealth countries are signatories to the UN Convention on the Rights of the Child (CRC), but not of its Optional Protocols.

The HRU has published the *Handbook on Ratification of Human Rights Instruments*, which simplifies and explains the process and consequences of ratification for member countries which have yet to ratify some of the above-mentioned instruments. Similarly, workshops and training are designed to encourage greater ratification and implementation of human rights treaties, for example the session held in March 2007 in Papua New Guinea for Commonwealth members in the Pacific region.

The HRU has also developed 'best practice' guidelines put together by expert groups in the Commonwealth on a range of topics, including the human rights considerations in 'treatment of victims of crime' and on 'strategies to combat the trafficking of women and children'.

Awareness raising and training

One of the main aims of the HRU's activities is to increase levels of awareness and understanding of human rights among key actors and agencies in member countries through education and training. The HRU identifies particular groups (governmental and others) whose activities touch closely on the human rights of Commonwealth country citizens or who stand to benefit the most from increased human rights educational activities. This strategy has been manifest in public sectors such as the police, judiciary and education.

In June 2006, the HRU published the *Commonwealth Handbook on Human Rights Training for Police*. The *Commonwealth Human Rights Training Programme*, which has so far reached police trainers from more than 25 member countries, is designed to provide trainers with the practical and normative tools to ensure that ordinary police procedures and actions are human rights compliant. On occasion, prisons trainers are included in the workshops.

The HRU has undertaken training and workshops for judges and lawyers, such as the June 2006 Fiji Colloquium, carried out in partnership with the Pacific regional office of the UN High Commissioner for Human Rights (UNHCHR), Interights and the Fiji National Human Rights Commission. The workshop examined the approach of judges and lawyers in a number of jurisdictions to the civil, cultural, economic, political and social rights embodied in international human rights treaties.

In December 2006, the HRU launched the *Model Human Rights Curriculum for Commonwealth Universities and Law Schools*, which assists teachers to raise the quality and quantity of human rights courses in Commonwealth law schools, colleges and universities. The HRU has also produced model short courses in human rights and is currently piloting a successful scheme with four Indian universities which are seeking to strengthen the availability of human rights education.

Mainstreaming human rights

Mainstreaming human rights in the Secretariat entails the deliberate infusion of human rights principles into the activities and work of the Secretariat. The Commonwealth Secretariat recognises that a human rights-based approach to development can help to meet the challenges of the Commonwealth in tackling poverty and inequality and lead to more sustainable long-term projects. The HRU assists in familiarising staff with international human rights standards and the Commonwealth mandate in human rights, and guides other divisions of the

Secretariat to incorporate human rights principles and practices in the design and execution of development projects.

Strengthening human rights mechanisms

The HRU offers institutional support to national human rights institutions (NHRIs) and works closely with national stakeholders and the Office of the UNHCHR, as well as other agencies and partners in the establishment and strengthening of NHRIs. In 2001, the HRU developed *Best Practice Principles for National Human Rights Institutions in the Commonwealth*, in line with the UN *Paris Principles*. These are now accepted and used by most Commonwealth countries and other non-Commonwealth countries in relation to the process of establishment and operation of national human rights bodies and their powers and mandates. The publication also offers guidance on specific aspects of human rights issues such as women's rights, as well as conflict, race, environment, refugees and young people. The guidelines have additionally been used by the Office of the UNHCHR in its work with NHRIs.

The HRU provides advice, training and other forms of technical assistance to governments to strengthen their NHRIs, as well as building capacity within relevant ministries, agencies and departments in mainstreaming human rights, and identifying and responding to human rights issues. This includes creating more effective complaints mechanisms with respect to human rights violations.

The HRU has also been instrumental in establishing important support networks between other Commonwealth NHRIs and other forums, regional bodies and the UN human rights system. At the Commonwealth Conference of NHRIs held in February 2007 the historic decision was taken to establish a Commonwealth Forum for NHRIs. A steering committee has been appointed to oversee the process of establishing the forum, and to look into the specific issues and modalities of doing so.

Publications and information

Information sharing is vital in the promotion of human rights and Commonwealth values

across the Commonwealth and beyond. The HRU publishes for the use and information of member countries literature on human rights developments and jurisprudence, as well as other educational materials to assist in the promotion, protection and justiciability of human rights.

Through the publication and dissemination of human rights information such as the newly redesigned *Human Rights Update* e-newsletter and the *Commonwealth Human Rights Law Digest*, the HRU assists countries to learn about human rights developments in the Commonwealth and the wider world and helps to develop policies in line with international human rights standards.

These publications include the 'best practice' guidelines described earlier.

HRU activities and women's rights

The HRU collaborates with other sections of the Secretariat that work on gender and women's rights, and will continue to raise awareness of women's human rights issues and support efforts to ensure greater respect for women's rights, including ending discrimination and violence. Recently the HRU participated in the Pan-Commonwealth Workshop on Addressing the Marginalisation of Indigenous and Tribal Women held in London, 12–13 April 2007. The HRU organised a workshop for the Asia Pacific region in January 2006 to strengthen the capacity of NHRIs to promote and protect women's economic, social and cultural rights.

The HRU is supporting the Secretariat's assistance to Uganda in hosting the forthcoming Commonwealth Women's Affairs Ministerial Meeting in Kampala, Uganda in June 2007.

The Secretariat's Gender Section, Justice Section and the HRU will be working jointly with the Ministry of Women and Children Affairs in Bangladesh to convene the Commonwealth Asia Colloquium on Gender, Culture and the Law in August 2007. This colloquium will be the second in the series that is being convened across the Commonwealth.

Cultural conservatism and cash constraints: a dual challenge for women's human rights advocates

Cassandra Balchin

Those working for gender equality in Commonwealth governments and in non-governmental organisations (NGOs) in Commonwealth countries have achieved some significant victories. But more and more in recent years this has been in spite of a general roll-back on gender rights following an increasingly socially conservative atmosphere at state and international level. This has combined with greater overall constraints in development funding, and the outcome has been growing challenges in the area of financing gender equality, which threaten advances made in previous decades.

In 2005–2006, the Association for Women's Rights in Development (AWID) conducted groundbreaking research on funding for women's rights.[1] AWID executive director Lydia Alpizar Duran noted in late 2006 that the level of access to resources for feminist movements and organisations mirrors women's general level of access to economic and financial resources globally.[2] What was reflected in AWID's research is not a positive picture: many women's organisations have had to close down programmes, scale down personnel, reduce activities and are continuing their rights work with great difficulty. The management of resources is taking up more and more time, while resources are increasingly conditional and competition for 'scarce' resources has created divisions.

Bilateral and multilateral development agencies are increasingly channelling funding through national governments, and it is clear that this is not reaching women's rights work as it should. Quite apart from the questionable commitment of many national governments to women's rights advocacy programmes which inevitably contain critiques of governance and democracy issues, a concern is that much of this funding is now destined for 'gender mainstreaming'. As AWID's research notes, gender mainstreaming has not had the desired consequence of strengthening action in respect of women's rights. Instead there are cases where mainstreaming has led to cutting gender equality specialists and women-specific programmes.[3] A number of women's organisations in Muslim contexts, linked through the international solidarity network Women Living Under Muslim Laws (WLUML), have played key roles in supporting, monitoring and proposing national gender mechanisms, leading WLUML to develop a collective project on the topic. Background desk research for the project by Jenny Morgan revealed a common pattern of resource constraints across Africa and in Commonwealth countries as diverse as Australia and India. Where national machineries are about to be set up, as in Sri Lanka,

the possibility of implementing the Convention on the Elimination of All Forms of Discrimination Against Women (CEDAW) is again severely constrained by, among other problems, insufficient financial resources.[4]

It is not just the amount of financing available that poses challenges. In relation to women's rights, certain long-standing issues continue to obstruct women's ability to advance themselves and contribute to their societies – for example, women's exclusion from political representation. New issues have emerged in addition to these, such as the gendered aspects of the HIV/AIDS pandemic. Yet those working on women's rights face the challenge of cyclical funding 'fashions'. The insecurities induced by this situation can hamper efforts to develop long-term programmes – vital in fields where advocacy is needed to bring about changes in social attitudes and/or changes in national policy. AWID's research has found that while over the past decade it has become significantly easier to raise funds for work on issues such as HIV-related health, gender-based violence and activities such as leadership, networking and communications, it is more difficult to raise funds for subjects such as reproductive rights, civil and political rights, lesbian, gay, bisexual and transgender (LGBT) rights, and health issues other than HIV/AIDS. It is also hard to obtain finance for budget heads such as staff salaries, administration, organisational capacity building, and research and documentation.[5]

Those working in the field have highlighted the use of specific articulations of culture in attempts to roll back gender equality and women's rights, and to undermine international agreement that reproductive rights and women's rights are human rights, as also are sexual rights,[6] even though sexual and reproductive health issues are among the most important issues in international human rights law.[7]

In the particular context of organisations such as WLUML, which addresses issues of culture and identity, there are yet further challenges. Against a background of rising religious fundamentalism across all cultures, women's rights advocates in Muslim contexts have often found the approach taken by development agencies towards the issues of gender and religion (and more widely political Islam) to be counterproductive.

Today, in international development policy religion is simultaneously seen as the primary developmental obstacle, the only developmental issue and the sole developmental solution.

The co-existence of these three – seemingly totally contradictory – approaches, which can often be found within a single bilateral or international development agency or NGO, is possible because they all stem from the same Orientalist presumption about the underdeveloped 'Other'.

I shall summarise a detailed critique I have made elsewhere (Balchin, 2003). In the first approach, which sees religion as the primary developmental obstacle, 'irrational' people are blamed for their own underdevelopment and other factors, such as the gross global trade inequalities perpetuated by the North, are ignored; in this approach custom is frequently conflated, inaccurately, with religion. In the second approach, factors that influence poverty, such as class, gender and racial discrimination, are ignored or downplayed. In the third approach, it is presumed that all 'proper' Indonesians, Ugandans, Moroccans, Pakistanis, etc. are 'religious'; secular initiatives are delegitimised and the work of many local service delivery and human rights groups that work across or irrespective of religious boundaries is ignored.

Meanwhile, in the 'war on terror' context, there is a tendency to overlook local women's own analysis of their needs and instead to engage with (invariably male) 'religious leaders' and promote 'moderate Muslims'. In contexts where the dominant male religious leadership seeks to preserve the inequitable status quo or only permit development projects that do not threaten existing social power structures, any diversion of development resources – national, bilateral or multilateral – away from local women's groups or national gender machineries towards 'religious organisations' can only undermine gender equality work.

In today's highly politically charged context, where political players have become increasingly sophisticated both in their discourse and the tools they use, the practical outcomes of financing gender equality work may not always be immediately understood. For example, one of the most common issues discussed today among WLUML networking organisations (and indeed more widely among those linked with AWID) is the cooption of the language of human rights by religious fundamentalists. In Latin America, church groups are supporting campaigns related to violence against women – but with a highly conservative agenda of preserving the patriarchal family. Meanwhile, certain self-labelled 'moderate Muslim' leaders are on record as supporting women's right to education and to work – accompanied by barely visible small print that this 'right' is strictly conditional on its beneficial impact on the family. I have discussed elsewhere how the current search for 'moderate Muslims' in development practice is sidelining progressive Muslim scholarship, ignoring secular trends within Muslim societies and helping to introduce a social conservatism on gender matters that is not 'traditional' in many contexts (Balchin, 2007).

An additional constraint on funding for gender equality work has come in the form of a general global trend away from supporting programme-based development work, which includes support for core costs, towards project-based funding. A 1998 article in the American liberal magazine, *The Nation*, discussed the trend's detrimental impact:

> *If a conservative genius wanted to disarm the left, he might have come up with the following plan: Dis [sic] progressive multi-issue groups like the Midwest Academy*

and Pacifica Radio and dispense money primarily to single-issue groups. Give each one just enough money to survive, but not enough to succeed. Spread your resources over thousands of projects, not key institutions, so that everyone is pitted against everyone else. Make sure the best thinkers and organisers are preoccupied with fundraising for their next paycheck rather than fighting for real change. Promote organising around obsolete political ideas rather than develop new ideas. And voila![8]

Although this relates to the US context and was written nearly a decade ago, the scenario is frighteningly familiar to those working on gender equality today.

In part, the demand for accountability and tangible development outcomes – resulting in a focus on things that can be counted, such as workshops and water pumps, rather than impossible-to-measure things such as a woman's greater sense of her own worth – is understandable. Taxpayers in the developed world want to know where 'their' money has gone. But rather than discussing some of the issues behind financing gender equality as raised in this article, governments, donors and even at times sections of the women's movement appear to find it easier to essentialise, through the media, images of 'women's continuing oppression in developing countries'. When, as in the case of women in Muslim contexts, images find their way into the mainstream media that do not fit the stereotype, they are nevertheless presented as exceptions rather than the norm, and the general taxpayer's understanding about the nature of social development, its challenges and solutions, remains clouded.

In part also, reluctance to fund the bigger picture may stem from the fact that universalism has fallen out of fashion and instead cultural specificity rules the day. While it is no doubt harmful to presume that 'sisterhood (as defined solely by women's rights advocates in the global North) is global', using the excuse of cultural specificity to avoid action on women's rights is equally inexcusable. Yet organisations such as WLUML, which work across cultural, geographical, linguistic and religious boundaries and which can link large organisations operating at the regional level with more localised groups, today find it increasingly hard to obtain funding, as has been shown by AWID's research.[9]

Moreover, the general development funding emphasis on reaching 'the poorest of the poor' has resulted in increasingly rigid insistence that women's international networks must explicitly 'target' their activities on Asia and Africa – or lose funding. Yet this overlooks factors such as human migration, whereby the boundaries between 'North' and 'South' are increasingly blurred. Take the case of women from the south Asian sub-continent or West Africa married to husbands settled in Britain. One of WLUML's activities is to provide advice and support to women in crisis, and the network is most commonly approached by women who have married across these boundaries. Simply because a woman is now located in a 'developed country' does not mean that her social problems are easier to solve; indeed, racism, isolation and language barriers can all compound the problems she experiences as a woman.

In the current climate, where cultural identities have become increasingly polarised, both in many societies where gender rights work remains to be done and in the minds of those who determine funding opportunities, women's groups such as WLUML that seek the difficult balance of highlighting commonalities while recognising diversities, appear to be losing out. As Lydia Alpizar Duran has noted, the fragmentation of women's movements into super-specialised movements around key issues means that in many cases women have lost the capacity to engineer the kinds of alliances that would help to define a broader agenda for social change.[10]

At their recent Plan of Action meeting in Dakar, Senegal, WLUML networkers identified the value they see in linking through the network. Among others reasons, they noted that:

> *More than the sum of its parts, the added value of a network lies in generating an analysis of women's rights violations that can only emerge once international networking has uncovered our diversities and similarities and how these can be used against women. Our coming together adds important new dimensions to our local understanding of local power dynamics.*

> *In other words, it is precisely an organisation that does not fit into the usual boxes that gives women greater possibilities of resisting and challenging gender inequality. And yet today WLUML, like so many other similar women's organisations, faces all of the challenges in raising funding for gender equality work discussed above.*[11]

While the current situation does threaten many of the gains women made in the heady 1990s, there is also room for measured optimism. Funding constraints for gender equality work may lead rights activists not only to be more innovative, but also to do some in-house 'spring-cleaning'. This is not an argument for corporate-style 'rationalisation' and 'streamlining', but a call to support ongoing efforts to reassess strategic planning and thinking. While cyclical funding 'fashions' may be here to stay, affecting both non-governmental as well as governmental women's rights work, an understanding of all social development issues as inherently interlinked means that clearly articulated and well-grounded gender justice goals can be achieved, whether through HIV/AIDS programmes or family law reform campaigns.

This is particularly so since it appears that the tide may be turning back to core and programme funding. AWID's research cites a publication on 21st-century philanthropic trends, *Looking Out for the Future*, which sees the growth of core support as an 'innovation' to watch.[12] AWID argues that as it becomes clearer that going overboard on demands for accountability and results defeats the very purpose of the voluntary sector, the pendulum might swing in the other direction.[13]

Meanwhile, there is some evidence that those voices within some national OECD policy-making circles who insist that the (mis)use of culture and religion to obstruct women's development requires a response more grounded in local women's knowledge are gaining in confidence and effectiveness. In funding circles the concept of 'multiple discriminations' is gaining ground, based on frontline feminist sociological theory which emphasises that effective strategies and policies to counter gender inequality must also take into account the fact that women, like men, have multiple intersecting identities; how they experiences their lives is determined not just by their gender, but also by their ethnicity or race, their class, age, sexual orientation, ability and, in some contexts, by how they identify religiously – or not, as the case may be.

Creating and protecting the spaces that will allow these positive trends to flourish is where the focus of discussion about the financing of gender equality work now needs to be directed.

BIBLIOGRAPHY

Balchin, C. (2003). 'With her feet on the ground: women, religion and development in Muslim communities', *Development* 46 (4): 39–49, Palgrave Macmillan, Basingstoke, England.

Balchin, C. (2007). '"Muslim Women" and "Moderate Muslims": British Policy and the Strengthening of Religious Absolutist Control over Gender Development', in Eyben, R. and Moncrieffe, J. (eds), *The Power of Labelling: How We Categorize and Why It Matters*, Earthscan Publications, London.

Clark, C., Sprenger, E. and VeneKlasen, L. (Just Associates) with Alpizar Duran, L. and Kerr, J. (AWID) (2006). *Where's the Money for Women's Rights: Assessing resources and the role of donors in the promotion of women's rights and support of women's organizations*, Association for Women's Rights in Development, Toronto.

ENDNOTES

1   http://www.awid.org/go.php?pg=where_is_money

2   http://www.awid.org/moneyandmovements/ppts/day1/opening_plenary/opening_plenary_la_en.doc

3   http://www.awid.org/publications/where_is_money/web_000.pdf

4   Bridge Report No. 66, *National Machineries for Women in Development: experiences, lessons and strategies*, Report prepared for the Ministry of Foreign Affairs, Denmark, by Emma Bell with Bridget Byrne, Julie Koch Laier, Sally Baden and Rachel Marcus, February 2002; Sixth African Regional Conference on Women, 22–26 November 1999, Addis Ababa, *Ethiopia: Mid-decade Review of the Implementation of the Dakar And Beijing Platforms for Action in the African Region, Assessment report on institutional mechanisms for the advancement of women*, Economic Commission for Africa, November 1999; CEDAW Committee comment on India, 4 February 2000. http://sim.law.uu.nl/SIM/Case Law/UNCom.nsf/89e6367c3ac1ba6fc12567b70027d9fb/f1e04b43b60 59b32c12568c0003992b9?OpenDocument; CEDAW Committee, on 1 February 2002 http://sim.law.uu.nl/SIM/CaseLaw/UNCom.nsf/

89e6367c3ac1ba6fc12567b70027d9fb/59bf0438ebab84ba41256bae 004b676d?OpenDocument; Paper presented to the Beyond Access Forum, Oxford 28 April 2004, Jill Blackmore, Professor of Education, Deakin University, *Gender Equity and Resourcing: Reflections from Australia*. http://www.ioe.ac.uk/schools/efps/GenderEducDev/Blackmore%20version%202.pdf

5   http://www.awid.org/publications/where_is_money/web_Annex04.pdf

6   Katherine McDonald, Executive Director, Action Canada for Population and Development http://www.publicservice.co.uk/propdf/EM2%20Action%20Canada%20PRO.pdf

7   Hunt, P. (2004). *2004 Report to the United Nations Commission on Human Rights*, report of UN Special Rapporteur on the Right to Health, UN Doc.E/CN.4/2004/49.

8   http://www.tni.org/detail_page.phtml?page=archives_shuman_nation

9   Clark et al. (2006), p. 8 http://www.awid.org/publications/where_is_money/web_book.pdf

10 http://www.awid.org/moneyandmovements/ppts/day1/opening_plenary/opening_plenary_la_en.doc

11 http://www.wluml.org/english/pubs/pdf/poa/senegal-2006-poa-en.pdf

12 Katherine Fulton and Andrew Blau (2005). *Looking Out for the Future, An Orientation for Twenty-First Century Philanthropists*, The Monitor Group.

13 Clark et al. (2006), p. 15, op. cit.

CASSANDRA BALCHIN is currently concentrating on networking, advocacy and policy work in the context of Muslim communities in Britain. She is a former journalist who has worked with women's groups in Pakistan. Her research and writing has focused on Muslim family law and law reform processes, and more recently on critiques of international development policy and practice regarding religion. She has been part of the network Women Living Under Muslim Laws since the early 1990s.

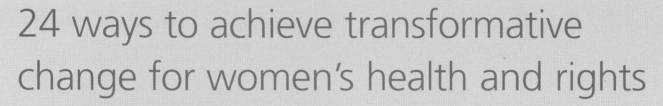

24 ways to achieve transformative change for women's health and rights

Asian-Pacific Resource and Research Centre for Women

The eight-country[1] study by the Asian-Pacific Resource and Research Centre for Women (ARROW), *Monitoring Ten Years of ICPD Implementation: The Way Forward to 2015*, revealed the fact that since 1994 two million women have died in these eight countries alone from pregnancy and childbirth-related causes. Of these, 259,530 died as a result of unsafe abortions, often caused by poverty. Annually, as many as 195,420 women continue to die from maternal mortality.

The figures were difficult to calculate, as country data are often not up to date or reliable and comparative baseline data are not easily available. Of the eight countries studied, China was the only one that achieved a 50% reduction in maternal mortality. In the six countries with high levels of maternal mortality, Cambodia (437 per 100,000 births), Indonesia (307), India (440), Nepal (905), Pakistan (500) and the Philippines (172), the target set by the International Conference on Population and Development (ICPD) of a rate of fewer than 125 deaths per 100,000 births by 2000 has not been met.[2]

To address this issue, it is critical that the primary health care system is strengthened, partly by increasing budgetary allocations. Maternal mortality and unsafe abortion need to be placed higher on the national policy agenda and dealt with more openly. An in-depth implementation progress needs to be more regularly monitored and government accountability and transparency must be vigorously acted upon.

Strategies to reduce maternal mortality

Below are some additional ideas for action:

1. Increase per capita government health expenditure, as recommended in the WHO Report of the Macroeconomic Commission on Health, to at least US$15 for developing countries. (This is the current level in Sri Lanka.)

2. Increase the proportion of public health investment to at least 3% of GDP and within this put up the allocations to be spent on reducing maternal mortality and unsafe abortion. (In India the current figure is 0.9% and in Pakistan 0.7%.)

3. Ensure that all related policies, such as national health, reproductive health, population, HIV/AIDS and women's empowerment policies, have detailed target figures and time schedules for the implementation of actions known to reduce maternal mortality. These include extending the number of functional emergency obstetric care facilities in all primary health care centres; increasing the availability and accessibility of fully functioning obstetric teams; making all existing clinic infrastructures fully functional with qualified and skilled staff, supplies and medication; increasing the number of adequately trained and equipped birth attendants and nurses; and ensuring that all clinics are also equipped for safe, legal abortion services, including 24-hour availability of blood banks.

4. Report annually on the progress of the implementation of plans to national and local stakeholders, including NGOs and UN agencies, using agreed indicators.

5. Review urgently restrictive abortion laws and reform them to at least allow abortion to save the life of the mother, for mental health reasons and for socio-economic reasons, especially poverty.

6. As a matter of urgency remove user fees for reproductive health services that have been introduced as part of health sector reforms, especially for childbirth, legal abortion and contraception.

Strategies to increase access to affordable and gender-sensitive health care for women

7. Policy-makers in governments, UN agencies and multilateral agencies need to ensure that health sector reforms are urgently evaluated and then regularly monitored, so that they can accurately assess the impact of the reforms on marginalised and poor sections of society and on the quality and affordability of health services.

8. Governments should remove user fees for priority reproductive health services (such as antenatal care, delivery, emergency obstetric care, abortion and family planning) for all women, including young people and marginalised groups such as migrant women. (The reduction of maternal mortality in Sri Lanka can be largely attributed to the provision of accessible and free services.)

9. In countries where social insurance has been introduced, the policy needs to cover reproductive health services and to be extended to the informal sector and to the poor and marginalised.

10. The introduction and review of health sector reform needs better assessment, including existing infrastructure and resources; targets committed to at the

Cairo and Beijing conferences and set by the Millennium Development Goals (MDGs); structured consultations/inputs from service providers, health clients (especially women) and local communities; optimal utilisation of resources available from federal and local budgets.

Strategies to increase rights-based and gender-sensitive services within policies and programmes

11. Governments need to strengthen their efforts and seek more technical assistance to ensure that a clear rights-based agenda and gender equality framework is included in the development of all population, reproductive health, HIV/AIDS and women's empowerment policies and programmes, and their implementation, monitoring and evaluation.

12. UN agencies need to swiftly fund, develop, provide and promote more models, tools, best practice and clear conceptual and practical rights and gender-sensitive frameworks in collaboration with women's NGOs.

13. There should be a policy requirement that governments must include women activists' NGOs in decision-making on new and revised laws, policies and plans, and ensure their representation and technical input on commissions and committees on population, reproductive health, women's health and HIV/AIDS.

14. UN agencies (particularly the UN Population Fund) should strengthen their role and be more active in clarifying, promoting and defending the ICPD human rights and reproductive rights framework in national laws, policies and programmes and in donor funding, beginning with a review of the content of these documents.

15. UN agencies, in collaboration with women's NGOs, should facilitate and provide more national and regional technical meetings, training and general technical assistance, beginning with top policy-makers.

16. National demographic surveys should use a rights-based and unmet needs framework and should therefore interview young and unmarried people, not just married women.

17. The provision of information and full reproductive health services to young people within the primary health care system should become a major policy objective.

Strategies to achieve the ICPD goals

18. Create a common regional and national monitoring system of the Beijing, Cairo and MDG objectives, with indicators agreed to by all stakeholders – governments, NGOs, UN agencies, researchers and parliamentarians.

19. Annual monitoring and public reporting of budgets and expenditure by local government bodies and the auditor general's office is required to ensure efficiency in resource use and progress in the achievement of the Beijing, Cairo and MDG objectives.

20. Designation of national focal points within the government (ministries of health and women's empowerment), who will host regular annual fora in which the presentation of government reports and dialogue with civil society on progress achieved will be an ongoing agenda.

21. Increased resources and technical assistance to the capacity building of politicians and government officials, including those in the remotest areas, in order to develop skills and commitment for working effectively as monitors of health services and women's rights.

22. Health ministries should initiate a coordination mechanism for women's health and reproductive health and rights for information sharing and project coordination, with a senior cabinet minister convening the initiative and including all relevant line ministries.

23. Introduce new dynamism by creating task forces composed of governmental organisations, parliamentarians, researchers and civil society organisation representatives to plan and monitor specific components of the national plan on women and the reproductive health and rights plan.

24. A national system for implementation of the Beijing agreement should include information and education dissemination up to the end user level and the establishment of an effective feedback loop involving NGOs.

BIBLIOGRAPHY

Asian-Pacific Resource and Research Centre for Women (2005a). *Monitoring Ten Years of ICPD Implementation: The Way Forward to 2015*, Asian Country Reports, ARROW, Kuala Lumpur, Malaysia.

Asian-Pacific Resource and Research Centre for Women (2005b). *Proceedings of the Women's Health and Rights Advocacy Partnership (WHRAP) Regional Policy Dialogue*, Unpublished report, ARROW, Kuala Lumpur, Malaysia.

Asian-Pacific Resource and Research Centre for Women (2003). *Access to Quality Gender-Sensitive Health Services; Women-Centred Action Research*, ARROW, Kuala Lumpur, Malaysia.

Asian-Pacific Resource and Research Centre for Women (2000). *Taking Up the Cairo Challenge: Country Studies in Asia-Pacific*, ARROW, Kuala Lumpur, Malaysia.

Ravindran, Sundari, T.K. and de Pinho, H. (eds) (2005). *The Right Reforms? Health Sector Reforms and Sexual and Reproductive Health*, Women's Health Project, School of Public Health, University of Witwatersrand, Parktown, South Africa.

ORGANISATIONAL NOTES

The Asian-Pacific Resource and Research Centre for Women (ARROW) is a regional organisation committed to promoting and protecting women's health and rights. Established in 1993, ARROW now works in 13 priority countries in the Asia-Pacific region to build partnerships for evidence-based advocacy, towards re-orienting policies and programmes, strengthening the women's movement and improving the lives of marginalised women across the region.

ENDNOTES

1 The countries are Cambodia, China, India, Indonesia, Nepal, Malaysia, Pakistan and the Philippines.

2 Asian-Pacific Resource and Research Centre for Women (2005a).

Using the law to combat domestic violence

Meena Shivdas

Introduction

Violence against women is disturbingly pervasive and persistent in the Commonwealth. Although the terms 'domestic violence', 'family violence', 'violence against women', 'sexual violence' and 'gender-based violence' are often used interchangeably, it is regularly argued that domestic violence is mainly encountered by women and that the violence is more often than not inflicted by their spouses or partners. However, there is a need to expand this definition as other forms of violence against women, including dowry killings, 'honour' killings and female genital mutilation, often occur within the home. More importantly, there is a need to understand that violence against women in domestic situations occurs within the broader context of gender discrimination and subordination in relation to education, resources, employment, opportunities and access to decision-making in the private and public spheres. There is recognition of the urgent need to frame human security in terms of accessing rights to resources and gaining a political voice to ensure that women's gender-intensified disadvantages and vulnerabilities do not exclude them from participation and decision-making in governance.

Concern about the socio-economic costs of domestic violence has led to actions by policy-makers at different levels – individual, household and community. The enactment and implementation of specific legislation addressing domestic violence has long been advocated as a policy solution. Most Commonwealth countries have either specific legislation which addresses the rights of women who are battered by their partners or broad legislation which covers domestic violence. In considering the various factors that result in women facing violence in their most intimate relationships, it must be recognised that abused and battered women turn to domestic violence legislation as a last resort. In most cases, it is only after they have exhausted all other avenues of help, including family and religious mediation and the intervention of social and health services, that abused and battered women turn to the law.

This article assesses whether specific legislation is an adequate vehicle for protecting the rights of battered and abused women by examining the implementation of the CARICOM Model Legislation on Domestic Violence[1] and identifies points for policy consideration.

International agendas

It was only in the 1990s that violence against women was recognised as a violation of women's human rights at the international level, when the 1993 World Conference on Human Rights in Vienna affirmed women's rights as human rights and expanded the international human rights agenda to include gender-specific violations. Consequently, the Vienna Declaration and Programme of Action[2] identified gender-specific abuses as human rights violations. Following this, the UN General Assembly adopted the Declaration on the Elimination of Violence against Women[3] in December 1993. Then in 1994 the UN Commission on Human Rights appointed a special rapporteur on violence against women, with the remit of integrating work relating to women's human rights into all UN activities.[4] The special rapporteur's 1996 report included a framework for model legislation on domestic violence. The Cairo Conference in 1994 and the Beijing Conference in 1995 further addressed violence against women within the framework of human rights and set out specific recommendations for consideration by states.

Since the Beijing Conference, the forms of violence against women have increased and new patterns are emerging. For example, while the issue of honour killings has been a concern in south Asia, including for certain Afghan[5] communities living as refugees in Pakistan, recently honour killings have also surfaced in south Asian diaspora communities, particularly in the UK. The trafficking of women and girls has also taken on new forms, facilitated by information and communications technologies. Consequently, governments may still be grappling with the extent of violations of women's rights, while at the same time they are trying to deal with new developments.

Does domestic violence legislation work?

Since 1991, countries in the Caribbean have enacted legislation which is intended to ensure protection for women in abusive domestic situations. To varying degrees the legislation is based on the CARICOM model. As pointed out by the United Nations Economic Commission for Latin America and the Caribbean (ECLAC)/UNIFEM review,[6] the CARICOM legislation was drafted so that countries could increase women's legal options when they were trying to protect themselves from further abuse. It was meant to complement the existing criminal justice system, as all forms of physical violation, including threats of violence against a partner or a stranger, were deemed to be a crime in the Caribbean. The CARICOM model legislation has succeeded in its intention, in that 16 Commonwealth Caribbean countries have now passed legislation to protect abused and battered women.[7]

The CARICOM model provides protection only for the spouse, parent, child or dependant of the respondent – women in visiting relationships are excluded. As a significant proportion of the adult female population in Caribbean countries do not enter residential unions even though they may be in long-term relationships, domestic violence legislation excludes many women. This limitation has been recognised by Trinidad and Tobago and by Dominica, where domestic violence legislation recognises visiting relationships.

Legislation in the Caribbean gives the victim/survivor the right to apply to the magistrates court for non-molestation, exclusion and occupation and tenancy orders. The law is therefore part of the civil process and steps are in place to ensure anonymity and confidentiality, as proceedings are conducted in closed courts.

How far has legislation helped women claim their rights?

Given the stigma and culture of silence surrounding domestic violence, domestic violence legislation allows others, including the parents of abused women, police officers and social workers (in the case of abused children) to move an application for protection. However, it has been found that despite the powers accorded to them, police officers rarely initiate applications for protection orders. The perception that domestic violence is a private matter still prevails. In some countries (Belize, Dominica, Grenada, St Kitts and Nevis, and Trinidad and Tobago) police accountability has been strengthened. This means that the police have to respond to every complaint or report, whether or not a report has been made by the victim. The police are also required to complete a report that is part of the domestic violence register in these countries, as well as in Guyana. Belize, Guyana and St Kitts and Nevis acknowledge the stigma and shame encountered by abused women, and recognise women's reluctance to come forward publicly to file complaints. Police are therefore required to interview women in a private area of police stations and ensure that confidentiality is maintained.

Despite detailed court procedures and steps to ensure the protection of abused women's identities, the ECLAC/UNIFEM study revealed that the limited use of legislation in comparison with the incidence of domestic violence is the result partly of a culture of discouragement. The stigma attached to the process of publicly outing one's spouse or partner by taking him to court, and the fact that many abused women are emotionally and financially dependent on abusive partners, are the strongest deterrents. The study also found that a significant number of cases had been withdrawn because women had been intimidated by their abusers. In many cases, couples have some sort of reconciliation. Another factor contributing to the limitation of legislation is lack of knowledge of the legislation. A further limitation of specific legislation is that presiding magistrates lack the power to grant custody and maintenance orders.

While there are still difficulties in implementing the legislation, there has been significant progress in building awareness of the issue and developing confidence in the judicial system. The ECLAC/UNIFEM study points out that the use of specific legislation by battered and abused women is highest in countries where public education is widely available and where there is access to the legal system. Women also tend to use the legislation in instances where they receive support from government and non-governmental organisations when they assert their rights. Another significant factor is the seriousness with which the courts treat applications for protection. A case in point is the Antigua and Barbuda experience, where speedy hearings and the granting of interim protection orders have been developed.

Domestic violence legislation: issues and challenges

Given the struggle to win acknowledgement of the fact that violence against women is a human rights issue, and the ongoing struggle to devise appropriate and effective policy measures to help women claim their rights, it is pertinent to set down some of the barriers, as listed below.

- The reluctance of the legal system to become involved in the domestic sphere, including domestic violence and marital rape.
- The gender bias of judges and police officers, which allows abuse to go unnoticed and unpunished.
- The mindsets of legislators, which tend to subscribe to the perpetuation of gender stereotyping and subordination, in accordance with prevailing societal norms.
- Entrenched cultural notions of women's subordination, which are evident in discriminatory and harmful practices directed at women.
- Women's lack of knowledge about their rights and their restricted access to legal recourse.
- The contradictions between civil laws and customary practices, which may have implications for the realisation of women's rights.
- The lack of political will in advancing gender equality and securing women's rights in all spheres.

Reviews and analyses of policy responses towards violence against women have shown that the struggle to legislate on domestic violence is ongoing and reflects both the need to define violence against women as a violation of women's human rights and to advocate for the recognition of all forms of violence deemed 'sensitive', including marital rape and some culturally 'accepted' forms of violence, as violations against women that must not be tacitly condoned.

International and regional women's rights instruments provide a framework for legislation on domestic violence. The African Union's Protocol on Women's Rights is an excellent example of a comprehensive framework that provides policy guidelines to legislators contemplating legislation on domestic violence.

Experience in the Commonwealth has shown that where strong legislation exists and where steps have been taken to ensure that prosecutions are followed through by providing battered women with the support they need to pursue justice, violence against women is increasingly perceived as a violation that calls for urgent action. The experience of Canada, New Zealand and the United Kingdom are cases in point. Effective laws, support for survivors of violence, a sensitised justice system, a proactive legislature, appropriate counselling, social and health services, community and religious mediation systems, trained police and rapid reporting procedures send out a strong message that violence against women will be addressed in a comprehensive manner.

The Commonwealth Secretariat's approach

The Commonwealth Secretariat advocates an integrated approach to the elimination of violence against women. This includes legislative measures, legal interventions, affirmative action, training of the police and judiciary, improved reporting, data collection and monitoring, public education, programmes targeted at abusive men, support services, health measures and protective mechanisms, and the intervention of community and religious leaders. Such an approach is women-centred and considers battered women's particular needs and interests within the framework of social relations and the realities of women's daily lives.

This approach requires commitment at the highest level of political office and an adequate allocation of resources. While countries take an incremental approach to the advancement of women's rights through specific action identified within broader development strategies and policy frameworks, national women's machineries which are tasked with the responsibility of advancing women's rights continue to be under-resourced and lack the power required to carry out this important mandate.

The approach's four key steps, which form the foundation for developing strategies to address violence against women that are appropriate for particular national contexts, are: conceptualisation; deeper understanding; action strategies and coordination; and the provision of a policy framework that addresses the issue in an integrated manner. This integrated approach has been adopted in several countries, including Kenya, Mauritius, Uganda and Zambia.

The Secretariat has promoted this integrated approach through national workshops on gender-based violence held in ten countries in east and southern Africa. It has also developed training and resource materials to address violence against women.

Conclusion

Legislation on domestic violence goes a long way towards helping abused and battered women assert their rights. However, legislation alone is not the answer. The integrated approach to the elimination of violence against women considers legislative measures, legal interventions, affirmative actions, training of the police and judiciary, improved reporting, data collection and monitoring, public education, programmes targeted at abusive men, support services, health measures and protective mechanisms.

The *Commonwealth Plan of Action for Gender Equality 2005–2015*[8] builds on this integrated approach by highlighting structural, systemic, cultural and ideological barriers to the realisation of women's rights. It underscores the fact that women and girls experience different forms of discrimination and disadvantage at different stages of their lives. The Plan of Action therefore calls for adequate support for women and girls throughout their life cycle so that progress made at one stage is not negated by adverse experiences and discrimination at a later stage.

This article is based on a paper delivered at a Commonwealth Parliamentary Association conference held in Abuja, Nigeria in August 2006.

ENDNOTES

1   The Commonwealth Secretariat's Economic and Legal Services Division, in collaboration with its Gender and Youth Affairs Division, supported the CARICOM Secretariat between 1989 and 1992 in the development of the CARICOM model legislation on eight areas of women's human rights: domestic violence; sexual offences; sexual harassment; equal pay; inheritance; equality for women in employment; citizenship; and maintenance and maintenance orders.

2   The UN Vienna Declaration and Programme of Action, Declaration paragraph 18, Programme of Action paragraphs 36–44, A/CONF.157/23, 1993.

3   UN General Assembly Resolution 48/104.

4   Resolution 1994/45.

5   See Johnston, N.L. (n.d.). 'Afghan refugee women: What room for manoeuvre? A study of the interface between space, politics and gender identity', unpublished dissertation, University of East Anglia, UK.

6   Clarke, R. and Sealy-Burke, J. (2003). *Eliminating Gender Based Violence, Ensuring Equality: ECLAC/UNIFEM Regional Assessment of Actions to End Violence against Women in the Caribbean*, ECLAC/UNIFEM.

7   The 16 countries are: Antigua & Barbuda (Domestic Violence Act, 1999); Bahamas (Sexual Offence and Domestic Violence Act, 1991); Barbados (Domestic Violence Act, 1992); Belize (Domestic Violence Act, 1992); Bermuda (Domestic Violence Act, 1997); British Virgin Islands (Domestic Violence Act, 1992); Cayman Islands (Summary Jurisdiction Law, 1992); Dominica (Protection against Domestic Violence Act, 2001); Grenada (Domestic Violence Act, 2001); Guyana (Domestic Violence Act, 1996); Jamaica (Domestic Violence Act, 1995); Montserrat (Family Act, 1998); St Kitts and Nevis (Domestic Violence Act, 2000); St Lucia (Domestic Violence Act, 1995); St Vincent and the Grenadines (Domestic Violence Act, 1995); Trinidad and Tobago (Domestic Violence Act, 1999, replacing the Domestic Violence Act, 1991).

8   The *Commonwealth Plan of Action for Gender Equality 2005–2015* was adopted by Women's Affairs Ministers in Fiji in June 2004 and was subsequently endorsed by the Commonwealth Heads of Government meeting held in Malta in November 2005. It is a comprehensive ten-year plan to advance gender equality, with four key areas of action: (1) democracy, peace and conflict; (2) human rights and the law; (3) poverty eradication and economic empowerment; and (4) HIV/AIDS. The Gender Section of the Commonwealth Secretariat is engaged in the implementation of the Plan.

promoting
peace and
democracy

Women's political participation in a democratic Commonwealth

The role of political and electoral systems

Elsie-Bernadette Onubogu and Khabele Matlosa

Overview

In 1996, the 53 countries of the Commonwealth adopted a goal of 30% of women in decision-making positions, following a similar target set by the 1995 UN Beijing Conference on Women. The target was based on an assumption that 30% would constitute a 'critical mass' – enough women to make a difference. *The Commonwealth Plan of Action for Gender Equality 2005–2015*[1] reiterated the target because to date only six Commonwealth countries have achieved it. The six countries are Mozambique, South Africa, Tanzania, Guyana, Grenada and New Zealand – three African countries, two Caribbean and one in the Pacific Region. The *Plan of Action* goes further, however, and sets a target of a *minimum* of 30% of women in decision-making in *all* spheres of life – in the public and private sector, not just politics. The Commonwealth recognises that women have a right to be equally represented in every area and at every level of society.

The *Plan of Action* is further guided by the priorities set out in the *Coolum Declaration for Commonwealth Action*, adopted by the 2002 Commonwealth Heads of Government Meeting (CHOGM) and supports the Convention on the Elimination of All Forms of Discrimination Against Women (CEDAW) and the Millennium Development Goals (MDGs).

Working within the framework provided by the *Updates* of the *Plan of Action*, the Commonwealth continues to play a major global advocacy role for gender mainstreaming, particularly in the area of promoting women's participation in government and decision-making. The Secretariat's strategy is based on working closely with National Women's Machineries (NWMs), such as ministries for women's affairs and gender. It has developed a practical framework, the Gender Management System (GMS), to apply gender analysis tools to priority sectors. It is currently documenting strategies to increase women's participation and representation, and lessons learnt from member countries. This study will be published soon.

Relevant frameworks: the *Plan of Action*, CEDAW and the MDGs

In the Commonwealth *Plan of Action*, ministers responsible for women's affairs reiterated that for women to be able to influence the decisions that affect their lives, their participation and representation was crucial. They therefore urged governments, political parties and civil society to strive to increase women's participation and representation at all levels to ensure the achievement of the minimum target of 30% endorsed by ministers and heads of government. The *Plan of Action* calls for countries that have already met the target to go on to achieve gender equality.

CEDAW

Political participation is a fundamental right of every person, including women. The International Covenant on Civil and Political Rights guarantees every citizen's right to participate in public affairs, vote or be voted into office and have access to public services within their country. The right of every woman to participate in the affairs of her country is further reaffirmed by the Charter on Human and People's Rights and by CEDAW. Ratification means that states have assumed an obligation to take all necessary measures to ensure women's effective participation in the public life of their country.

The Millennium Development Goals

In 2000, world leaders adopted the Millennium Development Goals. The relevant goal here is MDG 3 on the promotion of gender equality and women's empowerment. While the MDGs have been hailed as a positive strategy for stimulating development and promoting gender equality, they are not exhaustive, as issues such as peace, security and civil society involvement are not covered. Nor do the MDGs focus on rights. Despite this, experts agree that the MDGs provide important leverage to mobilise political will and resources for the achievement of the objectives of the 1995 UN World Conference on Women *Beijing Platform for Action* and CEDAW.

In an effort to address this apparent lacuna, experts have maintained that integrating a rights-based approach into the MDGs and the other relevant frameworks will help to address the rights of women and girls. The rights-based approach focuses on beneficiaries (women) as owners of rights; it provides for integrated responses in a holistic inclusive manner. The Commonwealth, therefore, speaks of 'representative democracy'. In political participation and decision-making such responses can ensure women's equal participation and representation, i.e. gender balance. In the Commonwealth, a rights-based approach is the preferred strategy for achieving gender equality.

These frameworks promote gender equality through gender mainstreaming strategies in order to ensure balanced representation of women, men and young people in the Commonwealth. As noted by the Commonwealth Secretary General, Rt. Hon. Don McKinnon: 'Gender equality is the fundamental premise which underlies any attempt to achieve representative democracy.'

The Southern African Development Community: a case study

Gender equality is essential for the entrenchment of intra-party democracy. The Southern African experience on the empowerment of women varies widely (Molokomme, 2000). In line with the mandate of the Commonwealth ministers responsible for women's affairs, Southern African Development Community (SADC) member states took a step forward in 1997 when they signed the *Declaration on Gender and Development* in Blantyre, Malawi. The states committed themselves individually and collectively to the following policy measures.

- Equal gender representation in all key organs of state, and at least 30% women in political and decision-making structures by 2005.

- Full women's access and control over productive resources to reduce female poverty levels.

- Repeal and reform of all laws and constitutions and changes in social practices that subject women to discrimination.

- Urgent measures to prevent the increasing levels of violence against women and children.

Electoral systems

Electoral systems set boundaries for parties' electoral contest for the control of state power by setting out the institutional framework for elections and defining formulae for the translation of votes into parliamentary seats. Evidence suggests that the two dominant electoral systems in Southern Africa, the British 'first-past-the-post' (FPTP)[2] and the proportional representation (PR)[3] models, have their own distinctive impact on the nature of party organisation and representation in the legislature.

Electoral systems in the SADC region reflect the institutional arrangements of the former colonial administrations. Almost all the countries which operate the FPTP electoral model have experienced political problems to which the FPTP model has contributed. It is also arguable that states which operate some form of PR have experienced fairly positive political development, particularly in respect of stability, even though issues around accountability remain a contested terrain. Unlike FPTP, PR systems have given representation to various political forces, including women and minority groups, and have enhanced the legitimacy and stability of political systems. Recent efforts to achieve electoral reform in Zambia, Zimbabwe and Malawi have shown a popular preference for moving away from the FPTP system to systems which have an element of proportionality.

Electoral systems perform three functions in a representative democracy.

1. They act as a conduit through which the electorate can hold their representatives in the legislature accountable.

2. They enable the national legislature to be constituted either through a proportionally determined vote count or through a simple plurality of votes.

3. Different electoral systems enable the public to express their opinions by giving a political party or a coalition of parties state power.

There is no consensus on which electoral system is best for democratic governance and political stability. Countries rarely make a deliberate decision to select a model that best suits their particular circumstances. Each political system has advantages and disadvantages in terms of the representation of different groups in society. States should endeavour to review and deliberately design electoral systems that suit their own conditions with a view to deepening democratic governance.

Women's participation

On the basis of this analysis, it is arguable that an electoral system can either facilitate or inhibit women's participation in governance. A PR system seems more likely to bring about gender equality in politics and increased participation by women. The converse is true for the FPTP system. Although PR does not guarantee that there will be more women members of the legislature, it is certainly a catalyst for gender equality. Table 1 shows women's participation in national assemblies in the SADC region and demonstrates that countries which have a PR system are doing much better than those using FPTP.

It is clear from the table that the two countries with the highest proportion of women in parliament are Mozambique (34.8%) and South Africa (32.8%), both of which operate a PR list system. The bottom two countries are Zimbabwe (10%) and Swaziland (3.1%), which have a FPTP (plurality) system. A plausible argument can therefore be made that PR is more conducive to gender equality in the legislature than FPTP. However, the South African and

Table 1 | Women's representation in SADC parliaments

Rank	Country	Electoral system	Lower or single house		
			Seats	Women	% Women
1	Mozambique	PR	250	90	34.8
2	South Africa	PR	400	131	32.8
3	Tanzania	FPTP	307	97	30.0
4	Namibia	PR	104	19	26.4
5	Mauritius	FPTP-block	70	12	17.0
6	Angola	PR	220	34	15.5
7	Malawi	FPTP	193	27	14.4
8	Lesotho	MMP	120	16	13.3
9	Botswana	FPTP	57	7	12.3
10	Zambia	FPTP	158	19	12.0
12	Zimbabwe	FPTP	150	15	10.0
13	Swaziland	FPTP	65	5	3.1

Source: Lowe-Morna, 2004:14 (updated by the author)

Mozambican experiences also demonstrate that PR systems need to be complemented by gender quotas. In part this explains why Tanzania ranks third among SADC countries in terms of gender representation, with 30% representation of women in the legislature, despite its FPTP system.

The role of political parties

Political parties are organised groups set up to contest control over state power and to direct the development process in line with their own ideological orientation and policy frameworks. Political parties are formed in all societies and states where the population actively participates in the political process. They enable party members to articulate their political will and strive for the realisation of their political aims as a group.

The challenges that confront political parties in terms of entrenching inner party democracy are many and varied. It has been argued that a lack of inner party democracy also constrains political competition among parties. Many African political parties, especially dominant ones, engage in internal 'dissent management', leading to autocracy. They restrict voices within the party and discipline MPs and other members who disagree with the leadership's positions, as well as exercising strict control over the selection of party officials and candidates for public office.

Leadership

The leadership of a political party is as important an issue as the way in which it is organised. The effectiveness and vibrancy of a party and the contribution it makes to a working democracy are heavily dependent on its leadership. In the majority of SADC countries the leadership issue remains problematic. Data from country studies suggest that political parties face daunting challenges in institutionalising accountable, transparent and visionary leadership that can inculcate a democratic culture both within the party and the nation at large.

Primary elections

Primary elections provide another litmus test of the extent and degree of inner party democracy. Often the process of nominating party candidates is fraught with controversy due to the manner in which it is executed by the party leadership. Problems in primary elections revolve around whether the process emphasises centralised leadership control or allows the party rank and file to influence the selection process. These problems are rife in almost all the SADC countries, irrespective of their electoral system. However, they are much more acute in the countries that operate FPTP. Parties need to open up to their rank and file membership the collective ownership of nominations and party lists.

Party alliances and coalitions

Party alliances and coalitions influence the operations of parties. Political parties in the region exhibit serious weaknesses in terms of forming alliances and coalitions at national level, with the exception of Mauritius, Malawi, South Africa and Mozambique. In other SADC countries, the experience of party alliances or coalitions at national level has been poor. There are also few sustainable intra-regional linkages among parties with similar perspectives.

Management of internal party affairs

Management of internal party affairs is an important yardstick of the extent to which inner party democracy exists within SADC states. The issue is inextricably linked to party leadership, which relates to how the day-to-day running of party affairs is managed, the building of national, provincial, district, community and village branches and the management of the party's resources. It also includes the development of manifestos and programmes, as well as the organisation of regular party meetings and conferences. In countries where the leadership of political parties is autocratic, party management is less accountable to the rank and file. In countries where the leadership is more open and democratic, party management is more transparent and accountable.

Policy and programme development

Policy and programme development determines the effectiveness of parties, especially in mobilising their support base and contesting state power. Many parties experience difficulties in developing policies and programmes. In most SADC countries the electorate is provided with inadequate information on which to base their choice of party when they cast their votes.

With regard to their internal functioning, political parties in Southern Africa are confronted with various challenges, including:

- party structure and internal governance
- party ideology and election manifestos
- policy development
- leadership selection and succession
- candidate nominations and primary elections
- party relations with civil society organisations and social movements
- party relations with electoral management bodies
- gender parity within parties
- mobilisation (especially targeting the youth)
- membership recruitment and managing the membership register
- public outreach and media liaison
- civic and voter education.

The challenge is for political parties to ensure wider inclusiveness at higher levels by bringing more women into positions of leadership. In general, both ruling and opposition parties in the region are led by men and executive committees are also dominated by men. We have yet to see women becoming party leaders rather than just cheerleaders. SADC member states should strive to achieve the benchmarks of the 1997 SADC *Declaration on Gender and Development*. Political parties should institute formal internal quotas or special measures to increase the number of women in their leadership structures, as well as quotas or measures to boost the number of women standing as electoral candidates.

Challenges in increasing women's representation in government across the Commonwealth

While notable progress continues to be recorded in different regions of the Commonwealth, particularly in the SADC region, challenges and obstacles remain. The low level of women's representation and participation has been attributed to various constraints. These include political structures that inhibit women's participation, negative attitudes towards women's involvement and traditional cultural expectations and assumptions. The constraints include: cultural assumptions, which create internal and external barriers; political and electoral systems; traditional and religious practices; low education levels and illiteracy; family responsibilities; financial considerations; and political will.

Recommendations

What needs to be done? To ensure effective and balanced representation, it is critical to engage in:

- constitutional reforms to ensure a rights-based perspective
- reform of electoral law
- legislative reform
- wider involvement in drawing up party manifestos
- quotas, affirmative action and measures targeted at increasing women's involvement
- attitudinal change
- training.

The 12 countries that have achieved the 30% benchmark of female representation in national parliaments have successfully lobbied for a quota system or had it mandated by law. Quota systems, however, are not enough. Additional measures are needed to address the structural and cultural barriers that stop women from participating in decision-making. Otherwise, when quota systems are abandoned, as in the former Soviet Union and Bangladesh, women's representation may fall.

Working in partnership with men

Making men advocates for change is very important; working with men is especially vital when women are not represented in decision-making at the highest level. Using men as spokespersons for campaigns that specifically target the attitudes of men and their behaviour has proved to be a powerful and effective strategy.

Training

Increasing the capacity of women to deliver when they are elected is also an important component of a programme designed to increase women's political participation. Among the areas on which training should focus are: advocacy and lobbying; campaign management; public speaking; media relations; community development; image building; leadership; conflict resolution skills; and gender sensitisation.

Awareness raising and advocacy on women's rights is essential.

Political parties

Increasingly, women around the world are beginning to hold political parties accountable for implementing regional or national mandates such as the 30% target adopted by ministers responsible for women affairs through 'women manifestos'. Such manifestos have been drawn up in Cameroon, Uganda and Sri Lanka. They call for specific measures geared to ensure a minimum of 30% representation for women at decision-making levels, including as candidates in elections.

Working with the media

The media are a potent political tool and should be encouraged to portray positive images of women, consult women as experts and give more air-time to stories celebrating women's achievements.

Encourage women's participation in decision-making at all levels

Campaigns designed to increase women's political participation should be conducted at local, national, regional and international levels. But research shows that for women to be actively engaged in politics, they need to be engaged at community level. Community-level engagement demonstrates that women have the capacity to fill positions of authority. Local government also provides an arena in which people are prepared for higher office. Women lack experience in local government and so do not gain the experience which would enable them to move into positions of higher office.

Awareness raising

Raising awareness is critical to increasing women's political participation. Many people are either unaware that women are under-represented or they do not think that increasing women's participation can make a difference.

Women's caucuses

In Namibia, women's groups came together and drew up an issue-oriented manifesto, which focused on HIV/AIDS and other key issues, and ran on this platform. They were able to effect change on issues as well as increase women's representation.

Family responsive employment policies

Family responsibilities inhibit women from participating in politics. Increasingly, women are raising children on their own. Quality, affordable childcare is critical if women are to be enabled to participate. Women parliamentarians must receive appropriate maternity rights and parliamentary business must be organised in such a way that it is compatible with women's childcare responsibilities.

Conclusion

From this analysis, it is evident that in most Commonwealth countries which have achieved the 30% benchmark of female representation in national parliaments and local government, women have successfully lobbied for specific measures such as quotas, affirmative action or changes in their national constitutions. However, specific measures and quotas are insufficient to ensure equal representation and participation of women in decision-making processes. Additional measures are necessary to address the structural, cultural, traditional, educational and financial barriers that impede women's participation. An important additional factor is political will.

Democracy must take into consideration the needs, diversity, challenges and contributions of its citizens in order to deliver tangible benefits to all. A key feature of any democratic system is that it acknowledges the rights of all individuals in society. We must therefore promote a rights-based perspective through constitutional reforms and the effective implementation of such provisions. Finally, the importance of women's full involvement and participation is not only central to the achievement of democracy. As the evidence shows, dichotomy between the political, social, economic and cultural areas is no longer tenable; democracy is closely linked to

the achievement of sustainable development. As Samoa's Minister of Education, Fiame Naomi Mataafa, has observed: 'Countries that have good representation by women are those with a healthy economy, an effective democratic government and an educated population.'

Six years into the 21st century, Africa recorded its first woman president, while New Zealand, Mozambique and Jamaica inducted female prime ministers. The global statistics on women in politics reveal large variations among regions and countries, and within countries. Some of the very best practice on women's political empowerment takes place in low- and middle-income countries where women have low human development indicators. The South therefore has much to teach the North, and it is not the case that high literacy levels, income and female labour force participation rates automatically translate into high percentages of female parliamentarians or women in decision-making. Irrespective of the progress that has been made, more needs to be done and the challenge remains to demonstrate the difference that women in government and decision-making can make to the lives of Commonwealth citizens.

REFERENCES

Lowe-Morna, C. (2004). *Gender in Southern African Politics: Ringing Up the Change*, Gender Links, Johannesburg, South Africa.

Molokomme, A. (2000). 'Gender and Democracy in SADC: A Regional Case Study, Paper presented to the Commonwealth Workshop on Gender and Democracy', Windhoek, Namibia.

ENDNOTES

1 Commonwealth Secretariat (2005). *Commonwealth Plan of Action for Gender Equality 2005–2015*, paras 3:1–3:13.

2 'First-past-the-post' is a system in which constituency seats are won by the candidate who wins the most votes – 'winner takes all'. Critics argue that this system is less likely to favour women, as political parties rarely nominate women as candidates.

3 Proportional representation is a system in which political parties draw up a list of candidates and voters choose among party lists. Seats are allocated to parties in accordance with the overall number of votes cast. The evidence tends to support the view that this system increases women's representation.

ELSIE-BERNADETTE ONUBOGU is responsible for work on gender, democracy, peace and conflict in the Social Transformation and Programmes Division of the Commonwealth Secretariat. Prior to joining the Secretariat, she worked with the United Nations on legal, gender and development issues. She has served with the UN Division for the Advancement of Women, investigated rape, sexual assault and other war crimes with the UN Tribunal for Rwanda, and worked as a consultant with the UNDP and UNIFEM on gender-based violence, violence against women and post-conflict reconstruction. She also served in UN peacekeeping missions in the former Yugoslavia and East Timor. She is a sociologist and international lawyer with expertise in the area of gender and human rights, and holds a degree from the Fletcher School of Law and Diplomacy, Boston, USA.

Women and democracy in Bermuda

Dame Jennifer Smith

The experience in the Caribbean is different in each of the countries of the Caribbean, Americas and Atlantic region.

My country, Bermuda, is Britain's oldest overseas territory. It is made up of about 150 islands and lies 917 km east of the coast of North Carolina. The total land area is 53.33 square km, with an estimated population in 2007 of 64,000. GDP per capita is approximately BMD$84,960, with an estimated growth rate in the range of 3.0 to 3.3%. Financial services (principally reinsurance) and tourism are the two main pillars of the economy, with e-commerce and telecommunications set to become a third.

Constitutionally, Bermuda is internally governed and is Britain's largest remaining overseas territory. The government comprises a governor, appointed by the Crown; a bi-cameral legislature, made up of the House of Assembly and the Senate; and a Cabinet consisting of the executive, headed by a premier and composed of members from the governing party.

Historical background

For many years white male property owners controlled Bermuda's legislature. Just before Emancipation Day on 1 August 1834, an Act was passed which doubled the property qualifications for voting in elections and for running for parliament and other important public offices, making it abundantly clear that the legislature of the day wanted to protect the status quo and guard against too rapid an assumption of political influence by ex-slaves.

Since Emancipation in 1834, racial issues have figured prominently in Bermudan elections: the majority black population had minimal civic rights until the second half of the 20th century.

The existence of a property qualification for voting and other privileges was instrumental in perpetuating the colony's power structure over the years. Racial discrimination and segregationist practices persisted long after slavery had officially ended in Bermuda, ensuring that the greatest impetus for change and progress came from the black community.

The formation of my political party, the Bermuda Progressive Labour Party (PLP), in 1963 was the culmination of a long struggle by courageous men and women against the exclusion of the majority of Bermudians from democratic participation in the running of their country. The PLP endured fluctuating fortunes. The number of PLP representatives elected to the legislature grew from five in 1964 to ten in 1968, then remained at ten in 1972. In 1976 the number grew to 14 and in 1980 to 18. Then in 1983, it went down to 14 and, worse, to a demoralising seven in 1985. In 1989, after a change of leaders, the number increased to 15 and then, in 1993, climbed back up to 18.

The political scene changed dramatically on 9 November 1998, when the PLP won its first General Election with a total of 26 seats. With only 14 seats in the House of Assembly, the United Bermuda Party assumed the role of opposition party for the first time in its 35 years of existence.

Women in politics

While women have always been the backbone of progress in Bermuda, in politics they are just beginning to become a force at the upper echelons of authority and power. Of 36 elected representatives, eight are women and of the 11 Senators in the appointed Upper House, only three are women.

Women in Bermuda, like women throughout the world, have come a long way. But ours is a relatively recent history which began with the women's suffrage movement in 1919. Women in Bermuda finally got the right to vote in 1944. Four years later in 1948 the first women were elected to parliament. Ten years passed before the next woman was elected. And it was not until 1963, when the franchise was finally extended to all those aged 25 years and over, that the first black woman was elected.

Women mentoring women is an important – even vital – part of the process of encouraging women to become involved in politics. In the PLP I follow in the footsteps of a great woman leader, Dame Lois Browne Evans, who has the distinction of being the first woman in a number of areas – including the first woman opposition leader in the Commonwealth, the first black woman elected to parliament in Bermuda, the first woman lawyer in Bermuda and the first woman elected as attorney-general.

As premier, I followed another woman, Pamela Gordon, who became the first woman premier in 1997.

It might seem that women in politics in Bermuda have not progressed very far in the years since they first began fighting for the right to vote. But this is untrue. Statistics reveal that, worldwide, women are not proportionally represented in democratic political institutions. This imbalance may be explained

by the fact that politics is about power; and power is still seen as a man's preserve by women and men alike.

The issue is the way in which women are perceived by this society. Motherhood, which emphasises the most basic difference between men and women, is not given the priority it deserves. Equality of pay and equality of opportunity in the workplace are not the same as recognising the equality of women and men in society. Traditional women's roles are as vital to the functioning of our society as any of the other roles we have acquired since our fight for equality.

If you do not believe this to be true, ask a mother who has stopped working for four or five years in order to raise a child how this time away from the workplace is regarded by employers when she tries to re-enter the workforce. There are very few employers who do not regard this as a negative; and the majority feel that such a woman, from a business point of view, has done nothing valuable with her time. Very few recognise that being a mother can actually improve a worker's personal management skills.

While governments can certainly play a role in strengthening marriages (the Bermuda Government has created a Family Life Council with a mandate to encourage healthy families by highlighting, reinforcing and rewarding best practice through seminars, conferences, support programmes and other activities), women must be committed to creating a value system that gives priority to motherhood and families.

Families are the nurturing place for the next generation and if families do not fulfil their role we have no future. When families are in trouble, our whole society is at risk. There are those who lay the blame for the breakdown in families squarely at the feet of women – after all, it is a woman's sacred destiny to be the mother of man and the keeper of his house. Others lay the blame for the breakdown in families squarely at the feet of men – who else can be blamed for the many young men who seem to have no role models and no pattern to follow into manhood?

Here in the Caribbean, Americas and Atlantic region, media reports do not give much hope for the future. There are too many examples that show that not all of our children are living in peace; too many examples of families failing and in disarray; too many examples of lives lost, futures ruined and human capital wasted. Yet, as signatories to the UN Convention on the Rights of the Child, we are all committed to ensuring that all children grow up in a safe, clean and nurturing environment.

To change the way society looks at women, we must change the way we look at ourselves. Then we can change the outlook and attitudes of men. As long as some of us believe that a woman who dresses a certain way or goes home with a man after a date is asking to be raped, society will continue to think of rape as a sex crime, rather than an abuse of power and an invasion of privacy. As long as some of us believe that marriage gives a man property rights over a woman, problems such as domestic violence will continue.

In the 21st century, women around the world continue to grapple with the determination of 'a woman's place'. Women around the world continue to look for the correct balance between career and family, while continuing to use to the full their talents and abilities.

As a female politician, I am convinced that politics offers the most effective pathway for massive global change that can promote human development through the promotion of women's rights. Over a hundred years ago, woman's suffrage proved to be the catalyst for the women's rights movement in the European democracies. The same women who campaigned for the vote campaigned for better schools, prisons, mental health care and welfare legislation.

Dr Najma Heptulla, President of the Council of the Inter-Parliamentary Union, had this to say at the launch of the report *Politics: Women's Insight*:

> *There is a need to recognise the global trend towards gender parity in all spheres of life, a trend that is even more significant in the parliamentary democracies. Parliaments reflect social attitudes. Hence, the need for greater political sensitivity and action to build political leadership among women. They should be educated in the dynamics of parliamentary politics and the functioning of government. The need for such training can no longer be under-estimated.*[1]

This, I submit, identifies the problem, the solution and the method to achieve social change on a global scale.

Education

Education is the key. It is the means by which women can reach their full potential and affect decisions that will contribute to the growth and well-being of those less fortunate.

The World Economic Forum's document *Women's Empowerment: Measuring the Global Gender Gap* notes that 'educational attainment is the most fundamental prerequisite for empowering women in all spheres of society …'.[2]

While the value of education cannot be overestimated, we must support and promote an agenda for human development. Violence represents the greatest human rights challenge faced by women. Women know what it means to be displaced, to bear the burden of child mortality and low rates of access to education and health care. Women know what it means to be excluded from public life and not recognised as full citizens.

Even in Bermuda, which has had two women premiers, three women leaders of the opposition, a woman attorney-general and several women government ministers, and where women outnumber men in the workplace, there is still violence against women in the form of incest, rape, and physical, verbal and emotional abuse.

Women's economic empowerment is crucial to the protection of women's human rights, including the right to education, work, health, housing, and sexual and reproductive rights. Increasing women's economic decision-making empowers women in all aspects.

More than ten years after Beijing, it is *still* a woman's face we see when we speak of poverty, of HIV/AIDS, of violent conflict and social upheaval, of trafficking in human beings.

Humanity's entry into the 21st century has been both painful and dangerous. In particular, terrorism and the 'war on terror' have made it clear that our destinies are linked and our lives intertwined. We must come together – as those brave women did more than a century ago to acquire the vote. Women who have the privilege of living in democracies have a duty to apply pressure on world leaders to help those who are less fortunate.

Although the Millennium Development Goal of promoting gender equality and empowering women has been diligently pursued by the Commonwealth Parliamentary Association, it has become all too clear that we will not achieve the target of women making up 30% of national parliaments until the year 2025 or gender parity until 2040.

Women in Bermuda, like women throughout the world, have come a long way in gaining equality – but the journey is not yet over: there is much more to be accomplished.

ENDNOTES

1 Waring, M., Greenwood, G. and Pintat, C. (2000). *Politics: Women's Insight*, Inter-Parliamentary Union, Geneva, Switzerland.

2 Lopez-Claros, A. and Zahidi, S. (2005). *Women's Empowerment: Measuring the Global Gender Gap*, World Economic Forum, Geneva, Switzerland.

DAME JENNIFER SMITH was Premier of Bermuda from 1998–2003 and was the first woman to become Premier after leading her party, the Bermuda Labour Party, to victory in a General Election. She entered politics in 1972 as the youngest woman ever to contest a seat in the House of Assembly, losing narrowly to her opponent. In 1980 she was appointed to the Senate and was first elected to the House of Assembly in 1989, serving as her party's spokesperson on education, health and social services, youth, sports, cultural and community affairs. From 1998–99 she also held the Education Portfolio. Outside politics her experience is in the arts, journalism and communications. Her community involvement has included work for the Bermuda TB, Cancer and Health Association, and the Bermuda Society of Arts. She is currently Deputy Speaker of the House of Assembly.

Women into politics

Jacqui Quinn-Leandro

It is now more than a decade since the 1995 Beijing conference identified 12 critical areas of concern for women's advance globally. They were: women and poverty; the education and training of women; women and health; violence against women; women and armed conflict; women and the economy; women in power and decision-making; institutional mechanisms for the advancement of women; human rights of women; women and the media; women and the environment; and the girl child. These formed the core of the Beijing Platform for Action.

Some years ago, Commonwealth Heads of Government set a target of 30% female representation in parliament. Since then, 12 Commonwealth countries have achieved women's representation of between 20 and 30%. But the slow rate of progress and the meagre funds allocated to gender mainstreaming and gender affairs generally make it clear that governments have not been serious about empowering women.

Weiner and Gunderson (1990) state that equity is 'designed to address a kind of *systemic discrimination* … found in employment systems'. But perhaps the best and simplest definition, which captures equity in all its variations, is one posited by Abrahamsson (1990). He states that equality means that 'women and men enjoy the same rights, bear the same responsibilities and have the same opportunities to have jobs that afford economic independence, care for their homes and families and take part in politics, union activities and other forms of civic life'.

The goal is a society in which women and men share equally and are accorded equal status; individuals must not feel confined or restrained by the 'traditional' conceptions of what is *fitting or appropriate* for females and males respectively in a given society. When we talk of equality or inequality, we are talking about the issue of power. In the context of the Commonwealth power means having a say in what happens in society and in the decision-making process.

Theorists have argued that feminism (and I would say here that I am not a feminist in the strict sense of the word – I am a woman-centric woman) embodies two simultaneous processes: a consciousness of the subordinate position in which women are viewed in society and the actions that those who regard themselves as activists take to redefine this unequal position. In assessing these processes, it is important to probe gender systems in order to determine the social roles assigned to men and women, cultural definitions of masculinity and femininity, the sexual division of labour within organisations, the rules regarding marriage and kinship behaviour between the sexes, the social significance of women's identification with the family and women's position relative to men in economic life.

According to the World Bank (2003): 'Even though Latin American and Caribbean women have almost reached the same level of education as men and in some countries have even surpassed them, they continue to participate less in the labour market and earn less than men.' The factors that contribute to this phenomenon include the large-scale participation of women in the service sector, which is generally the most poorly paid sector of the economy. In addition, the fact that women are generally responsible for caring for their families means that they often prefer to work part time and that they have a higher turnover rate in the labour force.

Workplace discrimination in the Caribbean is still rampant, despite the high percentage of women who are employed. In my own research on women's professional careers in Caribbean broadcasting it was clear that men still held the reins. The fact that in 2003 only 16% of top newsroom bosses were female means that women have little control over content, policy, money or direction. Men determine what news is and define how it is reported. In short, news in the Caribbean passes through a male filter. Women outnumber men in the newsroom in three places: on the bottom rung of the ladder as researchers and documentalists (88%); as news writers (86%); and as on-air reporters (63%).

Not surprisingly, the assessment made by the United Nations Development Programme (UNDP) in its Beijing Plus 10 review confirms that women are still greatly under-represented in political and bureaucratic posts around the world. The UNDP reports that women make up far less than half the decision-making structure of governments and state leaderships. In light of this, the Beijing Platform for Action called on governments, national bodies, the private sector, political parties, trade unions, employers' organisations, research and academic institutions, sub-regional bodies, and non-governmental and international organisations to 'implement measures to ensure women's equal access to and full participation in power structures and decision making; and increase women's capacity to participate in decision-making and leadership'.

As women leaders, we are well placed to insist on a mandate for our political parties of 30% female representation on party lists and

in internal party leadership positions. Whether it is called affirmative action, quotas or the zebra principle (as in Sweden), this is a small measure that can go a long way to increase women's participation and representation. In Antigua and Barbuda, and wherever I have a voice, I strongly advocate for these types of measures to be implemented in the local political system, because I believe that *it is at the political party structure that we must begin to redress the gender imbalance*.

Matland (2003) states that women have to overcome three hurdles to be elected to public office: first, they must be willing to stand for election; second, they must be nominated by their political party; and third, they must be elected by the voters. Matland argues that of these three barriers, nomination by the party is the most critical. I would like to see emanating from the eighth Women's Affairs Ministerial Meeting (WAMM) some of the proactive steps and measures that political parties *should* and *must* take to promote female participation and leadership.

One practical proposal that the WAMM should adopt is that girls and young women across the Commonwealth must be nurtured into believing that they are capable of doing *any* job, and be encouraged to pursue positions of political leadership. We women have toiled on the political campaign trail, organised fund-raising activities, fried the fish and barbecued the chicken, handed out the pamphlets, put up the posters and licked the stamps. But we lurk in the background and keep our traditional 'place' when it comes to challenging political leaderships and asserting our own personalities and abilities.

Too often women who are ordinarily bright, articulate and intelligent lower their eyes in humility, becoming rambling airheads

and defer to men because they are intimidated by them. Too often women are unwilling or unable to defend their side of an argument or debate a cause because they are afraid of being called 'aggressive' or masculine.

Although we women cry out and hanker for equality, when the time comes for us to step on the platform, too many of us fall back and make excuses. This may sound harsh, but it is a fact. We have many talkers who talk the talk of equity but refuse to walk the walk. Many women pontificate and criticise from a safe distance, but offer lame excuses when they are asked to lead a committee, run for office or take a practical stance for something they claim to believe in.

However, the real blame should be laid squarely at the door of the political parties. For decades the 'boys club' has paid lip service to equity, but has closed the door on capable, articulate and competent women who could easily out-run and out-perform their male counterparts, whose only qualification is that they are male.

For decades we have been fed the trifle that women are too soft for politics, that they are afraid of exposing their personal lives, that they are thin-skinned and their shoulders are not broad enough. For decades we have bought into the false notion that women do not support women. The 'boys club' has ridden on our dress tails, on our ability to organise, on our skills at planning and multi-tasking, our commitment to hard work and our dedication to a cause.

I am a realist and a firm believer that women's role in political leadership has been influenced by religious and cultural factors that shape popular perceptions of women's talents and possibilities. The cultural role of the male as protector and breadwinner of the family has reinforced the idea that men are the protectors of the national family. Structural difficulties are intertwined with cultural attitudes, norms and mores: many women have been brought up in a social environment in which they are taught to avoid risk and confrontation. Women are to be seen and not heard; they are expected to be submissive and compliant.

It is common knowledge that women politicians have had to overcome this kind of stereotypical or identity politics. Even as women forge ahead and make inroads into political representation, they are faced with the challenge of tearing down the cultural restrictions which dictate how they should look, speak and act, at the same time as they try to transform the political culture to create a genuinely *gender-fair* environment.

Rodriguez-Bello (2003), writing on women's political participation, describes a gender-fair environment as one that estimates women's capabilities not on how well they imitate 'male-speak' or how well they compete, but on their capacity for cooperation, vision and leadership.

It is critical that the WAMM discusses 'capacity'. How well or how badly women achieve in the political arena will turn largely on their capacity to perform; their capacity to accept criticism; their capacity to endure long and gruelling hours; their capacity to raise the requisite funds to run and win a campaign; their capacity to hear the cries of their sisters; and finally their capacity to lead from the front. I believe in the unlimited potential of women and I know that women do not need to be like men to be strong, capable leaders. Women can lead and be successful as they are.

The age-old beliefs about women's special attributes are presumed to bring to the political process integrity, cooperation, compassion, sensitivity and responsiveness to the concerns of all citizens; these are the traits that most women feel they bring to the public service. They are also the characteristics that the public seeks in its leaders. Interestingly, a study conducted by the US Lee Foundation found that voters overwhelmingly see women political leaders as more honest, less corrupt, less willing to cut political deals and less likely to be controlled by special interests.

When we look across the Commonwealth, we find more and more women candidates demonstrating forcefully that they can use the kinds of skills, tactics and messages needed to defeat male opponents and frame an agenda responsive to the needs of their constituents. The Caribbean region, for example, has some of the brightest female minds in the world, but sadly we are still playing catch-up. Women in the Caribbean have had to work twice as hard to prove what has always been known about us – that we have had to work like this just to take our places *among less than average men*. Women have worked in the background, believing that awful myth that their place is either behind their man or in the home.

As women, I challenge you to be committed to the struggle of breaking all the spoken and unspoken rules in this so-called 'man's world'. We must learn the rules, use the rules and change the system. Let us also look seriously at gender mainstreaming strategies that promote a culture of gender sensitivity in government; at our national machineries for women which have the primary role of leading and monitoring gender mainstreaming strategies; and at affirmative action. All these can assist in levelling the playing field.

Gender mainstreaming efforts mainstream gender perspectives and the goal of gender equality in government policy-making, planning, implementation and evaluation. This makes our governments more efficient in serving the needs of its citizens by ensuring that even seemingly neutral policies and programmes take into account women's concerns and needs.

As we toil in the vineyard encouraging, nurturing, and recommending gender equity in political participation, we must never tire; we must never become jaded in spreading the message of the need to get more and more women into political decision-making. We must bring up our daughters in the same way that we bring up our sons. They must believe that the sky in their world is no nearer or further away than the sky in their brother's world and that *that* is their limit also. Let us tell our daughters that there is no such thing as a glass ceiling: it is a myth. And, most importantly, we must lead by our example.

REFERENCES

Abrahamsson, U.B. (1990). 'Are we nearing the top of the hill?', Paper prepared for the XVIIth Conference of the International Association for Mass Communication Research, Stockholm, August 1990.

Matland, R. (2003). *Women in Parliament: Beyond Numbers*, Institute for Democracy and Electoral Assistance (IDEA), Stockholm, Sweden.

Rodriguez-Bello, C. (2003). 'Women and Political Participation', Women's Human Rights Net for the Advancement of Women (WHRNet), UN International Research and Training Institute, un-instraw.org/un/index.php

UNDP (2004). *10-year Review of the Implementation of the Beijing Platform for Action*, Economic Commission Preparatory Meeting, 14–15 December 2004.

United Nations (1995). *Platform for Action and the Beijing Declaration*, Fourth World Conference on Women, Beijing, China, 4–15 September 1995.

Weiner, N. and Gunderson, M. (1990). *Pay Equity: Issues, Options and Experiences*, Butterworths, Toronto, Canada.

World Bank (2003). *Challenges and Opportunities for Gender Equality in Latin America and the Caribbean*, World Bank, Washington, DC.

HON. DR JACQUI QUINN-LEANDRO is Minister of Labour, Public Administration and Gender Affairs of the Government of Antigua and Barbuda. She was the first woman to be elected as a member of the Antigua & Barbuda House of Representatives in March 2004, when she received the highest number of votes ever cast in a House of Representatives election. She is also the first woman to serve as Acting Prime Minister of Antigua and Barbuda. She is a graduate of the University of the West Indies, University of Cambridge and McGill University, Montreal, Canada. Dr Quinn-Leandro currently serves as the President of the Inter-American Commission of Women, a constituent body of the Organization of American States. She has a teenage daughter and a nine year-old son.

Financing for gender equality: post-conflict reconstruction and peace-building

Sherrill Whittington

Overview

The devastating impact of conflict results in widespread destruction of infrastructure, livelihoods, services, communities and massive dislocation of populations. Years of bad governance and fiscal breakdown leaves war-shattered failed states with no reserves and little capacity for financial management. Huge amounts of resources have been and continue to be expended on large and medium-level conflicts in countries such as Afghanistan, Liberia, Democratic Republic of Congo, former Yugoslavia, Iraq, Sri Lanka, Solomon Islands and Bougainville. Millions of dollars have been spent on attempts to reconstruct these countries with no guarantees of sustainable democratisation or economic development.

While massive costs are entailed in waging wars, the extreme poverty of vulnerable populations, particularly women and children, is always exacerbated by conflict. In many cases, following the cessation of hostilities there has been an outpouring of donor funding for post-conflict reconstruction and peace-building, but the extent to which this has promoted gender equality or benefited women and children has yet to be determined.

Women's involvement as equal players in national reconstruction is essential if they are 'to influence decisions that affect their lives and those of their families, and their political, social and economic empowerment must form part of the democratic ideal that contributes to sustainable development'.[1] In the immediate aftermath of conflict there exists a short, critical window for women to be 'included at the highest levels of peace-building, peacekeeping, conflict mediation, resolution, and post-conflict reconciliation and reconstruction activities'.[2]

This has to be translated into a gender-inclusive, participatory process of reconstruction with equal decision-making about, access to and allocation of resources. Achieving this raises a number of questions. What is the involvement of women in peace negotiations and donor conferences? To what degree are they, their priorities, concerns and values integrated into in-country donor needs assessments? Are they consulted in developing frameworks for national reconstruction and given serious consideration in defining priorities and resources? To what extent are systems of donor accountability for disbursement of funding during and after crises gender sensitive? How can a gender lens be applied to audit both the inputs and outputs of the billions of dollars spent globally for humanitarian aid, reconstruction and peace-building?

Post-conflict reconstruction: a window for gender equality

In the immediate aftermath of conflict and the conclusion of a peace agreement there is usually an influx of international actors charged with undertaking social and economic recovery in order to prevent a reversion to violent conflict. If planned and executed from a rights-based approach, this period of transition to sustainable peace can serve as a unique 'window of opportunity' to establish new norms and rules, engage new leaders and build new institutions with a focus on women's rights and their invaluable contribution to their nation's rebuilding. The period must be used not to reconstruct what has failed, but rather to build a new model of democratisation and development.

Yet from the very beginning of the reconstruction phase, the full and equal involvement of women is an issue of gender justice. This concept not only encompasses equitable treatment and participation of women in the negotiation of peace agreements, the planning and implementation of UN peace operations, the creation and administration of new governments (including agencies and institutions focused on the needs of women and girls), the provision of the full range of educational opportunities and the revival and growth of the economy, but also fostering a culture that enhances the talents, capabilities and well-being of women and girls.

Thus it is essential to engage all stakeholders in the reconstruction process, which begins with a peace agreement and is often followed by peacekeeping or peace support operations mandated to create conditions to restore internal security and repair communications, roads and transportation. The focus then shifts to restoring the rule of law, administration, governance, a judicial system and rebuilding basic social services such as health and education,[3] requiring substantial contributions by donors. These key players in national rebuilding, including the United Nations, World Bank, bilateral funders and non-governmental organisations (NGOs),[4] all have policies upholding the centrality of gender equality mainstreaming and should be in the forefront of ensuring that women are equal partners in, and equal beneficiaries of, all reconstruction programmes and activities.

This would give centrality to gender equality, which implies that the interests, needs and priorities of both women and men are taken into consideration from the outset,[5] because for women in particular

the peace table is a forum not only for negotiating an end to war, but also for laying the foundations of a new society guided by the principles of social justice, human rights and equality.[6] Participation can offer women the opportunity to secure gains on a wide range of issues, including economic security, social development and political participation, related to the advancement of women's rights and gender equality. While there is evidence that more recent peace agreements are starting to underscore the economic and security needs of women, such provisions are rarely backed by sufficient resources and will. Donors are in a powerful position not only to insist that women participate equally in all negotiations and to support their involvement, but also to ensure that gender budgetary frameworks are put in place to embed gender equality into every stage of reconstruction planning and implementation.

One of the most immediate ways in which this can be done is in the initial post-conflict aftermath during the disarmament, demobilisation, reintegration and rehabilitation (DDRR) phase. The 'invisibility' of many female ex-combatants and the definition of a 'combatant' as someone with weapons serve to compound the assumption that women who have undertaken supportive roles for male combatants are not entitled to benefits. This occurred in Timor-Leste in 2000, when the World Bank provided reintegration support and job training for former Fretilin[7] fighters with no benefit packages for the hundreds of women who had worked clandestinely supporting the 25-year liberation struggle. Before the official processes, women are often engaged in grassroots disarmament, as witnessed in Sierra Leone, Bougainville and the Solomon Islands.

Despite the fact that United Nations Security Council Resolution 1325 calls for all those involved in planning for disarmament,

demobilisation and reintegration to consider the different needs of female and male ex-combatants and to take into account the needs of their dependents, in Sierra Leone only 6% of DDRR participants were women and 0.6% girls, although women and girls constituted an estimated 12% of combatants. In northern Uganda, girls and young women maintained that education and skills training would be the most meaningful contribution that local and international agencies could provide to assist their reintegration. Yet few released from the Lord's Resistance Army (LRA)[8] have benefited from internationally funded reintegration programmes.

Article XXVIII, paragraph 2 of the Lomé Peace Accord,[9] which ended hostilities in Sierra Leone, stated that since women 'have been particularly victimized during the war, special attention shall be accorded to their needs and potentials in formulating and implementing national rehabilitation, reconstruction and development programmes, to enable them play a central role in the moral, social and physical reconstruction of Sierra Leone'. Yet despite such acknowledgements, support services and legal aid were rarely provided to women during the Truth and Reconciliation Commission (TRC)[10] and those involved in the judicial process were not provided with gender-sensitivity training to eliminate the gender bias which impeded women from receiving fair treatment as witnesses, as complainants and in investigations. If a donor-supported gender justice fund were to be made available to women and girls, with training resources and capacity-building provided for those involved in all such processes, then justice and reparations for victims of gender-based violence and other human rights abuses might be realised.

In order to heal war-torn societies, social justice, which also encompasses health and education issues, has to be accorded a high priority. Pre-conflict state failure diverts human and financial resources away from public health and other social services, a situation compounded by widespread destruction of facilities and resources during war. Not only does immediate attention have to be given to the plethora of injuries sustained, but also to the spread of disease, including increased rates of HIV transmission. While women and girls, along with men and boys, are victims of the general violence and lack of health care, they also experience the physical, psychological and societal repercussions of sexual violations. Special resources have to be allocated to addressing their rehabilitation and to the restoration of public health services, particularly in areas of reproductive health.

While immediate assistance is required to rebuild war-shattered economies, particular attention should be accorded to the gendered dimensions of economic reconstruction. Often during times of conflict women assume the role of bread-winner, taking on jobs traditionally undertaken by men. In addition to their domestic roles as primary care-givers, many women seek work outside the home in order to sustain their families as single parents. The percentage of female-headed households escalates during and after conflict, with widows often having no rights to the land they cultivate. With national reconstruction, many women lose their employment in the formal sector and return to working within the household or in the informal sector.

The establishment of peace support missions, coupled with the huge injection of foreign capital and influx of a short-term international community, results in the development of a dual economy, juxtaposing a wealthy foreign elite who enjoy a luxury lifestyle with a totally impoverished local population without access to basic goods and services. The gendered impact of this immediate, short-lived economic imbalance has yet to be fully analysed, but in many instances it inflates prices for local household items and foodstuffs. It also results in many women and girls seeking employment informally in the service sector, as household domestics or prostitutes. Lack of workplace contracts and conditions exposes them to abuse, as well as loss of family income with the downscaling of peacekeeping and donor operations. Failure to address income-generating skills training, short-term emergency credit provisions, and sustainable employment opportunities leads to a gender imbalance, with women excluded from economic reconstruction.

Post-conflict reconstruction programmes must prevent such discrimination by providing equal opportunities to men and women. While it is crucially important to focus on employing men, missing the opportunity to engage women in formal economic activities is a strategic oversight. The major development challenge is to take advantage of and assist in sustaining positive gender role changes regarding work by designing economic assistance programmes that build on newly acquired skills and encourage women and men to continue in their new activities.

Without economic support, women face huge barriers in attaining an equal voice in decision-making at a time of flux when they should play a key role in determining the nation's political future. Ensuring that non-discrimination and gender equality are embedded in new or revised constitutions is essential to build a legal and political framework based on rights. Lack of funding and capacity to build strong, unified civil society organisations and caucuses can prevent women making the most of the crucial

interim period between a peace agreement and the first post-conflict elections. While in many countries such as Rwanda, South Africa, Timor-Leste and Afghanistan, the post-conflict period witnessed a substantial increase in female parliamentary representation, in others, such as the Solomon Islands, it did not. A variety of factors are responsible and comparative studies need to be undertaken, but one of the key barriers facing women seeking political office, particularly those who contest as independents, is lack of financial support and capacity-building, regarded by women in the Solomon Islands as the key obstacle to their failure to secure a single seat in the 2006 elections.

Engendering post-conflict recovery and peace-building budgets

How can post-conflict gender gaps be redressed? The answer lies largely in adopting an inclusive, rights-based transformational approach to ensure constructive change, moving war-torn populations from extreme vulnerability and dependency to self-sufficiency and well-being. However, 'post-conflict reconstruction programmes rarely recognise the impact of decisions on resource allocations to different sectors on women, men and gender relations. Removing gender barriers in setting priorities may affect development outcomes significantly…'[11]

A key international instrument for ensuring that women are not marginalised is United Nations Security Council Resolution 1325 on Women, Peace and Security, which recognises that *peace is inextricably linked to equality between women and men*'.[12] The resolution addresses itself to all actors involved in negotiating and implementing peace agreements, calling on them to adopt a gender perspective, particularly regarding the special needs of women and girls during repatriation and resettlement and for rehabilitation, reintegration and post-conflict reconstruction, involving women in all the implementation mechanisms of the peace agreements. Special focus is accorded to ensuring the protection of and respect for the human rights of women and girls, particularly as they relate to the constitution, the electoral system, the police and the judiciary.[13]

The full budgetary implications of implementing Resolution 1325 have yet to be assessed. UN financing of post-conflict recovery, reconstruction and sustainable peace-building draws on a number of budgetary sources, most notably peacekeeping, the Consolidated Appeals Process (CAP), the recent Central Emergency Response Fund (CERF), covering all humanitarian crises, as well the budgets of UN agencies and funds which cover economic, social and political reconstruction. While there are numerous UN directives, mandates and resolutions on mainstreaming gender equality into all policies and programmes, there is as yet no gender budget for peacekeeping operations or peace-building. Nor do many reconstruction efforts and budgets specifically target women or undergo a gender-budget analysis. For example, in the United Nations Transitional Administration in East Timor (UNTAET),[14] the peacekeeping mission in Timor-Leste from 2000–2002, there was no budget allocated to the Gender Unit for programme implementation, all funding having to be raised independently from international external donors.[15] There are still no systems in place to monitor and evaluate the allocation and disbursement of funding to ensure that women and girls are equal partners in and equal beneficiaries of the full array of peacekeeping and national reconstruction programmes falling under the aegis of the UN.

The largest multilateral funder is the World Bank, which in its Operational Policy states that it 'aims to reduce gender disparities and enhance women's participation in the economic development of their countries by integrating gender considerations in its country assistance program'.[16] Through its Post-Conflict Fund (PCF), established in 1997 to enhance the World Bank's ability to support countries in transition from conflict to sustainable peace and economic growth, grants are made to a wide range of partners (institutions, NGOs, UN agencies, transitional authorities, governments and other civil society institutions) to provide earlier and broader World Bank assistance to post-conflict countries.[17] In a recent analysis of its role in conflict and development, the World Bank stated clearly that 'the design of post-conflict reconstruction programs needs to adopt an explicit gender focus…',[18] and that the PCF has played 'an important role in supporting innovative approaches to gender in conflict-affected countries'.[19] Among the initiatives supported have been community actions for the reintegration and recovery of youth and women in the DRC, employment projects for women in Bosnia and capacity-building for rural women leaders in South Africa, as well as a special project for war widows in Indonesia and Timor-Leste.

While specific women-focused projects can undoubtedly promote women's empowerment, such an approach fails to mainstream gender equality throughout all aspects of reconstruction and nation-building programmes. Although credit is a popular post-conflict reconstruction tool, it is a particularly difficult challenge for women without collateral. However, many credit programmes for post-conflict reconstruction have failed to integrate gender equality, as was seen in the World Bank Sierra Leone Economic Rehabilitation and Recovery Credit Project, which did not even acknowledge women's important role in the economy.[20]

Donor coordination is essential during this critical period if women's equal involvement is to be assured. A sudden huge injection of funding into countries that have been shattered economically, politically and socially has to be carefully managed. Unless a donor co-ordination mechanism is established which is able to monitor disbursement, duplication can occur. Women's organisations that may have been active as freedom fighters or peace-makers have to be able make the transition to promoting the role of women's rights in reconstruction. Unless a structured women's network is established and strengthened, the in-pouring of donor funding can lead to divisiveness, with new NGOs cropping up or others breaking away from a larger organisation in order to take advantage of the brief window of abundance. Both multilateral and bilateral donors, as well as other international actors, need to encourage unity of vision and a common agenda for women. This can be greatly facilitated by supporting a Women's Congress or National Women's Conference at the outset, as in Timor-Leste, Afghanistan and Iraq. Such inclusive conferences can produce a 'gender blueprint' for transformative reconstruction based on gender equality.

Despite commitments to the importance of gender equality, the percentages of donor funding actually allocated to women's economic, social and political empowerment in the wake of conflict remains miniscule compared with the total outlay. While there has been a recent recognition of the need for resource allocation to combat gender-based violence, other key women's rights areas in

the rule of law, governance and economic reconstruction are being neglected. If a gender audit were to be undertaken in selected post-conflict countries at various stages of redevelopment, it would be evident that when the overall impact of the reconstruction aid agenda is assessed, gender equality and women's rights have been largely overlooked.

Yet both the Inter-Agency Network on Women and Gender Equality (IANWGE) and the OECD-DAC Network on Gender Equality have recognised that gender equality and women's empowerment are critical for development effectiveness.[21] However, reviews of poverty reduction strategies, Millennium Development Goal progress reports and Sector Wide Approaches suggest that, with some notable exceptions, these have largely been gender-blind, take a very narrow perspective on gender, lack empirical evidence and/or fail to translate gender analysis into plans with budgets. There is a clear acknowledgement that to be effective in influencing the agenda, donors need to forge partnerships and develop clear goals and strategies for joint work to foster gender equality.[22] This is very relevant to the critical interim stage between the end of hostilities and building the foundations for a successfully operating state out of the ashes of one that has failed.

All post-conflict reconstruction programmes should support initial gender impact assessments, gender budget analyses and advocacy to improve spending patterns so that more donor funding benefits men and women equally.[23] The OECD *Principles for Good International Engagement in Fragile States*, in conjunction with the partnership commitments of the Paris Declaration,[24] can be engendered and applied as a guide to evaluating the effectiveness of such programmes. As considered by the OECD-DAC Network on Gender Equality and the OECD-DAC Working Party on Aid Effectiveness at their meeting in July 2006, one possible adaptation could be the following.

- *Ownership* can incorporate gender equality issues and women's concerns into the reconstruction agenda, with full support given to the strengthening and inclusion of women's national machineries and civil society organisations in implementation, monitoring and evaluation.

- *Alignment* necessitates donor acknowledgement of the application of mutual commitments to gender equality and international instruments to strengthen gender equality and women's empowerment.

- *Harmonisation* of ways of addressing gender equality in evolving new programme mechanisms and rationalisation of donor support for countries emerging from conflict should be undertaken.

- *Managing for results* should demonstrate gender equality results and impacts, with monitoring of the gender impacts of donor-funded reconstruction reflected in all performance assessment frameworks.

- *Mutual accountability* should be the responsibility of all multilateral and bilateral donors involved in post-conflict reconstruction programmes, with women included in the mechanisms; accountability must be monitored using gender-responsive indicators.[25]

The priorities of women in reconstructing their war-torn nation were very clearly enunciated in the Sudanese women's recommendations to the Oslo Donors Conference in April 2005, where they called for a commitment to principles of gender-responsive resource allocation so that at least 80% of budgetary allocations and resource support to Sudan's reconstruction met at least three of the following criteria.

- Directly benefiting women, contributing directly to women's empowerment and increasing women's capacities, opportunities and access to resources.

- Reducing gender inequalities in law, policy and practice.

- Directly benefiting young people, especially girls, in disadvantaged communities.

- Targeting rural areas.

The women also called for the provision of financial support for the hosting of an all-inclusive Sudanese Women's Conference that would define a coherent, long-term agenda and strategy for accelerating women's empowerment and gender equality.[26] They argued that for such an agenda to become a reality, donors and multilateral agencies would need to use their combined strengths and forge partnerships to foster gender equality as a clearly defined joint goal and shared task. This would necessitate a greater pooling of resources, increased use of programmatic approaches, joint analytical work, a clear division of roles and responsibilities, and agreements on strategic priorities and approaches by donors and multilateral agencies.[27]

Commonwealth commitment to transformative reconstruction

As a key international actor, the Commonwealth has long been an advocate of the integral importance of gender equality, regarding the principles of gender equality and inclusion as fundamental values on which every attempt at democracy and peace-building must be based. With a mandate encompassing human rights, promotion of democracy and good governance, electoral support to post-conflict countries and technical cooperation, the Commonwealth has also played a leading role in developing resources for gender budgeting.

The 1995 Commonwealth Plan of Action on Gender and Development endorsed by Commonwealth Heads of Government urged governments to 'take vigorous action to promote and defend women's rights, and advocate for their political participation in peace processes and democratic decision-making'.[28] The Sixth Women's Affairs Ministerial Meeting (WAMM), held in Delhi in 2000, recommended that 'the Commonwealth take action in collaboration with other international organisations and civil society to include women at the highest levels of peace-building, peacekeeping, conflict mediation, resolution, and post-conflict reconciliation and reconstruction activities'.[29] It encouraged a 30% target for women's participation in peace initiatives by the year 2005. The Commonwealth Plan of Action for Gender Equality 2005–2015 recognises that women's empowerment and gender equality are intrinsic to achieving sustainable development and democracy. It aims to advance Commonwealth action in gender, democracy, peace and conflict; gender, human rights and law; gender, poverty eradication and economic empowerment; and gender and HIV/AIDS. All of these four areas are critical to rebuilding war-torn states.

The many gender-responsive budgetary tools developed by the Commonwealth, including gender-aware policy appraisal, beneficiary assessment, gender-disaggregated expenditure incidence analysis and the gender-aware medium-term economic policy framework can be adapted to prepare a gender-responsive budget assessment of the application of funding resources in post-conflict reconstruction and peace-building. The capacities of national machineries for women and women's civil society organisations can be developed to examine and monitor inputs, activities, outputs and impacts of multilateral and bilateral donor interventions and provide comprehensive feedback on the effectiveness and efficiency of donor expenditure.[30] Gender budgeting models such as those undertaken in Rwanda and South Africa can be further developed and improved, and adapted to other Commonwealth countries such as the Solomon Islands, Bougainville and Sierra Leone, which are currently developing good governance programmes.

Both the Commonwealth Fund for Technical Cooperation (CFTC) and the Commonwealth Parliamentary Association (CPA) have direct experience in furthering Commonwealth principles in post-conflict development and democratisation. The CFTC regards itself as a force for peace, democracy, equality and good governance[31] and is utilised to fund policy advice, build capacity, develop resource materials and give technical assistance.[32] The CPA works in the fields of good governance, democracy, elections and human rights, with special attention paid to gender sensitising.[33] Such capacity for outreach and direct involvement in post-conflict transitions enables these Commonwealth bodies to undertake a key role in evaluating the extent of resource allocation for women's empowerment and gender equity.

Conclusions

In order to advance gender equality, women's rights and women's empowerment in post-conflict reconstruction, adequate resources must be earmarked, monitored and evaluated to determine to what extent they are advancing equality for development and democracy. Gender-disaggregated measures of inputs, outputs and outcomes for reconstruction budgets need to be developed and gender audits undertaken in countries at various stages of recovery and rehabilitation.

The Commonwealth is in a prime position to evaluate existing gender budgetary resources, experiences and expertise. It can take the initiative in developing inclusive budgetary frameworks and models for rebuilding war-torn countries. With its direct access to governments, it can work to build the capacity of women's ministries and national machineries to work with finance ministries, civil society organisations and international donors to develop appropriate gender equality objectives and strategies. The capacity of women parliamentarians to monitor budgetary expenditure can also be developed and strengthened.

Failure to ensure that reconstruction and peace-building budgets are consultative, inclusive and equitable will result in rebuilding from a flawed perspective. Peace-building must be a participatory process that does not reconstruct what has failed, but develops a new paradigm based on gender equality and the protection of women's social, economic and political rights.

BIBLIOGRAPHY

Aid Modalities and the Promotion of Gender Equality. Summary Report of the Joint meeting of the Inter-Agency Network on Women and Gender Equality (IANWGE) and the OECD-DAC Network on Gender Equality, 30–31 January, 2006.

Anderlini, S. (2000). *Women at the Peace Table, Making a Difference*, United Nations Development Fund for Women, New York.

Anderlini, S. (2004). *Inclusive Security, Sustainable Peace: A Toolkit for Advocacy and Action*, Women Waging Peace, International Alert, p. 52.

Baksh-Soodeen, R. and Etchart, L. (2003). *Gender Mainstreaming in Conflict Transformation: Building Sustainable Peace*, Commonwealth Secretariat, London.

Budlender, D. and Hewitt, G. (2004). *Engendering Budgets: A Practitioner's Guide to Understanding and Implementing Gender-Responsive Budgets*, Commonwealth Secretariat, London.

Commonwealth Secretariat (2005). *The Commonwealth Plan of Action for Gender Equality 2005–2015*, Commonwealth Secretariat, London.

Network on Gender Equality. *Paris Declaration Commitments and Implications for Gender Equality and Women's Empowerment*, OECD-DAC Network on Gender Equality DCD/DAC/GEN, 23 June 2006.

Sweetman, C. (ed.) (2005). *Gender, Peacebuilding and Reconstruction*, Oxfam Great Britain, Oxford.

World Bank (2002). *Integrating Gender into the World Bank's Work: A Strategy for Action*, World Bank, Washington, DC.

World Bank (2004). *The Role of the World Bank in Conflict and Development: An Evolving Agenda*, World Bank, Washington, DC.

ENDNOTES

1 *Commonwealth Plan of Action for Gender Equality*, 2005–2015, p. 26.

2 Ibid., para. 3.10. p. 28.

3 Anderlini, S. (2004), p. 52.

4 NGOs such as Oxfam, CARE and Save the Children Fund.

5 Office of the Special Advisor on Gender Issues and Advancement of Women, 'Gender mainstreaming: strategy for promoting gender equality', United Nations, New York, August 2001. http://www.un.org/womenwatch/osagi/pdf/factsheet1.pdf.

6 Anderlini, S. (2000), p. 10.

7 Fretilin (Revolutionary Front for an Independent East Timor) was the resistance movement that fought for independence in East Timor, first from the Portuguese and then from Indonesia, 1974–98.

8 Nearly all captive girls, including those who are pregnant and who have small children, are trained as fighters in the LRA.

9 The Lomé Peace Agreement was signed between the Government of Sierra Leone and the Revolutionary United Front in July 1999.

10 A TRC was also established in Sierra Leone by an Act of Parliament on 10 February 2000. It directs that that TRC pays 'special attention to the subject of sexual abuse'.

11 Sweetman (2005), p. 5.

12 Former UN Secretary-General Kofi Annan, in the United Nations Security Council debate introducing Resolution 1325, 20 October 2000.

13 United Nations Resolution 1325 (2000), S/RES/1325 (2000), adopted by the Security Council at its 4213th meeting, on 31 October 2000.

14 UNTAET, 1999–2002.

15 As Head of the UNTAET Gender Unit, the author was responsible for developing proposals and raising external funding for gender mainstreaming projects in the transitional administration, dealing with gender-based violence, situational analysis of the documentation of the impact of conflict on women and women's political training for elections.

16 World Bank (2002), p. 30.

17 www.worldbank.org

18 World Bank (2004), p. 20.

19 Ibid., p. 21.

20 Ibid., p. 6.

21 *Aid Modalities and the Promotion of Gender Equality* (2006), p. 4.

22 Network on Gender Equality (2006).

23 Ibid., p. 6.

24 The Paris Declaration on Aid Effectiveness, signed in March 2005, established global commitments for donor and partner countries to support more effective aid in a context of significant scaling up of aid. Ibid, p. 1.

25 Network on Gender Equality (2006), p. 5.

26 Sudanese Women's Priorities and Recommendations to the Oslo Donors Conference on Sudan 11–12 April 2005, Oslo Donors Conference on Sudan, 2005.

27 Network on Gender Equality (2006), p. 6.

28 http://www.thecommonwealth.org

29 Ibid.

30 Budlender and Hewitt (2004).

31 Commonwealth Secretariat (2005).

32 Ibid.

33 The Commonwealth Parliamentary Association (CPA), http://www.cpahg.org

SHERRILL WHITTINGTON has worked on gender issues and programmes for women for more than 15 years, mostly through the UN and the Commonwealth of Learning. As a member of the UNICEF gender team, she was responsible for the development of a guide for institutional gender equality mainstreaming, and developed training materials to address the rights of women and children in emergencies and conflict. As senior adviser for the UN Fourth World Conference on Women, she designed and implemented a global programme to incorporate youth issues into preparations for the conference. At field level, she was head of the Gender Affairs Office in UNTAET, and established Timor-Leste's national machinery for women. More recently, she has worked on UNICEF programmes in post-conflict West Africa, worked as team leader for an AusAID study on the barriers to women in post-conflict government in the Solomon Islands and developed a brief for the Commonwealth Secretariat on women's parliamentary representation. She is a Visiting Professor in Gender and Peace-building at the United Nations University for Peace in Costa Rica. She has a Master's Degree in International Relations and a Master of Letters Degree in Asian History.

the role of
the public
sector

The role of national women's machineries in financing gender equality

Auxilia Ponga

Good governance requires an effective separation of powers between the legislature, the judiciary and the executive organs of government. While it may be difficult to define good governance, it requires the state to act responsibly and take into account the interests of the people (Yaya Mansaray, 2004). Good governance requires the participation of women and men in public life as it must relate to society as a whole in its quality and functions. Governance has to do with how power is exercised, how citizens acquire a voice and how decisions are made on issues of public concern.

Ever since the first UN conference on women held in Mexico in 1975, it has been felt that women were not fully participating in governance and the development process, and that greater women's participation was needed. As a result of the 1975–1985 UN Decade for Women governments set up desks, units, departments and even ministries to address the issue and ensure that the experiences of women, their concerns and their perspectives were incorporated in governance structures. These were to be mechanisms, processes and institutions through which women were to articulate their interests, exercise their legal rights, meet their obligations and mediate their differences. This was in agreement with the fourth point of the 1991 Harare Declaration, which affirmed women's equality and that they must be able to 'exercise their full and equal rights'.

National women's machineries

Many Commonwealth countries established national women's machineries (NWMs) in the period 1975–1985, although these vary in size, influence and location in the government structure, as well as in the funding they receive. NWMs are supposed to take a leading role in ensuring that their governments recognise the importance of mainstreaming gender equality concerns into the planning, implementation, monitoring and evaluation of government programmes and projects. NWMs are supposed to provide policy advice and support for capacity building for mainstreaming gender in all government sectors. They coordinate a network of structures and processes that attempt to mainstream gender equality concerns in their country. NWMs work across all sectors to facilitate the advancement of gender-aware policies and programmes at all levels.

Nearly 20 years have passed since the first NWMs were set up and an in-depth study is currently being conducted to assess how they have performed. Overall, the activities of NWMs have had a positive impact in increasing public awareness of gender issues and concerns. Achievements include the formulation of national gender policies and the establishment of national women's structures for gender mainstreaming characterised by gender focal points (GFPs) in line ministries and departments at national and provincial level. Toolkits consisting of a collection of gender sensitisation and training tools have been developed to assist the GFPs in their work. A set of checklists, criteria and evaluation frameworks for 'seeing' women's and men's participation, needs and realities more clearly have also been developed and have been used in the provision of technical support to GFPs.

Challenges include inadequate communication systems between NWMs, GFPs and cooperating partners, and GFPs' lack of technical back-up from NWMs. Difficulties faced by most NWMs, especially those from developing countries, range from insufficient funding to lack of capacity in staff. Staff in NWMs usually face structures that are not supportive to gender mainstreaming. A case in point is the way in which an NWM within one ministry depends on staff in other ministries for mainstreaming gender. The members of staff of sector ministries generally have other responsibilities and are expected to mainstream gender in addition to their normal work. The work of mainstreaming gender is often not captured in the job description of sector ministry staff, nor is gender one of the key result areas on which they are appraised.

The budgets that GFP personnel have for their normal daily work do not include work on mainstreaming gender, which is treated as additional and peripheral. This makes them ineffectual and often very little mainstreaming, if any, takes place. GFP personnel are usually not part of the management structure and therefore do not participate in decision-making. In terms of institutions, national mechanisms are in place to promote gender concerns, but ministries of women's affairs rely heavily on donor funding and the work of GFPs in other ministries is often unsupported by management.

Whereas much work has been done to build the technical capacity of GFP personnel so that they can mainstream gender at national and regional levels, as yet not much can be seen in terms of impact. NWMs have no control over the staff of other ministries and these are transferred or promoted or given other responsibilities, often without the NWM being consulted, leading to a high turnover of GFP personnel.

Financing for gender equality

So how can countries move on to ensure that financing for gender equality is made available? This question needs to be addressed by all NWMs in Commonwealth countries. The timing could not be more opportune, as public sector reforms to make public expenditure more 'results based' are part of the good governance agenda. NWMs can play a leading role in championing a framework that looks at what governments want to achieve. This approach fits well with the aims of gender-responsive budget initiatives and their concern with the impact of budgetary allocations on women and men. To be effective, a radical change is required in the conventional model. An important aspect of this is to reassess the meanings of economy, efficiency and effectiveness from a gender perspective, and to add a fourth 'e', equity.

The role of NWMs will be made easier if governments begin to create greater consistency between social commitments and economic goals and how they try to achieve these. The aim of this article is not to provide answers to the question of how gender equality can be financed, but to inspire government officials, policy-makers, donor agencies and civil society groups to engage in gender-responsive budget initiatives by demonstrating both equity and efficiency gains. As Budlender et al. (2002) have argued:

Gender-responsive budget initiatives are mechanisms for mainstreaming gender into public expenditure and public revenue decision-making, which can lead to more effective policy design and outcomes. However, the technical nature of much gender budget work can obscure the political nature of the budget process and hence the need for advocacy strategies. Political support is crucial, particularly from finance ministries and officials in key sectoral ministries. Ministers responsible for women's affairs are important advocates but often lack political influence to mobilize support and lack the capacity to address macroeconomic issues. Recommendations include the need for broad-based coalitions, sex-disaggregated indicators, the development of tools for revenue analysis, and more work at the sub-national level.

In any discussion of the placement, role and functions of NWMs and their partnership with other line ministries, it is important to address the linkages with processes that bring broader public accountability for fiscal policy in ways that are sensitive to the needs of poor women and men. Gender-responsive budget initiatives seek to widen governance and accountability structures by giving women a voice in discussions on public spending, revenue-raising and debt. NWMs are key players in ensuring that the debate on accountability and governance is gender responsive. Accountability in the context of budgets involves four core issues:

- which players are involved in policy formulation and to what extent

- how responsive government is to inputs from external stakeholders

- how transparent the budget process is

- how credible policy commitments are when assessed against budgetary priorities.

The representation and participation of the people, including women, who are directly affected by budget allocation decisions is important, partly because it is a way of strengthening democracy. However, gender-responsive budget initiatives not only seek to increase women's participation in decision-making, but also seek to strengthen women's capacity for effective participation and government's capacity to undertake gender analyses and engender macroeconomic policies. The key questions that gender-responsive budget initiatives address are: What impact does this fiscal measure have on gender equality? Does it reduce gender inequality, increase it or leave it unchanged? Is there consistency between economic goals and social commitments? Gender-responsive budgeting demonstrates the potential of participatory budgeting and analysis to make governments accountable to international and national commitments, and bring about a fairer distribution of public resources (Sharp, 2003).

Conclusion

While the institutionalisation of gender concerns from 1985 onwards in Commonwealth member states is documented in *Gender Equality: A Decade of Commonwealth Action*, the challenge now is how to finance gender equality for development and democracy. NWMs are encouraged to document the work of women in development/gender units and gender mainstreaming activities within the context of member countries, focusing on policy developments, organisational forms and activities over time. Second, their role is to appraise gender mainstreaming efforts at country level through an examination of the organisational set-up and gender mainstreaming efforts. Third, they should ensure that when the financing of gender equality is addressed, NWMs are strengthened and women in development/gender concerns in Commonwealth countries are financed through some of the approaches discussed earlier. Only then can we hope for a world in which women and

men have equal rights and opportunities at all stages of their lives and where they can express their creativity in all fields of human endeavour. Only then will women be respected and valued as equal and able partners. It has become clear that fiscal policies and budgets that are gender-blind potentially widen inequality between women and men in areas such as health, income, education, nutrition, democracy and peace or the lack of it.

REFERENCES

Budlender, D., Elson, D., Hewitt, G. and Mukhopandhyay, T. (2002). *Gender Budgets Make Cents: Understanding Gender Responsive Budgets*, Commonwealth Secretariat, London.

Commonwealth Secretariat (2005). *Gender Equality: A Decade of Commonwealth Action: A Reference Book for Gender Ministers*, Commonwealth Secretariat, London.

Sharp, R. (2003). *Budgeting for Equity: Gender Budget Initiatives within a Framework of Performance Oriented Budgeting*, UNIFEM, New York.

Yaya Mansaray, K. (2004). 'Achieving Good Governance: The Role of Women in Policy Making', in Onimode, B. et al. (eds), *African Development and Governance Strategies in the 21st Century*, Zed Books, London.

AUXILIA BUPE PONGA has a PhD from the University of Manchester, UK, and is a gender adviser responsible for the public sector and governance in the Social Transformation Programmes Division of the Commonwealth Secretariat. She was previously Permanent Secretary for Gender in the Development Division of the Cabinet Office, Government of Zambia, where she was the chief adviser on gender and led delegations to the UN and other international meetings. She has worked as a consultant with UN agencies, the World Bank and other bilateral agencies in Zambia. She has wide experience of working with civil society organisations in Zambia and in the SADC region.

gender
profiles
of member
countries

Antigua and Barbuda

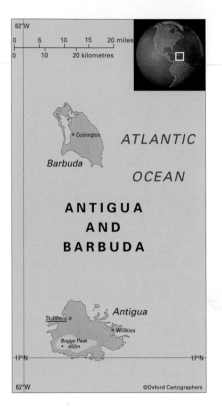

KEY FACTS

Joined Commonwealth: 1981

Capital: St John's

GDP growth (%): 1.6% p.a. 1990–2004

Official language: English

Time: GMT minus 4 hours

Currency: Eastern Caribbean dollar
(EC$)

Main telephone lines/1,000 people: 488

Mobile phones/1,000 people: 490

National Women's Machinery

Antigua and Barbuda acceded to CEDAW in 1989 and to its Optional Protocol in 2006. Its National Women's Machinery is the Department of Women's Affairs in the Ministry of Labour, Public Administration and Empowerment.

Since its inception in 1982, the Department has experienced frequent location shifts between ministries; these shifts have often resulted in chronic discontinuity of work plans and implementation strategies and marginalisation within a new ministry. The Department of Women's Affairs has responsibility for promoting the social, political and economic interests of women and consequently their role in development. Training and education are focus areas for the Department: it provides a number of training schemes to promote awareness of the issue of gender and empowerment training for women.

To guide the work of the Department, an Advisory Committee was established in 1991. This comprised of a number of senior professional women in the public service and representatives of the Co-ordinating Council of Women, an umbrella group for women.

In consultation with NGOs and the private sector, the Directorate revised its national Plan of Action for Gender Affairs in 1997.

Antigua and Barbuda is ranked at 59 in the Gender-related Development Index (GDI) in the *UNDP Human Development Report 2006*.

Priority concerns for mainstreaming gender issues

Among the 12 critical areas of concern outlined in the 1995 *Beijing Platform for Action*, the Government of Antigua and Barbuda has identified the following, in order of priority, for national action:

1. Education and training of women

2. Women in power and decision-making

3. Women and poverty

4. Violence against women

5. Human rights of women

Followed by: 6. Women and health; 7. The girl-child; 8. Women and the environment; 9. Institutional mechanisms for the advancement of women; 10. Women in the media; 11. Women and the economy; 12. Women and armed conflict.

Women in power and decision-making

In 2004, Antigua and Barbuda had its first female elected representative in Parliament; there are also two women in the Upper House of the Senate. Women are well-represented in the public service, and several have risen to the top of the civil service and the teaching services.

Cultural attitudes are still resistant to the idea of women participating in politics at the highest levels. The Department of Women's Affairs has hosted a series of training workshops and other activities that highlighted the need for women to be partners in the governance of Antigua and Barbuda. Activities have included training and education, networking and advocacy and research and data collection on women in politics and decision-making.

Education

Public spending on education was 3.8% of GDP in 2002/03. There are 12 years of compulsory education starting at age five. The school year starts in September.

Health

91% of the population uses an improved drinking water source and 95% adequate sanitation facilities (2002). The country has a general hospital (220 beds), a private clinic, seven health centres and 17 associated clinics. Government finances visits by specialists in diabetics, heart disease, hypertension and glaucoma. A new hospital was built in the late 1990s. Infant mortality was 11 per 1,000 live births in 2004.

Religion

Mainly Christians (Anglicans and other Protestants; some Roman Catholics).

Media

Antigua Sun and *Daily Observer* are dailies; *The Worker's Voice* (Antigua Labour Party) is published twice weekly, and *The Sunday Scoop* weekly (from September 2004). There are 10,000 internet users (2002).

Concerns for the future

There will be continued focus on women in politics and decision-making, who can work to further promote gender mainstreaming through policies and programmes at a high level. There will be focus on improving education and skills, in order to improve the economic status of women and families, and to work towards eradicating poverty. Violence against women, and the health and welfare of women will continue to be addressed through training programmes, education, support services and legal reform.

Key contacts

- Senator Gwendolyn Tonge
  Special Adviser to Hon Minister for
  Health & Social Improvement
  Cecil Charles Building
  Cross Street
  PO Box 548
  St John's
  Antigua and Barbuda
  Tel: +1 268 4639252
  Fax: +1 268 463 9251
  Email: women@candw.ag

- Ms Sheila Roseau
  Directorate of Gender Affairs
  Executive Director
  Minister for Health & Social Improvement
  Cecil Charles Building
  Cross Street
  PO Box 548
  St John's
  Antigua and Barbuda
  Tel: +1 268 462 9664
  Fax: +1 268 462 9664
  Email: gender@antigua.gov.ag
         gender@candw.ag

Antigua and Barbuda | Summary of gender profile

Gender profile			1990	2000	2004
Population	Total population (000)		63	77	80
	Female population (% of total)		...	...	...
Labour force participation	Female labour force (% of total)		...	...	...
	Female unemployment (% of female labour force)		5.6	...	...
Education	Adult illiteracy rate (% of people aged 15+)	Female	...	...	...
		Male	...	...	...
	Net primary enrolment ratio (% of age group)	Female	...	...	...
		Male	...	...	...
	Net secondary enrolment ratio (% of age group)	Female	...	...	...
		Male	...	...	...
	Gross tertiary enrolment ratio (% of age group)	Female	...	...	...
		Male	...	...	...
Health	Life expectancy at birth (years)	Female	76	78	78
		Male	71	72	73
	Infant mortality rate (per 1,000 live births)		...	13	...
	Prevalence of HIV (% of people aged 15–24)	Female	...	...	...
		Male	...	...	...

Australia

KEY FACTS

Joined Commonwealth: 1931 (Statute of Westminster)

Capital: Canberra

GDP growth (%): 2.5% p.a. 1990–2004

Official language: English

Time: GMT plus 8–11 hours

Currency: Australian dollar (A$)

Main telephone lines/1,000 people: 542

Mobile phones/1,000 people: 720

National Women's Machinery

Australia acceded to CEDAW in 1983. Its National Women's Machinery is the Office for Women (OFW), located in the Department for Family and Community Services, and Indigenous Affairs. All work is founded on the goal of mainstreaming women's issues; this means working to ensure that a focus on women's experiences, issues or perspectives becomes everyone's business. The OFW provides high level advice to the Minister assisting the Prime Minister for Women's Issues; administers programmes; advises on legislative issues relating to women; provides the principal focus for consultation between the women's sector and government; and represents government at national and international forums.

The OFW funds national women's organisations to provide National Secretariat services on behalf of women in Australia. The Secretariats work collaboratively to provide informed and representative advice to the government on policy issues, development and implementation relevant to the diverse views and circumstances of women.

The National Council of Women of Australia instigated the formation of the Australian Women's Coalition by drawing together women's organisations which work co-operatively together to establish priorities for women and to increase communication between Government and the women of Australia. The National Rural Women's Coalition (NRWC) is a collaborative national voice for women living in rural, regional and remote Australia, established in 2002.

Australia is ranked at 3 in the Gender-related Development Index (GDI) in the *UNDP Human Development Report 2006*, the highest ranked Commonwealth member country.

Institutional mechanisms for the advancement of women

Australia has a comprehensive range of social, economic, political and legal frameworks that seek to advance the status of women and eliminate discrimination and violence against women and girls. Key institutional government measures include the Sex Discrimination Act 1984; Equal Opportunity for Women in the Workplace Act 1999; Workplace Relations Act 1996; Equal Opportunity for Women in the Workplace Agency; and Parliamentary Advisory Group on Women. In line with international best practice, the Australian Government has pursued a strategy of integrating women's issues into mainstream policy making and practice across all government agencies.

Priority concerns for mainstreaming gender issues

The Government of Australia advances gender equality in all critical areas of concern outlined in the 1995 *Beijing Platform for Action*.

Women in power and decision-making

Increasing women's participation in leadership and decision-making, including politics, is a major government priority. Since 1996, the Government has increased its activities to maximise the number of women appointed on merit to senior positions of power and decision-making. The number of women elected to Parliament continues to increase. In the 2004 elections, there were 37 female MPs, constituting nearly 25% of the House. There is over 35% female representation in the Senate.

Women in Australia are also well-represented in other key leadership and decision-making positions. In 2003, women in Australia occupied 34 per cent of senior positions on government boards. OFW provides an executive search service, AppointWomen, to ministers, government departments and agencies to promote the representation of women on government boards.

Violence against women

The Australian Government has nominated domestic violence as an issue of national importance. The government works with state and territory governments, business and the community to help prevent violence against women in all its forms. The Australian Government committed $50 million over the years 2001–2005 to the Partnerships Against Domestic Violence (PADV) initiative. PADV is managed by OFW to gather knowledge and find better ways of preventing and addressing domestic violence in the community. Some grants have been awarded to specifically assist indigenous NGOs to work with local communities to help them develop and implement grassroots culturally appropriate projects which will strengthen their capacity to prevent and address family violence.

Education

Responsibility for education lies with the states and systems vary slightly. Public spending on education was 4.9% of GDP in 2002/03. There are 11 years of compulsory education starting at age five. Net enrolment ratios are 97% for primary and 88% for secondary. The school year starts in January. About 74% of the relevant age group is enrolled in tertiary education (67% of males and 82% of females, 2002/03). There is virtually no illiteracy among people aged 15–24.

Health

Health facilities are the responsibility of the states, although the federal government administers the Medicare insurance scheme, introduced in 1984. Infant mortality was 5 per 1,000 live births in 2004 (20 in 1960).

Women and health

The National Women's Health Programme identifies seven priority health issues for women. These are reproductive health and sexuality; health of ageing women; women's emotional and mental health;

violence against women; occupational health and safety; the health needs of women as carers; and the health effects of sex role stereotyping. All Australian governments and the community and health sectors recognise the importance of working to stem the incidence of HIV/AIDS. In 2005, 16,000 people were infected with HIV and there were 500 deaths from the disease.

Religion

Christians 70% (Roman Catholics 27%, Anglicans 22%), small minorities of Muslims, Buddhists and Jews (1996 census).

Media

National daily newspapers are *The Australian* and *Australian Financial Review*. Regional newspapers include *The Advertiser* (Adelaide), *The Age* (Melbourne), *The Courier-Mail* (Brisbane), *The Daily Telegraph* (Sydney), *Herald-Sun* (Melbourne), *The Sydney Morning Herald*, and *The West Australian* (Perth). There are 722 TV sets and 602 personal computers per 1,000 people, and 11.3 million internet users (2003).

Australia | Summary of gender profile

Gender profile			1990	2000	2004
Population	Total population (000)		17,065	19,153	19,942
	Female population (% of total)		50.1	50.7	50.6
Labour force participation	Female labour force (% of total)		41	44	45
	Female unemployment (% of female labour force)		7.1	5.5	5.5
Education	Adult illiteracy rate (% of people aged 15+)	Female	...	...	...
		Male	...	...	...
	Net primary enrolment ratio (% of age group)	Female	99	93	95
		Male	99	92	95
	Net secondary enrolment ratio (% of age group)	Female	81	90	85
		Male	81	90	86
	Gross tertiary enrolment ratio (% of age group)	Female	43	72	82
		Male	36	59	67
Health	Life expectancy at birth (years)	Female	80	82	83
		Male	74	76	77
	Infant mortality rate (per 1,000 live births)		8	5	5
	Prevalence of HIV (% of people aged 15–24)	Female	...	0.0	...
		Male	...	0.1	...

Concerns for the future

There have been great gains for Australian women in recent years, although some areas of challenge remain. Key areas where efforts will continue to be focused are family/domestic violence and sexual assault against women and girls; the concentration of women in some fields/sectors/occupations; and the under-representation of women in high-level decision-making.

Key contacts

- Ms Julia Burns
  Executive Director
  Office for Women
  Department of Family & Community Services
  Bonner House
  PO Box 7788
  Canberra Mail Centre, ACT 2610
  Australia
  Tel: +61 2 6212 2400
  Fax: +61 2 6212 2497
  Email: women@facs.gov.au
  Email: julia.burns@facsia.gov.au

- Gabrielle Burrell
  Section Manager International, Indigenous &Rural Office for Women
  Department of Family and Community Services
  Bonner House
  PO Box 7788
  Canberra Mail Centre, ACT 2610
  Australia
  Tel: +61 2 6212 9011
  Email: gabrielle.burrell@facsia.gov.au
          anne.orourke@facsia.gov.au

The Bahamas

KEY FACTS

Joined Commonwealth: 1973

Capital: Nassau

GDP growth (%): 0.2% p.a. 1990–2003

Official language: English

Time: GMT minus 5 hours

Currency: Bahamian dollar (B$)

Main telephone lines/1,000 people: 415

Mobile phones/1,000 people: 367

National Women's Machinery

The Bahamas acceded to CEDAW in 1993. Its National Women's Machinery is the Bureau of Women's Affairs in the Ministry of Social Services and Community Development. The Bureau of Women's Affairs is responsible for creating and maintaining an environment conducive to gender equality in The Bahamas. The Bureau monitors and advises government on the legal, economic and social status of women in The Bahamas, and ensures that these conform to international treaties and standards set by the United Nations and other international organisations, to which The Bahamas has committed itself.

The Bureau of Women's Affairs has led educational campaigns with the public, including local women's NGOs, on legislation and other issues that impact on women. The Family and Child Protection Act, 2006 was passed after extensive consultation with citizens.

The Bahamas is ranked at 52 in the Gender-related Development Index (GDI) in the *UNDP Human Development Report 2006*.

Priority concerns for mainstreaming gender issues

Among the 12 critical areas of concern outlined in the 1995 *Beijing Platform for Action*, the Government of The Bahamas has identified the following, in order of priority, for national action:

1. Violence against women

2. Women and health

3. Education and training of women

4. Women and poverty

5. Human rights of women

Followed by: 6. Women and the economy; 7. The girl-child; 8. Women in power and decision-making; 9. Institutional mechanisms for the advancement of women; 10. Women and the environment; 11. Women in the media; 12. Women and armed conflict.

Women in power and decision-making

The Bahamas has not implemented any quotas to ensure equal representation of women in Parliament; however, the number of women in Parliament and other executive positions in the country is very encouraging. 20% of MPs are female, along with seven senators, and there are four female cabinet ministers.

Violence against women

Violence against women remains an area of concern to The Bahamas. Approximately 85% of domestic abuse complaints made to the police are made by women. Compounding the problem is the slow justice due to a backlog of cases at the criminal justice system and constant complaint withdrawals by the victims themselves.

The Government intends to introduce a Domestic Violence (Protection Orders) Act. The proposed Act will address the shortcomings of the existing Sexual Offences and Domestic Violence Act, which has been in place since 1991. Areas of particular interest in the new legislation are the expanded definitions of a spouse, harassment and stalking and the ability of the court to mandate counselling for the offender.

Education

There are 12 years of compulsory education starting at age five (2002/03). Net enrolment ratios are 86% for primary and 76% for secondary. The pupil–teacher ratio for primary is 17:1 and for secondary 15:1. The school year starts in September.

Health

New Providence has the Princess Margaret Hospital, mental hospital and rehabilitation unit, geriatric hospital, private hospital, with an emergency facility, and private clinic which undertakes plastic surgery. Grand Bahama has a general hospital and the Out Islands have cottage hospitals. In addition there are medical centres and clinics, and a flying doctor and dentist service covers the islands. 97% of the population uses an improved drinking water source and 100% have adequate sanitation facilities (2002). Infant mortality was 10 per 1,000 live births in 2004 (51 in 1960). At the end of 2003, 3% of people age 15 to 49 were HIV-positive.

Women and health

AIDS has been the leading cause of death in The Bahamas since 1994. The National HIV/AIDS Program continues to focus on information, education and communication to prevent HIV infections and reduce stigma and discrimination. At the end of 2005, there were a total of 6,800 cases of HIV and 500 deaths from the disease.

The Bureau of Women's Affairs continues to support the National AIDS Centre as one of the agencies educated for HIV prevention, reduction in stigma discrimination and as a partner in care efforts. Other agencies involved in the area include faith-based organisations, trade unions, human resource managers, women's groups and the media.

Religion

Mainly Christians (Baptists 32%, Anglicans 20%, Roman Catholics 19%, Methodists, Church of God).

Media

Daily newspapers are *The Bahama Journal*, *Freeport News*, *The Nassau Guardian* and *The Tribune*; *The Punch* is published twice weekly, and there are several weeklies. There are 84,000 internet users (2003).

Concerns for the future

The Bahamas will focus on initiatives to combat HIV/AIDS, improving women's health and education, and on violence against women.

Key contacts

- Mrs Phedra Rahming
  First Assistant Secretary & Officer in Charge
  Ministry of Social Services & Community Development
  Frederick House, Frederick St
  PO Box N-3206
  Nassau
  The Bahamas
  Tel: +1 242 356 0244/6
  Fax: +1 242 328 4917
  Email: womenbureau@bahamas.gov.bs

The Bahamas | Summary of gender profile

Gender profile			1990	2000	2004
Population	Total population (000)		255	301	319
	Female population (% of total)		50.5	51.1	51.3
Labour force participation	Female labour force (% of total)		45	49	50
	Female unemployment (% of female labour force)		12.5	9.7	11.1
Education	Adult illiteracy rate (% of people aged 15+)	Female	4.2	5.5	...
		Male	5.9	6.7	...
	Net primary enrolment ratio (% of age group)	Female	91	88	85
		Male	88	87	83
	Net secondary enrolment ratio (% of age group)	Female	...	80	78
		Male	...	75	70
	Gross tertiary enrolment ratio (% of age group)	Female	...	...	...
		Male	...	...	...
Health	Life expectancy at birth (years)	Female	73	72	74
		Male	64	65	67
	Infant mortality rate (per 1,000 live births)		24	14	10
	Prevalence of HIV (% of people aged 15–24)	Female	...	3	...
		Male	...	2.6	...

Bangladesh

KEY FACTS

Joined Commonwealth: 1972

Capital: Dhaka

GPD growth (%): 3.1% p.a. 1990–2003

Official language: Bangla

Time: GMT plus 6 hours

Currency: taka (Tk)

Main telephone lines/1,000 people: 6

Mobile phones/1,000 people: 10

National Women's Machinery

Bangladesh acceded to CEDAW in 1984 and to its Optional Protocol in 2000. The National Women's Machinery is the Ministry of Women's and Children's Affairs.

The Ministry of Women Affairs was established in 1978 to fulfil government commitments toward women development. In 1994, the Government reallocated the work and responsibilities of the Ministry, and was renamed the Ministry of Women and Children Affairs. The activities of the Ministry can be divided into two broad categories: policy formulation and advocacy; and programme implementation. Its objectives are to mainstream women in the development process and elevate their status in society; and to raise awareness about child rights and development of the latent potential of children.

Since women's development is a cross-cutting issue, the Ministry alone cannot be solely responsible for women's development. All sectors are equally involved in the integration of gender concerns, needs and interests into their policies, plans and programmes. The following institutional measures are in place:

- National Council for Women's Development (NCWD), established in 1995. The NCWD is the most high-powered committee for women's development and is headed by the Prime Minister;

- The Parliamentary Standing Committee for MWCA, established to fulfil the commitments of the National Policy;

- The Women's Development Monitoring and Evaluation Committee, established in 1998 to monitor the progress of the National Action Policy and other women in development (WID) activities;

- The WID Focal Points, established in different sectoral ministries to ensure incorporation of gender concerns and needs in policies, plans and programmes;

- District and sub-district level (Upazila) WID Coordination Committees, set up to ensure co-ordination between policy and implementation. The District and sub-district level officers and representatives from local civil society are members of this committee.

The National Action Plan (NAP) for the Advancement of Women was prepared and approved by Government. The formulation process brought together the government, NGOs and women's organisations. The goals of the NAP are to make women's development an integral part of the national development programme; to establish women as equal partners in development with equal roles in policy and decision making in the family, community and the national at large; and to remove legal economic, political or cultural barriers that prevent exercising equal rights by undertaking policy reforms and strong affirmative actions.

Bangladesh is ranked at 137 in the Gender-related Development Index (GDI) in the *UNDP Human Development Report 2006*.

Priority concerns for mainstreaming gender issues

The major goals of the Bangladesh National Policy for the Advancement of Women are to:

1. Establish equality between men and women in all spheres;

2. Eliminate all forms of discrimination against women and girls;

3. Establish women's human rights;

4. Develop women as a human resource;

5. Recognise women's contribution in social and economic sphere.

Followed by: 6. Eliminate poverty among women; 7. Establish equality between men and women in administration, politics, education, games, sports and all other socio-economic spheres; 8. Eliminate all forms of oppression against women and girls; 9. Ensure empowerment of women in politics; 10. Develop appropriate technology for women; 11. Ensure adequate health and nutrition for women; 12. Provide housing and shelter for women; 13. Create positive images of women in the media; and 14. Adopt special measures for women's equality in especially disadvantaged situations.

Women in power and decision-making

Ensuring participation at grassroots level power and decision-making is a vital area of national life. Women working in various administrative positions regularly receive training. A few women have been promoted to senior level government positions through lateral entry. Women participation in the executive body of different organisations has increased. Women's progress in politics is hindered by a lack of appropriate and adequate organisational arrangements in political parties for women's participation, a low inclusion of women, especially in decision-

making hierarchies, and a lack of political training. Despite these constraints, after the 2001 election, 52 of 345 parliamentary seats were held by women.

Violence against women

Violence against women is increasing despite efforts to curb it. The Women and Children Repression Prevention Act 2000 was formulated by the Parliament to address the problem of violence. It provides capital punishment for offenders.

Some noteworthy measures undertaken by the government are, establishing special cells for women in the police headquarters; establishing committees for the prevention of violence against women at the national, district and Upazila levels; providing training for the Law Enforcing Agencies; providing legal aid for the victims of violence; setting up shelter homes for abused and tortured women and strengthening awareness raising programmes.

Education

Public spending on education was 2.4% of GDP in 2002/03. There are five years of compulsory education starting at age six. Almost all primary schools are government-

managed. Secondary schools (11–16) and higher secondary colleges (17–18) are mostly private, often government-subsidised. Net enrolment ratios are 84% for primary and 44% for secondary. The pupil-teacher ratio for primary is 56:1 and for secondary 34:1. The school year starts in January.

About 6% of the relevant age group is enrolled in tertiary education (8% of males and 4% of females, 2002/03). A parallel system of education – *Madrasah* education – offers Islamic instructions from primary level up to postgraduate level. Illiteracy among people aged 15–24 is 50.3% (42.2% for males and 58.9% for females, 2002).

Health

Public sector medical facilities remain scarce, though there are clinics run by a major NGO, BRAC. To provide safe drinking water, between the 1970s and the mid-1990s some 5 million wells were drilled and in 2002 the UN estimated that 75% of the population was using an improved drinking water source and 48% adequate sanitation facilities (40% and 4% in the early 1980s). However, from 1996 naturally occurring arsenic was detected in the ground water

Bangladesh	Summary of gender profile				
Gender profile			1990	2000	2004
Population	Total population (000)		104,047	128,916	139,215
	Female population (% of total)		48.5	48.8	48.9
Labour force participation	Female labour force (% of total)		40	38	37
	Female unemployment (% of female labour force)		0.9	3.3	...
Education	Adult illiteracy rate (% of people aged 15+)	Female	76.3	...	...
		Male	55.7	...	...
	Net primary enrolment ratio (% of age group)	Female	...	...	...
		Male	...	...	...
	Net secondary enrolment ratio (% of age group)	Female	...	48	51
		Male	...	46	45
	Gross tertiary enrolment ratio (% of age group)	Female	...	4	4
		Male	...	8	9
Health	Life expectancy at birth (years)	Female	55	62	63
		Male	55	61	64
	Infant mortality rate (per 1,000 live births)		100	66	56
	Prevalence of HIV (% of people aged 15–24)	Female	...	0.6	...
		Male	...	0.4	...

(supplying over 1 million tube wells), putting at least 40% of the population at risk. By the 2000s there was an epidemic of health problems caused by arsenic poisoning.

Bangladesh has maintained a high level of immunisation coverage against diseases such as diphtheria, whooping cough, tetanus and measles. The infant mortality rate was 56 per 1,000 live births in 2004 (149 in 1960).

Women and health

The health of women is a crucial factor in the health of children, but gender discrimination leaves women particularly vulnerable to disease and death. The poor nutritional status of female children at birth is compounded by a lack of access to various services, resources and opportunities associated with high workloads and lack of rest. All this results in poor health, and low birth weight of babies, who tend to go on to be more malnourished in childhood and beyond.

The prevalence of HIV/AIDS is also a concern. In 2005, there were a total of 11,000 cases, 1,400 cases were in women, and there were 500 deaths from the disease.

Religion

Muslims 83%, Hindus 16%, a few Buddhists and Christians; Islam is the state religion (1998).

Media

Bangladesh has a lively and thriving press, with more than 100 daily newspapers and very many weeklies in circulation. Leading English-language newspapers are *The Bangladesh Observer* (since 1949), *The Daily Star*, *New Age*, *The New Nation*, *The Dhaka Courier* (weekly), and *The Independent*. Dailies in Bengali include *Ittefaq*, *Prothom Alo* and *Jugantor*. There are 59 TV sets and eight personal computers per 1,000 people, and 243,000 internet users (2002/2003).

Concerns for the future

Maternity is still considered as an aspect of the reproductive role of women and not perceived as a social function. Such stereotypes are reflected in electronic media and is sustained by the culture. The Government is gradually trying to sensitise media to change the prevailing perception about women's role.

In spite of all efforts at curbing, all forms of violence including trafficking are still growing. Actions need to be strengthened

with collaborative efforts of the government and NGOs. Some of the basic issues are, traditional attitudes that contribute to the vulnerability and insecurity of women, and the involvement of regional and global networks in trafficking. Full implementation of relevant laws and inadequate judicial structure still poses a challenge to be overcome.

In spite of significant developments, women's participation in the political process faces some problems. However, the reservation of seats of women in the elected bodies should have a positive impact in ensuring some representation of women and enabling women to learn about the organisation of different bodies and the political process as a whole.

Key contacts

- Mr Mahfulzul Islam
  Secretary
  Ministry of Women's & Children's Affairs
  Bangladesh Secretariat
  Block No. 6, 2nd & 3rd Floor
  Dhaka
  Bangladesh
  Fax: +880 2 861 1012
  Tel: +880 2 861 1012
  Email: plau@global-bd.net

Barbados

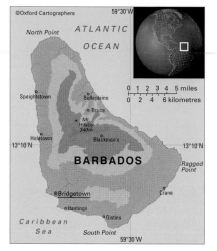

KEY FACTS

Joined Commonwealth: 1966

Capital: Bridgetown

GDP growth (%): 1.4% p.a. 1990–2003

Official language: English

Time: GMT minus 4 hours

Currency: Barbados dollar (Bds dollar)

Main Telephone Lines/1,000 people: 497

Mobile Phones/1,000 people: 519

National Women's Machinery

Barbados was one of the first Commonwealth countries to ratify CEDAW in 1980. Its National Women's Machinery is the Bureau of Gender Affairs in the Ministry of Social Transformation. The Bureau provides advice and direction to government agencies and NGOs on legislation and other policy matters; monitors the impact of policies; creates programmes to further the development of gender equity in areas such as public education and human resource development; and liaises with local, regional and international agencies.

The Bureau has implemented a programme of training and sensitisation for the inter-ministerial gender focal points, which assist with the implementation of gender management systems in all government Ministries and departments.

Barbados is ranked at 31 in the Gender-related Development Index (GDI) in the *UNDP Human Development Report 2006*.

Priority concerns for mainstreaming gender issues

Among the 12 critical areas of concern outlined in the 1995 *Beijing Platform for Action*, the Government of Barbados has identified the following, in order of priority, for national action:

1. Institutional mechanisms for the advancement of women

2. Women and health

3. Violence against women

4. Women and poverty

5. Women in power and decision-making

Followed by: 6. Women and the economy; 7. The girl-child; 8. Human rights of women; 9. Education and training of women; 10. Women and the environment; 11. Women in the media; 12. Women and armed conflict.

Women in power and decision-making

The equal participation of both women and men in decision-making is key to achieving a balance that reflects the composition of Barbadian society, this balance is needed in order to strengthen democracy and promote its proper functioning. Equality in political decision-making is integral to the achievement of the integration of a gender perspective in government policy making. A number of initiatives are in place to facilitate women's participation in public life. Among these was a leadership training programme implemented by the Bureau, in collaboration with the School of Continuing Studies focusing on 'Education for Women in Politics'. After the 2003 election, women held four out of 30 seats in Parliament.

Violence against women

The government recognises that violence against women remains prevalent. In the fight to reduce and eventually eradicate this plague from our society, the Bureau of Gender Affairs has implemented a number of programmes which aim to combat and eliminate violence against women. These programmes are being conducted at three levels: the elimination of inequalities between men and women; the provision of services for victims and offenders; and the provision of funding to women groups to engage in education and support services.

In 1999, the Barbados Government established a shelter for battered women in fulfilment of its commitment to provide services to improve the welfare of abused women. A Victim Support Group was established by the Royal Barbados Police Force. It is a non-profit voluntary organisation, established in December 1998 to offer emotional and practical support to nationals, non-nationals and their families and friends, who have suffered traumatic experiences as a result of various crimes such as robbery, sexual offences and burglary.

Women and poverty

In Barbados, pockets of poverty continue to exist alongside prosperity, and more women than men tend to fall below the poverty line. As a result, the government has established a number of institutional mechanisms to assist persons who are living below the poverty line. The Poverty Alleviation Bureau was established in October 1998, to develop a strategy for the alleviation and eventual eradication of poverty through community involvement. It aims to assist in the alleviation and eradication of poverty through the empowerment of individuals and groups, and by the provision of economic and financial opportunities as well as educational and vocational training. It has established an effective working relationship with government agencies, NGOs, civil society organisation, individuals and community groups in an effort to reduce inefficiencies, duplication of efforts and wastage of resources.

Education

Public spending on education was 7.6% of GDP in 2002/03. There are 11 years of compulsory education starting at age four. Net enrolment ratios are 100% for primary and 90% for secondary. The pupil–teacher ratio in primary education is 16:1 and for secondary 15:1. Computers are widely available to schools. The school year starts in September.

About 38% of the relevant age group is enrolled in tertiary education (2000/01). There is virtually no illiteracy among people aged 15–24.

Health

Barbados has a national health service and the general health profile and life expectancy of a developed country; virtually the entire population uses an improved drinking water source and adequate sanitation facilities (2002). Infant mortality was 10 per 1,000 live births in 2004 (74 in 1960). At the end of 2003, 1.5% of people aged 15–49 were HIV-positive.

Women and health

Gender inequality is a critical factor in the increasing incidence of HIV/AIDS in Barbados. The Bureau of Gender Affairs has implemented a training programme on the gender dimensions of HIV/AIDS, to provide information on the gender relations and the gender dynamics of HIV/AIDS, in order to reduce the levels of vulnerability. In 2005, there were a total of 2,700 cases of HIV/AIDS infections, 1,000 cases were in women.

Religion

Mainly Christians (Anglicans 40%, Pentecostals 8%, Methodists 7%, Roman Catholics 4%), with small Jewish, Hindu and Muslim communities.

Media

Dailies are *Barbados Advocate/Sunday Advocate*, and *The Nation*, and weeklies, *Broad Street Journal* (business) and *Weekend Investigator*; *Caribbean Week* is a fortnightly. There are 104 personal computers per 1,000 people, and 100,000 internet users (2002/2003).

Concerns for the future

The Government of Barbados has acknowledged the critical role of women to national development, which has led to the implementation of a number of projects and programmes aimed at improving the status of women. However, the Bureau of Gender Affairs is confronted with numerous challenges in fulfilling its mandate. Among

Barbados	Summary of gender profile				
Gender profile			*1990*	*2000*	*2004*
Population	Total population (000)		257	266	269
	Female population (% of total)		52.1	51.7	51.7
Labour force participation	Female labour force (% of total)		47	48	47
	Female unemployment (% of female labour force)		20.7	11.5	12.6
Education	Adult illiteracy rate (% of people aged 15+)	Female	0.7	...	...
		Male	0.6	...	...
	Net primary enrolment ratio (% of age group)	Female	80	100	99
		Male	81	100	100
	Net secondary enrolment ratio (% of age group)	Female	...	89	98
		Male	...	90	93
	Gross tertiary enrolment ratio (% of age group)	Female	30	56	...
		Male	24	21	...
Health	Life expectancy at birth (years)	Female	78	78	78
		Male	73	73	73
	Infant mortality rate (per 1,000 live births)		14	12	10
	Prevalence of HIV (% of people aged 15–24)	Female	...	...	...
		Male	...	...	...

the most constant are the prevailing values, beliefs and structures which are deeply embedded in the psyche of our people. These beliefs need to be challenged and people must be encouraged to rethink the way they do things in order to facilitate the process of transformation.

There is a need for the development of a national policy statement on gender and for the continued institutional strengthening of the Bureau of Gender Affairs. The Bureau will continue to mobilise the NGO sector for collaboration on social and economic issues, advocate for the amendment of legislation to reflect gender equality, advocate for the empowerment of at-risk persons and develop a monitoring and evaluation device to see the effectiveness of its programmes and initiatives. There will be a continued focus on combating violence against women, efforts to reduce the prevalence of HIV/AIDS, and strategies to improve women's health and education.

Key contacts

- Mr John Hollingsworth
  Director of the Bureau of Gender Affairs
  Ministry of Social Transformation
  2nd Floor Old National Insurance Building
  Fairchild Street, Bridgetown
  Barbados
  Tel: +1 246 431 0850/51
  Fax: +1 246 431 0850
  Email: genderbureau@caribsurf.com

Belize

KEY FACTS

Joined Commonwealth: 1981

Capital: Belmopan

GDP growth (%): 2.3% p.a. 1990–2003

Official language: English

Time: GMT minus 6 hours

Currency: Belizean dollar (Bz$)

Main telephone lines/1,000 people: 113

Mobile phones/1,000 people: 205

National Women's Machinery

Belize acceded to CEDAW in 1990 and to its Optional Protocol in 2002. Its National Women's Machinery is the Women's Department in the Ministry of Human Development, Women and Youth.

The Department facilitates opportunities for women through gender-sensitive education and training programmes, and advocates for gender-sensitive policies, plans, programmes and projects. The Department achieves its goals through a wide variety of education and training programmes, designed to create opportunities for full women's participation in national development. This task is supported by the involvement of civil society organisations, the Women's Commission and other partners in development. Women Development Officers are assigned to all districts, operating out of the Human Development Office, where they consult, develop and execute local and national programmes.

Belize is ranked at 95 in the Gender-related Development Index (GDI) in the *UNDP Human Development Report 2006*.

Priority concerns in mainstreaming gender issues

Among the 12 critical areas of concern outlined in the 1995 *Beijing Platform for Action*, the Belize Government has identified the following, in order of priority, for national action:

1. Violence against women

2. Education and training of women

3. Women and poverty

4. Women and health

5. Women in power and decision-making

Followed by: 6. Women and the economy; 7. Human rights of women; 8. Institutional mechanisms for the advancement of women; 9. The girl-child; 10. Women in the media; 11. Women and the environment; 12. Women in armed conflict.

Women in power and decision-making

In 2006, Belize swore in its first female Justice of the Supreme Court. This has been a crucial step in recognising the crucial role women play in the judicial, social, cultural, political and economic arenas.

Municipal elections held in 2006 indicated an overwhelming increase in female candidates resulting in the election of the first female Mayor in Belize City. There continues to be, however, the need to address the whole question of how to broaden decision-making processes so that women as well as men have full input into the definition of what issues require priority, and how to strengthen gender equality and women's participation in all political, economic and social policies.

Violence against women

Much of the work of the Women's Department is focused on addressing violence against women. A Domestic Violence Task Force was established, and efforts were made to involve and sensitise all sectors of the community. Police stations were provided with basic furniture to operate special units to deal with family violence cases, training was provided to police officers countrywide, and to para-professionals. Family violence committees were established in each district and a national registration form was created to keep records of reported incidents. The Department has held workshops with schools and communities, radio and TV programs, and disseminated pamphlets and brochures on domestic violence.

Education

Public spending on education was 5.2% of GDP in 2002/03. There are ten years of compulsory education starting at age five. Net enrolment ratios are 99% for primary education and 69% for secondary. The pupil–teacher ratio for primary is 21:1 and for secondary 23:1. The school year starts in September.

About 2% of the relevant age group is enrolled in tertiary education (1% of males and 3% of females, 2002/03). Illiteracy among people aged 15–24 is 15.8% (16.1% for males and 15.5% for females, 2000 census).

Health

There are government hospitals in Belize City, Belmopan and other main towns, and health-care centres and mobile clinics in rural areas. Malaria requires constant surveillance. The National Primary Healthcare Centre organises preventive programmes. 91% of the population uses an improved drinking water source and 47% adequate sanitation facilities (2002). Infant mortality was 32 per 1,000 live births in 2004 (74 in 1960). At the end of 2003, 2.4% of people age 15 to 49 were HIV-positive.

Women and health

Statistics indicate that HIV infections are increasing, with around 25% of the affected being women. To address this epidemic a National AIDS Commission has been legally established to co-ordinate education programmes and awareness-raising. In 2005, the Sexual and Reproductive Health Policy was launched which focuses on interventions to protect and promote sexual and reproductive health and rights.

Religion

Mainly Christians (Roman Catholics 50%, Pentecostals 7%, Seventh-day Adventists 5%, Anglicans 5%, Mennonites, Methodists); small minorities of Baha'i, Muslims and Jews (2000).

Media

Weekly newspapers include *Amandala*, *The Belize Times* (People's United Party), *The Guardian* (United Democratic Party), *The San Pedro Sun*, and *The Reporter*. There are 127 personal computers per 1,000 people and 30,000 internet users (2002).

Concerns for the future

The Government of Belize remains committed to the eradication of poverty, elimination of violence, advancement of women, the pursuit of gender equality and women's access to justice. While much progress has been made, there is more to urgently be done in the areas of HIV/AIDS, gender-based violence including rape and sexual abuse, maternal mortality, teenage pregnancy, and trafficking.

Key contacts

- Ms Anita Zetina
  Director, Women's Department
  Ministry of Human Development,
  Women & Youth
  26 Albert Street
  PO Box 846
  Belize City
  Belize
  Tel: +501 2 227 7397/227 3888
  Fax: +501 2 227 1275
  Email: womensdept@btl.net

Belize | Summary of gender profile

Gender profile			1990	2000	2004
Population	Total population (000)		189	250	264
	Female population (% of total)		49.2	4924	49.5
Labour force participation	Female labour force (% of total)		27	32	34
	Female unemployment (% of female labour force)		...	20.3	15.3
Education	Adult illiteracy rate (% of people aged 15+)	Female	11.8	6.8	...
		Male	10	6.7	...
	Net primary enrolment ratio (% of age group)	Female	93	96	100
		Male	95	96	99
	Net secondary enrolment ratio (% of age group)	Female	33	61	73
		Male	29	57	70
	Gross tertiary enrolment ratio (% of age group)	Female	1	...	4
		Male	1	...	2
Health	Life expectancy at birth (years)	Female	74	75	74
		Male	71	70	69
	Infant mortality rate (per 1,000 live births)		39	34	32
	Prevalence of HIV (% of people aged 15–24)	Female	...	2	...
		Male	...	1.1	...

Botswana

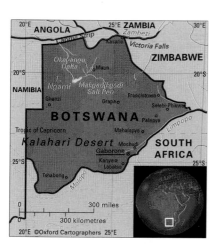

KEY FACTS

Joined Commonwealth: 1966

Capital: Gaborone

GDP growth (%): 2.2% p.a. 1990–2003

Official languages: Setswana, English

Time: GMT plus 2 hours

Currency: Botswana pula (BWP)

Main telephone lines/1,000 people: 75

Mobile phones/1,000 people: 297

National Women's Machinery

Botswana acceded to CEDAW in 1996 and to its Optional Protocol in 2007. Its National Women's Machinery is the Women's Affairs Department (WAD) in the Ministry of Labour and Home Affairs.

The National Women's Machinery was established initially as a unit in 1981, upgraded to a division in 1991, and finally upgraded to a full government department in 1996 as a reflection of the importance of the full integration of women's issues in national socio-economic development. WAD has developed a comprehensive advocacy and social mobilisation strategy for the National Gender Programme, providing a comprehensive strategy for consensus building, resource mobilisation, and sustained commitment to the National Gender Programme.

All ministries have a Gender Focal Point in order to ensure that the gender perspective is integrated into policies and programmes throughout government.

WAD has actively sought to establish partnership within NGOs in order to facilitate the implementation of the National Gender Programme. Through the Women's NGO Coalition different NGOs have taken responsibility for different aspects of the programme.

Botswana is ranked at 131 in the Gender-related Development Index (GDI) in the *UNDP Human Development Report 2006*.

Priority concerns for mainstreaming gender issues

Among the 12 critical areas of concern outlined in the 1995 *Beijing Platform for Action*, the Botswana Government has identified the following, in order of priority, for national action:

1. Women in poverty/women and the economy

2. Women in power and decision-making

3. Education and training of women

4. Women and health

5. The girl-child

6. Violence against women/human rights of women

Women in power and decision-making

Women's equal participation in political life plays a pivotal role in the general process of the advancement of women. There was a target of 30% representation for women in parliament for the 2004 elections. This was not achieved – there was only 11% representation. The major challenges are the prevailing gender stereotypes and the absence of a comprehensive affirmative Action Plan focusing on promoting gender equality in all organisations both in the public and private sectors.

Violence against women

A major challenge is that violence against women is on the increase and there is an absence of a comprehensive policy and laws dealing with gender violence. Efforts made to date include the following:

- Women in Law in Southern Africa undertook a number of studies on women and the administration of justice including advocacy and change of attitude among the police, health and court officials dealing with victims of violence;

- Networking among key stakeholders on gender violence;

- A Women's Shelter House established to assist battered women and children;

- Rape cases are now being heard on camera;

- Provision of limited support to NGOs such as the Women's Shelter;

- Women Against Rape (legal literacy and aid for women and girls);
- Implementing the Commonwealth integrated approach to combating gender based violence.

Education

Public spending on education was 2.2% of GDP in 2000/01. There are ten years of compulsory education starting at age six. Net enrolment ratios are 81% for primary and 54% for secondary (2002/03). The pupil–teacher ratio for primary education is 27:1 and for secondary 16:1. The private sector provides about one-third of secondary places. The school year starts in January.

About 5% of the relevant age group is enrolled in tertiary education (2002/03). Illiteracy among people aged 15–24 is 10.9% (14.5% for males and 7.2% for females, 2002).

Health

There are some 30 hospitals and over 500 clinics and health centres. Malaria is endemic in northern Botswana. 95% of the population uses an improved drinking water source and 41% adequate sanitation facilities (2002). Infant mortality was 84 per 1,000 live births in 2004, having risen sharply since the late 1990s due to AIDS (118 in 1960). At the end of 2003, 37.3% of people aged 15–49 were HIV- positive. Full AIDS control and prevention programmes are now in place.

Women and health

Progress has been made in several areas including: maternal and child health and family planning facilities are now available in every clinic; safe motherhood programmes exist; implementation of counselling and home-based care for HIV/AIDS sufferers; creation of programmes to prevent mother to child transmission of HIV in some hospitals; and the establishment of The National AIDS Council.

Major challenges include the increasing rate of HIV/AIDS within the population, in 2005, 52% of those infected were women.

Religion

Most people are Christians or hold traditional beliefs. Traditional religions incorporate some Christian practices.

Media

The government-owned *Daily News* is published in English and Setswana and *Mmegi* is an independent daily. There are several privately-owned weeklies including *The Botswana Gazette* (Wednesday, since 1985), *Botswana Guardian* (weekend) and *The Midweek Sun*. Botswana Television was launched in 2000. There are 44 TV sets and 41 personal computers per 1,000 people, and 60,000 internet users (2002).

Concerns for the future

Gender equality in access to education and productive resources continues to remain a challenge. Cultural and social influence on gender equality in access to education is also an important influence, in some cultures girls are forced into pre-arranged marriages at puberty stage forcing them to leave school early. The impact of inadequate participation of women in decision-making poses the challenge of improving the economic status of women, and there is a clear connection between poverty and exclusion from policy making and decision-making. Combating the prevalence of HIV/AIDS will also remain a priority.

Botswana | Summary of gender profile

Gender profile			1990	2000	2004
Population	Total population (000)		1,429	1,754	1,769
	Female population (% of total)		51	51	50.9
Labour force participation	Female labour force (% of total)		45	44	42
	Female unemployment (% of female labour force)		17.3	17.1	...
Education	Adult illiteracy rate (% of people aged 15+)	Female	39.7	...	18.2
		Male	34.3	...	19.6
	Net primary enrolment ratio (% of age group)	Female	87	81	84
		Male	80	78	80
	Net secondary enrolment ratio (% of age group)	Female	39	62	63
		Male	32	56	56
	Gross tertiary enrolment ratio (% of age group)	Female	3	3	6
		Male	4	4	7
Health	Life expectancy at birth (years)	Female	67	44	35
		Male	62	41	36
	Infant mortality rate (per 1,000 live births)		45	74	64
	Prevalence of HIV (% of people aged 15–24)	Female	...	34.3	...
		Male	...	15.8	...

Key contacts

- Ms M I Legwaila
  Director
  Women's Affairs Department
  Ministry of Labour and Home Affairs
  Private Bag 00107
  Gaborone
  Botswana
  Tel: +267 397 103/391 2290
  Fax: +267 3911944
  Email: mlegwaila@gov.bw
          tmenyatso@gov.bw;
          cokello-wengi@gov.bw

Brunei Darussalam

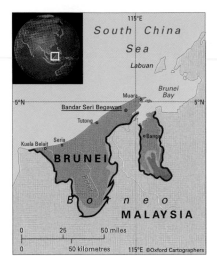

KEY FACTS

Joined Commonwealth: 1984

Capital: Bandar Seri Bagawan

GDP growth (%): –0.7% p.a. 1990–2003

Official language: Malay

Time: GMT plus 8 hours

Currency: Brunei Dollar

Main telephone lines/1,000 people: 256

Mobile phones/1,000 people: 401

National Women's Machinery

Brunei Darussalam acceded to CEDAW in 2006. Its National Women's Machinery is the Department of Community Development in the Ministry of Culture, Youth and Sports.

The Department's functions range from protecting, counselling women and girls, to providing welfare allowances and emergency relief. The Department is strongly supported by the Council of Women of Brunei Darussalam, which is an NGO founded in 1984, which aims to represent the rights of Bruneian women, improve the status of women in all fields, disseminate and collect information pertaining to women, and provide a forum for exchanging views.

Brunei Darussalam is ranked at 34 in the Gender-related Development Index (GDI) in the *UNDP Human Development Report 2006*.

Priority concerns for mainstreaming gender issues

Among the 12 critical areas of concern outlined in the 1995 *Beijing Platform for Action*, the Government of Brunei Darussalam has identified the following, in order of priority, for national action:

1. Women and poverty/women and health/ violence against women/the girl-child

2. Education and training of women

3. Women and the economy

Women in power and decision-making

Women's educational achievement has enabled them to take up employment opportunities in various specialised professions. An increasing number of them are holding senior positions and also involved in policy and decision-making.

Violence against women

An area of concern is an increase in domestic violence and abuse against women. The National Committee for Handling Social Issues, established in 2000, has implemented programmes which among others, include protection and rehabilitation of women and girls; public awareness campaigns on family harmony; and counselling services. The Domestic Violence Order is being drafted to ensure that women and children are protected.

Education

Public spending on education was 4.4% of GDP in 1998/99. There are 12 years of compulsory education starting at age five. The pupil–teacher ratio for primary is 13:1 and for secondary 11:1 (2002/03). The school year starts in January.

About 13% of the relevant age group is enrolled in tertiary education (9% of males and 17% of females, 2002/03). Illiteracy among people age 15–24 is 1.1% (2001 census).

Health

There are ten hospitals, health clinics, travelling clinics and a flying doctor service. Infant mortality was 8 per 1,000 live births in 2004 (63 in 1960). Malaria has been completely eradicated.

Religion

Official religion is Islam; minorities of Buddhists (13%), Christians (10%), Confucians and Taoists. The national ideology, Melayu Islam Beraja (MIB, Malay Muslim monarchy) fuses Islamic values and Brunei Malay culture.

Media

Borneo Bulletin is an English-language daily newspaper. *Media Permata* is published daily in Malay, and *Brunei Direct* is an online news service. There are 77 personal computers per 1,000 people and 35,000 internet users (2001/2002).

Concerns for the future

Focus will be put on advancing women in the economy, women in decision-making, and institutional mechanisms for the advancement of women.

Key contacts

- Ms Adina Othman
  Head of Social Affairs Services Unit
  Ministry of Culture, Youth and Sports
  Kampung Pulaie
  Jalan Kebangsaan 3786
  Bandar Seri Begawan
  Brunei Darussalam
  Tel: +673 2 240585
  Fax: +673 2 380 869/380042
  Email: adina@brunet.bn
         cokello-wengi@gov.bw

Brunei Darussalam	Summary of gender profile				
Gender profile			1990	2000	2004
Population	Total population (000)		257	333	366
	Female population (% of total)		47.1	47.9	48.1
Labour force participation	Female labour force (% of total)		32	34	34
	Female unemployment (% of female labour force)		...	...	...
Education	Adult illiteracy rate (% of people aged 15+)	Female	20.6	11.9	9.8
		Male	9	5.4	4.8
	Net primary enrolment ratio (% of age group)	Female	91	...	...
		Male	93	...	...
	Net secondary enrolment ratio (% of age group)	Female	75	...	...
		Male	67	...	...
	Gross tertiary enrolment ratio (% of age group)	Female	...	16	17
		Male	...	8	10
Health	Life expectancy at birth (years)	Female	76	79	79
		Male	72	74	75
	Infant mortality rate (per 1,000 live births)		10	8	8
	Prevalence of HIV (% of people aged 15–24)	Female	...	...	...
		Male	...	...	...

Cameroon

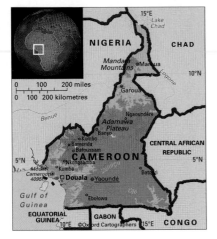

KEY FACTS

Joined Commonwealth: 1995

Capital: Yaoundé (constitutional); Douala (economic)

GDP growth (%): –0.2% p.a. 1990–2003

Official languages: French, English

Time: GMT plus 1 hour

Currency: CFA franc (CFAfr)

Main telephone lines/1,000 people: 7

Mobile phones/1,000 people: 66

National Women's Machinery

Cameroon acceded to CEDAW in 1994 and to its Optional Protocol in 2005. Its National Women's Machinery is the Ministry of Women's Affairs. It is responsible for responsible for drafting and implementing measures relating to respect of women's rights and strengthening guarantees of gender equality in the political, economic, social and cultural spheres.

The policy declaration on the Integration of Women in Development, the Multi-sectoral Plan of Action on Women and Development, and the National Plan of Action on the Integration of Women in Development were adopted by the Government in 1999, in order to advance the status of women in the economic and socio-cultural areas. The policies were prepared with the participation of the main actors in the cause of women's advancement – the administration, the private sector, and civil society. The policies are being implemented on a multi-sectoral across-the-board basis and co-ordinated by the Ministry of Women's Affairs.

Cameroon is ranked at 144 in the Gender-related Development Index (GDI) in the *UNDP Human Development Report 2006.*

Priority concerns for mainstreaming gender issues

Among the 12 critical areas of concern outlined in the 1995 *Beijing Platform for Action*, the Government of Cameroon has identified the following, in order of priority, for national action:

1. Institutional mechanisms for the advancement of women

2. Human rights of women

3. Women and poverty

4. Women and health

5. Education and training of women

Followed by: 6. The girl-child; 7. Women and the economy; 8. Women in power and decision-making; 9. Violence against women; 10. Women and armed conflict.

Institutional mechanisms for the advancement of women

There are external services in the provinces, departments and districts, which ensure extensive coverage of the Ministry of Women's Affairs' activities. Rural group leaders also provide leadership and guidance to grass-roots women's groups in their various activities. Women's Advancement Centres have also been established, these are neighbourhood structures that provide leadership and training in simple trades and dispense informal education to women and girls. Women are still very under-represented in Parliament, only 16 out of 180 MPs are women.

Education

Public spending on education was 3.8% of GDP in 2002/03. There are six years of compulsory education starting at age six. The pupil–teacher ratio for primary education is 57:1 and for secondary 21:1. School attendance is lower in the Far North province, where the population is partly nomadic. The school year starts in September. About 5% of the relevant age group is enrolled in tertiary education (2002/03).

Health

There are three referral hospitals, some 70 general hospitals, some 50 private hospitals and a wide network of public and private health centres, some of which are for the treatment of leprosy. 63% of the population uses an improved drinking water source and 48% adequate sanitation facilities (2002). Infant mortality was 87 per 1,000 live births in 2004 (151 in 1960). At the end of 2003, 6.9% of people aged 15–49 were HIV-positive.

Women and health

The government has implemented the health strategy document, adopted in 2001, in order to improve the population's health situation. There is emphasis on the importance of women to combat sexually transmitted diseases and HIV/AIDS. Women not only form the section of the population most affected by the epidemic, 57% in 2005, but they also represent the most vulnerable social group. Accordingly, prevention of the transmission of HIV/AIDS from mother to child and encouragement of the use of condoms and sheaths appear prominently among the strategies recommended in the health strategy document.

Religion

Mainly Christians (about half of whom are Roman Catholics), with a substantial

minority of Muslims, and a dominant attachment to traditional beliefs.

Media

Cameroon Tribune (daily in French and English editions) is the official newspaper. *Le Messager* is the leading independent daily in French, published in Douala since 1979. Other independent papers include *Mutations* (published daily in French), *The Herald* (three times weekly, in English) and *The Post* (twice weekly, in English). There are 75 TV sets and six personal computers per 1,000 people, and 60,000 internet users (2002).

Concerns for the future

The phenomenon of violence against women and girls is a social reality in Cameroon. It produces a negative impact on the victims, the perpetrators, the development of the family and, indeed, on the country as a whole. An Act is being drafted, designed to combat violence

against women and girls. Improving education and training, and combating poverty, is seen as central to wider political, economic and social development. Better educated women are also important to efforts to improve health and standards of the family, and to the improved participation of women in the decision-making process. Emphasis will be placed on developing policies for the education of girls, and lowering the drop-out rate.

Key contacts

- Dr Tanda Robert
  Director of Commonwealth Affairs
  Commonwealth Department
  Ministry of External Affairs
  Yaounde
  Cameroon
  Tel: +237 2210691/2201133
  Fax: +237 2210691
  Email: tandarob@yahoo.fr

Cameroon	Summary of gender profile				
Gender profile			1990	2000	2004
Population	Total population (000)		11,651	14,856	16,038
	Female population (% of total)		50.4	50.4	50.3
Labour force participation	Female labour force (% of total)		42	40	40
	Female unemployment (% of female labour force)		...	...	...
Education	Adult illiteracy rate (% of people aged 15+)	Female	52.5	...	40.2
		Male	31.3	...	33
	Net primary enrolment ratio (% of age group)	Female	69	...	...
		Male	79	...	...
	Net secondary enrolment ratio (% of age group)	Female	...	...	...
		Male	...	...	...
	Gross tertiary enrolment ratio (% of age group)	Female	...	4	4
		Male	...	6	6
Health	Life expectancy at birth (years)	Female	54	48	47
		Male	51	46	45
	Infant mortality rate (per 1,000 live births)		85	88	87
	Prevalence of HIV (% of people aged 15–24)	Female	...	7.8	...
		Male	...	3.8	...

Canada

KEY FACTS

Joined Commonwealth: 1931 (Statute of Westminster)

Capital: Ottawa

GDP growth (%): 2.2% p.a. 1990–2003

Official languages: English, French

Time: GMT minus 8–3 hours

Currency: Canadian dollar

Main telephone lines/1,000 people: 651

Mobile phones/1,000 people: 419

National Women's Machinery

Canada is a federal state comprising ten provinces and three territories. Many of the critical areas of concern outlined in the 1995 *Beijing Platform for Action* are interconnected rather than separate, and a number are shared areas of responsibility or fall primarily within provincial or territorial legislation. Due to its constitutional structure the Status of Women Canada (SWC) is the central agency of its National Women's Machinery, but is not the sole component. Each federal government ministry is responsible for implementing the Government's commitment to gender-based policy. There are also women's machinery offices in provincial and territorial governments.

Created in 1976, SWC reports to the Secretary of State (Status of Women), who is responsible for representing gender equality interests in Cabinet. Since 1995, the various mechanisms within the federal government to advance women's equality have been consolidated into SWC. The goals of this consolidation are: to strengthen the government's efforts to advance women's equality by creating a single-window operation; to enhance access to government; and to strengthen links with local, regional and national women's organisations, other NGOs and other representatives of civil society.

SWC's primary responsibilities include: conducting gender-based analysis of legislation, policies and programmes; making recommendations for changes, and using other tools and information to ensure that government decisions promote gender equality; promoting gender-based analysis throughout the federal government; representing Canada internationally on gender equality issues; supporting policy research and its use in policy development; providing financial assistance to women's

and other voluntary organisations; and assessing trends and progress.

Canada acceded to CEDAW in 1981 and to its Optional Protocol in 2003. Canada is ranked at 6 in the Gender-related Development Index (GDI) in the *UNDP Human Development Report 2006*.

Priority concerns for mainstreaming gender issues

Canada has highlighted those areas of concern that reflect the priorities of the national women's machinery, and for which there is common recognition across jurisdictions of where attention has been focused. These include:

- Women and the economy, including women in poverty

- Human rights of women and violence against women

- Institutional mechanisms for the advancement of women

Women in power and decision-making

Women's empowerment has many dimensions and women can be involved in decision-making in many ways – as parents and family members, community activists, consumers, employees, union members, business owners and members of government, non-government and private sector organisations. Most women in Canada now participate in the labour force and have access to their own income, which enhances their influence in the household and in public life. They still spend more time caring for children and household, however, which increases their time pressure. Women are continuing to make progress in attaining high-level positions in the public and private sectors. Women MPs make up 20% of the current parliament.

Violence against women

The incidence of, and even the severity of, spousal violence against women appears to have declined slightly over the past decade, which may be the result of several factors, including increased confidence in the administration of the criminal justice system (more reports to police), reduced societal tolerance for spousal violence and the increased availability of shelters and other needed services. In 2003, Ministers placed priority attention on the circumstances of Aboriginal women both on- and off-reserve, with violence as one of the priorities, and agreed to develop a plan of action to guide their work in this important area.

Education

Public spending on education was 5.2% of GDP in 2000/01. There are 11 years of compulsory education starting at age six. Net enrolment ratios are 100% for primary education and 98% for secondary. The pupil–teacher ratio for primary is 17:1 and for secondary 18:1. Most primary and secondary schooling is publicly funded. The school year starts in September.

About 59% of the relevant age group is enrolled in tertiary education (2000/2001).

Post-secondary education expanded rapidly during the 1980s and 1990s; women have shown the faster increase, and now outnumber men. There is virtually no illiteracy among people aged 15–24. There are more than 1,000 public libraries, containing more than 70 million volumes.

Health

Health insurance, provided by the provinces with federal government financial support, covers all the population. The entire population uses an improved drinking water source and adequate sanitation facilities (2002). The leading causes of death are circulatory system diseases, cancer, respiratory diseases and accidents. Serious health problems include AIDS. Smoking has declined dramatically, from over half of men to a minority. Infant mortality was 5 per 1,000 live births in 2004 (28 in 1960).

Religion

84% of people adhere to a religion; 74% of people are Christians (Roman Catholics 43%, Protestants 29%, Eastern Orthodox 1.6%), 2.0% Muslims, 1.1% Jews, 1.0% Hindus, 1.0% Buddhists and 0.9% Sikhs.

Media

Among some 100 dailies, the leaders include *The Globe and Mail* (Toronto, but distributed nationally), *National Post*, *Toronto Star*, *Vancouver Sun*, and *Le Devoir* and *La Presse* (in French). *Maclean's* is a weekly news magazine. There are 691 TV sets and 487 personal computers per 1,000 people, and 15.2 million internet users (2002).

Concerns for the future

Progress has been made in establishing a positive environment for implementing the policy commitment to gender-based analysis, and in increasing understanding and debate both within and outside government on a broader range of policy options. There is, however, room for further progress. Major challenges include: adapting to a changing government and economic environment; making effective use of limited resources for stimulating gender-based analysis; and promoting exchanges and common understanding among stakeholders. Further work is also required to refine indicators, and to develop indicators that reflect the social diversity of the population and recognize that factors

Canada | Summary of gender profile

Gender profile			1990	2000	2004
Population	Total population (000)		27,791	30,770	31,958
	Female population (% of total)		50.4	50.5	50.4
Labour force participation	Female labour force (% of total)		44	46	46
	Female unemployment (% of female labour force)		8.1	6.7	6.8
Education	Adult illiteracy rate (% of people aged 15+)	Female	...	...	...
		Male	...	...	...
	Net primary enrolment ratio (% of age group)	Female	98	99	...
		Male	98	98	...
	Net secondary enrolment ratio (% of age group)	Female	89	94	...
		Male	88	94	...
	Gross tertiary enrolment ratio (% of age group)	Female	...	69	66
		Male	...	51	49
Health	Life expectancy at birth (years)	Female	81	82	83
		Male	74	76	77
	Infant mortality rate (per 1,000 live births)		8	7	6
	Prevalence of HIV (% of people aged 15–24)	Female	...	0.1	...
		Male	...	0.3	...

such as Aboriginal status, disability, race, age, family status, and rural or urban location, can interact with gender in different ways.

Promoting further policy links and mutual respect between governments and non-governmental organisations, and holding consultations on policy issues and options with women's and other equality-seeking organizations, as well as civil society, is an important part of gender-based analysis.

Key contacts

- Ms Florence Ievers
  Co-ordinator, Status of Women Canada
  McDonald Building, 10th Floor
  123 Slater Street
  Ontario K1P 1H9
  Canada
  Tel: +1 613 995 7838
  Fax: +1 613 943 0449
  Email: florence.ievers@swc-cfc.gc.ca

- Sheila Regehr
  Coordinator, Status of Women Canada
  McDonald Building, 10th Floor
  123 Slater Street
  Ontario K1P 1H9
  Canada
  Tel: +1 613 995 3891
  Fax: +1 613 947 0530
  Email: Sheila.Regehr@swc-cfc.gc.ca

Republic of Cyprus

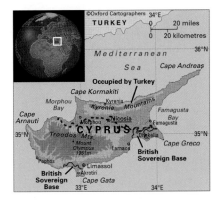

KEY FACTS

Joined Commonwealth: 1961

Capital: Nicosia

GDP growth (%): 3.2% p.a. 1990–2003

Official languages: Greek, Turkish

Time: GMT plus 2–3 hours

Currency: Cyprus pound (C£); Turkish lira in occupied north

Main telephone lines/1,000 people: 572

Mobile phones/1,000 people: 744

National Women's Machinery

Cyprus is an island country divided following the illegal occupation of the north by Turkish troops in 1974.

Cyprus acceded to CEDAW in 1985 and to its Optional Protocol in 2002. Its National Women's Machinery is the Department of Gender Equality in the Ministry of Justice and Public Order. The Department deals with all matters concerning women, focusing on the elimination of legal discrimination against women and the promotion of real equality between men and women. It advises the Council of Ministers on policies, programmes and laws promoting women's rights. It monitors, co-ordinates and evaluates the implementation and effectiveness of these programmes and laws, carries out research on gender issues, promotes education and training programmes on relevant issues, and supports and subsidises women's organisations.

The Department is a system of four bodies:

- The Council for Women's Rights, consisting of representatives of major women's and trades union organisations;

- The Inter-Ministerial Committee, consisting of the Competent Officers for Women's Rights appointed in all ministries and the Planning Bureau;

- The National Committee for Women's Rights, which consists of all the members of the Council for Women's Rights and the Competent Offices for Women's Rights, and other organisations promoting gender equality;

- The General Secretariat, which provides administrative and scientific support for the Department and promotes and implements its decisions.

Cyprus is ranked at 29 in the Gender-related Development Index (GDI) in the *UNDP Human Development Report 2006*.

Priority concerns for mainstreaming gender issues

Among the 12 critical areas of concern outlined in the 1995 *Beijing Platform for Action*, the Government of Cyprus has identified the following, in order of priority, for national action:

1. Violence against women

2. Women and the economy

3. Women in power and decision-making

4. Institutional mechanisms for the advancement of women

5. Education and training of women

Followed by: 6. Women and health; 7. Women and armed conflict; 8. Human rights of women; 9. The girl-child; 10. Women in the media; 11. Women and the environment; 12. Women in poverty.

Women in power and decision-making

Despite the increasing number of women actively involved in politics, women are under-represented in the Government, Parliament, judiciary and almost all decision-making bodies in general. In the 2001 elections, there were only six women elected out of 56 available seats in Parliament. Research has shown that both male and female Cypriot voters do not fully trust women yet, who remain 'invisible' for a variety of reasons. Another research carried out by the Women's Organisation of the United Democrats Party reveals that the main reason for the low representation and participation of women in politics is due to the conservative traditional features of the Cyprus society. The education system, the media, as well as the family are not very supportive and encouraging to women's efforts to enter the political scene. The Government put in place a set of measures to increase women's participation in political and public life, including providing training seminars on issues such as 'Women in Politics'.

Violence against women

There is an increased awareness of and commitment towards preventing and combating violence against women and girls, including domestic violence, which for a number of years was a taboo. This has been achieved mainly through improved legislation, policies, programmes and setting up and strengthening of the necessary structures for the protection of victims of violence. The pioneering initiatives of civil society, in particular women's organisations, in the field of preventing violence against women and offering assistance to girl and women-victims of domestic violence, has played an important role in the provision of support services to women victims of violence and in promoting awareness-raising campaigns. As regards trafficking and exploitation of women, which internationally is becoming increasingly worrying, there is an increased sensitivity witnessed both among the public and the government authorities. This has been achieved mainly due to the joint efforts of governmental and NGOs.

Insufficient understanding of the root of the problem and of its real dimensions, as well as inadequate data, further impedes informed analysis and policy making. The effective implementation of the law depends heavily on the sensitisation and specialisation of all professionals involved in the handling of cases of violence. Lack or insufficiency of these factors constitutes a major difficulty. It also relies on the level of co-ordination and co-operation among all services involved, i.e. police, social workers, doctors, etc., which may not always be adequate. Another major obstacle is the reluctance of women, victims of violence and/or trafficking and exploitation, to report violence against them and seek support and assistance.

Education

Public spending on education was 6.3% of GDP in 2002/03. There are nine years of compulsory education starting at age six. Net enrolment ratios are 96% for primary education and 93% for secondary. The pupil–teacher ratio for primary is 19:1 and for secondary 12:1. There are many private schools. The school year starts in September. The occupied north also has free education to the age of 15.

About 60% of school leavers go on to university, many studying overseas. Greek Cypriots have one of the world's highest proportions of graduates. About 32% of the relevant age group is enrolled in tertiary education (2002/03). There is virtually no illiteracy among people aged 15–24.

Health

In the Republic, medical care is free for government employees, refugees and low-income families, including in all about 65% of the population. The government has proposed a national health insurance scheme. A new general hospital was built in Nicosia in the latter 1990s. The entire population uses an improved drinking water source and adequate sanitation facilities (2002). Overall, the infant mortality rate was 5 per 1,000 live births in 2004 (30 in 1960).

The health service in the occupied north is nationalised, though complicated surgery is done abroad, or the UN arranges treatment in the Republic.

Women and health

Cyprus remains a low prevalence country for HIV/AIDS, particularly for women, who

Republic of Cyprus	Summary of gender profile				
Gender profile			1990	2000	2004
Population	Total population (000)		681	786	826
	Female population (% of total)		50.2	50.8	51.2
Labour force participation	Female labour force (% of total)		38	41	45
	Female unemployment (% of female labour force)		…	7.4	4.6
Education	Adult illiteracy rate (% of people aged 15+)	Female	9	…	4.9
		Male	2.3	…	1.4
	Net primary enrolment ratio (% of age group)	Female	87	96	96
		Male	87	95	96
	Net secondary enrolment ratio (% of age group)	Female	70	89	94
		Male	68	87	91
	Gross tertiary enrolment ratio (% of age group)	Female	13	22	33
		Male	12	17	31
Health	Life expectancy at birth (years)	Female	79	81	81
		Male	74	76	77
	Infant mortality rate (per 1,000 live births)		12	6	5
	Prevalence of HIV (% of people aged 15–24)	Female	…	…	…
		Male	…	…	…

are outnumbered by 6 to 1 by men with regard to HIV infection. The main concern for the Ministry of Health has been to prevent the further spread of the virus. The National AIDS Programme has continued to be implemented according to the principles for prevention of the transmission of the virus and the reduction of the social and personal consequences of HIV infection. A new strategic plan for prevention of AIDS has also been prepared for the period 2004–2008.

Religion

Most Greek Cypriots belong to the autocephalous Cypriot Orthodox Church; most Turkish Cypriots are Sunni Muslims. There are minorities of Maronites, Armenians, Roman Catholics and Anglicans.

Media

There are several daily papers, including one evening paper, most in Greek but *Cyprus Mail* is in English. Of the several bi-weekly, weekly and fortnightly papers, two (*Cyprus Weekly* and *Cyprus Financial Mirror*) are in English. There are 270 personal computers per 1,000 people and 250,000 internet users (2002/2003).

Concerns for the future

The Government of Cyprus considers that the main challenges ahead pertain to implementation and thus, efforts, should concentrate on how to promote further and successful implementation of gender equality issues. It is important to find creative ways to secure high political level of support for the national co-ordination mechanism, efficient and effective

monitoring mechanisms, accountability of the different actors involved in the promotion of gender mainstreaming policies, visibility of gender equality and gender mainstreaming actions, empowerment of women and creation of gender sensitive environment for all social and political structures and processes.

Key contacts

- Mrs Maro Varnavidou
  Secretary General
  National Machinery for Women's Rights
  Ministry of Justice & Public Order
  125 Athalassas Ave.
  1461 Nicosia
  Republic of Cyprus
  Tel: +357 22 805930/805955
  Fax: +357 22 518356/349
  Email: womens.rights@mjpo.gov.cy

Dominica

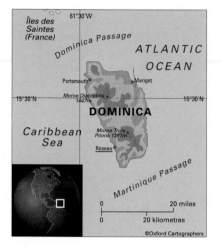

KEY FACTS

Joined Commonwealth: 1978

Capital: Roseau

GPD growth (%): 1.2% p.a. 1990–2003

Official language: English

Time: GMT minus 4 hours

Currency: Eastern Caribbean dollar (EC$)

Main telephone lines/1,000 people: 304

Mobile phones/1,000 people: 120

National Women's Machinery

Dominica was one of the earliest Commonwealth countries to accede to CEDAW, in 1980. Its National Women's Machinery is the Women's Bureau in the Ministry of Community Development and Gender Affairs.

The Women's Bureau works in partnership with NGOs and civil society groups, as well as the private sector and public sector for support of gender equality and empowerment of women. It also works closely with women's organisations, especially the umbrella organisation Dominica National Council of Women.

Dominica is ranked at 68 in the Gender-related Development Index (GDI) in the *UNDP Human Development Report 2006*.

Priority concerns for mainstreaming gender issues

Among the 12 critical areas of concern outlined in the 1995 *Beijing Platform for Action*, the Government of Dominica has identified the following, in order of priority, for national action:

1. Women and poverty

2. Violence against women

3. The girl-child

4. Women and health

5. Education and training of women

Followed by: 6. Institutional mechanisms for the advancement of women; 7. Women and the economy; 8. Women in power and decision-making; 9. Human rights of women; 10. Women in the media; 11. Women and the environment; 12. Women and armed conflict.

Women in power and decision-making

Women are generally under-represented in power and high-level decision-making positions, where they can sufficiently influence policy decisions that affect their own lives and help bring to the fore consideration for the plight of women. In the 2005 elections, only four out of 31 seats in Parliament were won by women.

Violence against women

There has been much work and effort which has gone into addressing this social ill which negatively impacts on the family and the entire society. The Legal Aid Clinic ensures legal representation for all vulnerable groups, including women and children, in situations of violence. Many interventions have been spearheaded by the Women's Bureau and the Dominica National Council of Women in order to increase public awareness and education at community and national level, and also providing lobbying and advocacy.

Education

There are 12 years of compulsory education starting at age five. Net enrolment ratios are 81% for primary education and 92% for secondary (2002/03). The pupil–teacher ratio for primary is 19:1 and for secondary 17:1. The school year starts in September.

Further education is provided at a teacher-training college, a nursing school and at the regional University of the West Indies, which has a branch in Dominica and main campuses in Barbados, Jamaica, and Trinidad and Tobago.

Health

The health system operates through local clinics, larger health centres, a polyclinic in Roseau, and the national referral hospital, the Princess Margaret Hospital. There is a smaller hospital at Portsmouth, and cottage hospitals at Marigot and Grand Bay. 97% of the population uses an improved drinking water source and 83% adequate sanitation facilities (2002).

Infant mortality was 13 per 1,000 live births in 2004.

Women and health

There are initiatives aimed at the following: improving maternal and child health care; childhood immunisation; reproductive health; reduction of mother to child transmission of HIV; and healthy lifestyles programmes. 47% of all cases of HIV/AIDS infection in 2005 were women. There are problems with accessibility and cost of anti-retroviral drugs in order to combat this problem.

Religion

Mainly Christians (about 70% Roman Catholics).

Media

The Chronicle (founded in 1909), *The Tropical Star* and *The Sun* are all weekly. There are 90 personal computers per 1,000 people and 12,500 internet users (2002).

Concerns for the future

There is a lack of adequate gender analysis in research which is a barrier to implementing development strategies and programmes. Dominica will also continue to focus of violence against women, empowerment of women, health issues, and eradicating poverty.

Key contacts

- Ms Rosie Browne
  Director
  Women's Bureau
  Ministry of Community Development,
  Gender Affairs and Information
  The Globe Building
  106 Independence Street
  Roseau
  Dominica
  Tel: +1 767 448 2401 Ex: 3344
  Tel/Fax: +1 767 449 8220
  Email: wbint@cwdom.dm

Dominica | Summary of gender profile

Gender profile			1990	2000	2004
Population	Total population (000)		72	73	79
	Female population (% of total)		...	50	...
Labour force participation	Female labour force (% of total)		...	...	...
	Female unemployment (% of female labour force)		18.3	...	...
Education	Adult illiteracy rate (% of people aged 15+)	Female	...	...	...
		Male	...	...	...
	Net primary enrolment ratio (% of age group)	Female	...	90	88
		Male	...	93	87
	Net secondary enrolment ratio (% of age group)	Female	...	84	92
		Male	...	78	89
	Gross tertiary enrolment ratio (% of age group)	Female	...	...	...
		Male	...	...	...
Health	Life expectancy at birth (years)	Female	75	78	79
		Male	71	74	75
	Infant mortality rate (per 1,000 live births)		15	13	13
	Prevalence of HIV (% of people aged 15–24)	Female	...	...	...
		Male	...	...	...

Fiji Islands

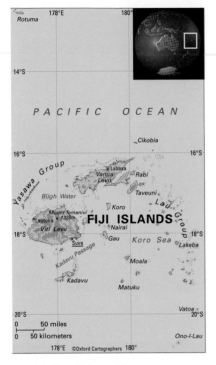

Fiji Islands' military regime was suspended from the councils of the Commonwealth on 8 December 2006, pending restoration of democracy and the rule of law in the country.

KEY FACTS

Joined Commonwealth: 1970 (rejoined in 1997 after10 year lapse)

Capital: Suva

GDP growth (%): 1.5% p.a. 1990–2003

Official language: English

Time: GMT plus 12–13 hours

Currency: Fiji Island dollar

Main telephone lines/1,000 people: 124

Mobile phones/1,000 people: 133

National Women's Machinery

Fiji Islands ratified CEDAW in 1995. Its National Women's Machinery is the Department of Women in the Ministry of Women, Culture and Heritage, and Social Welfare. The Ministry is the primary advisor to Government on public policies that affect women, is the key catalyst for the implementation of the Women's Plan of Action, and assists the Government work towards the full and active participation of women in society. The Ministry provides policy advice, including a gender analysis of the various public policy issues that affect women and on a wide range of issues relating to women's development. It provides ministerial support services, including the preparation of speech notes and speeches, advisory support to the Minister in Cabinet Committees, preparation of press releases, and administrative support to the Minister as Chair of the National Women's Advisory Council. The Ministry also provides gender advisory services to assist other ministries/departments to develop gender-inclusive approaches in order to mainstream women and gender concerns in their policies, programmes, and practices.

The Women's Plan of Action 1999–2008 includes strategic objectives and directions for the five taskforce areas: action in mainstreaming of women's and gender concerns in the planning process and all policy areas; women and the law; micro-enterprise; balancing gender in decision-making; and violence against women.

Fiji Islands is ranked at 90 in the Gender-related Development Index (GDI) in the *UNDP Human Development Report 2006*.

Priority concerns for mainstreaming gender issues

Among the 12 critical areas of concern outlined in the 1995 *Beijing Platform for Action*, the Government of Fiji Islands has identified the following, in order of priority, for national action:

1. Institutional mechanisms for the advancement of women

2. Women in power and decision-making

3. Women and the economy

4. Human rights of women

5. Violence against women

Followed by: 6. Women and poverty; 7. Women and health; 8. Education and training of women; 9. Women and armed conflict; 10. Women and the environment; 11. The girl-child; 12. Women in the media.

Women in power and decision-making

The Ministry has created the Nominations Service, which is a computerised directory of skilled and experienced women who are available for nomination for government bodies. It provides to ministers and government the names of women suitable for appointment to statutory boards and committees.

Women and the economy

The Ministry has developed and implemented the Women's Social and Economic Development Program (WOSED). WOSED is a micro-enterprise programme being conducted in selected areas throughout Fiji. The objective of the programme is to enhance the social, economic and political status of women so they can participate confidently and meaningfully at all levels of the development process.

Violence against women

Domestic violence in Fiji is prevalent, and there is a high level of tolerance. Women themselves appear to be culturally and socially conditioned to believe that violence inflicted upon them is justified under certain circumstances. One of the taskforces of the Ministry is responsible for combating violence against women. Counselling centres for both victims and perpetrators of violence have been established, and there have been training programmes implemented in the community and for law enforcement officials, on how to deal with such violence.

Education

Public spending on education was 5.6% of GDP in 2001/02. There are ten years of compulsory education starting at age six. Net enrolment ratios are 100% for primary education and 76% for secondary. The pupil–teacher ratio for primary is 28:1 and for secondary 17:1. The school year starts in January. Illiteracy among people age 15–24 is 0.7% (0.9% for males and 0.6% for females, 1996 census).

Health

There is a comprehensive system providing universal health and dental services for nominal fees. There are 25 hospitals. The country is free of malaria. Infant mortality was 16 per 1,000 live births in 2004 (1 in 1960).

Women and health

Women in Fiji's rural areas are serviced by health centres and nursing stations providing only basic health services. Women's access to the range of reproductive health services are limited as the wider range of services are available at the district hospitals which can be difficult to get to because of cost. There needs to be more appropriate, high-quality health information made available to people in the rural areas.

There is a Strategic Plan on HIV/AIDS, half of all reported cases are in women. There is a need to develop a policy on the treatment and care of HIV/AIDS patients, and to provide support in the community to sufferers and carers. There must be an increase in budgetary allocations to provide the necessary treatment. The majority of health care providers of AIDS patients are women who have no support.

Religion

Christians 52% (mainly Methodist), Hindus 38%, Muslims 8%, small number of Sikhs (1986).

Media

Daily English-language newspapers are *Fiji Times* (founded 1869), *Fiji Sun* and *Daily Post* (1989, partly state-owned). The publishers of *Fiji Times* also produce weekly Fijian and Hindi papers, while a fortnightly Fijian paper is available from Sun Publishers. There are 51 personal computers per 1,000 people and 55,000 internet users (2003).

Concerns for the future

History has shown that every time a conflict breaks out, women, in their communities, mobilise for peace. Women and women's groups play key roles as activists and peace-makers in each conflict situation, while at the same time holding together their families and communities.

Whether it takes the form of silent protest, prayer and peace vigils, protest marches and public actions, the feminisation of conflict and peace can no longer be disregarded in decision making forums. Since the military coup in 2006, Fiji will need to work to promote and enhance the recognition and contribution of women to detect early conflict warning via intervention, resolution strategies and post

Fiji Islands | Summary of gender profile

Gender profile			1990	2000	2004
Population	Total population (000)		724	811	841
	Female population (% of total)		49.2	49.2	49.2
Labour force participation	Female labour force (% of total)		38	38	38
	Female unemployment (% of female labour force)		...	...	...
Education	Adult illiteracy rate (% of people aged 15+)	Female	14.5	...	8.6
		Male	8.4	...	5.5
	Net primary enrolment ratio (% of age group)	Female	...	99	96
		Male	...	100	97
	Net secondary enrolment ratio (% of age group)	Female	...	80	81
		Male	...	73	75
	Gross tertiary enrolment ratio (% of age group)	Female	6	...	17
		Male	10	...	14
Health	Life expectancy at birth (years)	Female	69	70	70
		Male	65	65	66
	Infant mortality rate (per 1,000 live births)		25	18	16
	Prevalence of HIV (% of people aged 15–24)	Female	...	...	...
		Male	...	...	...

conflict progress. Sustainable development and peace building must encompass the rights of men and women and boys and girls and that there needs to be equal distribution of development benefits. Men and women bring different perspectives to peace negotiations, because of the unique experiences that have shaped them and influenced their priorities.

Fiji will need to constructively address difficult and sensitive issues including underlying causes of tensions and conflict (ethnicity, socio-economic disparities, and lack of good governance, land disputes and erosion of cultural values), while also reiterating the belief in the liberty of the individual under the law, in equal rights for all citizens regardless of gender, race, colour, creed or political belief and in the individual's inalienable right to participate by means of free and democratic political process in framing the society in which he or she lives.

Key contacts

* Department of Women
  Ministry of Women, Culture and
  Heritage, and Social Welfare
  PO Box 14068
  Suva
  Fiji Islands
  Tel: +679 331 2199
  Fax: +679 330 3829

The Gambia

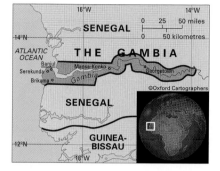

KEY FACTS

Joined Commonwealth: 1965

Capital: Banjul

GDP growth (%): 0.1% p.a. 1990–2003

Official language: English

Time: GMT

Currency: dalasi (D)

Main telephone lines/1,000 people: 29

Mobile phones/1,000 people: 75

National Women's Machinery

The Gambia ratified CEDAW in 1993. Its National Women's Machinery is made up of the Women's Bureau in the Department of State for Women's Affairs, and the National Women's Council. The National Women's Council functions as the national assembly for women, while the Women's Bureau serves as the Secretariat to the National Women's Council. The Bureau focuses on information gathering, dissemination, research and analysis. The Bureau assists the Council in monitoring trends and forging links with other institutions on the socio-economic and political front, reviewing bills, legislation, policies, programmes, new technologies and providing relevant information for informed decision-making.

The Women's Bureau and the National Women's Council are the principal actors in the implementation at the National Policy for the Advancement of Gambian Women 1997–2007. The Policy's goals are two fold: to catalyse all possible courses of action necessary to eliminate all forms of inequality between women and men; and to facilitate the creation of an enabling environment for the promotion of women's participation and contribution, for equal opportunities and access to existing initiatives aimed at promoting the advancement of women and the girl-child.

The Gambia is ranked at 155 in the Gender-related Development Index (GDI) in the *UNDP Human Development Report 2006*.

Priority concerns for mainstreaming gender issues

Among the 12 critical areas of concern outlined in the 1995 *Beijing Platform for Action*, the Government of The Gambia has identified the following, in order of priority, for national action:

1. Education and training of women

2. Women and health

3. Women and the economy

4. Women in poverty

5. The girl-child

Followed by: 6. Women in power and decision-making; 7. Institutional mechanisms for the advancement of women; 8. Human rights of women; 9. Women and the environment; 10. Violence against women; 11. Women in the media; 12. Women and armed conflict.

Women in power and decision-making

More females are taking up leadership positions. In the last election, 13.2% of MPs were female, whereas they only made up 2% in 1999. In the NGO and private sector there has been marked improvement in the number at decision-making levels. However, the changes and gains achieved at central level have not been reflected at local decentralised levels. As yet there are no female Divisional Commissioners or District Head Chiefs, although there are a few female village heads. The media is critical in promoting women's access to development.

Violence against women

Violence in any form, whether sexual harassment, or psychological or physical abuse perpetrated against females is recognised in The Gambia as a violation of human rights. Under the laws of The Gambia, violence against women is covered under assault, there is no separate provision set aside for the maltreatment of women. Consequently, such cases are often regarded as family problems and in most cases forwarded to the Department of Social Welfare. At other times, such cases of violence are not even reported for action to the necessary authorities. However, law enforcement bodies and human rights groups have contributed significantly in trying to eliminate violence against women.

Three main factors have been identified in the increasing trends in violence against women: traditional and socio-cultural beliefs; religious barriers; and low levels of education. There is a need for additional constitutional provision on the issues of sexual harassment and domestic disputes involving women. Such legislation will strengthen the current efforts of the police in trying to curb the incidence of violence against women.

Education

Public spending on education was 2.8% of GDP in 2002/03. There are six years of primary education and six years of secondary. Net enrolment ratios are 79% for primary education and 33% for secondary. The pupil–teacher ratio for primary is 38:1 and for secondary 25:1. The school year starts in September.

Health

The country relies partially on expatriate doctors: when Chinese doctors working in the country were recalled in 1995, Cuban doctors replaced them. There are hospitals at Banjul, Bansang and a new one at Farafenni opened in 1998. In addition there are health centres and dispensaries.

Traditional healers and midwives are well established in rural areas. There is a leprosy control programme. 82% of the population uses an improved drinking water source and 53% adequate sanitation facilities (2002). Infant mortality was 89 per 1,000 live births in 2004 (207 in 1960). At the end of 2003, 1.2% of people aged 15–49 were HIV positive.

Women and health

The Gambia Government is a signatory to the Alma Ata Declaration, and has committed itself through the Primary Health Care strategy to improve the quality of health of the population. The current National Health Policy seeks to ensure that health services are both accessible and responsive to the needs of the population, particularly those in the rural areas. The health care delivery system operates at three levels: primary, secondary and tertiary.

The Maternal and Child Health and Family Planning Unit of the Department of State for Health has developed strategies to reduce the high incidence of maternal mortality, which include the early identification of 'at risk mothers', improved case management of both ante-natal and post-natal patients and adolescent sexual

health. There is a high incidence of HIV/AIDS throughout the population, with 55% of those infected in 2005 being women. The Government has implemented the HIV/AIDS Rapid Response Programme, and established the National AIDS and Population Secretariats in order to increase gender sensitisation of issues related to the disease, and women's health and reproductive rights.

Religion

Muslims about 90%, the rest mostly Christians. Traditional animist religions are often practised alongside both of these religions.

Media

Newspapers are in English and include *Observer* (daily), *Foroyaa*, *The Independent* and *The Point*. There are 15 TV sets and 14 personal computers per 1,000 people, and 25,000 internet users (2002).

Concerns for the future

The Gambia need to implement further macro and sectoral policies and programmes that are sensitive to gender and poverty issues through the

The Gambia | Summary of gender profile

Gender profile			1990	2000	2004
Population	Total population (000)		936	1,316	1,478
	Female population (% of total)		50.7	50.5	50.4
Labour force participation	Female labour force (% of total)		43	42	42
	Female unemployment (% of female labour force)		...	12.2	...
Education	Adult illiteracy rate (% of people aged 15+)	Female	80.3	70.3	...
		Male	68.3	56.3	...
	Net primary enrolment ratio (% of age group)	Female	40	62	...
		Male	56	71	...
	Net secondary enrolment ratio (% of age group)	Female	...	22	27
		Male	...	32	39
	Gross tertiary enrolment ratio (% of age group)	Female	...	0	0
		Male	...	2	2
Health	Life expectancy at birth (years)	Female	52	56	58
		Male	49	53	55
	Infant mortality rate (per 1,000 live births)		103	92	89
	Prevalence of HIV (% of people aged 15–24)	Female	...	2.2	...
		Male	...	0.9	...

mainstreaming process. There needs to be increased advocacy, awareness creation and campaigns that encourage positive attitudes and behaviour towards gender equality, equity and the empowerment of woman and the girl child. Access to the required resources, particularly financial and technical, needs to be addressed, and properly targeted and utilised.

Key contacts

- Mrs Ida Fye-Hydara
Executive Director
Women's Bureau
Department of State for Women's Affairs
14/15 Marina Parade
Banjul
The Gambia
Tel: +220 422 8730/33
Fax: +220 422 7214/4229846/
           992 2071
Email: womensb@qanet.gm

Ghana

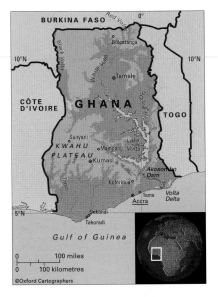

KEY FACTS

Joined Commonwealth: 1957

Capital: Accra

GDP growth (%): 2.1% p.a. 1990–2003

Official language: English

Time: GMT

Currency: cedi (C)

Main telephone lines/1,000 people: 14

Mobile phones/1,000 people: 36

National Women's Machinery

Ghana ratified CEDAW in 1986 and signed to its Optional Protocol in 2000. Its National Women's Machinery is the Ministry of Women and Children's Affairs.

The National Women's Ministry was first established in 1975 and underwent several structural changes until it was elevated to the status of a Ministry in 2001. The main task of the Ministry is to support government-wide mainstreaming of a gender-equality perspective in all policy areas. It works in collaboration with NGOs, civil society organisations and professional bodies to promote the issues and interests of women. Progress for women has been made through greater resource allocation by government, multilateral and donor agencies for training, technology transfer, credit support, health programmes, and organisational capacity building. Efforts are being made to make the transition from a Women In Development (WID) approach to the Gender and Development (GAD) approach adopted by NGOs, to work for women's well-being. This is a pragmatic step to challenge and review institutions that are inimical to progressing women's issues throughout the country, as many social and cultural customs were left unchallenged under the WID approach. The main strategy for modifying these customs has been through negotiation, implementation of policies and enactment of new laws.

Ghana is ranked at 136 in the Gender-related Development Index (GDI) in the *UNDP Human Development Report 2006*.

Priority concerns for mainstreaming gender issues

Among the 12 critical areas of concern outlined in the 1995 *Beijing Platform for Action*, the Government of Ghana has identified the following, in order of priority, for national action:

1. Women in poverty/women and the economy

2. Violence against women/women and health/education and training of women/the girl-child

3. Human rights of women/institutional mechanisms for the advancement of women

4. Women in power and decision-making

5. Women and the environment/women in the media

6. Women and armed conflict

For ease of implementation, Ghana has placed equal priority on some of the critical areas.

Women and the economy/women in poverty

The Ghana Poverty Reduction Strategy (GPRS) is the Government's response to tackling poverty. The Government has adopted strategies to deal with the effects of poverty on the household, and on women in particular. These have included introducing exemptions from paying hospital fees for pregnant, poor and elderly women; mitigating the social costs of adjustment; and introducing micro-credit schemes.

Women in power and decision-making

Traditional biases continue to limit women's access to education and training, and decision-making roles in the family and public life. Women's limited participation in politics and public service does not allow their full integration into national decision-making. Women's participation in parliament is still very low and stands at about 10%. Few women stand for election as they know little about constitutional provision, though they are beginning to become more politically aware of their civil rights.

Violence against women

The Government and NGOs have intensified efforts to address violations of women's human rights, particularly in the area of violence against women. There are a number of Women and Juvenile Units across the administrative regions, which is helping to break the silence associated with reporting domestic violence issues. There are several legislative processes underway in order to further address the issue of violence, as well as affirmative action policies to correct gender imbalance.

Education

Public spending on education was 4.1% of GDP in 1999/2000. There are nine years of compulsory education starting at age six. Net enrolment ratios are 59% for primary education and 36% for secondary (2003/04). The pupil–teacher ratio for primary is 32:1 and for secondary 19:1. The school year starts in September.

About 3% of the relevant age group is enrolled in tertiary education (4% of males and 2% of females, 2003/04). There are five universities, including the most recently established University for Development Studies at Tamale. There are many teacher-training colleges, polytechnics and specialised tertiary institutions.

The girl-child

The Education Strategic Plan 2003–2015 has provided for a capitation graduated in favour of girls, in order to cover the costs prescribed under school levies, thus minimising the cost of education to the family. Provisions have been made to ensure access and participation of all children, especially the girl-child. Education facilities in all districts are undergoing rehabilitation, and additional schools are being created in areas where such services are lacking.

The Girl's Education Unit was established in 1997 to facilitate and advocate for the education of girls. It has developed a programme that promotes education of girls as a means of attaining gender parity throughout the rest of society.

Health

Public hospital and other medical care is provided at nominal rates. As well as public hospitals and clinics, some are private and some operated by religious missions. 79% of the population uses an improved drinking water source and 58% adequate sanitation facilities (2002). Infant mortality was 68 per 1,000 live births in 2004 (126 in 1960). AIDS, malaria and tuberculosis pose serious problems, and there have been cases of yellow fever, bilharzia and intestinal worms in rural areas. At the end of 2003, 3.1% of people age 15 to 49 were HIV-positive.

Women and health

Women's health is determined by three main factors: geographical access to health-care facilities; financial access; and socio-cultural access. Approximately 60% of Ghanaians are within 8kms of the nearest health care facility, but there is a lack of access in some northern regions. Poor women are less likely to be capable of accessing health care, there has been an exemption policy implemented for pre-natal visits to assist in this regard.

Women's health is a priority and is being addressed under the National Reproductive Health Programme. The programme comprises safe motherhood practices including infant health, family planning and management of STI/HIV/AIDS infections and reproductive health. 56% of HIV/AIDS infections affect women.

Ghana	Summary of gender profile				
Gender profile			1990	2000	2004
Population	Total population (000)		15,479	19,867	21,664
	Female population (% of total)		49.6	49.5	49.4
Labour force participation	Female labour force (% of total)		49	49	48
	Female unemployment (% of female labour force)		…	8.7	…
Education	Adult illiteracy rate (% of people aged 15+)	Female	52.8	…	50.2
		Male	29.9	…	33.6
	Net primary enrolment ratio (% of age group)	Female	50	60	62
		Male	57	62	62
	Net secondary enrolment ratio (% of age group)	Female	…	29	33
		Male	…	34	39
	Gross tertiary enrolment ratio (% of age group)	Female	0	1	2
		Male	2	4	4
Health	Life expectancy at birth (years)	Female	58	57	58
		Male	55	56	57
	Infant mortality rate (per 1,000 live births)		75	68	68
	Prevalence of HIV (% of people aged 15–24)	Female	…	3.4	…
		Male	…	1.4	…

Religion

Christians 63%, Muslims 16%, and traditional animist religions are often practised alongside both of these religions.

Media

Daily Graphic and *Ghanaian Times* (both state-owned), and The *Accra Daily Mail* are daily newspapers. The *Ghanaian Chronicle* publishes three times a week, and *Ghana Palaver*, *The Independent*, *The Mirror* and *Sunday Herald* are weeklies. There are 53 TV sets and 4 personal computers per 1,000 people, and 170,000 internet users (2002).

Concerns for the future

Ghana will continue to focus on education and training for women, implementing health strategies, and programmes to tackle poverty among women. Though affirmative action, the government hopes to increase the numbers of women participating in all levels of decision-making.

Key contacts

- Mrs Marian A Tackie
  Executive Director and Head
  Ministry of Women and Children's Affairs
  PO Box M-186
  Accra
  Ghana
  Tel: +233 21 688 180/7
  Fax: +233 21 688 182

Grenada

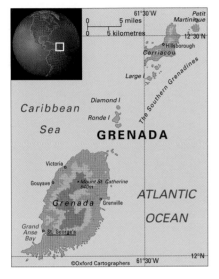

KEY FACTS

Joined Commonwealth: 1981

Capital: St John's

GDP growth (%): 1.6% p.a. 1990–2004

Official language: English

Time: GMT minus 4 hours

Currency: Eastern Caribbean dollar (EC$)

Main telephone lines/1,000 people: 488

Mobile phones/1,000 people: 490

National Women's Machinery

Grenada acceded to CEDAW in 1990. Its National Women's Machinery is the Department of Gender and Family Affairs in the Ministry of Social Development.

Grenada is ranked at 85 in the Gender-related Development Index (GDI) in the *UNDP Human Development Report 2006*.

Priority concerns for mainstreaming gender issues

Among the 12 critical areas of concern outlined in the 1995 *Beijing Platform for Action*, the Government of Grenada has identified the following, in order of priority, for national action:

1. Institutional mechanisms for the advancement of women

2. Women and poverty

3. Education and training of women

4. Violence against women

5. Women and health

Followed by: 6. Women and the economy; 7. Women in power and decision-making; 8. Human rights of women; 9. Women in the media; 10. Women and the environment.

Women and the economy

Grenada has one of the highest unemployment rates in the Caribbean. Unemployment is particularly high among young people and people living in rural areas. The causes of poverty in Grenada are complex. They are related to historical and economic factors, including the vulnerability of the economy because of the country's small size and its exposure to natural disaster. The destructive tropical storms and hurricanes that roar through the islands are a factor in keeping poor people from overcoming poverty. In

Grenada, as in much of the Caribbean, a large number (about 45 per cent) of households are headed by women. This is often the result of out-migration by men in search of employment. Teenage pregnancy is also common, and many young mothers have to end their schooling and look for work to provide for their children. Poverty and the limitations of a small island economy affect rural youth, restricting their opportunity to complete schooling or to find employment.

Education

Public spending on education was 5.1% of GDP in 2002/03. There are 12 years of compulsory education starting at age five. The net enrolment ratio is 96% for secondary education. The pupil–teacher ratio for primary education is 19:1 and for secondary 20:1. The school year starts in September.

Health

There are three hospitals: General Hospital (St George's), Princess Alice Hospital (St Andrew's) and Princess Royal Hospital (Carriacou). There are homes for handicapped children and geriatric patients. Health centres and district medical stations undertake maternity and child welfare work under the charge of a nurse/midwife. Government hospitals and clinics provide free medical and dental treatment. There is a piped-water supply to all the towns and to many of the villages and 95% of the population uses an improved drinking water source and 97% adequate sanitation facilities (2002). Infant mortality was 18 per 1,000 live births in 2004.

Religion

Mainly Christians (Roman Catholics 53%, Anglicans 14%, Seventh Day Adventists, Methodists).

Media

There are no daily newspapers, but *The Grenada Guardian*, *The Grenada Informer*, *The Grenada Times*, *Grenada Today* and *The Grenadian Voice* are weeklies. There are 132 personal computers per 1,000 people and 19,000 internet users (2002/2003).

Concerns for the future

There will be continued focus on women and poverty, and education and training of women.

Key contacts

- The Hon Yolande Bain-Joseph, MP
  Minister
  Ministry of Social Development
  Ministerial Complex, Botanical Gardens
  Tanteen
  St George's
  Grenada
  Tel: +1 473 440 7952
  Fax: +1 473 440 7990
  Email: grenwomen@caribsurf.com
          mhousing@hotmail.com

Grenada | Summary of gender profile

Gender profile			1990	2000	2004
Population	Total population (000)		94	101	102
	Female population (% of total)		…	…	…
Labour force participation	Female labour force (% of total)		…	…	…
	Female unemployment (% of female labour force)		12.8	21.3	…
Education	Adult illiteracy rate (% of people aged 15+)	Female	…	…	…
		Male	…	…	…
	Net primary enrolment ratio (% of age group)	Female	…	80	…
		Male	…	89	…
	Net secondary enrolment ratio (% of age group)	Female	…	…	…
		Male	…	…	…
	Gross tertiary enrolment ratio (% of age group)	Female	…	…	…
		Male	…	…	…
Health	Life expectancy at birth (years)	Female	…	76	76
		Male	…	69	70
	Infant mortality rate (per 1,000 live births)		30	21	18
	Prevalence of HIV (% of people aged 15–24)	Female	…	…	…
		Male	…	…	…

Guyana

©Oxford Cartographers

KEY FACTS

Joined Commonwealth: 1966

Capital: Georgetown

GDP growth (%): 3.6% p.a. 1990–2003

Official language: English

Time: GMT minus 4 hours

Currency: Guyana dollar (G$)

Main telephone lines/1,000 people: 92

Mobile phones/1,000 people: 99

National Women's Machinery

Guyana ratified CEDAW in 1980. Its National Women's Machinery is the Women's Affairs Bureau in the Ministry of Human Services and Social Security. The Women's Affairs Bureau is the de facto coordinating mechanism for all policy implementation relating to gender equality. In addition to the Bureau there are two further bodies that are key to the implementation of gender equality measures: the Inter-Ministry Committee on Gender, which ensures that the programmes of their respective ministries and agencies are gender sensitive and non-discriminatory; and the Women and Gender Equality Commission.

There are also Regional Women's Desks in the ten administrative regions of Guyana, each with an appointed Regional Women's Affairs Officer. These Officers are mandated to address matters relating to women's concerns at a regional level. The aim of this initiative is to strengthen the implementation capacity of the regional mechanisms for regional project and programme delivery.

Guyana is ranked at 103 in the Gender-related Development Index (GDI) in the *UNDP Human Development Report 2006.*

Priority concerns for mainstreaming gender issues

The Government of Guyana's critical areas of concern under its National Plan of Action, which also link with components of the 1995 *Beijing Platform for Action* are:

- Women and poverty

- Education and training

- Women and health

- Violence against women

- Women in power and decision-making

- Women with disabilities

- Situation of indigenous women

- The girl-child.

Women in power and decision-making

While some rights have been accorded to women through the constitution and the electoral system, the opportunity for equal status of women resulted from strong lobbying by women's groups. The number of women in Parliament increased from 18.5% in 2000 to 29% in 2006. There is no formal mechanism which prevents the representation of women at national and international levels, although women are not adequately represented in top-level decision-making positions. Women have improved their professional and technical status through their educational endeavours, but are still in the minority in the national administration. Measures to promote the advancement of women have included a National Democratic Institute training programme for parliamentarians and women in local government. There is greater participation of women at the community level.

Education

Public spending on education was 8.4% of GDP in 2002/03. There are ten years of compulsory education starting at age six. The net enrolment ratio is 99% for primary education. The pupil–teacher ratio for primary education is 27:1 and for secondary 20:1. The school year starts in September. About 6% of the relevant age group is enrolled in tertiary education (2002/03).

Health

The Public Hospital at Georgetown is the national referral hospital; there are some 30 hospitals and many health centres throughout the country, with both public and private care available, the former usually free. 83% of the population uses an improved drinking water source and 70% adequate sanitation facilities (2002). Infant mortality was 48 per 1,000 live births in 2004 (100 in 1960). At the end of 2003, 2.5% of people age 15 to 49 were HIV-positive.

Women and health

The core objectives of the health sector are to increase the life span for all Guyanese, to reduce disparities among social groups, to improve the nation's access to health care, improve the quality of care offered and to ensure that health services are provided at an affordable cost. The Ministry of Health is developing programmes to address gender-specific health issues such as reproductive health, the impact of STDs and HIV/AIDS, cancer, poor nutrition, and maternal morbidity and mortality. Gender-sensitivity analysis is also being included in the planning, implementation, monitoring and evaluation of all health programmes. Information systems are being designed to provide adequate gender-differentiated information in support of policy and decision-making processes.

Guyana has a Strategic Plan for HIV/AIDS in order to provide a co-ordinated response to the HIV/AIDS epidemic. Women have become a particularly vulnerable group due to poverty, lack of education and unemployment. 55% of all HIV/AIDS cases are women. The Women's Affairs Bureau mobilises women through NGO and civil society involvement, collaborating with the National AIDS Secretariat in the implementation of the Strategic Plan. The Government has allocated additional financial resources to the health sector for the HIV/AIDS control programmes.

Religion

Christians 50%, Hindus 35%, Muslims 10%.

Media

The state-owned *Guyana Chronicle/Sunday Chronicle* and privately-owned *Stabroek News* are dailies. The *Catholic Standard* and *Kaieteur News* are weekly, and *Mirror* twice weekly. There are 27 personal computers per 1,000 people and 125,000 internet users (2002).

Concerns for the future

There will be continuing focus on empowerment of women through education and training, reform of legislation to continue to improve the participation of women in decision-making positions and strategies to eliminate violence against women.

Key contacts

- Ms Hymawattie Lagan
  Administrator
  Ministry of Human Services & Social Security
  1 Water and Cornhill Streets
  Georgetown
  Guyana
  Tel: +592 225 4362/9162
  Fax: +592 225 3497

Guyana | Summary of gender profile

Gender profile			1990	2000	2004
Population	Total population (000)		729	744	750
	Female population (% of total)		51.4	51.5	51.5
Labour force participation	Female labour force (% of total)		33	36	37
	Female unemployment (% of female labour force)		18.1	14.3	...
Education	Adult illiteracy rate (% of people aged 15+)	Female	3.6	1.9	...
		Male	2	1.1	...
	Net primary enrolment ratio (% of age group)	Female	89	97	99
		Male	89	100	100
	Net secondary enrolment ratio (% of age group)	Female	69	72	...
		Male	65	68	...
	Gross tertiary enrolment ratio (% of age group)	Female	4	8	9
		Male	8	12	14
Health	Life expectancy at birth (years)	Female	59	64	64
		Male	59	62	63
	Infant mortality rate (per 1,000 live births)		80	68	62
	Prevalence of HIV (% of people aged 15–24)	Female	...	4	...
		Male	...	3.3	...

India

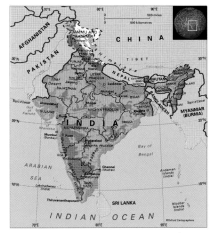

The designations and the presentation of material on this map, based on UN practice, do not imply the expression of any opinion whatsoever on the part of the Commonwealth Secretariat or the publishers concerning the legal status of any country, territory or area, or of its authorities, or concerning the delimitation of its frontiers or boundaries. There is no intention to define the status of Jammu and/or Kashmir, which has not yet been agreed upon by the parties.

KEY FACTS

Joined Commonwealth: 1947

Capital: New Delhi

GDP growth (%): 4.0% p.a. 1990–2003

Official languages: Hindi, English

Time: GMT plus 5.5 hours

Currency: rupee (Rs)

Main telephone lines/1,000 people: 46

Mobile phones/1,000 people: 25

National Women's Machinery

India ratified CEDAW in 1993. Its National Women's Machinery is the Department of Women Development in the Ministry of Women and Child Development. In addition to formulating policies and programmes, it enacts and amends legislation affecting women and children, and co-ordinates the efforts of government and NGOs. There are four autonomous organisations working under the Department:

- The National Commission for Women (NCW), which supports the Department in protecting women's rights and privileges;

- The National Institute of Public Co-ordination and Child Development, which undertakes research and training;

- The Rashtriya Mahila Kosh (RMK), which has links for women in the informal sector for entrepreneurial activities;

- The Central Social Welfare Board (CSWB), an umbrella body for networking with state social welfare boards and voluntary organisations.

Gender mainstreaming is one of the cornerstones of budgeting and policy initiatives in India. To ensure gender-sensitive resource allocation and engender macroeconomic policy, the importance of gender issues is reflected not only in the National Policy for the Empowerment of Women, but also in the Tenth Five Year Plan (2002–2007).

India is ranked at 126 in the Gender-related Development Index (GDI) in the *UNDP Human Development Report 2006*.

Priority concerns for mainstreaming gender issues

Among the 12 critical areas of concern outlined in the 1995 *Beijing Platform for Action*, the Government of India has identified the following, in order of priority,

for national action:

1. Education and training of women

2. Women and health

3. The girl-child

4. Women and poverty

5. Women and the economy

Followed by: 6. Institutional mechanisms for the advancement of women; 7. Human rights of women; 8. Violence against women; 9. Women in power and decision-making; 10. Women and armed conflict; 11. Women in the media; 12. Women and the environment.

Women in power and decision-making

The Government has taken several initiatives, including affirmative action, to overcome the historical and political disadvantages faced by women, enabling them to enter and effectively participate in the decision-making process. Though women have been entering the political arena, the number of women holding positions of power is extremely low. In the 2004 elections, the number of women MPs was 44 out of 539, a decrease from 49 women in the previous parliament.

Institutional mechanisms for the advancement of women

The National Policy for the Advancement of Women aims to bring about the advancement, development and empowerment of women. It aims to create an environment for the full development of women through positive economic and social policies, enabling them to realise their full potential, ensure equal access to health care, education, employment, social security, and participation in decision-making. The policy ascribes affirmative action in areas such as the legal system, decision-making structures, access to micro-credit, and the development of gender-development indices.

Violence against women

Swadhar was launched in 2001, as a flexible and innovative approach to catering for the requirements of women in difficult circumstances. It focuses on the rehabilitation of sex workers, women offered to temples, women in social and moral danger, single/elderly/disabled/widowed women and all other women in difficult situations. The scheme provides shelter, counselling and training for women in those circumstances who do not have any social or economic support.

Violence against women is also being addressed through the Tenth Five Year Plan, through a well-planned programme of action, with short- and long-term evaluatory measures at national and state levels. The Government also aims to bring about the necessary amendments to the Indian Penal Code and other legislations.

Women and the economy

The Government has initiated a number of direct and indirect measures for the economic empowerment of women. The

National Policy for the Empowerment of Women includes a framework within which efforts are taken to ensure the inclusion of women's perspectives in the design and implementation of macro-economic, industrial and development policies. Women's contribution in economic development as entrepreneurs, producers and workers has been formally recognised in the formal and informal sectors.

Education

Public spending on education was 4.1% of GDP in 2000/01. There are nine years of compulsory education starting at age six. The primary net enrolment ratio is 88%. The pupil–teacher ratio for primary education is 41:1 and for secondary 33:1 (2002/03). The school year starts in April.

About 12% of the relevant age group is enrolled in tertiary education (14% of males and 10% of females, 2002/03). There are over 200 universities, 9,000 colleges and 1,000 polytechnics, including some 150 medical colleges. There are schemes to reserve places for scheduled (lowest) castes and scheduled tribes in certain colleges and universities, and special boarding schools for talented children with priority given to those from rural areas. Illiteracy among

people age 15–24 is 23.6% (15.8% for males and 32.3% for females, 2001 census).

Health

Primary health care is provided in rural areas by more than 20,000 centres, backed by sub-centres, community health centres and dispensaries. Western medicine predominates, although Ayurvedic medicine is also practised. The Ayurvedic tradition also gave rise to homeopathy (some 365,000 practitioners). 86% of the population uses an improved drinking water source and 30% adequate sanitation facilities (2002). Infant mortality was 62 per 1,000 live births in 2004 (146 in 1960). National health programmes have been established to combat malaria, filaria, sexually transmitted diseases (including AIDS), leprosy and tuberculosis. Family welfare centres give advice and education on family planning. At the end of 2003, 0.9% of people aged 15–49 were HIV-positive.

Women and health

The National Health Policy facilitates increased access to basic health care and provides holistic health care for women. It

India — Summary of gender profile

Gender profile			1990	2000	2004
Population	Total population (000)		849,515	1,015,923	1,087,124
	Female population (% of total)		48.4	48.6	48.7
Labour force participation	Female labour force (% of total)		30	28	28
	Female unemployment (% of female labour force)		...	20.3	...
Education	Adult illiteracy rate (% of people aged 15+)	Female	64.1	...	52.2
		Male	38.1	...	26.6
	Net primary enrolment ratio (% of age group)	Female	...	75	84
		Male	...	91	90
	Net secondary enrolment ratio (% of age group)	Female	...	...	...
		Male	...	...	...
	Gross tertiary enrolment ratio (% of age group)	Female	4	8	9
		Male	8	12	14
Health	Life expectancy at birth (years)	Female	59	64	64
		Male	59	62	63
	Infant mortality rate (per 1,000 live births)		80	68	62
	Prevalence of HIV (% of people aged 15–24)	Female	...	0.6	...
		Male	...	0.4	...

commits high priority to the funding of initiatives relating to women. Improvement in the health status of women is sought to be achieved through access and utilisation of health, family welfare and nutrition services, with special focus on the underprivileged segments of the population. Government has committed to increasing public investment in programmes to control all communicable diseases, and to provide leadership efforts to control HIV/AIDS. 28% of all HIV/AIDS infections are in women.

Religion

Hindus 81%, Muslims 12%, Christians 2%, Sikhs 2%, Buddhists, Jains.

Media

The leading English-language dailies are *Deccan Herald* (Bangalore), *The Hindu* (Chennai), *The Hindustan Times* (New Delhi), *The Indian Express* (New Delhi), *The Pioneer* (New Delhi), *The Statesman* (Kolkata) and *The Times of India* (Mumbai), and *India Today* and *Outlook* are weekly news magazines. There are more than 4,000 daily newspapers published in some 90 languages. Private TV channels have been allowed since 1992 and private radio stations since 2000, though publicly owned All India Radio is the only radio network permitted to broadcast news. There are 83 TV sets and seven personal computers per 1,000 people, and 18.48 million internet users (2002/2003).

Concerns for the future

Despite the constitutional mandate of equal status for men and women, there is still much to be done to achieve this. There will be continued efforts focused on addressing illiteracy, social practices, cultural norms based on patriarchal hierarchy, poor representation of women in policy-making, poverty, regional disparity in development and lack of access to information and resources.

Key contacts

- Ms Parul Debi Das
  Joint Secretary
  Department of Women
  Ministry of Women and Child
  Development
  Jeeva Deep Building, Parliament Street
  New Delhi 110001
  India
  Tel: +91 11 2338 1654
  Fax: +91 11 2307 0480
  Email: pddas@sb.nic.in

- Mrs Katruri Gupta Menon
  Under Secretary
  Department of Women
  Ministry of Women and Child
  Development
  Shastri Bhavan, 'A' Wing,
  Dr Rajendra Prasad Rd
  New Delhi 110001
  India
  Tel: +91 11 2338 2747
  Fax: +91 11 2307 0480
  Email: secy.wcd@sb.nic.in

Jamaica

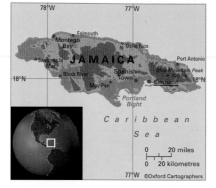

KEY FACTS

Joined Commonwealth: 1962

Capital: Kingston

GDP growth (%): 0.0% p.a. 1990–2003

Official language: English

Time: GMT minus 5 hours

Currency: Jamaican dollar (J$)

Main telephone lines/1,000 people: 169

Mobile phones/1,000 people: 681

National Women's Machinery

Jamaica acceded to CEDAW in 1984. Its National Women's Machinery is the Bureau of Women's Affairs in the Office of the Prime Minister.

Jamaica is ranked at 104 in the Gender-related Development Index (GDI) in the *UNDP Human Development Report 2006*.

Priority concerns for mainstreaming gender issues

Among the 12 critical areas of concern outlined in the 1995 *Beijing Platform for Action*, the Government of Jamaica has identified the following, in order of priority, for national action:

1. Violence against women

2. Women in poverty

3. Women and health

4. Human rights of women

5. Education and training of women

Followed by: 6. Institutional mechanisms for the advancement of women; 7. Women in power and decision-making; 8. Women and the economy; 9. The girl-child.

Women and the economy

Women need expanded economic opportunities, through avenues such as education and skills training, so as to take advantage of emerging market opportunities and to realise their productive potential. One agency geared towards advancing the economic empowerment of women is the Jamaica Network of Rural Women Producer (PNRWP). It was established in 1999 and its objectives include promoting co-operation among rural women, and creating partnerships with institutions and the private sector in support of micro-credit development, and to create sustainable employment opportunities for its members.

Women in power and decision-making

Although women have been making strides professionally and using their educational opportunities to good effect, they still continue to be under-represented at the highest levels of governance, power and decision-making. In the 2002 elections, only seven out of 60 elected were women. The composition of corporate boards in Jamaica remain male-dominated.

Violence against women

The Domestic Violence Act was passed in 1995, with a view to providing additional remedies for the victims of domestic violence. The passage of this Act allowed for domestic violence to be specifically recognised, with the provision of civil remedies, such as injunctive relief and awards of damages.

Trafficking in women and girls for the purpose of the sex trade, and also sex tourism are issues of concern. Women and girls who are subject to trafficking and sex tourism, face an increased risk of violence as well as increased risk of further violation, unwanted pregnancies, STIs and HIV infection.

In order to address the problems of violence against women in all spheres, the government will focus on rehabilitation, prevention, free education and training, and taking account of the special needs of the girl-child.

Education

Public spending on education was 4.9% of GDP in 2002/03. There are six years of compulsory education starting at age six. Net enrolment ratios are 95% for primary education and 75% for secondary. The pupil–teacher ratio for primary education is 30:1 and for secondary 20:1. The school year starts in September.

About 17% of the relevant age group is enrolled in tertiary education (10% of males and 25% of females, 2002/03). Illiteracy among people age 15–24 is 5.5% (8.7% for males and 2.2% for females, 2002).

Health

There are more than 20 hospitals, mostly public, and many health centres. Hospital services and government medical care are subsidised, patients paying modest fees related to their income. Around 9% of the population has private health insurance. 93% of the population uses an improved drinking water source and 80% adequate sanitation facilities (2002). Infant mortality was 17 per 1,000 live births in 2004 (56 in 1960). At the end of 2003, 1.2% of people age 15 to 49 were HIV positive.

Religion

Mainly Christians (Church of God 21%, Baptists 9%, Seventh Day Adventists 9%, Pentecostals 8%, Anglicans 6%), and there is also a significant Rastafarian community.

Media

National dailies are *The Gleaner*, *Jamaica Observer* and *Daily Star* (evenings), and all have weekend editions. *Sunday Herald* is a weekly. There are 374 TV sets and 54 personal computers per 1,000 people, and 600,000 internet users (2002).

Concerns for the future

Violence against women continues to be a major social and human rights problem, despite the initiatives at government, private and NGO levels. More public education is needed about the dangers of unprotected sex in order to address the growing problem of HIV/AIDS.

Key contacts

- Faith Webster
  Director
  The Bureau of Women's Affairs
  4 Ellesmere Road
  Kingston 10
  Jamaica
  Tel: +1 876 929 6244/0542
  Fax: +1 876 929 0549
  Email: jbwa@cwjamaica.com

Jamaica | Summary of gender profile

Gender profile			1990	2000	2004
Population	Total population (000)		2,390	2,589	2,639
	Female population (% of total)		51	50.7	50.6
Labour force participation	Female labour force (% of total)		47	45	44
	Female unemployment (% of female labour force)		23.1	22.3	15.7
Education	Adult illiteracy rate (% of people aged 15+)	Female	13.9	...	14.1
		Male	22.1	...	25.9
	Net primary enrolment ratio (% of age group)	Female	96	90	89
		Male	96	90	88
	Net secondary enrolment ratio (% of age group)	Female	65	79	77
		Male	62	76	74
	Gross tertiary enrolment ratio (% of age group)	Female	6	20	26
		Male	8	11	12
Health	Life expectancy at birth (years)	Female	73	73	73
		Male	70	69	69
	Infant mortality rate (per 1,000 live births)		17	17	17
	Prevalence of HIV (% of people aged 15–24)	Female	...	0.6	...
		Male	...	0.4	...

Kenya

KEY FACTS

Joined Commonwealth: 1963

Capital: Nairobi

GDP growth (%): –0.6% p.a. 1990–2003

Official language: English

Time: GMT plus 3 hours

Currency: Kenyan shilling (KSh)

Main telephone lines/1,000 people: 10

Mobile phones/1,000 people: 50

National Women's Machinery

Kenya acceded to CEDAW in 1984. Its National Women's Machinery is the Department of Gender in the Ministry of Gender, Culture, Sports and Social Services. The Department has a broad mandate for co-ordinating and mainstreaming gender issues in all spheres of development. There are also gender focal points in a number of key ministries to ensure that the gender perspective is incorporated into all relevant policies and programmes.

The National Policy on Gender and Development provides a framework for the advancement of women in the political, economic, social and cultural areas. It also provides a mechanism for the initiation, lobbying and advocating for legal reforms on issues affecting women, and can formulate laws, policies and programmes that eliminate all forms of discrimination against women in all institutions.

Kenya is ranked at 152 in the Gender-related Development Index (GDI) in the *UNDP Human Development Report 2006*.

Priority concerns for mainstreaming gender issues

Among the 12 critical areas of concern outlined in the 1995 *Beijing Platform for Action*, the Government of Kenya has identified the following for priority action:

- Women and poverty

- Violence against women

- Education and training of women

- Women and health.

Women and the economy

Efforts are being made by the government and community support organisations to enable women to access micro-finance credit. The challenges that women continue to face include lack of capacity in terms of skills and other managerial competencies that would allow them to effectively utilise funds to operate micro-enterprise. There are programmes in place that seek to build the capacity of women in entrepreneurship.

Women in power and decision-making

There has been a progressive increase in women's participation in strategic decision-making positions such as Parliament, Central Government, Local Authorities, Trade Unions, Professional Bodies and Land Boards. In the 2002 elections, 16 out of 219 MPs elected were women. Some of the factors that continue to impede women's participation in politics are inadequate resources, social-cultural attitudes which do not encourage women, violence and the patronage-based nature of politics in Kenya.

Education

Public spending on education was 7.0% of GDP in 2002/03. There are eight years of compulsory education starting at age six. Net enrolment ratios are 66% for primary education and 25% for secondary. The pupil–teacher ratio for primary education is 30:1 and for secondary 26:1. The school year starts in January.

About 3% of the relevant age group is enrolled in tertiary education (2001/02). Illiteracy among people age 15–24 is 19.7% (20.2% for males and 19.3% for females, 2000).

Health

62% of the population uses an improved drinking water source and 48% adequate sanitation facilities (2002). Infant mortality was 79 per 1,000 live births in 2004 (122 in 1960). Malaria is the main endemic health problem, and AIDS is a severe problem. At the end of 2003, 6.7% of people age 15 to 49 were HIV positive.

Women and health

The health status of the population has been steadily improving, but there are still challenges facing the Government, such as the decline in life expectancy due to HIV/AIDS. 57% of those with the disease are women.

Kenya has implemented a health policy framework to address health care service delivery including curative services, preventative and information services, increased health personnel, and drugs and pharmaceutical supplies. The Government has pledged to improve maternal and child health services, to provide immunisation against vaccine preventable diseases, and to improve nutrition standards of the vulnerable.

Religion

Christians 78% (mainly Protestants and Roman Catholics), Muslims 10%, and most of the rest hold traditional beliefs.

Media

English-language daily newspapers are *Daily Nation*, *Kenya Times* (owned by Kenya African National Union), *East African Standard* and *The People Daily*. *Taifa Leo* is published daily in Kiswahili. Weeklies include *The East African* (for an international audience). There are 26 TV sets and 7 personal computers per 1,000 people, and 400,000 internet users (2002).

Concerns for the future

New and continuing challenges include the problem of female genital mutilation, which, since it was prohibited, has meant that women are under pressure to undergo the rite in adulthood. There has also been an increase in violence against women, particularly sexual violence. HIV/AIDS will also continue to be a health and socio-economic concern.

Key contacts

- Mrs Juliet Kola
  Head, Women's Bureau
  Ministry of Gender, Sports, Culture & Social Services
  NSSF Building
  P O Box 30276
  Nairobi
  Kenya
  Tel: +254 20 608 741
  Fax: +254 20 608 741
  Email: genderdep@nbnet.co.ke

Kenya | Summary of gender profile

Gender profile			1990	2000	2004
Population	Total population (000)		23,430	30,689	33,467
	Female population (% of total)		50.2	50.2	50
Labour force participation	Female labour force (% of total)		46	44	44
	Female unemployment (% of female labour force)		...	...	...
Education	Adult illiteracy rate (% of people aged 15+)	Female	39.2	...	29.8
		Male	19.1	...	22.3
	Net primary enrolment ratio (% of age group)	Female	...	68	77
		Male	...	66	76
	Net secondary enrolment ratio (% of age group)	Female	...	23	...
		Male	...	23	...
	Gross tertiary enrolment ratio (% of age group)	Female	1	3	...
		Male	2	3	...
Health	Life expectancy at birth (years)	Female	60	48	47
		Male	56	49	49
	Infant mortality rate (per 1,000 live births)		64	77	79
	Prevalence of HIV (% of people aged 15–24)	Female	...	13	...
		Male	...	6.4	...

Kiribati

KEY FACTS

Joined Commonwealth: 1979

Capital: Tarawa

GDP growth (%): 2.7% p.a. 1990–2003

Official language: English

Time: GMT plus 12–14 hours

Currency: Australian dollar

Main telephone lines/1,000 people: 51

Mobile phones/1,000 people: 6

National Women's Machinery

Kiribati acceded to CEDAW in 2004. Its National Women's Machinery is Aia Maea Ainen Kiribati (AMAK) which is a semi-governmental body working within the Ministry of Internal and Social Affairs.

Priority concerns for mainstreaming gender issues

Among the 12 critical areas of concern outlined in the 1995 *Beijing Platform for Action*, the Government of Kiribati has identified the following, in order of priority, for national action:

1. Human Rights of Women

2. Women in Power and Decision-making

3. Women and the Economy

4. Women and Health

5. Violence Against Women

Followed by: 6. Education and Training of Women; 7. The Girl-child; 8. Women and Poverty; 9. Institutional Mechanisms for the Advancement of Women; 10. Women and the Environment; 11. Women in the Media; 12. Women and Armed Conflict.

Women and the economy

Kiribati has made some significant progress in gender equity, notably through the education system. The socio-economic status of women is improving with more equal access to education. However, the role of women on the outer islands is still confined largely to domestic duties and food duties, land tenure and local politics are reserved mainly for men.

Education

There are 10 years of compulsory education starting at age six. The pupil–teacher ratio for primary is 22:1 (2002/03). The school year starts in January.

Health

64% of the population uses an improved drinking water source and 39% adequate sanitation facilities (2002). Infant mortality was 49 per 1,000 live births in 2004. Tuberculosis is a serious public health problem; there are regular outbreaks of dengue fever and occasional cases of leprosy and typhoid. The first AIDS case was reported in Tarawa in 1991.

Religion

Christianity is the predominant religion, more than 50% of the people being Roman Catholic. Tamara and Arorae are mostly Protestant. There is a small Baha'i minority.

Media

Te Uekera, a weekly newspaper published by the Broadcasting and Publications Authority, is mainly in I-Kiribati, but with main news items also in English. *Kiribati Newstar* is an independent weekly. The Roman Catholic and Protestant churches publish newsletters. There is no national television service. There are 2,000 internet users (2002).

Concerns for the future

There is a lack of financial and human resources for promoting gender equality, and the national women's machinery will need to be strengthened in order to further advance gender issues throughout the country. Policies, legislations and programmes need to be evaluated in order to ensure that they take account of women's rights. Areas of focus will be tackling the prevalence of HIV/AIDS, improving access to education and training, especially in the outer islands, implementing strategies to increase participation of women in the decision-making process, combating violence against women including trafficking, and improving the collecting and dissemination of sex-disaggregated data to inform policies and programmes.

Key contacts

• Mr Manikaoti Timeon
  Deputy Secretary
  Ministry of Internal & Social Affairs
  PO Box 75, Bairiki
  Tarawa
  Kiribati
  Tel: +686 21092
  Fax: +686 21133
  Email: homeaffairs@tskl.net.ki

Kiribati | Summary of gender profile

Gender profile			1990	2000	2004
Population	Total population (000)		72	91	97
	Female population (% of total)		...	49.5	...
Labour force participation	Female labour force (% of total)		...	...	...
	Female unemployment (% of female labour force)		...	...	...
Education	Adult illiteracy rate (% of people aged 15+)	Female	...	...	...
		Male	...	...	...
	Net primary enrolment ratio (% of age group)	Female	...	...	...
		Male	...	...	...
	Net secondary enrolment ratio (% of age group)	Female	...	...	...
		Male	...	...	...
	Gross tertiary enrolment ratio (% of age group)	Female	...	...	...
		Male	...	...	...
Health	Life expectancy at birth (years)	Female	59	65	66
		Male	55	59	60
	Infant mortality rate (per 1,000 live births)		65	52	49
	Prevalence of HIV (% of people aged 15–24)	Female	...	...	...
		Male	...	...	...

Lesotho

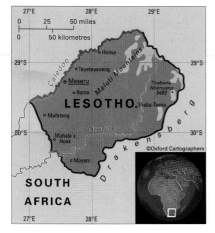

KEY FACTS

Joined Commonwealth: 1966

Capital: Maseru

GDP growth (%): 2.4% p.a. 1990–2003

Official languages: Sesotho, English

Time: GMT plus 2 hours

Currency: loti, plural maloti (M)

Main telephone lines/1,000 people: 16

Mobile phones/1,000 people: 47

National Women's Machinery

Lesotho acceded to CEDAW in 1995 and to its Optional Protocol in 2004. Its National Women's Machinery is the Department of Gender in the Ministry of Gender and Youth, Sports and Recreation.

The Department of Gender ensures equality of all opportunities between women, men, girls and boys, so that development efforts have an equal impact on all gender issues. The aim is to facilitate proper integration of gender issues in development to ensure full involvement, participation and partnership of women and men, girls and boys in both their productive lives. The Department takes gender concerns into account in all national and sectoral policies, programmes, budgets and plans in order to achieve gender equality in the development process.

In order to carry out its mandate, the Department is organised into three areas of operation which are very closely inter-related; economic empowerment, which is concerned with poverty eradication;, social empowerment, which deals with the fight against gender-based violence and HIV/AIDS; and political empowerment; which advocates for equal representation and participation of women and men in politics and decision-making positions of society.

The work of the Department is essentially one of advocacy for gender equality in all aspects of development in the country. Since advocacy calls for public awareness and education, the Department makes its services available to the public through the print and electronic media, workshops and meetings, public activities and commemoration of special dates.

The Gender and Development Policy aims to advance gender equity and equality through capacity building, socio-economic and political empowerment, as well as networking with government, civil society organisations and NGOs.

Lesotho is ranked at 149 in the Gender-related Development Index (GDI) in the *UNDP Human Development Report 2006.*

Priority concerns for mainstreaming gender issues

Among the 12 critical areas of concern outlined in the 1995 *Beijing Platform for Action*, the Government of Lesotho has identified the following, in order of priority, for national action:

1. Women and Poverty / Women and the Economy

2. Education and Training of Women / Institutional Mechanisms for the Advancement of Women

3. Women and Armed Conflict / Women in Power and Decision-making / Human Rights of Women

4. Women and Health

5. Violence Against Women / The Girl-child

Followed by: 6. Women in the Media; 7. Women and the Environment.

Some areas of concern have been linked as they fall under one priority area in the Lesotho Gender and Development Policy.

Women and poverty

The Poverty Reduction Strategy aims to address the part of the population that lives below the poverty line. It aims to create jobs, increase governance, improve infrastructure, health and social welfare, and increase public service delivery.

Education

Public spending on education was 10.4% of GDP in 2001/02. There are seven years of compulsory education starting at age six. Net enrolment ratios are 86% for primary and 22% for secondary (2002/03). The pupil–teacher ratio for primary is 47:1 and for secondary 23:1. The school year starts in March.

About 3% of the relevant age group is enrolled in tertiary education (2% of males and 4% of females, 2002/03). The National University of Lesotho is at Roma, 35km from Maseru.

Health

76% of the population uses an improved drinking water source and 37% adequate sanitation facilities (2002). Infant mortality was 61 per 1,000 live births in 2004 (137 in 1960). Lesotho is vulnerable to AIDS and other sexually-transmitted diseases; a high proportion of young men work in other countries with serious AIDS problems. At the end of 2003, 28.9% of people age 15 to 49 were HIV positive.

Women and health

The HIV/AIDS infection rate is increasing, in 2005, over half of all cases were in females. The National HIV/AIDS policy has been implemented to try and create universal awareness of the pandemic. The Department of Gender has also run advocacy campaigns, hosted radio programmes and held public gatherings on the subject. The National Health Policy also includes provision for special attention to be given to those living with HIV/AIDS.

Religion

Mainly Christians (Roman Catholics 56%, and Lesotho Evangelicals and Anglicans 24%), and the rest hold traditional beliefs, which often coexist with Christianity.

Media

There are several independent weekly newspapers including *Mopheme/The Survivor* (Sesotho/English), *The Mirror* and *Public Eye* (English), and *Makatolle*, *MoAfrica* and *Mohlanka* in Sesotho. The government newspaper is *Lentsoe la Basotho* in Sesotho. There are 35 TV sets per 1,000 people and 30,000 internet users (2002/2003).

Concerns for the future

There will continue to be focus on HIV/AIDS, violence against women, poverty and economic empowerment, increasing the number of women in decision-making positions, and addressing human rights of women.

Key contacts

- Ms Matau Futho-Letsatsi
  Director – Gender Affairs
  Ministry of Gender, Youth, Sports & Recreation
  PO Box 10993
  Maseru 100
  Lesotho
  Tel: +266 22 314 763
  Fax: +266 22 310506
  Email: CGO@mgysr.gov.ls
         mataufutho@hotmail.com

Lesotho | Summary of gender profile

Gender profile			1990	2000	2004
Population	Total population (000)		1,593	1,788	1,798
	Female population (% of total)		53.6	53.6	53.5
Labour force participation	Female labour force (% of total)		46	45	45
	Female unemployment (% of female labour force)		…	…	…
Education	Adult illiteracy rate (% of people aged 15+)	Female	10.5	…	9.7
		Male	34.6	…	26.3
	Net primary enrolment ratio (% of age group)	Female	79	85	88
		Male	64	78	83
	Net secondary enrolment ratio (% of age group)	Female	20	24	28
		Male	10	14	18
	Gross tertiary enrolment ratio (% of age group)	Female	2	3	3
		Male	1	2	2
Health	Life expectancy at birth (years)	Female	59	44	37
		Male	55	39	35
	Infant mortality rate (per 1,000 live births)		74	75	80
	Prevalence of HIV (% of people aged 15–24)	Female	…	26.4	…
		Male	…	12.1	…

Malawi

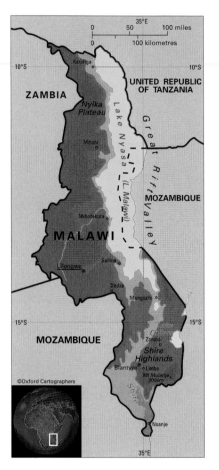

KEY FACTS

Joined Commonwealth: 1964

Capital: Lilongwe

GDP growth (%): 1.0% p.a. 1990–2003

Official language: English

Time: GMT plus 2 hours

Currency: Malawi kwacha (MK)

Main telephone lines/1,000 people: 8

Mobile phones/1,000 people: 13

National Women's Machinery

Malawi acceded to CEDAW in 1987 and to its Optional Protocol in 2000. Its National Women's Machinery is the Department for Gender Affairs in the Ministry of Gender, Child Welfare and Community Services. Its main mandate is to spearhead the formulation, implementation, co-ordination, collaboration, monitoring and evaluation of gender policy, programmes and activities at all levels. Its goal is to mainstream gender in the national development process to enhance participation of men, women, boys and girls, for sustainable and equitable development for poverty eradication.

In order to operate its mandate, the Department of Gender Affairs identified gender focal points in all the public, private, parastatal and NGO sectors, whose role is to ensure that the gender perspective is integrated into the stakeholders business.

The National Gender Policy was launched in 2000, and identified sixth thematic areas for focus; education and training; reproductive health; food and nutrition security; natural resources and environmental management; governance and human rights; and poverty eradication and economic empowerment.

Malawi is ranked at 166 in the Gender-related Development Index (GDI) in the *UNDP Human Development Report 2006*.

Priority concerns for mainstreaming gender issues

Among the 12 critical areas of concern outlined in the 1995 *Beijing Platform for Action*, the Government of Malawi has identified the following, in order of priority, for national action:

1. Women and Poverty

2. Education and Training of Women

3. Women and Health

4. Violence Against Women

5. Women in Power and Decision-making

Following by: 6. The Girl-child; 7. Institutional Mechanisms for the Advancement of Women; 8. Human Rights of Women; 9. Women and the Economy; 10. Women in the Media; 11. Women and the Environment; 12. Women and Armed Conflict.

Women in power and decision-making

Even though there is a conducive environment for non-discriminatory civil and political participation, there are insufficient mechanisms to address the impediments of women in Malawi. More women than men fail to participate in civil and political activities due to low levels of education, and there is a stereotyped perception that those roles are traditionally masculine. Since independence, Malawi law has required the use of English in Parliament, and this requirement for fluency tends to be at the disadvantage of women. In the 2004 election, only 26 out of 191 parliamentary positions were taken up by women.

Violence against women

Violence in the workplace requires attention; sexual harassment of women by male worker is rampant, which is a reflection of socially constructed roles and images that exist in society. The woman is regarded as inferior and a sex object. Not many women are aware that sexual harassment is unacceptable.

Other forms of violence include forced prostitution, trafficking, and harmful cultural practices. There are mechanisms in place to support the rehabilitation of victims, and the reform of offenders, but they are currently inadequate and being readdressed.

Education

Public spending on education was 6.0% of GDP in 2002/03. There are eight years of compulsory education starting at age six. The secondary net enrolment ratio is **29%**. The pupil–teacher ratio for primary is 62:1 and for secondary 46:1. The school year starts in January. Illiteracy among people aged 15–24 is 23.7% (17.9% for males and 29.3% for females, 1998 census).

Education and training of women

Access to education, retention of pupils and students, content and delivery of education, and attainment by pupils and students has been low. Vocational guidance and education are limited, particularly for women. Adult and continuing education are in high demand, particularly amongst rural women.

The Government has attempted to eliminate gender stereotyping through the curriculum. The curriculum in both primary and secondary schools incorporate not only gender issues, but also HIV/AIDS, family planning and health.

Health

67% of the population uses an improved drinking water source and 46% adequate sanitation facilities (2002). Malaria, dysentery, bilharzia, measles, tuberculosis and hepatitis are common. There has been a successful campaign against leprosy. Infant mortality was 110 per 1,000 live births in 2004 (205 in 1960) – still among the highest in the world.

Since the 1990s, the incidence of HIV/AIDS has been among the highest in the world and AIDS treatment continues to make very heavy demands on health resources. At the end of 2003, 14.2% of people age 15 to 49 were HIV positive.

Women and health

Health facilities are provided by the government, the Christian Health Association of Malawi, the private sector, and traditional health providers. The number of health services, personnel and access to adequate facilities has been a problem for a long time. There is also discrimination based on economic and cultural status, particularly against women. Malawi is heavily affected the HIV/AIDS pandemic, and 53% of cases are in women. The prevalence rate is among the worst in the world. Programmes co-ordinated by the National AIDS commission to raise awareness of the disease include the use of media, public meetings, youth programmes, and information, education and communication. People who are least knowledgeable about HIV/AIDS are women, and usually in rural areas.

Religion

Christians (Protestants 55%, Roman Catholics 20%), Muslims 20%; the Ngoni are predominantly Christians, while many of the Yao people are Muslims.

Media

The *Daily Times* and *The Nation/Weekend Nation* are dailies; *Malawi News* is weekly, and *Boma Lathu* monthly in Chichewa. Television Malawi began broadcasting in March 1999 – every evening, initially to main population centres. There are 4 TV sets and 2 personal computers per 1,000 people, and 36,000 internet users (2002/2003).

Malawi | Summary of gender profile

Gender profile			1990	2000	2004
Population	Total population (000)		9,459	11,512	12,608
	Female population (% of total)		50.9	50.6	50.4
Labour force participation	Female labour force (% of total)		50	50	50
	Female unemployment (% of female labour force)		...	...	...
Education	Adult illiteracy rate (% of people aged 15+)	Female	63.8	...	46
		Male	31.2	...	25.1
	Net primary enrolment ratio (% of age group)	Female	47	98	98
		Male	50	100	93
	Net secondary enrolment ratio (% of age group)	Female	...	26	23
		Male	...	36	27
	Gross tertiary enrolment ratio (% of age group)	Female	0	0	0
		Male	1	0	1
Health	Life expectancy at birth (years)	Female	47	41	40
		Male	44	40	40
	Infant mortality rate (per 1,000 live births)		146	117	110
	Prevalence of HIV (% of people aged 15–24)	Female	...	15.3	...
		Male	...	7	...

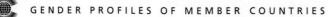

Concerns for the future

Malawi will concentrate on gender mainstreaming and budgeting in the public sector, reviewing legislation, economic empowerment of women through entrepreneurial development and training; further programmes to combat HIV/AIDS, and improving health care services.

Key contacts

• Mrs Isabel Matenje
  Director for Gender
  Ministry of Gender, Youth & Community Services
  Private Bag 330
  Lilongwe 3
  Malawi
  Tel: +265 784198/770411
  Fax: +265 780826/782334
  Email: imatenje@yahoo.com
          icmatenje@yahoo.com

Malaysia

KEY FACTS

Joined Commonwealth: 1957

Capital: Kuala Lumpur

GDP growth (%): 3.4% p.a. 1990–2003

Official language: Malay

Time: GMT plus 8 hours

Currency: ringgit or Malaysian dollar (M$)

Main telephone lines/1,000 people: 182

Mobile phones/1,000 people: 442

National Women's Machinery

Malaysia ratified CEDAW in 1995. Its National Women's Machinery is the Ministry of Women, Family and Community Development. It is mandated to ensure the effective implementation and co-ordination of programmes for women and families.

A National Advisory Council on Women, Inter-Ministerial Committee on Women, Technical Working Groups, and other state level liaison and consultative committees have been established to monitor and evaluate the implementation of the National Women's Policy and the National Plan for the Advancement of Women.

The Ninth Malaysia Plan 2006–2010 includes a further concentration of mainstreaming gender issues into national development. Efforts will be undertaken to equip women with the necessary skills and knowledge to enable them to be more competitive and versatile to meet the challenges of a knowledge-based economy.

To further strengthen the national machinery and improve its effectiveness, the Cabinet Committee on Gender Equality was established in 2004 to provide policy direction and monitor activities pertaining to women and family development. Gender focal points were appointed in all ministries and agencies to ensure the integration of the gender perspective in the formulation and implementation of policies and programmes and the removal of any form of discrimination against women.

Malaysia is ranked at 61 in the Gender-related Development Index (GDI) in the *UNDP Human Development Report 2006*.

Priority concerns for mainstreaming gender issues

Among the 12 critical areas of concern outlined in the 1995 *Beijing Platform for Action*, the Government of Malaysia has identified the following, in order of priority, for national action:

1. Institutional mechanisms for the advancement of women

2. Violence against women

3. Human rights of women

4. Women and poverty

5. Women and health

Followed by: 6. Education and training of women; 7. Women and the economy; 8. Women in power and decision-making; 9. Women in the media; 10. The girl-child; 11. Women and the environment; 12. Women and armed conflict.

Women and poverty

Various economic, social and training programmes have been implemented by the Government and NGOs to reduce the incidence of poverty among women, including single mothers and female-headed households. Through these programmes, the incidence of poverty among female-headed households declined from 12.5 per cent in 2002 to 11.5 per cent in 2004.

Violence against women

Efforts have been undertaken to stem the increasing number of cases of violence against women. In addition to reviewing existing and introducing new legislation, preventive and rehabilitative programmes have been implemented. Concerted efforts will be undertaken to increase awareness that ensuring the safety and well-being of women and families is the responsibility of all. Awareness and training programmes relating to understanding gender roles and expectations, preventing abuse and violence, resolving conflicts and maintaining family harmony will continue to be implemented by the Government and NGOs.

Education

Public spending on education was 8.1% of GDP in 2002/03. With effect from January 2003, there were six years of compulsory education starting at age six. Net enrolment ratios are 93% for primary education and 70% for secondary. The pupil–teacher ratio for primary education is 19:1 and for secondary 18:1. The school year starts in January and comprises two terms.

About 29% of the relevant age group is enrolled in tertiary education (26% of males and 33% of females, 2002/03). Illiteracy among people age 15–24 is 2.8% (2.8% for males and 2.7% for females, 2000 census).

Education and training of women

The social and economic advancement of women has been furthered by equal access to educational opportunities. Enrolment of females in primary and secondary schools reflects the gender ratio in the country, accounting for about half of the total enrolment in 2005. As part of efforts to enable women to improve themselves and take advantage of opportunities in the job market, various skills and entrepreneur

training programmes are being implemented.

Health

95% of the population uses an improved drinking water source (2002). Infant mortality was 10 per 1,000 live births in 2004 (73 in 1960).

Women and health

The maternal and child health programme, aimed at reducing maternal and child mortality and morbidity, improving pre-natal and ante-natal health care, as well as providing health and nutrition education, continues to be implemented.

In addition, emphasis is given to ensuring access to safe delivery services. In view of the fact that women, especially young women, are in the high risk category in terms of their vulnerability to HIV/AIDS, emphasis has been given to increasing awareness, as well as providing information and education. Despite these efforts, women made up 11.6% of those with HIV infection in 2005 (up from 7.9% in 2001). The programme on the prevention of mother-to-child transmission of HIV as well as the provision of care and support for

those infected, including counselling, will be continued. Education on sexuality, living skills and behaviour change programmes will be intensified.

Religion

Muslims 54%, Taoists 22%, Buddhists 17%, Hindus and Christians. Islam is the official religion; freedom of worship is guaranteed under the constitution.

Media

Leading English-language dailies are *New Straits Times*, *The Star*, *The Malay Mail* and *Business Times*. *Malaysiakini* is an online news service. There are 210 TV sets and 167 personal computers per 1,000 people, and 8.66 million internet users (2002/2003).

Concerns for the future

During the Ninth Plan period (2006–2010) efforts will continue to be undertaken to address issues confronting women to enable them to realise their potential and participate more effectively as partners in development. The strategic thrusts for the further advancement of women during the Plan period will be as follows: promoting greater female participation in the labour

Malaysia	Summary of gender profile				
Gender profile			1990	2000	2004
Population	Total population (000)		17,845	22,997	24,894
	Female population (% of total)		49.3	49.2	49.2
Labour force participation	Female labour force (% of total)		35	35	36
	Female unemployment (% of female labour force)		...	3.1	3.6
Education	Adult illiteracy rate (% of people aged 15+)	Female	25.6	...	14.6
		Male	13.1	...	8
	Net primary enrolment ratio (% of age group)	Female	...	97	93
		Male	...	97	93
	Net secondary enrolment ratio (% of age group)	Female	...	73	74
		Male	...	66	66
	Gross tertiary enrolment ratio (% of age group)	Female	...	27	33
		Male	...	25	25
Health	Life expectancy at birth (years)	Female	72	75	76
		Male	68	70	71
	Infant mortality rate (per 1,000 live births)		16	11	10
	Prevalence of HIV (% of people aged 15–24)	Female	...	0.1	...
		Male	...	0.6	...

force; increasing education and training opportunities; enhancing participation in business and entrepreneurial activities; reviewing laws and regulations to promote the status of women; improving further the health status and well-being of women; reducing violence against women; reducing incidence of poverty and improving quality of life; strengthening national machinery and institutional capacity; and advancing issues pertaining to women at the international level.

Key contacts

• Datuk Faizah Mohd Tahir
Secretary-General
Ministry of Women, Family and
Community Development
Level 3, Block E
Bukit Perdana Government Complex
Jalan Dato' Onn
50515 Kuala Lumpur
Malaysia
Tel: +60 3 2690 4008
Fax: +60 3 2693 8498
Email: faizah@kpwk.gov.my

Maldives

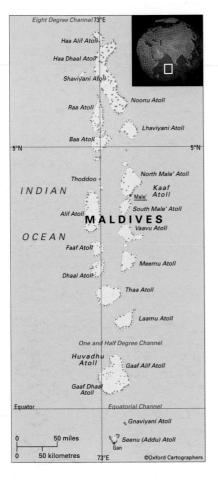

KEY FACTS

Joined Commonwealth: 1982

Capital: Malé

GDP growth (%): 4.5% p.a. 1990–2003

Official language: Dhivehi

Time: GMT plus 5 hours

Currency: Maldivian rufiyaa (MRf)

Main telephone lines/1,000 people: 102

Mobile phones/1,000 people: 149

National Women's Machinery

Maldives ratified CEDAW in 1993 and acceded to its Optional Protocol in 2006. Its National Women's Machinery is the Ministry of Gender and Family.

Maldives is ranked at 98 in the Gender-related Development Index (GDI) in the *UNDP Human Development Report 2006*.

Priority concerns for mainstreaming gender issues

Among the 12 critical areas of concern outlined in the 1995 *Beijing Platform for Action*, the Maldives Government has identified the following, in order of priority, for national action:

1. Institutional mechanisms for the advancement of women

2. Education and training of women

3. Women and health

4. Violence against women

5. The girl-child

Followed by: 6. Women in poverty / Women in the economy; 7. Women in power and decision-making; 8. Women in the media; 9. Human rights of women; 10. Women and the environment; 11. Women and armed conflict.

Women in power and decision-making

The employed population by industry and sex, still shows that most women are concentrated in sectors such as agriculture, manufacturing and social service provisions such as education and health. Few women are found in other sectors. Women are being recruited by the government to leadership training courses, which primarily trains people for high-level positions in the islands. In the 2005, only 12% of MPs elected were women.

Violence against women

A significant amount of work has been done to establish a rudimentary support service for victims of domestic violence. This is the most overt form of discrimination found in the Maldives. The major reason for this is possibly the negligent judicial system in the form of both legislation and in implementation. Most of the work to strengthen action on domestic violence and violence against women has been on building the human resource base necessary to build a support system. Social workers have been trained within the community and gender-based violence counselling training has been provided at the main hospital and in the referral hospitals in the atolls.

Education

Public spending on education was 3.7% of GDP in 1998/99. There are seven years of compulsory education starting at age six. All administrative atolls have government primary schools and an education centre providing education for all age groups. Most of the many private schools receive state subsidies and are run by the community. Net enrolment ratios are 92% for primary and 51% for secondary (2002/03). The pupil–teacher ratio for primary is 20:1 and for secondary 15:1. The school year starts in January. Illiteracy among people age 15–24 is 1.8% (2.0% for males and 1.7% for females, 2000 census).

Health

84% of the population uses an improved drinking water source and 58% adequate sanitation facilities (2002). Infant mortality was 35 per 1,000 live births in 2004 (180 in 1960). Malaria has been practically eradicated and diarrhoeal diseases have been considerably reduced.

Women and health

Programmes are being conducted through mass media to address women's health issues, malnourishment, and reproductive health. The geographical layout of the country and small island populations, make it difficult to establish health care facilities, especially specialist care, on every island. There is a high level of knowledge about HIV/AIDS and how it is transmitted, and the incidence of the disease is low, 4,100 cases in total were reported in 2005, 1,000 of these being infected women.

Religion

Sunni Muslims.

Media

The leading Dhivehi dailies are *Aafathis*, *Haveeru* and *Miadhu*, which post daily online news bulletins in English. There are 71 personal computers per 1,000 people and 15,000 internet users (2002).

Concerns for the future

More work is required to deal with violence against women. There needs to be more public awareness, political advocacy and legal literacy in this area. The judicial system will also need to be reviewed and strengthened to facilitate support for violence victims.

Health care services in the atolls will need to be addressed, and other methods explored in order to ensure adequate facilities, such as the mobile team approach.

Key contacts

- Ms Maana Raafiu
  Director-General
  Ministry of Gender & Family
  Umar Shopping Arcade
  Chandhani Magu
  Male' 20-02
  Maldives

  Tel: +960 317759/323687
  Fax: +960 331 6237
  Email: kamana@dhivehinet.net.mv
  planning@mgf.gov.mv

Maldives | Summary of gender profile

Gender profile			1990	2000	2004
Population	Total population (000)		216	290	321
	Female population (% of total)		48.7	48.6	48.7
Labour force participation	Female labour force (% of total)		19	33	38
	Female unemployment (% of female labour force)		...	2.7	...
Education	Adult illiteracy rate (% of people aged 15+)	Female	5.4	...	3.6
		Male	5	...	3.8
	Net primary enrolment ratio (% of age group)	Female	...	97	90
		Male	...	96	89
	Net secondary enrolment ratio (% of age group)	Female	...	43	55
		Male	...	37	48
	Gross tertiary enrolment ratio (% of age group)	Female	...	...	...
		Male	...	...	...
Health	Life expectancy at birth (years)	Female	59	65	67
		Male	62	66	68
	Infant mortality rate (per 1,000 live births)		79	45	35
	Prevalence of HIV (% of people aged 15–24)	Female	...	0.5	...
		Male	...	0.3	...

Malta

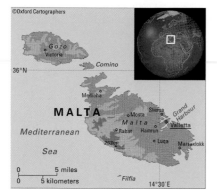

KEY FACTS

Joined Commonwealth: 1964

Capital: Valletta

GDP growth (%): 3.6% p.a. 1990–2003

Official languages: Maltese, English

Time: GMT plus 1–2 hours

Currency: Maltese lira (Lm)

Main telephone lines/1,000 people: 521

Mobile phones/1,000 people: 725

National Women's Machinery

Malta acceded to CEDAW in 1991. Its National Women's Machinery is the National Commission for the Promotion of Equality in the Ministry for the Family and Social Solidarity. Its mandate is to promote gender equality and the advancement of women in the political, social, economic and cultural spheres of Maltese society. It ensures that legislation reinforces the principles of gender equality, provides protection against discrimination and enables women to achieve equality in practice.

Malta is ranked at 32 in the Gender-related Development Index (GDI) in the *UNDP Human Development Report 2006*.

Priority concerns for mainstreaming gender issues

Among the 12 critical areas of concern outlined in the 1995 *Beijing Platform for Action*, the Government of Malta has identified the following, in order of priority, for national action:

1. Women and the economy

2. Institutional mechanisms for the advancement of women

3. Women in power and decision-making

4. Women and the environment

5. Violence against women

Followed by: 6. Education and training of women; 7. Women and health.

Women in power and decision-making

The representation of women in decision-making is crucial to gender equality, and the number of women in high-level positions is low. The national women's machinery has undertaken measures aimed at increasing women's participation in politics, both at national and local level. It has lobbied political parties to encourage women to overcome cultural barriers in the field of politics. The number of women candidates standing in elections has increased, but their actual election remains low. In the 2003 election, only 6 out of 65 seats in Parliament were won by women.

Violence against women

Under Maltese domestic law, provisions against gender-based violence, together with remedies, are provided for under both the Criminal and Civil Codes. Legislation specifically targeting violence against women is being prepared. The APPOGG is an agency that falls under the umbrella of the Ministry for Social Policy, and offers services to victims through its Domestic Violence Unit. It was established to provide support to victims of abuse, help them find shelter when requested, and link them to other necessary services. The Domestic Violence Unit has also formulated guidelines for doctors, nurses, police, social works and the clergy, to enable them to detect violent abuse of women, and deal with it appropriately.

Education

Public spending on education was 4.6% of GDP in 2002/03. There are 11 years of compulsory education starting at age five. The numerous church schools are subsidised by the government. Net enrolment ratios are 96% for primary and 87% for secondary. The pupil–teacher ratio for primary is 18:1 and for secondary 10:1. The school year starts in September.

About 30% of the relevant age group is enrolled in tertiary education (25% of males and 35% of females, 2002/03). Illiteracy among people age 15–24 is 4.0% (5.6% for males and 2.2% for females, 1995 census).

Health

The entire population uses an improved drinking water source and adequate sanitation facilities (2002). Infant mortality was 5 per 1,000 live births in 2004 (37 in 1960). Summer dust, and sand carried on the wind from North Africa, sometimes cause respiratory problems.

Religion

Virtually all Christians (Roman Catholics).

Media

There are daily and weekly newspapers in English, including *Malta Independent* (seven days a week), *Times of Malta*, *The Sunday Times* and *Malta Business Weekly*, and daily – including *In-Nazzjon* and *L-Orizzont* – and weekly papers in Maltese. Italian as well as Maltese radio and television are received. Cable TV was introduced in 1992 and by the early 2000s more than 70% of households were connected. There are 255 personal computers per 1,000 people and 120,000 internet users (2002).

Concerns for the future

There are several areas which require further commitment in order to achieve gender equity: mainstreaming gender equality; the reconciliation of work and family responsibilities; the increase of women in decision-making; the elimination of violence against women; and giving women the tools to overcome social problems related to single parenthood, drug and alcohol abuse, and gambling.

Key contacts

- Ms Sina Bugeja
  Executive Director
  National Commission for the Promotion of Equality for Men and Women
  Gattard House
  National Road
  Blata l-Bajda HMR 02
  Malta
  Tel: +356 2590 3850
  Fax: +356 2590 3851
  Email: gender.equality@gov.mt

Malta	Summary of gender profile				
Gender profile			1990	2000	2004
Population	Total population (000)		353	390	400
	Female population (% of total)		50.6	50.5	50
Labour force participation	Female labour force (% of total)		25	28	...
	Female unemployment (% of female labour force)		2.3	5.4	...
Education	Adult illiteracy rate (% of people aged 15+)	Female	11.1	7.3	...
		Male	12.1	8.7	...
	Net primary enrolment ratio (% of age group)	Female	98	98	...
		Male	99	98	...
	Net secondary enrolment ratio (% of age group)	Female	79	80	...
		Male	80	79	...
	Gross tertiary enrolment ratio (% of age group)	Female	12	28	...
		Male	14	22	...
Health	Life expectancy at birth (years)	Female	78	81	...
		Male	73	76	...
	Infant mortality rate (per 1,000 live births)		11	5	5
	Prevalence of HIV (% of people aged 15–24)	Female	...	...	...
		Male	...	...	...

Mauritius

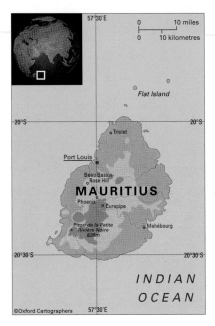

KEY FACTS

Joined Commonwealth: 1968

Capital: Port Louis

GDP growth (%): 4.0% p.a. 1990–2003

Official language: English

Time: GMT plus 4 hours

Currency: Mauritian rupee (MRs)

Main telephones lines/1,000 people: 285

Mobile phones/1,000 people: 267

National Women's Machinery

Mauritius acceded to CEDAW in 1984 and to its Optional Protocol in 2001. Its National Women's Machinery is the Women's Unit in the Ministry of Women's Rights, Child Development, Family Welfare and Consumer Protection. The main objectives of the Women's Unit is to promote and defend women's rights, to work for the elimination of all forms of discrimination against women, and to ensure that legal measures are taken to promote equality between men and women; and to implement gender sensitive policies.

The National Women's Council was established in 1985 to promote the interests and advancement of women, to support women's organisations, and to ensure that government policy and action meets the needs of women at grass-root level.

Mauritius is ranked at 63 in the Gender-related Development Index (GDI) in the *UNDP Human Development Report 2006*.

Priority concerns for mainstreaming gender issues

Among the 12 critical areas of concern outlined in the 1995 *Beijing Platform for Action*, the Government of Mauritius has identified the following, in order of priority, for national action:

1. Violence against women

2. The girl-child

3. Women and the economy

4. Education and training of women

5. Women and poverty

Followed by: 6. Human rights of women; 7. Women and health; 8. Institutional mechanisms for the advancement of women; 9. Women in power and decision-making; 10. Women in the media; 11. Women and the environment; 12. Women and armed conflict.

Education

Public spending on education was 4.7% of GDP in 2002/03. There are six years of compulsory education starting at age six. Net enrolment ratios are 97% for primary and 74% for secondary. The pupil–teacher ratio for primary is 25:1 and for secondary about 19:1. The school year starts in January.

About 15% of the relevant age group is enrolled in tertiary education (13% of males and 18% of females, 2002/03). Illiteracy among people age 15–24 is 5.5% (6.3% for males and 4.6% for females, 2000 census).

Health

Overall, the health profile is similar to that of developed countries. Health care in the public sector is free to all Mauritians. As well as some 13 hospitals, there are area and community health centres. Virtually the entire population uses an improved drinking water source and adequate sanitation facilities (2002). Infant mortality was 14 per 1,000 live births in 2004 (67 in 1960). Malaria was substantially eradicated in the 1950s. A national AIDS prevention and control programme has been running since 1987.

Religion

Hindus 52%, Christians (mainly Roman Catholics) 28%, Muslims 17%.

Media

Daily newspapers and periodicals are published in French, English, Hindi, Urdu and Chinese. The leading dailies are *L'Express*, *Le Matinal* and *Le Mauricien* (afternoon). There are 299 TV sets and 149 personal computers per 1,000 people, and 150,000 internet users (2002/2003).

Concerns for the future

Institutional measures adopted towards the development and advancement of women have been extensive and widespread, and essential for the empowerment of women. Women have become more independent, can aspire to earn a living of their own, and can work outside of the home. However, margins of difference between men and women still remain strong despite considerable achievements. Therefore there will be a high priority on the girl-child, violence against women, and eradicating poverty.

Key contacts

- Mr P Jhugroo
  Permanent Secretary
  Ministry for Women's Rights, Child
  Development, Family Welfare and
  Consumer Protection
  2nd Floor CSK Building
  Corner of Remy Ollier & Emmanuel
  Anquetil Streets
  Port Louis
  Mauritius
  Tel: +230 206 3732
  Fax: +230 216 2061
  Email: Premhans@intnet.mu

Mauritius | Summary of gender profile

Gender profile			1990	2000	2004
Population	Total population (000)		1,057	1,187	1,233
	Female population (% of total)		50.1	50.2	50.3
Labour force participation	Female labour force (% of total)		34	34	35
	Female unemployment (% of female labour force)		3.6	9.6	12.6
Education	Adult illiteracy rate (% of people aged 15+)	Female	25	...	19.5
		Male	15.2	...	11.6
	Net primary enrolment ratio (% of age group)	Female	92	97	96
		Male	91	96	94
	Net secondary enrolment ratio (% of age group)	Female	...	68	78
		Male	...	71	72
	Gross tertiary enrolment ratio (% of age group)	Female	3	7	20
		Male	5	8	14
Health	Life expectancy at birth (years)	Female	73	75	76
		Male	66	68	69
	Infant mortality rate (per 1,000 live births)		20	16	14
	Prevalence of HIV (% of people aged 15–24)	Female	...	0	...
		Male	...	0	...

Mozambique

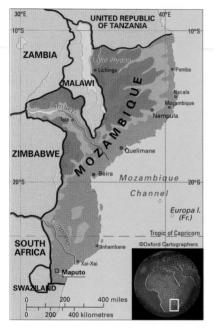

KEY FACTS

Joined Commonwealth: 1995

Capital: Maputo

GDP growth (%): 4.6% p.a. 1990–2003

Official language: Portuguese

Time: GMT plus 2 hours

Currency: Mozambique metical (MT)

Main telephone lines/1,000 people: 5

Mobile phones/1,000 people: 23

National Women's Machinery

Mozambique acceded to CEDAW in 1997. Its National Women's Machinery is the Ministry of Women and Social Action.

Mozambique is ranked at 168 in the Gender-related Development Index (GDI) in the *UNDP Human Development Report 2006*.

Priority concerns for mainstreaming gender issues

Among the 12 critical areas of concern outlined in the 1995 *Beijing Platform for Action*, the Government of Mozambique places priority on the following:

- Women in the economy

- Women in power and decision-making / Women in the media

- Women in poverty / Violence against women / Human rights of women

- Women and health / Women and the environment

- Education and training of women / The girl-child

- Institutional mechanisms of the advancement of women.

Education

Public spending on education was 2.4% of GDP in 1999/2000. There are seven years of compulsory education starting at age six. Net enrolment ratios are 55% for primary and 12% for secondary (2002/03). The pupil–teacher ratio for primary is 67:1 and for secondary 27:1. The school year starts in January.

About 1% of the relevant age group is enrolled in tertiary education (1999/2000). Illiteracy among people age 15–24 is 37.2% (23.4% for males and 50.8% for females, 2002).

Health

The national health service lost its monopoly of health care in 1992. 42% of the population uses an improved drinking water source and 27% adequate sanitation facilities (2002). Infant mortality was 104 per 1,000 live births in 2004 (180 in 1960). Malaria and AIDS are serious problems. At the end of 2003, 12.2% of people age 15 to 49 were HIV positive – and there are regular outbreaks of cholera.

Religion

Christians 30% (mainly Roman Catholics), Muslims 20% (mainly in the north), most of the rest holding traditional beliefs, which incorporate some Christian practices.

Media

The daily newspapers are *Notícias* (largest and oldest and partly government-owned) and *Diário de Moçambique* (independent), both in Portuguese. *Demos*, *Domingo*, *Fim de Semana*, *Savana* and *Zambeze* are published weekly in Portuguese. There are 14 TV sets and 5 personal computers per 1,000 people, and 50,000 internet users (2002).

Concerns for the future

Mozambique will continue efforts to lift women out of poverty, work towards eradicating violence against women, and work towards creating opportunities for women in the economy.

Key contacts

- Ms Josefa Lopes Langa
  Director of National Directorate of
  Women
  Ministry of Women and Social Action
  67 Carlos Albers Street
  Maputo
  Mozambique
  Tel: +258 21 310650
  Fax: +258 21 310650
  Email: jvilanga@yahoo.com.br

- Mr Sansao Buque
  Deputy Director of National Directorate
  of Women
  Ministry of Women and Social Action
  67 Carlos Albers Street
  Maputo
  Mozambique
  Tel: +258 21 310650
  Fax: +258 21 310650
  Email: Sbuque@hotmail.com

- Mr Pita Bongece Alfandega (POC of
  Commonwealth)
  Head of Multilateral Cooperation
  Ministry of Women and Social Action
  67 Carlos Albers Street
  Maputo
  Mozambique
  Tel: +258 21 497901/3
  Email: Bongece@hotmail.com

Mozambique | Summary of gender profile

Gender profile			1990	2000	2004
Population	Total population (000)		13,429	17,911	19,424
	Female population (% of total)		52.2	52	51.7
Labour force participation	Female labour force (% of total)		54	54	54
	Female unemployment (% of female labour force)		...	...	...
Education	Adult illiteracy rate (% of people aged 15+)	Female	81.6	...	...
		Male	50.7	...	...
	Net primary enrolment ratio (% of age group)	Female	38	50	67
		Male	48	61	75
	Net secondary enrolment ratio (% of age group)	Female	...	3	4
		Male	...	4	5
	Gross tertiary enrolment ratio (% of age group)	Female	...	...	1
		Male	...	...	2
Health	Life expectancy at birth (years)	Female	45	44	42
		Male	42	41	41
	Infant mortality rate (per 1,000 live births)		158	122	104
	Prevalence of HIV (% of people aged 15–24)	Female	...	14.7	...
		Male	...	6.7	...

Namibia

KEY FACTS

Joined Commonwealth: 1990

Capital: Windhoek

GDP growth (%): 0.9% p.a. 1990–2003

Official language: English

Time: GMT plus 1–2 hours

Currency: Namibia dollar (N$)

Main telephone lines/1,000 people: 66

Mobile phones/1,000 people: 116

National Women's Machinery

Namibia acceded to CEDAW in 1992 and to its Optional Protocol in 2000. Its National Women's Machinery is the Directorate of Gender Equality in the Ministry of Gender Equality and Child Welfare. It works to ensure the empowerment of women, men and children and the equality between men and women as prerequisites for full participation in political, legal, social, cultural and economic development; to ensure the active participation of women in regional, national and international forums, with a view to enhancing their capacity in various activities at all levels; and to monitor projects and programmes.

The Namibian Government adopted the National Gender Policy in 1997, with the aim of redressing the inequalities between women and men. The policy identifies ten critical areas of concern, and it provides a vision to improve women's living conditions including practical and forward-looking guidelines and strategies for the implementation, monitoring and evaluation of the constitutional provisions for gender equality. Additionally the National Gender Plan of Action was developed to support the policy, it was approved by Cabinet in 1998, and is a programme aimed at speeding up the implementation process of the National Gender Policy. Within the framework of the policy, the following monitoring mechanisms were established:

- Gender Focal Points – to oversee that all policies and programmes, which are developed in the Ministries and other Governmental Institutions and bodies at National, Regional and Local Levels, are gender focused;

- Gender Sectoral Committee – to advise the Ministry of Women Affairs and Child Welfare on issues related specifically to their areas of focus;

- Gender network co-ordinating committee and the National information-sharing forum.

Namibia is ranked at 125 in the Gender-related Development Index (GDI) in the *UNDP Human Development Report 2006*.

Priority concerns for mainstreaming gender issues

Among the 12 critical areas of concern outlined in the 1995 *Beijing Platform for Action*, the Government of Namibia has identified the following, in order of priority, for national action:

1. Institutional mechanisms for the advancement of women

2. Women in power and decision-making

3. Violence against women

4. Women and health

5. Education and training of women

Followed by: 6. Women and poverty / Women and the economy; 7. The girl-child; 8. Human rights of women; 9. Women in media; 10. Women and the environment.

Violence against women

The Ministry of Women's Affairs has adopted a National Plan of Action on Combating Gender Based Violence in 2001, which is being implemented with all the relevant stakeholders. The Women and Child Protection Units have been established to provide temporary safety shelters, counselling services and legal advice for abused women and children due to the escalation of domestic violence in Namibia.

Women and poverty/Women and the economy

Agricultural programs and interventions target women at community level. Communal allocation of land by Traditional

Authority prevails in some areas where women have no direct rights to land. Several services and measures have been implemented aimed at enhancing agricultural extension capacity and outreach programs to communal farmers, including female-headed households. The services include the provision of information and advisory services aimed at changing societal perceptions and attitudes. This is done through workshops on gender awareness conducted to empower Extension Officers with gender analytical skills.

Education

Public spending on education was 7.2% of GDP in 2002/03. There are 10 years of compulsory education starting at age six. Net enrolment ratios are 78% for primary and 44% for secondary. The pupil–teacher ratio for primary is 28:1 and for secondary 24:1. The school year starts in January. In 1993, English became the main language of instruction.

About 7% of the relevant age group is enrolled in tertiary education (2002/03). Illiteracy among people age 15–24 is 7.7% (8.8% for males and 6.5% for females, 2001 census). There are extensive adult literacy programmes.

Health

80% of the population uses an improved drinking water source and 30% adequate sanitation facilities (2002). Tuberculosis and malaria are widespread in the north. Infant mortality was 47 per 1,000 live births in 2004 (129 in 1960). HIV infection has increased rapidly and, at the end of 2003, 21.3% of people age 15 to 49 were HIV positive.

Women and health

Women account for 53% of all reported HIV/AIDS cases. The Ministry of Health introduced a National Program for the prevention of mother-to-child HIV transmission in 2001 using anti-retroviral drugs. The service is now available for pregnant women in most regions of the country. The Third Mid-Term Plan on HIV/AIDS for the period 2004–2009 is being implemented. The document provides the framework for all the relevant actors to collaborate and guide the implementation process needed for an effective multi-sectoral HIV/AIDS response.

Religion

Christian majority (predominantly Lutherans).

Media

Daily newspapers include *The Namibian* (in English and Oshivambo), *Namibia Economist*, *New Era* (government-owned), *Die Republikein* (in Afrikaans) and *Allgemeine Zeitung* (in German). *Windhoek Observer* is published weekly. There are 269 TV sets and 99 personal computers per 1,000 people, and 65,000 internet users (2002/2003).

Concerns for the future

Although Namibia has adopted the National Gender Policy and the Plan of Action, a lot still needs to be done with regard the implementation of this policy. Although the gender focal points are in place, these structures are not very effective, mainly due to budgetary provisions for gender programmes within sector ministries which are not always available. Other key challenges in relation to the critical areas of concern include the effective implementation of programmes by NGOs working in partnership with the government on gender issues is hampered by lack of funds. Poverty is still a major problem that needs to be overcome, although Namibia is considered to be food

Namibia	Summary of gender profile				
Gender profile			1990	2000	2004
Population	Total population (000)		1,398	1,894	2,009
	Female population (% of total)		51	51	50
Labour force participation	Female labour force (% of total)		44	44	44
	Female unemployment (% of female labour force)		19	39	...
Education	Adult illiteracy rate (% of people aged 15+)	Female	27.6	18.8	...
		Male	22.6	17.2	...
	Net primary enrolment ratio (% of age group)	Female	93	77	76
		Male	86	71	71
	Net secondary enrolment ratio (% of age group)	Female	36	42	43
		Male	26	30	32
	Gross tertiary enrolment ratio (% of age group)	Female	4	7	7
		Male	2	8	6
Health	Life expectancy at birth (years)	Female	63	54	48
		Male	60	51	47
	Infant mortality rate (per 1,000 live births)		60	50	47
	Prevalence of HIV (% of people aged 15–24)	Female	...	19.8	...
		Male	...	9.1	...

secure at the national level, many households are still vulnerable to chronic or acute food insecurity due to low agricultural production, recurrent drought, low incomes and limited off-farm employment opportunities due to the loss of productive labour forces at the household level due to AIDS. Women's subordinated position in society makes them more vulnerable to HIV infection, and their economical status forces them to indulge in unprotected sex. Ignorance and men's attitude towards women's health and reproductive rights also renders women more vulnerable to sexual infections including HIV. Despite the enactment of laws dealing with domestic violence and rape, the incidences of gender-based violence are still escalating. There are insufficient shelters for battered/abused women and children, and there are very few programmes targeted at the perpetrators of gender-based violence. Namibia being a patriarchal society is also characterised by the patriarchal male domination attitudes that play a major role in the extent that women participate in decision-making positions. Much still needs to be done to remove social and legal barriers that impede on women's full and equal participation in all developmental activities at all levels.

Key contacts

- Ms Sirkka Ausiku
  Permanent Secretary
  Ministry of Gender Equality and Child Welfare
  Private Bag 13359/13339
  Windhoek
  Namibia
  Tel: +264 61 283 3111
  Fax: +264 61 238 941/226
  Email: sausiku@mgecw.gov.na

Nauru

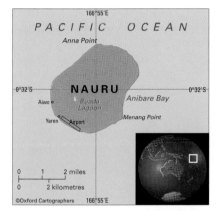

KEY FACTS

Special Member: Nauru is a Special Member, having become one officially on 1 July 2005

Joined Commonwealth: 1968

Official language: English

Time: GMT plus 12 hours

Currency: Australian dollar

Main telephone lines/1,000 people: 160

Mobile phones/1,000 people: 130 (2004)

National Women's Machinery

Nauru is not a state party to CEDAW. Its National Women's Machinery is the Women's Affairs Section in the Office of the President.

Priority concerns for mainstreaming gender issues

Among the Government of Nauru's priority areas for action on gender equality are:

- Ensuring equal access to education

- Eradicating illiteracy among women

- Improving women's access throughout their life-cycle to affordable quality health care

- Increasing community awareness of the importance of women's human rights and legal rights

- Introducing education programmes of women and the environment.

Women in power and decision-making

The law grants women the same freedoms and protections as men. The Government officially provides equal opportunities in education and employment, and women are free to own property and pursue private interests. However, in practice, societal pressures limit opportunities for women to exercise these rights fully. There are no legal impediments to participation in politics by women. However, the dominance of traditional clans in national politics limit participation by women, and there are no women in the 18-seat Parliament or in the Cabinet. Participation by women in party-based politics has increased, and women held many senior civil service positions, including Permanent Secretary and Cabinet Secretary-level jobs.

Women and poverty/Women and the economy

The economy depends almost entirely on the country's declining phosphate deposits. These were depleted in 2000 on a large-scale commercial basis; however, small-scale mining is still occurring. The main challenge to alleviating poverty in Nauru is the establishment of an alternate economic activity. A further challenge is the organisation and management of a modern state that promotes a performance-oriented public service, an increasingly competitive and productive private sector, and good governance that can underpin public and private investment.

Education

There are 11 years of compulsory education starting at age six. The school year starts in January. Adult illiteracy is around 5%.

Health

There is a high incidence of diabetes, cancer and heart disease. There is no malaria. Medical and dental treatment is free for all Nauruans and for government employees and their families. There are two hospitals, one for Nauruans and one provided by the Nauru Phosphate Corporation which is mainly for employees of the corporation. A pure water supply is provided by the Nauru Phosphate Corporation's desalination plant. Infant mortality was 25 per 1,000 live births in 2004.

Religion

Mainly Christians (predominantly Protestants).

Media

There is no daily newspaper. The *Nauru Bulletin* is published weekly in Nauruan and English by the government, and *Central*

Star News and *The Nauru Chronicle* fortnightly. The Nauru Broadcasting Service, state-owned and non-commercial, was founded in 1968. Radio broadcasts are in English and Nauruan and include material from Radio Australia and the BBC. Since 1991, Nauru Television (NTV) has broadcast programmes from New Zealand via satellite and on video-tape. There are 300 internet users (2002).

Concerns for the future

Institutional arrangements for promoting gender equality have proven problematic in the Pacific. Government women's development agencies have had great difficulty in implementing international commitments, as all are starved of resources and human capacity, and are given low priority in budget allocations. Renewed attention on the question of best approaches to promoting gender equality is warranted.

Key contacts

- Ms Joy Heine
  Director
  Women's Affairs Section
  Government Offices
  Yaren District
  Nauru
  Tel: +674 444 3133/3109/3090
  Fax: +674 444 3788/3195/3820/3105
  Email: sechealth@cenpac.net.nr

Nauru — Summary of gender profile					
Gender profile			*1990*	*2000*	*2004*
Population	Total population (000)		...	12	13
	Female population (% of total)		...	...	...
Labour force participation	Female labour force (% of total)		41	...	...
	Female unemployment (% of female labour force)		...	...	...
Education	Adult illiteracy rate (% of people aged 15+)	Female	...	...	...
		Male	...	...	...
	Net primary enrolment ratio (% of age group)	Female	...	82	...
		Male	...	80	...
	Net secondary enrolment ratio (% of age group)	Female	...	56	...
		Male	...	52	...
	Gross tertiary enrolment ratio (% of age group)	Female	...	...	...
		Male	...	...	...
Health	Life expectancy at birth (years)	Female	...	65	...
		Male	...	57	...
	Infant mortality rate (per 1,000 live births)		...	25	25
	Prevalence of HIV (% of people aged 15–24)	Female	...	...	...
		Male	...	...	...

New Zealand

KEY FACTS

Joined Commonwealth: 1931 (Statute of Westminster)

Capital: Wellington

GDP growth (%): 2.1% p.a. 1990–2003

Official languages: English, Maori

Time: GMT plus 12–13 hours

Currency: New Zealand dollar (NZ$)

Main telephone lines/1,000 people: 449

Mobile phones/1,000 people: 648

National Women's Machinery

New Zealand ratified CEDAW in 1985 and acceded to its Optional Protocol in 2000. Its National Women's Machinery is the Ministry of Women's Affairs. The Ministry was established in 1984, and is the smallest core government agency. It is mandated to provide advice on policy solutions to improve the status of women; recommend suitable women nominees for state sector boards; and manage New Zealand's international obligations in relation to the status of women.

The work of the Ministry is guided by The Action Plan for New Zealand Women, a five year whole-of-government plan launched in 2004. The plan focuses of three main areas of work: economic sustainability, work-life balance, and well-being.

The Ministry of Women's Affairs Nominations Service aims to increase the number of women leaders and decision-makers on state sector governance boards and committees. The Nominations Service maintains a database of women with relevant skills and experience that is used to identify potential candidates for director positions on state sector boards.

New Zealand is ranked at 20 in the Gender-related Development Index (GDI) in the *UNDP Human Development Report 2006*.

Priority concerns for mainstreaming gender issues

Among the 12 critical areas of concern outlined in the 1995 *Beijing Platform for Action*, the Government of New Zealand has identified the following, in order of priority, for national action:

1. Institutional mechanisms for the advancement of women

2. Women and the economy

3. Women and poverty

4. Women in power and decision-making

5. Violence against women

Followed by: 6. Women and health; 7. Human rights of women; 8. Education and training of women; 9. The girl-child; 10. Women in the media; 11. Women and armed conflict; 12. Women and the environment.

Violence against women

The Government is continuing to pay special attention to the prevention of the trafficking and sexual exploitation of young people. It is also concerned to help illegal immigrants from being trapped into prostitution. The focus of the criminal law is on those who exploit prostitutes; whereas a harm-reduction focus is applied to prostitutes themselves, rather than the sanction of the criminal law.

Women, and in particular Maori women, are more likely than men to experience violence and sexual assault. Objectives have been formulated to target these issues.

Women in power and decision-making

There are three types of local government in New Zealand: regional, territorial (cities and districts) and unitary (which combines the functions of a regional and territorial council). Since 1989, the overall number of women local government candidates has increased, and as a consequence of the 2005 elections, 39 women were elected to parliamentary positions. Women's overall representation in the public service also increased from 56% in 2002 to 59% in 2004. The high proportion of female employment in the public service is mainly because the public service includes a number of occupations in which women tend to work (such as social workers, case workers and clerical staff). The Government recognises that if women are to sustain a reasonable standard of living and provide for, or help provide for, the future of their families, they require access to a good level of income and the skills and knowledge that will help them maximise their financial resources.

Education

Public spending on education was 6.7% of GDP in 2002/03. There are 12 years of compulsory education starting at age five. Net enrolment ratios are 100% for primary and 93% for secondary. The pupil–teacher ratio for primary is 18:1 and for secondary 13:1. The school year starts in January.

About 74% of the relevant age group is enrolled in tertiary education (59% of males and 90% of females, 2002/03). There is virtually no illiteracy among people age 15–24.

Health

Treatment in public hospitals is free for everyone. Infant mortality was 5 per 1,000 live births in 2004 (22 in 1960).

Women and health

The Government's over-arching objectives for the health and disability sector are to improve the health of all New Zealanders and to reduce health inequalities, that is, to improve not just the length of life but people's length of life free from pain or disability. The Government has developed a number of broad strategies to improve the health status of New Zealanders. Many of these strategies are particularly relevant to women, such as those dealing with sexual and reproductive health and mental health. The Government also continues to provide a number of health services specific to women, such as free screening for breast and cervical cancer and free maternity care. The Government is committed to improving women's health, and will continue to monitor and develop health services and strategies to achieve this goal. Women continue to live longer than men, however there are differences in life expectancy across ethnic groups. Also, there are gender and ethnicity differences in illness and lifestyle factors that affect morbidity and mortality.

Religion

70% of people adhere to a religion; 59% of people are Christians (Anglicans 17%, Roman Catholics 14%, Presbyterians 12%, Methodists 3.5%); others include Ratana (Maori) 1.4%, Buddhists 1.2% and Hindus 1.1% (2001 census).

Media

Largest dailies are *The New Zealand Herald* (Auckland, the main national newspaper), *The Dominion Post* (Wellington), *The Press* (Christchurch) and *Otago Daily Times* (Dunedin). Around 30 daily papers – mostly evening editions – are published locally and regionally. The principal Sunday papers are *Sunday Star Times* and *Sunday News*. The Maori monthly *Kia Hiwa Ra* has a readership of over 15,000; and there is a fortnightly Maori paper *Te Maori News*. More than 2,300 magazines circulate on a regular basis, including the bi-monthly Maori *Mana* magazine. There are 574 TV sets and 414 personal computers per 1,000 people, and 2,110,000 internet users (2002/2003).

Concerns for the future

The Women's Plan of Action will continue to be implemented with the focus on economic stability, work-life balance and well-being.

New Zealand	Summary of gender profile				
Gender profile			*1990*	*2000*	*2004*
Population	Total population (000)		3,448	3,858	3,989
	Female population (% of total)		50.7	51.1	51
Labour force participation	Female labour force (% of total)		43	45	46
	Female unemployment (% of female labour force)		7.3	5.8	4.4
Education	Adult illiteracy rate (% of people aged 15+)	Female	...	...	...
		Male	...	...	...
	Net primary enrolment ratio (% of age group)	Female	97	100	100
		Male	98	99	100
	Net secondary enrolment ratio (% of age group)	Female	86	93	94
		Male	84	90	91
	Gross tertiary enrolment ratio (% of age group)	Female	48	81	86
		Male	48	56	58
Health	Life expectancy at birth (years)	Female	78	81	81
		Male	73	76	71
	Infant mortality rate (per 1,000 live births)		8	6	5
	Prevalence of HIV (% of people aged 15–24)	Female	...	0	...
		Male	...	0.1	...

Key contacts

- Ms Carolyn Risk
  Strategy Development Leader
  Ministry of Women's Affairs
  Level 2, 48 Mulgrave Street
  PO Box 10049
  Wellington
  New Zealand
  Tel: +64 4 915 7112
  Fax: +64 4 915 1604
  Email: mwa@mwa.govt.nz
           risk@mwa.govt.nz

- Cherie Engelbrecht
  Senior Policy Analyst
  Ministry of Women's Affairs
  Level 2, 48 Mulgrave Street
  Thorndon
  PO Box 10049
  Wellington
  New Zealand
  Tel: +64 4 915 7112
  Email: engelbrecht@mwa.govt.nz

- Ms Shenagh Gleisner
  Chief Executive
  Ministry of Women's Affairs
  Level 2, 48 Mulgrave Street
  PO Box 10049
  Wellington
  New Zealand
  Tel: +64 4 916 5825
  Fax: +64 4 916 1604
  Email: mwa@mwa.govt.nz
           gleisner@mwa.govt.nz

Nigeria

KEY FACTS

Joined Commonwealth: 1960
(suspended 1995–99)

Capital: Abuja

GDP growth (%): 0.0% p.a. 1990–2003

Official language: English

Time: GMT plus 1 hour

Currency: Naira (N)

Main telephone lines/1,000 people: 7

Mobile phones/1,000 people: 26

National Women's Machinery

Nigeria acceded to CEDAW in 1985 and to its Optional Protocol in 2004. Its National Women's Machinery is the Federal Ministry of Women's Affairs. It serves as the national vehicle to bring about speedy and healthy development of Nigeria women in the mainstream of the national development process and to ensure the survival, protection, development and participation of all children as preparation for meaningful adult life. The Ministry is divided into three divisions to undertake and co-ordinate activities that stimulate the advancement of women and development. These divisions are: human resources and capacity building; women organisation; and economic services.

The Federal Ministry of Women Affairs operates at national level, but networks with state, local government and ward levels through the following structures:

- State Ministry of Women's Affairs (SMWA), in each of the 36 states, structured like the Federal Ministry, but essentially autonomous;

- Women Development Unit (WDU) at each local government council level;

- Gender Focal Points at ward level.

A National Policy on Women was adopted in 2000, which includes provisions for affirmative action to increase to 30% women's representation in the legislative and executive arms of the Government; translation of the Convention into the three major Nigerian languages; the production of information, education and communication materials for creating awareness and educating the public about women's rights; and empowerment programmes targeting women, institutions, students and the general public, as well as professional groups and traditional and religious institutions.

Nigeria is ranked at 159 in the Gender-related Development Index (GDI) in the *UNDP Human Development Report 2006*.

Priority concerns for mainstreaming gender issues

Among the 12 critical areas of concern outlined in the 1995 *Beijing Platform for Action*, the Government of Nigeria has identified the following, in order of priority, for national action:

1. Human rights of women

2. Violence against women

3. Women in power and decision-making

4. The girl-child

5. Women and the economy

Followed by: 6. Women and health; 7. Education and training of women; 8. Women and poverty; 9. Women and armed conflict; 10. Women in the media; 11. Women and the environment; 12. Institutional mechanisms for the advancement of women.

Women in power and decision-making

The National Policy on Women includes a stipulation for 30% representation of women in public office, but this has not yet been achieved. There is a low number of women in political and public life, especially in leadership and decision-making positions. After the 2003 elections, women represented only 6% of MPs. The persistence of stereotypical and patriarchal attitudes, which view men as natural leaders, preclude women from seeking positions of leadership.

Education

There are six years of compulsory education starting at age six. Net enrolment ratios are 67% for primary education and 29% for secondary (2002/03). The pupil-teacher ratio for primary education is 42:1 and for secondary 35:1. The school year starts in September. About 8% of the relevant age group is enrolled in tertiary education (10% of males and 7% of females, 2002/03). Illiteracy among people aged 15–24 is 11.4% (9.3% for males and 13.5% for females, 2002).

Health

60% of the population uses an improved drinking water source and 38% adequate sanitation facilities (2002). Infant mortality was 101 per 1,000 live births in 2004 (123 in 1960). At the end of 2003, 5.4% of people age 15 to 49 were HIV-positive.

Women and health

There are insufficient and inadequate healthcare facilities and family planning services, and a lack of access to such facilities and services in some areas of Nigeria. Traditional practices that are harmful to the physical and mental health of women and girls persist. A multi-sectoral approach has been taken against the rising HIV/AIDS infection rate, where women account for 55% of all cases.

Religion

Muslims (mainly in the north and west) 50%; Christians (mainly in the south) 40%; the rest of the population hold traditional beliefs.

Media

There are more than 100 national and regional newspapers, some state-owned, as well as Sunday papers, business weeklies and news magazines. Established titles with national distribution include *The Guardian*, *New Nigerian* (government-owned with Lagos and Kaduna editions), *Newswatch* (weekly), *Post Express*, *The Punch*, *Tell* (weekly), *This Day* (Lagos), *Daily Times* (Lagos), *Daily Trust* (Abuja) and *Vanguard* (Lagos). There are state-run radio stations in all 36 states and state-run TV in most. There are 103 TV sets and seven personal computers per 1,000 people, and 750,000 internet users (2002/2003).

Concerns for the future

There will be a continuing focus on strengthening institutional mechanisms which are a prerequisite for mainstreaming gender into all areas of national development. Efforts will also be targeted towards addressing deep-rooted discriminatory practices, eliminating violence against women and increasing the number of women in high-level decision-making positions.

Key contacts

- Dr Habiba Muda Lawan
  Director
  Federal Ministry of Women's Affairs
  New Federal Secretariat Complex
  Shehu Shagari Way
  Maitama
  P M B 229
  Central District
  Garki, Abuja
  Nigeria
  Tel: +234 9 523 8341
  Fax: +234 9 523 3644/7112
  Email: genderaffairsdeptnig@yahoo.co.uk
  lawhab@yahoo.co.uk

Nigeria | Summary of gender profile

Gender profile			1990	2000	2004
Population	Total population (000)		90,557	117,608	128,709
	Female population (% of total)		49.8	50.7	49
Labour force participation	Female labour force (% of total)		36	35	35
	Female unemployment (% of female labour force)		5.3	...	...
Education	Adult illiteracy rate (% of people aged 15+)	Female	61.6	43.9	...
		Male	40.6	27.8	...
	Net primary enrolment ratio (% of age group)	Female	...	...	81
		Male	...	...	95
	Net secondary enrolment ratio (% of age group)	Female	...	...	25
		Male	...	...	31
	Gross tertiary enrolment ratio (% of age group)	Female	...	2	7
		Male	...	6	13
Health	Life expectancy at birth (years)	Female	48	44	44
		Male	45	43	43
	Infant mortality rate (per 1,000 live births)		120	107	107
	Prevalence of HIV (% of people aged 15–24)	Female	...	5.1	...
		Male	...	2.5	...

Pakistan

The designations and the presentation of material on this map, based on UN practice, do not imply the expression of any opinion whatsoever on the part of the Commonwealth Secretariat or the publishers concerning the legal status of any country, territory or area, or of its authorities, or concerning the delimitation of its frontiers or boundaries. There is no intention to define the status of Jammu and/or Kashmir, which has not yet been agreed upon by the parties.

KEY FACTS

Joined Commonwealth: 1960
(suspended 1995–99)

Capital: Abuja

GDP growth (%): 0.0% p.a. 1990–2003

Official language: English

Time: GMT plus 5 hours

Currency: Naira (N)

Main telephone lines/1,000 people: 7

Mobile phones/1,000 people: 26

National Women's Machinery

Pakistan acceded to CEDAW in 1996. Its National Women's Machinery is the Ministry of Women's Development. It plays the role of advocate, planner and co-ordinator of women, children, elderly and special persons. It is responsible for the formulation of policies and laws to meet the special needs of women, ensuring that their interests and needs are adequately represented in public policy formulation by various organisations and agencies of government, the promotion and undertaking of projects for the development of women, matters relating to equality of opportunity in education, training and employment, and facilities in health care and community development.

The National Policy for Advancement and Empowerment of Women was launched in 2002 to serve as a guide for the Government to initiate focused programmes to enhance women's participation in socio-economic development. It also contributes to enhancing the status of women through mass awareness campaigns and gender mainstreaming. The policy provides medium- and long-term visions for women's development, together with measures for implementation.

The National Commission on the Status of Women was established in July 2000. Its main functions are to examine the policy, programmes and other measures taken by the Government for women's development and gender equality, to assess implementation and make suitable recommendations to the concerned authorities where these are considered necessary.

The Gender Reform Action Plan (GRAP) is a comprehensive plan, founded on the concept of affirmative action, to help speed women's integration into the national mainstream. It specifically addresses and makes recommendations for special measures to facilitate women's entry and progress in such fields as government service and politics. The objective is to sensitise the government machinery at the federal and provincial levels to the needs of women and stimulate thinking on how these should be addressed.

Pakistan is ranked at 134 in the Gender-related Development Index (GDI) in the *UNDP Human Development Report 2006*.

Priority concerns for mainstreaming gender issues

Among the 12 critical areas of concern outlined in the 1995 *Beijing Platform for Action*, the Government of Pakistan has identified the following, in order of priority, for national action:

1. Women in power and decision-making

2. Education and training of women

3. Violence against women

4. Women and health

5. Women in poverty

Followed by: 6. Women and the economy; 7. Human rights of women; 8. Institutional mechanisms for the advancement of women; 9. Women in the media; 10. Women and the environment; 11. The girl-child; 12. Women and armed conflict.

Violence against women

The Ministry of Women's Development, with assistance from the UK Department for International Development and the Gender Equality Umbrella Project/UN Development Programme, is launching the Family Protection Complex project to address the serious national issue of violence against women which is rampant in Pakistan. The family protection services will connect existing women's shelters (such as Dar-ul-Amaan) and crisis centres. This functional unit will co-ordinate with the women's police and judicial lock-ups. The project is premised on a holistic approach which builds horizontal linkages between government agencies to enable an integrated response to the issue.

Women and poverty

The Ministry of Women's Development is preparing a large project to address issue of gender and poverty. This will be closely linked with the Government's devolution plan and the Zakat and Bait ul Mal programmes to reach the target beneficiaries, the poorest and most marginalised segments of the population. The project is likely to benefit 20,000 women through the provision of financial assistance and training in multiple skills, including information technology. The project will be executed through district santazars and the NGOs involved in extension of micro-credit to women.

Women in power and decision-making

The Ministry of Women's Development launched the National Programme for Women's Political Participation to build upon the breakthrough provided by the reservation of 33% seats for women in

local bodies and 17% seats in the provincial and federal legislatures. Under the programme newly elected women legislators and councillors are provided with orientation to the political system, the legislative mechanism, constituency servicing, research and documentation, and networking.

Education

Public spending on education was 1.8% of GDP in 2000/01. There are five years of compulsory education starting at age five. The primary net enrolment ratio is 59%. The pupil–teacher ratio for primary education is 40:1 (2002/03). The school year starts in April.

About 3% of the relevant age group is enrolled in tertiary education (2002/03). Illiteracy among people aged 15–24 is 35.5% (25.2% for males and 46.1% for females, 2004 (Labour Force Survey). There is an extensive literacy programme.

Health

The network of medical services includes hospitals, dispensaries, rural health centres and basic health units. Family planning services are provided at family welfare

centres. 90% of the population uses an improved drinking water source and 54% have adequate sanitation facilities (2002 figures). Malaria remains a serious problem. Infant mortality was 80 per 1,000 live births in 2004 (down from 139 in 1960).

Women and health

The main barrier to information about health issues, including reproductive health, is illiteracy. All maternal and child health centres are expected to provide information on sexual and reproductive health, particularly contraception, to women who approach them. The Government adopted a National Health Policy in 2001 to bring about an overhaul of the health sector. An important aspect of the policy is the focus on the health needs of women and girls. This includes reducing the prevalence of communicable diseases, a national immunisation programme, creating more health work for both urban and rural health centres, and providing more reproductive health services.

Religion

Muslims 97%, the majority of whom are Sunni, with a minority (of about 20%) of Shia. There are small communities of

Pakistan	Summary of gender profile					
Gender profile				1990	2000	2004
Population	Total population (000)			108,000	138,100	154,794
	Female population (% of total)			47.7	48.2	49
Labour force participation	Female labour force (% of total)			23	25	26
	Female unemployment (% of female labour force)			0.9	15.8	16.4
Education	Adult illiteracy rate (% of people aged 15+)	Female		79.9	72.1	64
		Male		50.7	42.6	37
	Net primary enrolment ratio (% of age group)	Female		39	...	56
		Male		82	...	76
	Net secondary enrolment ratio (% of age group)	Female		12	24	...
		Male		24	42	...
	Gross tertiary enrolment ratio (% of age group)	Female		2	...	3
		Male		4	...	3
Health	Life expectancy at birth (years)	Female		60	64	66
		Male		58	62	64
	Infant mortality rate (per 1,000 live births)			100	85	80
	Prevalence of HIV (% of people aged 15–24)	Female		...	0	...
		Male		...	0.1	...

Hindus, Christians, Qadianis and a few Parsis (Zoroastrians).

Media

The first Urdu journal appeared in 1836. In 1991 there were 2,204 newspapers and periodicals, including 271 dailies and 508 weeklies. The main newspapers in Urdu are *Jang* (Karachi), *Nawa-e-Waqt*, *Ausaf*, *Sahafat*, *Din*, *Khabrain*, *Pakistan*, *Asas* and *Al-Akhbar*. Leading English-language papers are *Dawn* (Karachi), *Daily Times*, *The Nation* and *The News* (Lahore), and *The Frontier Post* (Peshawar/Quetta). The principal news magazines are *Akhbar-e-Jehan*, *Herald*, *MAG*, *Newsline* and *Takbeer* (Karachi), *Pakistan and Gulf Economist* and *Pulse* (Islamabad), *The Friday Times* and *Zindagi* (Lahore). There are 150 TV sets and four personal computers per 1,000 people, and 1,500,000 internet users (2001/2002).

Concerns for the future

The main challenge Pakistan faces in the promotion and protection of women's rights is to ensure that international obligations, constitutional provisions, the laws enacted, the implementation machinery, monitoring mechanisms created and various programmes actually bring about a positive change in the lives of Pakistani women. This challenge has not yet been overcome because of a multiplicity of factors. The state suffers from a serious impoverishment of resources. There is also a lack of awareness and entrenched societal attitudes relating to women and women's rights. This affects the range and quality of initiatives that can be taken. The low level of literacy has an aggravating effect. Even when men are aware of the rights of women, many are not willing to recognise them. There is an incorrect understanding of the role women play in the national development process. A number of

stereotypes still prevail. This sometimes results in constitutional and legal guarantees against discrimination not being fully implemented. As in most other countries, domestic affairs are considered a private matter and incidents within the family, including violence, are usually not reported and often not treated with appropriate seriousness by the relevant authorities.

Key contacts

- Mr Mahmood Salim Mahmood
  Secretary
  Ministry of Women Development
  Statelife Building No.V
  China Chowr, Blue Area
  Islamabad
  Pakistan
  Tel: +92 51 920 6695
  Fax: +92 51 920 5831
  Email: szafarhm@hotmail.com
          szafarhma@gmail.com

Papua New Guinea

KEY FACTS

Joined Commonwealth: 1975

Capital: Port Moresby

GDP growth (%): 0.2% p.a. 1990–2003

Official language: English

Time: GMT plus 10 hours

Currency: kina (K)

Main telephone lines/1,000 people: 11

Mobile phones/1,000 people: 3

National Women's Machinery

Papua New Guinea acceded to CEDAW in 1995. Its National Women's Machinery is the Gender and Development Division in the Department of Community Development.

Papua New Guinea is ranked at 139 in the Gender-related Development Index (GDI) in the *UNDP Human Development Report 2006*.

Priority concerns for mainstreaming gender issues

The Government of Papua New Guinea has identified the following as priority areas for national action on gender equality:

- Institutional strengthening and upgrading of the National Women's Machinery

- Economic empowerment of women

- Shared decision-making and good governance

- Integration of gender issues in government planning of policies and programmes.

Women and the economy

Because of economic stagnation, as well as widespread evidence of deterioration in public services, especially in the rural areas, living standards for a significant number of Papua New Guineans has declined since 1990. In spite of the increasing cost of living, salaries have changed very little over a long period, which has contributed to a static or possibly worsening poverty situation, particularly in the urban sector. Papua New Guinea is now developing a poverty reduction strategy that is intended to give an added focus to poverty in the existing national Medium-Term Development Strategy (2003–2007).

Education

Public spending on education was 2.3% of GDP in 2000/01. There are nine years of compulsory education starting at age six. Net enrolment ratios are 73% for primary education and 24% for secondary (2001/02). The pupil–teacher ratio for primary education is 35:1 and for secondary 23:1 (2002/03). The school year starts in January. Illiteracy among people aged 15–24 is 33.3% (30.9% for males and 35.9% for females, according to the 2000 census).

Health

Health care is provided by state- and church-run hospitals, dispensaries and clinics, with charges low and related to ability to pay. 39% of the population uses an improved drinking water source and 45% have adequate sanitation facilities (2002). Infant mortality was 68 per 1,000 live births in 2004 (down from 143 in 1960).

Women and health

Communicable diseases remain the major causes of morbidity and mortality in all age groups. However, significant progress has been made in some areas. In 2000, the country was declared poliomyelitis-free. However, around 50% of all mortality is still due to communicable diseases. Malaria is the leading cause of all outpatient visits, the third leading cause of hospital admissions and deaths, and is now endemic in every province, including those that were once malaria-free. Papua New Guinea was declared to have a generalised HIV/AIDS epidemic in 2003. Women make up 56% of reported cases of HIV. Incidence of sexually transmitted infections is rising; incidence of sexual assaults on women is also high, which increases their risk of STIs.

A major challenge to improving health in Papua New Guinea is related to perceptions of illness and health among the general population. There is a widespread lack of awareness of risk-related and health-promoting behaviour, and little involvement by local communities in health-promoting activities. Rural health services are poor and deteriorating.

Religion

Christians 90% (predominantly Protestants), though Christian beliefs often coexist with traditional beliefs.

Media

There are two daily papers, *Post-Courier* and *The National*, and a weekly, *The Independent*, are published in English. There are 23 TV sets and 59 personal computers per 1,000 people, and 75,000 internet users (2002/2003).

Concerns for the future

Papua New Guinea continues to face huge development challenges. Current GDP growth is not considered sufficient to keep pace with population growth. Priority issues facing Papua New Guinea include insufficient health, education, transport and public utilities infrastructures, major law and order problems, difficult land ownership and access issues, corruption and inefficient government, the threat of environmental degradation and unsustainable resource management by both domestic and foreign operators. Another issue with potential serious consequences for Papua New Guinea is the rapid spread of HIV/AIDS.

Key contacts

- Mr Joseph Klapat
  Secretary (Department Head)
  Gender & Development Division
  Department of Community Development
  Kumul Avenue, Waigani
  PO Box 7354
  Boroko NCD
  Papua New Guinea
  Tel: +675 325 5727
  Fax: +675 325 0133/323 0554
  Email: g-tatsi@hotmail.com

- Ms Molly Willie
  Acting Assistant Secretary
  Women's Division
  Department of Provincial & Local Govt Affairs
  PO Box 7354, Boroko
  Papua New Guinea
  Tel: +675 325 4566
  Fax: +675 325 0553

Papua New Guinea | Summary of gender profile

Gender profile			1990	2000	2004
Population	Total population (000)		4,114	5,229	5,772
	Female population (% of total)		47.3	48.5	48
Labour force participation	Female labour force (% of total)		46	48	48
	Female unemployment (% of female labour force)		5.9	1.3	...
Education	Adult illiteracy rate (% of people aged 15+)	Female	51.8	43.2	...
		Male	35.6	29.4	...
	Net primary enrolment ratio (% of age group)	Female	...	74	...
		Male	...	82	...
	Net secondary enrolment ratio (% of age group)	Female	...	20	...
		Male	...	25	...
	Gross tertiary enrolment ratio (% of age group)	Female	1	1	...
		Male	4	3	...
Health	Life expectancy at birth (years)	Female	54	55	57
		Male	51	54	55
	Infant mortality rate (per 1,000 live births)		74	70	68
	Prevalence of HIV (% of people aged 15–24)	Female	...	0.2	...
		Male	...	0.1	...

St Kitts and Nevis

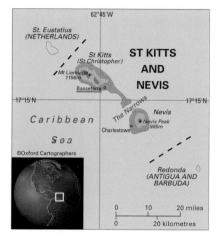

KEY FACTS

Joined Commonwealth: 1983

Capital: Basseterre

GDP growth (%): 3.2% p.a. 1990–2003

Official language: English

Time: GMT minus 4 hours

Currency: Eastern Caribbean dollar (EC$)

Main telephone lines/1,000 people: 500

Mobile phones/1,000 people: 106

National Women's Machinery

St Kitts and Nevis acceded to CEDAW in 1985 and to its Optional Protocol in 2006. Its National Women's Machinery is the Department of Gender Affairs in the Ministry of Social and Community Development and Gender Affairs.

St Kitts and Nevis is ranked at 51 in the Gender-related Development Index (GDI) in the *UNDP Human Development Report 2006*.

Priority concerns for mainstreaming gender issues

Among the 12 critical areas of concern outlined in the 1995 *Beijing Platform for Action*, the Government of St Kitts and Nevis has identified the following, in order of priority, for national action:

1. Education and training of women

2. Women in power and decision-making

3. Violence against women

4. Women in poverty

5. Institutional mechanisms for the advancement of women

Followed by: 6. Women and the economy; 7. The girl-child; 8. Human rights of women; 9. Women and health; 10. Women in the media; 11. Women and the environment; 12. Women and armed conflict.

Violence against women

Legislative amendments have been enacted which increase the penalties for all forms of sexual abuse. This legal development mirrors a widespread awareness of the seriousness of such forms of abuse. The Domestic Violence Act has been enacted to increase women's legal options; it ensures access to the courts for the purpose of seeking protective relief from all forms of domestic abuse. The Government has instituted mandatory gender-sensitive modules on human rights and violence against women within the police-training programme. In addition, training has been provided for health personnel, guidance counsellors and childcare workers to enhance their capacity to provide supportive and gender sensitive services to victims of violence.

Women in power and decision-making

On the issue of political and public life, strong extended family networks have enabled women to participate in public life and more recently, political activities. Unfortunately, the breakdown of family networks due to migration and single parent households has meant that traditional support services for women also collapse. While women have a strong voice in shaping the political direction of the country, women are not found commensurate with their numbers in decision-making positions, there are no women in parliament for example.

Religion

Mainly Christians (Anglicans, Methodists, Roman Catholics, Moravians and others).

Media

Newspapers include *Sun St Kitts/Nevis* (daily, privately owned), *Democrat* (weekly of People's Action Movement), *The Labour Spokesman* (twice weekly of St Kitts-Nevis Trades and Labour Union), and *The St Kitts and Nevis Observer* (weekly). There are 192 personal computers per 1,000 people and 10,000 internet users (2002).

Education

Public spending on education was 3.2% of GDP in 2002/03. There are 12 years of compulsory education starting at age five, offered by state, private and church schools.

Net enrolment ratios are 100% for primary education and 95% for secondary. The pupil–teacher ratio for primary education is 17:1 and for secondary 10:1. The school year starts in September.

Health

There are general hospitals at Basseterre in St Kitts and Charlestown in Nevis, and many health clinics. 99% of the population uses an improved drinking water source and 96% have adequate sanitation facilities (2002). Infant mortality was 18 per 1,000 live births in 2004.

Concerns for the future

There is a misconception that women already enjoy a high degree of empowerment, and has created a belief that the empowerment of women is not necessary. St. Kitts and Nevis is still very much a patriarchal society and the culture that supports this pervades professional and social relationships between men and women. Most of the data that might be helpful in decision-making with regard to gender policy is not disaggregated by sex.

Key contacts

- Ms Ingrid Charles-Gumbs
  Director of Gender Affairs
  Ministry of Social and Community
  Development, and Gender Affairs
  Government Headquarters
  Church Street, PO Box 186
  Basseterre
  St Kitts and Nevis
  Tel: +1 869 465 2521 Ex: 1020/1277
  Fax: +1 869 466 8244
  Email: mwaskn@caribsurf.com
          ingrid_charles_gumbs@
          hotmail.com

St Kitts and Nevis | Summary of gender profile

Gender profile			1990	2000	2004
Population	Total population (000)		40	41	42
	Female population (% of total)		...	...	...
Labour force participation	Female labour force (% of total)		...	...	...
	Female unemployment (% of female labour force)		...	...	...
Education	Adult illiteracy rate (% of people aged 15+)	Female	...	...	...
		Male	31.3	20.9	...
	Net primary enrolment ratio (% of age group)	Female	...	100	...
		Male	...	91	...
	Net secondary enrolment ratio (% of age group)	Female	...	100	...
		Male	...	83	...
	Gross tertiary enrolment ratio (% of age group)	Female	...	...	...
		Male	...	...	...
Health	Life expectancy at birth (years)	Female	69	73	74
		Male	65	68	69
	Infant mortality rate (per 1,000 live births)		30	21	18
	Prevalence of HIV (% of people aged 15–24)	Female	...	...	...
		Male	...	...	...

St Lucia

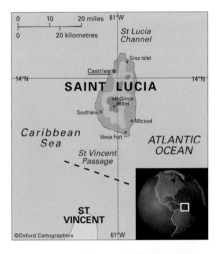

KEY FACTS

Joined Commonwealth: 1979

Capital: Castries

GDP growth (%): 0.2% p.a. 1990–2003

Official language: English

Time: GMT minus 4 hours

Currency: Eastern Caribbean dollar (EC$)

Main telephone lines/1,000 people: 273

Mobile Phones/1,000 people: 529

National Women's Machinery

St Lucia acceded to CEDAW in 1982. Its National Women's Machinery is the Division of Gender Relations in the Ministry of Health, Human Services, Family Affairs and Gender Relations. It exists to promote and facilitate the redistribution of resources and power at all levels, and a redefinition of roles and responsibilities to improve the relationship between men and women. The goal is to enhance the quality of women's lives and allow both men and women to reach their full potential.

St Lucia is ranked at 71 in the Gender-related Development Index (GDI) in the *UNDP Human Development Report 2006*.

Priority concerns for mainstreaming gender issues

Among the 12 critical areas of concern outlined in the 1995 *Beijing Platform for Action*, the Government of St Lucia has identified the following, in order of priority, for national action:

1. Violence against women

2. Women and health

3. Education and training of women

4. Women and poverty

5. Women and the economy

Followed by: 6. The girl-child; 7. Institutional mechanisms for the advancement of women; 8. Women in power and decision-making; 9. Women and the environment; 10. Human rights of women; 11. Women in the media; 12. Women and armed conflict.

Violence against women

The Division of Gender Relations has developed a three-pronged approach to combating violence against women: public awareness, education and sensitisation; safety and rehabilitation of victims; and therapeutic intervention for the perpetrator. It has provided domestic violence sensitisation education and training for all ranks of the police force; members of the judiciary; human resource managers in the public and private sectors; leaders of faith-based organisations; and school principals and teachers. To provide safety and rehabilitation for victims of domestic violence, the Women's Support Centre was opened in October 2001. The Centre accepts women and their children who are fleeing from life-threatening domestic violence situations. The Centre offers a homely and secure environment to its clients, providing them with counselling services, and assists them in developing personal safety plans. It offers support in helping them to rebuild their lives.

Women in power and decision-making

Women in St Lucia have the right to stand as candidates in general elections. They are eligible to be candidates on the same terms as men, but women do not fully utilise or exercise these rights. The political arena continues to be dominated by men; in the last election only 11% of elected parliamentary MPs were women. Some of the reasons cited for the limited number of women involved in politics include: the poor quality of political campaigning – women do not want to subject themselves to slander and abuse on political platforms; women's skills and experience are not recognised as being 'suitable' for a political career; women underestimate themselves and their ability to become good parliamentarians; women will not be able to withstand the pressures of combined family responsibilities and the demands of a political career.

Religion

Mainly Christians (Roman Catholics more than 80%, Anglicans, Methodists, Seventh Day Adventists, Baptists).

Media

The main newspapers are *The Voice of St Lucia*, *The Star* (three times weekly), *The Crusader*, *The Mirror* and *The Vanguard*. There are 150 personal computers per 1,000 people (2002).

Education

Public spending on education was 7.7% of GDP in 2002/03. There are 12 years of compulsory education starting at age five. Net enrolment ratios are 99% for primary education and 76% for secondary. The pupil–teacher ratio for primary education is 22:1 and for secondary 16:1. The school year starts in September. Illiteracy among people age 15–24 is 4.6% (5.2% for males and 4.1% for females, 2001 census).

Health

The Victoria Hospital and the new Tapion Hospital provide a range of medical treatment, and the Golden Hope Hospital caters for psychiatric cases. There are cottage hospitals at Vieux Fort, Dennery and Soufrière and more than 20 health centres. 98% of the population uses an improved drinking water source and 89% have adequate sanitation facilities (2002). Infant mortality was 13 per 1,000 live births in 2004.

Women and health

Emphasis has been placed on increasing access to health care, improving reproductive health services and mental health. The removal of user fees for certain health care services and the establishment of a polyclinic in a highly populated area in the north of the country have been part of the action taken to increase access to health care. These activities are particularly beneficial to women as the major users of health services. The issue of reproductive health is being addressed by both government and NGOs. Particular emphasis has been placed on breast and cervical cancer, sexually transmitted diseases, including HIV/AIDS, adolescent health and sexuality, family life education and counselling, family planning and contraceptive usage. The success of some health programmes has been hampered by social, cultural and spiritual beliefs and practices. For much of its history, St Lucia has been a predominantly Catholic nation, and today it continues to be predominantly Christian. The impact of this religious context has been the non-support of family planning methods, particularly the use of contraceptives, by various religious institutions, and resistance to or clandestine acceptance of family planning methods by women and other individuals.

Concerns for the future

Although there have been some positive changes in legislation which seek to correct inequalities, there are no special measures or mechanisms to enforce these laws in order to ensure the desired equality between men and women. There are also discriminatory laws which remain in effect.

Key contacts

- Mrs Lera Pascal
  Director, Gender Relations
  Ministry of Health, Human Services,
  Family and Gender Relations
  Walcott Building
  Jeremie St
  Castries
  St Lucia
  Tel: +1 758 453 0557
  Fax: +1 758 453 0938
  Email: womendiv@candw.lc

St Lucia	Summary of gender profile				
Gender profile			1990	2000	2004
Population	Total population (000)		134	156	159
	Female population (% of total)		51.6	51.3	51
Labour force participation	Female labour force (% of total)		39	41	41
	Female unemployment (% of female labour force)		...	20.7	51
Education	Adult illiteracy rate (% of people aged 15+)	Female	...	...	...
		Male	...	...	...
	Net primary enrolment ratio (% of age group)	Female	94	95	96
		Male	97	94	99
	Net secondary enrolment ratio (% of age group)	Female	...	72	62
		Male	...	56	63
	Gross tertiary enrolment ratio (% of age group)	Female	6	...	22
		Male	4	...	6
Health	Life expectancy at birth (years)	Female	73	74	75
		Male	69	70	72
	Infant mortality rate (per 1,000 live births)		20	17	13
	Prevalence of HIV (% of people aged 15–24)	Female	...	...	...
		Male	...	...	...

St Vincent and the Grenadines

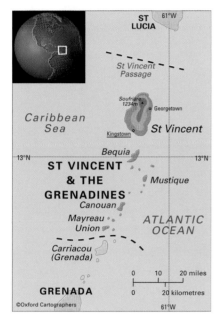

KEY FACTS

Joined Commonwealth: 1979

Capital: Kingstown

GDP growth (%): 3.0% p.a. 1990–2003

Official language: English

Time: GMT minus 4 hours

Currency: Eastern Caribbean dollar (EC$)

Main telephone lines/1,000 people: 273

Mobile phones/1,000 people: 529

National Women's Machinery

St Vincent and the Grenadines acceded to CEDAW in 1981. Its National Women's Machinery is the Gender Affairs Department in the Ministry for Social Development, Co-operatives, the Family, Gender and Ecclesiastical Affairs. The objectives of the Department are to implement an action plan that will ensure gender integration into all policies, procedures and programmes; work to prevent and eradicate domestic violence; create an environment where the educational, social, cultural and economic growth marginalised people can be sustained; and monitor and evaluate gender-sensitisation programmes.

St Vincent and the Grenadines is ranked at 88 in the Gender-related Development Index (GDI) in the *UNDP Human Development Report 2006*.

Priority concerns for mainstreaming gender issues

Among the 12 critical areas of concern outlined in the 1995 *Beijing Platform for Action*, the Government of St Vincent and the Grenadines has identified the following, in order of priority, for national action:

1. Violence against women

2. Institutional mechanisms for the advancement of women

3. Women in power and decision-making

4. Women and health

5. Education and training of women

Followed by: 6. Human rights of women; 7. Women and poverty; 8. Women and the economy; 9. The girl-child; 10. Women in the media; 11. Women and the environment; 12. Women and armed conflict.

Violence against women

Violence against women remains a serious problem. The law does not criminalise domestic violence, but rather provides protection for victims. Cases involving domestic violence are normally charged under assault, battery or other similar laws. The Gender Affairs Department provides a referral and information service to domestic violence victims, educating victims on the role of the police, legal affairs, and the family court in dealing with domestic violence, as well as providing information about possible assistance from various NGOs.

Women in power and decision-making

Women in St Vincent have been able to attain top administrative positions, but they find that they are still not involved actively in policy and decision-making within their organisations. This is particularly true of women who are administrators within the public service. Their positions entitle them to implement rather than influence directly the formulation of policies and decisions. The low visibility of women continues to be characteristic of political life. In the 2005 elections, women were elected to only four out of 22 parliamentary positions.

Education

Public spending on education was 10% of GDP in 2002/03. There are 11 years of compulsory education starting at age five. Net enrolment ratios are 90% for primary education and 58% for secondary. The pupil–teacher ratio for primary education is 18:1 and for secondary 22:1. The school year starts in September.

Health

As well as Kingstown General Hospital, there are district hospitals and health centres. Infant mortality was 18 per 1,000 live births in 2004.

Women and health

The Ministry of Health is attempting to reduce childbearing by very young women through public education and public health measures. Radio messages and newspaper articles, directed to men as well as women, are attempting to educate the public on the modern view of teenage pregnancy. Health clinics are equipped to distribute several types of contraceptives for women, but traditional attitudes hamper the promotion of contraceptives. Clinic nurses are directed to supply contraceptives to any girl or woman who asks for them and to advise them about birth control, but the attitude that it is not appropriate for schoolgirls to be sexually active prompts nurses to refuse to give them contraceptives or to inform their mothers, or other persons, about their sexual activity.

HIV/AIDS has emerged as a major challenge. Transmitted mainly through heterosexual contact, the general infection rate is estimated at around 2% and is growing rapidly. Adolescents and young adults, especially girls between 15–19 years old, are particularly vulnerable, due in part to early sexual initiation. In some instances, teenage girls outnumber boys by five to one for new infections, and 4.5 to one for reported AIDS cases.

Religion

Mainly Christians (mainly Anglicans, but also Methodists, Roman Catholics and others).

Media

The Herald is a daily paper; weekly newspapers include *The News*, *Searchlight* and *The Vincentian*. There are 120 personal computers per 1,000 people and 7,000 internet users (2002).

Key contacts

- Ms Miriam Roache
  Co-ordinator
  Gender Affairs Department
  Ministry for Social Development,
  Cooperatives, the Family, Gender and
  Ecclesiastical Affairs
  Egmont Street
  Kingstown Post Office
  Kingstown
  St Vincent and the Grenadines
  Tel: +1 784 457 2789
  Fax: +1 784 457 2476
  Email: corwoman@caribsurf.com
         mariamroache@hotmail.com

St Vincent and the Grenadines | Summary of gender profile

Gender profile			1990	2000	2004
Population	Total population (000)		109	116	118
	Female population (% of total)		50.4	50	50
Labour force participation	Female labour force (% of total)		36	39	40
	Female unemployment (% of female labour force)		22.1	...	...
Education	Adult illiteracy rate (% of people aged 15+)	Female	52.5	36.3	...
		Male	31.3	20.9	...
	Net primary enrolment ratio (% of age group)	Female	...	88	92
		Male	...	93	95
	Net secondary enrolment ratio (% of age group)	Female	23	62	63
		Male	33	54	62
	Gross tertiary enrolment ratio (% of age group)	Female	1	4	...
		Male	5	6	...
Health	Life expectancy at birth (years)	Female	72	73	74
		Male	67	68	69
	Infant mortality rate (per 1,000 live births)		22	21	18
	Prevalence of HIV (% of people aged 15–24)	Female	...	7.8	...
		Male	...	3.8	...

Samoa

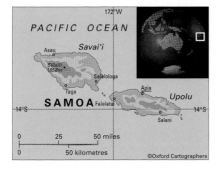

KEY FACTS

Joined Commonwealth: 1970

Capital: Apia

GDP growth (%): 3.1% p.a. 1990–2003

Official language: Samoan

Time: GMT minus 11 hours

Currency: tala or Samoan dollar (T)

Main telephone lines/1,000 people: 73

Mobile phones/1,000 people: 58

National Women's Machinery

Samoa acceded to CEDAW in 1992. Its National Women's Machinery is the Ministry of Women, Community and Social Development. It works to provide equality of outcomes for women in all their fields of interest and involvement; creates improvements in the opportunities available to women for equal participation in all spheres of community and economic life; forges links at the village level with a national network of women's groups; and co-ordinates women's programmes and policy development so as to minimise potential duplication of activities.

Samoa is ranked at 75 in the Gender-related Development Index (GDI) in the *UNDP Human Development Report 2006*.

Priority concerns for mainstreaming gender issues

Among the 12 critical areas of concern outlined in the 1995 *Beijing Platform for Action*, the Government of Samoa has identified the following, in order of priority, for national action:

1. Education and training of women

2. Women and health

3. Violence against women

4. Women and the economy

5. Women and poverty

Followed by: 6. Human rights of women; 7. Women in power and decision-making; 8. Institutional mechanisms for the advancement of women; 9. Women and the environment; 10. Women in the media; 11. The girl-child.

Education

Public spending on education was 4.8% of GDP in 2001/02. There are 10 years of compulsory education starting at age five. As well as state schools, there are several mission schools. Net enrolment ratios are 98% for primary education and 62% for secondary (2002/03). The pupil–teacher ratio for primary education is 27:1 and for secondary 21:1. The school year starts in February.

About 7% of the relevant age group is enrolled in tertiary education (2001/02). Illiteracy among people aged 15–24 is 0.5% (0.6% for males and 0.5% for females, 2002).

Health

The national hospital in Apia, four district hospitals and health centres. Most medical training is undertaken at the Fiji School of Medicine. Patterns of illness and death are shifting to those of a developed country, with longer life expectancy and a rising incidence of lifestyle diseases. 88% of the population uses an improved drinking water source and 100% have adequate sanitation facilities (2002). Infant mortality was 25 per 1,000 live births in 2004 (down from 134 in 1960).

Religion

Mainly Christians (Congregationalists 47%, Roman Catholics 20%, Methodists 15%).

Media

Samoa Observer and *Samoa Times* are dailies. *Le Samoa* (weekly), *Savali* (fortnightly), and *Talamua Magazine* (monthly) are in both Samoan and English. There are seven personal computers per 1,000 people and 4,000 internet users (2002).

Concerns for the future

Gender issues, such as the promotion and protection of women's rights, gender equity and women and HIV/AIDS are of high importance in Samoan society. Women have always been recognised in Samoa as significant contributors to the economic and social well-being of Samoan society. Programmes will need to be developed and implemented at all levels of society to break the traditional attitudes towards women and their roles. Up-skill training will need to be conducted and community development services provided for women in order to strengthen their capacity so as to improve their standards of living. The women's committees in the villages will need to be strengthened through policy implementation. The Ministry of Women, with the Education Department and other Academic Institutions, will also work to raise the level of awareness about employment opportunities at an earlier stage.

Key contacts

- Mrs L Foisaga Eteuati Shon
  Chief Executive Officer
  Ministry of Women, Community & Social Development
  FMFM II Building, 4th Floor
  PO Box 872
  Apia
  Samoa
  Tel: +685 63410
  Fax: +685 23639
  Email: foisaga@lesamoa.net

Samoa | Summary of gender profile

Gender profile			1990	2000	2004
Population	Total population (000)		161	177	184
	Female population (% of total)		47.6	48	48
Labour force participation	Female labour force (% of total)		32	32	32
	Female unemployment (% of female labour force)		...	...	...
Education	Adult illiteracy rate (% of people aged 15+)	Female	2.6	1.7	...
		Male	1.5	1.1	...
	Net primary enrolment ratio (% of age group)	Female	...	93	94
		Male	...	92	94
	Net secondary enrolment ratio (% of age group)	Female	...	69	70
		Male	...	60	62
	Gross tertiary enrolment ratio (% of age group)	Female	5	7	...
		Male	5	8	...
Health	Life expectancy at birth (years)	Female	68	72	73
		Male	65	66	67
	Infant mortality rate (per 1,000 live births)		40	28	25
	Prevalence of HIV (% of people aged 15–24)	Female	...	...	...
		Male	...	...	...

Seychelles

KEY FACTS

Joined Commonwealth: 1976

Capital: Victoria

GDP growth (%): 2.2% p.a. 1990–2003

Official languages: Creole, English and French

Time: GMT plus 4 hours

Currency: Seychelles rupee (SRs)

Main telephone lines/1,000 people: 256

Mobile phones/1,000 people: 595

National Women's Machinery

Seychelles ratified CEDAW in 1992 and signed to its Optional Protocol in 2002. Its National Women's Machinery is the Social Development Division in the Ministry of Social Affairs and Employment. The Gender Unit is adopting an integrated approach to development in Seychelles. It is the focal point for gender in Seychelles and there is a continued effort in the sharing of information and resources with all stakeholders. The Gender Unit, in collaboration with local and international organisations, has accomplished sensitisation activities in the form of workshops, lectures, debates, presentations, research, radio and TV programmes.

Seychelles is ranked at 47 in the Gender-related Development Index (GDI) in the *UNDP Human Development Report 2006*.

Priority concerns for mainstreaming gender issues

Among the 12 critical areas of concern outlined in the 1995 *Beijing Platform for Action*, the Government of Seychelles has identified the following, in order of priority, for national action:

1. Violence against women

2. Women and poverty

3. Institutional mechanisms for the advancement of women

4. Women and health

5. Women in power and decision-making

Followed by: 6. Women and the economy; 7. Human rights of women; 8. The girl-child; 9. Education and training of women; 10. Women in the media; 11. Women in the environment; 12. Women and armed conflict.

Women in power and decision-making

There is a need for more qualitative research to understand the underlying causes for the poor representation of women in politics. Many women admit having problems reconciling family responsibilities with the heavy demands of public life. There is insufficient data and research on how domestic responsibilities are shared between men and women in the home. Women parliamentarians themselves lack the lobbying and advocacy skills to promote greater gender equality. There is also a need for more positive portrayal of women in politics by the media.

Education

Public spending on education was 5.2% of GDP in 2002/03. There are ten years of compulsory education starting at age six. Net enrolment ratios are 100% for primary education and 100% for secondary. The pupil–teacher ratio for primary education is 14:1 and for secondary 14:1. The school year starts in January. Teaching is in Creole, French and English. Illiteracy among people age 15–24 is 0.9% (1.2% for males and 0.6% for females, 2003 census).

Health

A network of polyclinics provides general medical care, dentistry and other services. There are also private general practitioners. The public health service depends heavily on medical personnel from overseas. 87% of the population uses an improved drinking water source (2002). There is no malaria, yellow fever or bilharzia. Infant mortality was 12 per 1,000 live births in 2004 (43 in 1978).

Women and health

There are a large number of serious challenges and constraints in pursuing a

comprehensive national HIV/AIDS response. Persistent risky sexual behaviour has been rife despite raised awareness on HIV/AIDS in the population. Resource mobilisation has been scaled up but is still insufficient in terms of human and material capacity in several areas. There is a need for a larger and more effective unit for the AIDS Prevention and Control Programme. While the legal situation is not prejudicial towards the reproductive health status of adolescents and youth, the practice and interpretation of certain laws means that adolescents and youth may not benefit as much as they could from access to services.

Religion

90% of the population are Roman Catholics and there are small numbers of other Christians, and even smaller communities of Muslims and Hindus. Belief in the supernatural and in gris-gris, the old magic of spirits, often co-exists with Christian belief. Sorcery was outlawed in 1958.

Media

There is a government-controlled daily newspaper, *Seychelles Nation*, in English, French and Creole. The opposition-owned *Regar* is published weekly. The Seychelles Broadcasting Corporation provides radio and TV broadcasts in Creole, French and English. There are 155 personal computers per 1,000 people and 11,700 internet users (2002).

Concerns for the future

Areas of focus include: encouraging women to become active role models, especially in parliamentary positions, and proposing laws that further facilitate the participation of women in public life; encouraging the media to promote positive images of women in politics and challenge stereotypes; extending training programmes organised for women at grass roots levels by NGOs and facilitating the setting up of small home businesses; reviewing

arrangements for increasing micro-credit facilities for women; commissioning more qualitative and participatory research to understand social and cultural factors underlying persisting inequalities; and promoting a zero-tolerance policy towards domestic violence.

Key contacts

- Ms Antoinette Jolicsew
  Permanent Secretary
  Ministry of Social Affairs and Employment
  PO Box 190
  Unity House
  Victoria
  Seychelles
  Tel: +248 281 500/704/322 321
  Fax: +248 224 765
  Email: psmsamd@seychelles.net
         popunit@seychelles.net
         mesa@seychelles.net

Seychelles	Summary of gender profile				
Gender profile			*1990*	*2000*	*2004*
Population	Total population (000)		70	81	80
	Female population (% of total)		...	49.4	...
Labour force participation	Female labour force (% of total)		...	...	...
	Female unemployment (% of female labour force)		...	...	...
Education	Adult illiteracy rate (% of people aged 15+)	Female	...	...	...
		Male	...	...	...
	Net primary enrolment ratio (% of age group)	Female	...	100	99
		Male	...	100	100
	Net secondary enrolment ratio (% of age group)	Female	...	100	97
		Male	...	97	100
	Gross tertiary enrolment ratio (% of age group)	Female	...	...	...
		Male	...	...	...
Health	Life expectancy at birth (years)	Female	74	76	77
		Male	67	69	69
	Infant mortality rate (per 1,000 live births)		17	13	12
	Prevalence of HIV (% of people aged 15–24)	Female	...	...	...
		Male	...	...	...

Sierra Leone

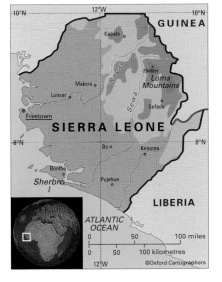

KEY FACTS

Joined Commonwealth: 1961

Capital: Freetown

GDP growth (%): –5.2% p.a. 1990–2003

Official language: English

Time: GMT

Currency: leone (Le)

Main telephone lines/1,000 people: 5

Mobile phones/1,000 people: 14

National Women's Machinery

Sierra Leone ratified CEDAW in 1998 and signed its Optional Protocol in 2002. Its National Women's Machinery is the Ministry of Social Welfare, Gender and Children's Affairs. The specific mandate of the Ministry is to co-ordinate activities related to the integration of gender issues into mainstream national and sectoral development plans and programmes; to address relevant issues in policy and law; and to promote the recognition of the full value of the social, political and economic contribution of women in national development.

The National Policy on Advancement of Women provides a conducive environment which will allow women to improve their status and participation, and provides integrated guidelines for evaluating the activities of agencies engaged in implementing CEDAW. The goals of the policy are to fully integrate women in the development process, to empower them and enhance their capabilities in economic, social and political development, and to ensure that all forms of discrimination against women are eliminated.

The Gender Mainstreaming Policy has the overall goal of incorporating a gender perspective in all legislative measures, policies, programmes and projects.

Sierra Leone is ranked at 176 in the Gender-related Development Index (GDI) in the *UNDP Human Development Report 2006*.

Priority concerns for mainstreaming gender issues

Among the 12 critical areas of concern outlined in the *1995 Beijing Platform for Action*, the Government of Sierra Leone places priority on the following:

- Peace (includes the issues violence against women, human rights of women, and women and armed conflict)
- Women and poverty
- Education and training of women
- Women and health.

Peace was chosen as a label to include three priority areas of concern affected by the decade of war against rebels.

Women in power and decision-making

In 2000 the 50/50 Group was established with the support of the British Council, Sierra Leone. Its mission is to increase the level of female participation in government and to ensure gender parity in all walks of life. It has been involved in the training of both old and new budding women politicians. Many beneficiaries of such training have gone on to run for political office in the 2004 local government elections. The group is also involved in lobbying government and political parties for the adoption of conditions that would enable women to participate in politics.

Violence against women

Women and girls became particular targets of malice and violence during the civil conflict in Sierra Leone. They suffered abduction and exploitation at the hands of the various factions. They were raped, forced into sexual slavery and endured acts of gross sexual violence. They were taken from their homes and villages by force. The Family Support Unit (FSU) of the Sierra Leone Police was set up in 2003 specifically to handle cases of rape, other sexual offences and domestic violence. It is specially trained in the collection of evidence for the prosecution of such crimes and the handling of victims of abuses. FSU branches have been opened in all police stations in the main towns. This has created a supportive environment to address domestic violence. Female genital mutilation (FGM) is deeply rooted in the cultural practices of Sierra Leone. Advocacy for its eradication has received a high degree of hostility in the country in all spheres. FGM continues to keep women oppressed; it implies that women and girls are to be subordinate to men in matters of sexuality. There are currently no national policies and educational measures to discourage and prohibit FGM. In an effort to combat trafficking of persons into the sex trade, government authorities have become more vigilant in their efforts to close brothels, which are perceived as perpetuating trafficking. The government has also begun to publicise trafficking issues through government-sponsored radio programmes and official statements in the press.

Education

Public spending on education was 3.7% of GDP in 2000/01. There are six years of primary education and six years of secondary. The pupil–teacher ratio for primary education is 37:1 and for secondary 27:1. The school year starts in September.

About 2% of the relevant age group is enrolled in tertiary education (2001/02). Illiteracy among people aged 15–24 is

61.8% (53.1% for males and 70.1% for females, 2000).

Education and training of women

Culture and tradition in Sierra Leone has in the past prevented women, particularly those in rural provinces, from accessing education. The practice in rural communities, where most people live below the poverty line, is usually to favour the education of men and boys at the expense of women and girls. In the provinces, the location of schools has been far from the neediest rural communities, resulting in long journeys by children from their homes to school. This has discouraged parents and guardians from sending their children and wards to school. Such reluctance appears to have affected the enrolment and attendance of girls more than boys, which has contributed to the particularly low literacy of women in the provinces. High levels of illiteracy have also had implications at a political level, where women's issues have generally been relegated to the back burner. There has always been a lack of awareness of the need for women to participate in issues

affecting their lives, even among the women themselves.

Health

57% of the population uses an improved drinking water source and 39% have adequate sanitation facilities (2002). Climatic conditions are conducive to the spread of tropical diseases (notably malaria and guinea worm), and civil war has made the country vulnerable to cholera. There was a high incidence of maiming during the civil war. Infant mortality was 165 per 1,000 live births in 2004, the highest rate in the world for that year (220 in 1960). At the end of 2001, 7% of people aged 15–49 were estimated to be HIV-positive.

Women and health

Women have long experienced unequal access to basic health services, as well as unequal opportunities for the protection, promotion and maintenance of their health. Traditional practices such as venerating women because of their childbearing capabilities and encouraging them to increase the number of children they bear, tend to put their health at risk while

Sierra Leone — Summary of gender profile

Gender profile			1990	2000	2004
Population	Total population (000)		4,078	4,509	5,336
	Female population (% of total)		50.9	50.9	51
Labour force participation	Female labour force (% of total)		39	39	38
	Female unemployment (% of female labour force)		...	...	...
Education	Adult illiteracy rate (% of people aged 15+)	Female	...	...	75.6
		Male	...	...	53.1
	Net primary enrolment ratio (% of age group)	Female	37	...	...
		Male	50	...	...
	Net secondary enrolment ratio (% of age group)	Female	...	24	...
		Male	...	29	...
	Gross tertiary enrolment ratio (% of age group)	Female	0	1	1
		Male	2	3	3
Health	Life expectancy at birth (years)	Female	40	42	43
		Male	37	39	40
	Infant mortality rate (per 1,000 live births)		175	167	165
	Prevalence of HIV (% of people aged 15–24)	Female	...	2.9	...
		Male	...	1.2	...

satisfying societal standards. Tradition and culture have also prohibited women from enjoying sexual and reproductive rights. As a result of increased understanding of the medical causes of maternal health, attention has been focused on developing strategies to reduce the high levels of maternal mortality. The Government's key concerns are outlined in the National Health Policy formulated in 2002. The Government recognises the need to treat citizens with particular vulnerability resulting from gender, poverty, conflict and specific health problems. Among the national priority health problems identified in the policy are unsatisfactory reproductive health, especially maternal mortality, and other health concerns including STIs, HIV/AIDS and nutrition-related diseases. Over 54% of HIV/AIDS infections are in women.

Religion

Muslims 60%, Christians 10%; most of the rest of the population hold traditional beliefs, which often coexist with other religions.

Media

There are many newspapers including *Awoko*, *Concord Times*, *The Democrat* and *Standard Times*. There are 13 TV sets per 1,000 people and 8,000 internet users (2002).

Concerns for the future

Sierra Leone is emerging from an 11-year civil war that destroyed most of the country's social, economic and physical infrastructure, resulting in a breakdown of civil and political authority. This has had a devastating impact on the social and economic fabric of the nation. Rebuilding the country's economic and social infrastructure to provide security and livelihood while guaranteeing the promotion and protection of rights for its citizens is a daunting challenge. The Ministry's five- year strategic 2002–2007 Plan of Action for the Advancement of Women has been undermined by inadequate financial and human resources, and competing government priorities. Little

has been done to publicise the plan; this needs to be done rapidly for gender mainstreaming to advance. Education and training will be crucial in ensuring the development and advancement of women.

Key contacts

- Permanent Secretary
  Ministry of Gender and Children's Affairs
  Youyi Building, 9th Floor
  Brookfields
  Freetown
  Sierra Leone
  Tel: +232 22 242301
  Fax: +232 22 242301

Singapore

KEY FACTS

Joined Commonwealth: 1965

Capital: Singapore

GDP growth (%): 3.5% p.a. 1990–2003

Official languages: English, Chinese (Mandarin),

Malay, Tamil

Time: GMT plus 8 hours

Currency: Singapore dollar (S$)

Main telephone lines/1,000 people: 450

Mobile phones/1,000 people: 853

National Women's Machinery

Singapore acceded to CEDAW in 1995. Its National Women's Machinery is the Women's Desk in the Ministry of Community Development, Youth and Sports.

The Women's Desk was established in 2002, and serves as the national focal point on gender policy matters and international co-operation pertaining to women. It adopts a 'many helping hands' approach to work with voluntary welfare organisations, NGOs, and the private sector to enhance the status of women in Singapore.

The Inter-Ministry Committee on CEDAW was set up in 1996 to monitor Singapore's implementation of the Convention. Where appropriate the Committee facilitates gender analysis and the implementation of gender-sensitive measures. The Women's Desk is the Secretariat to the Inter-Ministry Committee on CEDAW.

The Women's Desk has formed six women's workgroups comprising women from the private and public sector to look into gender equality issues. The six areas of focus are: leadership and mentoring; re-skilling; micro and social enterprise; women and health; work family harmony; and volunteerism and philanthropy.

The Women's Desk has identified key partners to enhance state and civil society collaboration and synergy on gender issues. These partners are:

- Singapore Council of Women's Organisations, the umbrella body for women's groups;

- The National Trades Union Congress Women's Committee, which champions women's interests pertaining to labour issues;

- The People's Association Women Integration Network Council, which

runs programmes for women at community level.

The memberships of these organisations represent more than 90% of all women's groups in Singapore and are therefore a good platform through which to advance key gender matters.

Singapore is ranked at 25 in the Gender-related Development Index (GDI) in the *UNDP Human Development Report 2006*.

Priority concerns for mainstreaming gender issues

The Singapore Government has identified all the critical areas of concern outlined in the 1995 *Beijing Platform for Action* as of equal priority (except for women and armed conflict, which is not applicable).

Women in power and decision-making

Equal opportunities based on the principles of meritocracy and access to education have resulted in women occupying important leadership positions in various capacities, such as judges, senior civil servants, diplomats, commanders of army and air force units, and trade union leaders. Recruitment into the public sector is open and transparent, and the development of every individual, female or male, is based on merit. The opportunities in the civil service are open to both men and women. There is a higher proportion of women in the civil service, compared to men.

Women and the economy

The JUMPstart Programme equips women, particularly non-working women from low-income households, with skills such as budgeting, financial planning and IT literacy, which will enable them to better manage their limited finances and enter the work force if they wish to.

Education

Strong policy emphasis had led by the 1990s to virtually universal primary education. There are 11 years of compulsory education starting at age six. The school year starts in January. Secondary education is streamed at three levels, according to measured ability, leading to junior college or vocational institutions. Illiteracy among people aged 15–24 is 0.5% (0.6% for males and 0.4% for females, 2000 census).

Education and training of women

The Government remains committed to providing all Singaporeans, both girls and boys, with equal access to quality education which will develop them fully and empower them to choose their own careers and shape their futures. Singapore believes that education is a fundamental resource which must be given to girls and boys in order that they become women and men who are well-educated, share economic and social responsibility, and are well-ranked in all fronts globally.

Health

Private health care predominates in the primary sector; 80% of hospital care is through public provision. There are more than 20 hospitals, 10 of which are government run. Employees pay into a health insurance fund known as Medisave (which is part of the wider social welfare provision of the Central Provident Fund). The entire population uses an improved drinking water source and has adequate sanitation facilities (2002). Infant mortality was three per 1,000 live births in 2004, the lowest rate in the world (down from 31 in 1960).

Women and health

The Government places a high priority on healthcare in Singapore. It not only grants women equal access to healthcare resources, but also pays attention to the special healthcare needs of women. The high standards of Singapore's healthcare system is demonstrated by increasing life expectancy for women, decreasing maternal mortality, and a low infant mortality rate. Healthcare in public institutions is heavily subsidised and affordable to all Singaporeans. No Singaporean is denied care due to lack of ability to pay. There are specific programmes targeted at women, e.g. subsidised breast and cervical cancer screenings.

Religion

Buddhists (28%), Muslims, Christians, Taoists, Hindus, Sikhs.

Media

There are several daily newspapers, among which *The Straits Times* (founded in 1845), *Business Times*, *The New Paper* and *Today* are in English. Other dailies are in Chinese, Tamil or Malay. There are 303 TV sets and 622 personal computers per 1,000 people, and 2,135,000 internet users (2002/2003).

Concerns for the future

There are three main issues facing women in Singapore: equipping women with new skills or updating their existing skills for life-long employability; addressing the work-life balance; and financial literacy.

Singapore | Summary of gender profile

Gender profile			1990	2000	2004
Population	Total population (000)		3,047	4,018	4,273
	Female population (% of total)		49.7	48.7	50
Labour force participation	Female labour force (% of total)		39	40	40
	Female unemployment (% of female labour force)		1.3	5.1	5.3
Education	Adult illiteracy rate (% of people aged 15+)	Female	16.8	11.7	11.4
		Male	5.6	3.8	3.4
	Net primary enrolment ratio (% of age group)	Female	...	...	...
		Male	...	...	...
	Net secondary enrolment ratio (% of age group)	Female	...	...	...
		Male	...	...	...
	Gross tertiary enrolment ratio (% of age group)	Female	17	...	...
		Male	24	...	...
Health	Life expectancy at birth (years)	Female	77	80	81
		Male	72	76	77
	Infant mortality rate (per 1,000 live births)		7	3	3
	Prevalence of HIV (% of people aged 15–24)	Female	...	0.2	...
		Male	...	0.2	...

Key contacts

- Mrs Tan Hwee Seh
  Coordinating Director
  Ministry of Community Development,
  Youth and Sports
  No 18-00 MCDS Building
  512 Thomson Road 298136
  Singapore
  Tel: +65 6354 8510/ 6355 6373
  Fax: +65 6354 8151
  Email: Maureen_goh@mcds.gov.sg
         tan-hwee_seh@mcys.gov.sg
         mcds_women_desk@mcds.gov.sg

- Mrs Tisa Ng
  President
  Singapore Council of Women's
  Organisations
  SCWO Centre
  96 Waterloo Street, 187967
  Singapore
  Tel: +65 6837 0611
  Fax: +65 6837 0081
  Email: sheila_koh@mcys.gov.sg

Solomon Islands

KEY FACTS

Joined Commonwealth: 1978

Capital: Honiara

GDP growth (%): –2.8% p.a. 1990–2003

Official language: English

Time: GMT plus 11 hours

Currency: Solomon Islands dollar (SI$)

Main telephone lines/1,000 people: 13

Mobile phones/1,000 people: 3

National Women's Machinery

Solomon Islands acceded to CEDAW and its Optional Protocol in 2002. Its National Women's Machinery is the Ministry of Youth, Sports and Women's Affairs.

Solomon Islands is ranked at 128 in the Gender-related Development Index (GDI) in the *UNDP Human Development Report 2006*.

Priority concerns for mainstreaming gender issues

Among the 12 critical areas of concern outlined in the 1995 *Beijing Platform for Action*, the Government of Solomon Islands has identified the following, in order of priority, for national action:

1. Women in power and decision-making

2. Education and training of women

3. Women and armed conflict

4. Human rights of women

5. Women and health

Followed by: 6. Institutional mechanisms for the advancement of women; 7. Women and the economy; 8. Violence against women; 9. Women and poverty; 10. Women and the environment; 11. The girl-child; 12. Women in the media.

Women in power and decision-making

Despite their exclusion from formal decision-making processes, Solomon Islander women have moved between the different combatant groups persuading men to lay down arms; women negotiators took on the traditional go-between role, which is a traditional method of conflict resolution in the Solomon Islands. The National Council of Women and other women's organisations were heavily involved in voter awareness programmes during the elections held in 2002 and 2006.

They are also active in carrying out awareness and advocacy work on human rights in the communities.

Violence against women

Violence against women, including rape and domestic abuse, remains a serious problem. Among the reasons cited for the failure to report many incidents of abuse were pressure from male relatives, fear of reprisals, feelings of shame and cultural taboos on discussion of such matters. In 2005, the police established a sexual assault unit, staffed mostly by female officers, to combat the problem. The unit was well received by the public; women felt more comfortable reporting abuses. NGOs conducted awareness campaigns on family violence during the year. There are church-run facilities for abused women and an NGO supported family centre that provides counselling, legal assistance and other support services for women.

Women and the economy

While international and regional efforts have focused on social issues affecting women, not enough attention has been paid to economically empowering women. This situation was made worse by the ethnic and armed conflict, which brought about a downturn of the economy due to lawlessness, a closure of major businesses and disruption to basic services, especially in the education and health sectors. The poor economic situation forced government to restructure and saw a massive redundancy of public officers. It also forced government to place a freeze on new recruitment. The fact that women's issues are cross-cutting also meant that other priority areas for women that need to be addressed could not be adequately attended to.

Education

Public spending on education was 3.4% of GDP in 2000/01. There are six years of primary education and seven years of secondary. The school year starts in January. Adult literacy is around 62%.

Health

The government runs six hospitals, as well as clinics and clinical aid posts. The churches run two hospitals as well as clinics. 70% of the population uses an improved drinking water source and 31% have adequate sanitation facilities (2002). Infant mortality was 34 per 1,000 live births in 2004 (120 in 1960).

Malaria remains the main health problem.

Religion

Mainly Christians (Church of Melanesia Anglicans 45%, Roman Catholics 18%, Methodists, Presbyterians, Baptists and Seventh Day Adventists).

Media

Solomon Star is a daily newspaper, and *Solomon Times* and *Solomons Voice* are weekly. TV broadcasting is available via satellite. There are 41 personal computers per 1,000 people and 2,500 internet users (2002/2003).

Concerns for the future

Women play a vital role in creating and maintaining peace at the community level in the Solomon Islands, and they have been greatly affected by the conflict through displacement, vulnerability to rape, harassment, and economic hardship. As a country emerging from a conflict situation, improving the welfare of women is an indispensable requirement for sustainable security and development. A major constraining factor in the implementation of the gender plan for action has been the lack of resources in terms of finance and capacity within the national women's machinery to effectively play a facilitation, implementation, coordination and monitoring role.

Key contacts

- Ms Ruth Liloqua
  Permanent Secretary
  Department of Home Affairs
  Ministry of Youth, Sports & Women's Affairs
  PO Box G11
  Honiara
  Solomon Islands
  Tel: +677 28601/2559
  Fax: +677 25591
  Email: wdd@welkam.solomon.com.sb
            falu51@hotmail.com

- Ms Janet Tuhaika
  Director
  Women's Development Division (WDD)
  Ministry of Youth, Sports & Womens Affairs
  PO Box G11
  Honiara
  Solomon Islands
  Tel: +677 27529
  Fax: +677 27529
  Email: pacfaw@solomon.com.sb

Solomon Islands | Summary of gender profile

Gender profile			1990	2000	2004
Population	Total population (000)		317	419	466
	Female population (% of total)		48.3	48	48
Labour force participation	Female labour force (% of total)		39	39	39
	Female unemployment (% of female labour force)		...	...	...
Education	Adult illiteracy rate (% of people aged 15+)	Female	41.7	67.9	...
		Male	19.6	43.7	...
	Net primary enrolment ratio (% of age group)	Female	...	...	79
		Male	...	...	80
	Net secondary enrolment ratio (% of age group)	Female	...	16	24
		Male	...	19	29
	Gross tertiary enrolment ratio (% of age group)	Female	...	...	...
		Male	...	...	...
Health	Life expectancy at birth (years)	Female	62	62	63
		Male	60	61	62
	Infant mortality rate (per 1,000 live births)		38	36	34
	Prevalence of HIV (% of people aged 15–24)	Female	...	...	...
		Male	...	...	...

South Africa

KEY FACTS

Joined Commonwealth: 1931 (Statute of Westminster; left in 1961, rejoined in 1994)

Capital: Tshwane formerly Pretoria

GDP growth (%): 0.2% p.a. 1990–2003

Official languages: 11 official languages, including Afrikaans, English, isiNdebele, isiXhosa, isiZulu, Sesotho sa Leboa, Sesotho, Setswana, siSwati, Tshivenda and Xitsonga

Time: GMT plus 2 hours

Currency: rand (R)

Main telephone lines/1,000 people: 107

Mobile phones/1,000 people: 364

National Women's Machinery

South Africa ratified CEDAW in 1996 and acceded to its Optional Protocol in 2005.

The National Women's Machinery is a comprehensive structure which consists of structures in the executive, legislative, independent bodies set up by statutory law and non-governmental organisations. The role played by NGOs and civil society institutions is also defined as part of the national mechanism for the promotion of gender equality and empowerment of women. The components of the gender machinery are the facilitators of the gender programme and all have co-ordinating roles.

Within the Executive Branch, the machinery comprises the following.

- The Cabinet: The Cabinet Cluster Committee is responsible for ensuring the adoption and implementation of the National Gender Policy and guaranteeing that Cabinet discussion are engendered, and that Ministers actively assert the implementation of the gender policy. The Committee is also required to provide access to information; ensure that the integrated coordination framework results in measurable sector-specific outputs; and make recommendations on policy and legislation.

- The Office on the Status of Women (OSW): The OSW is located in the Presidency and was established in 1997 as the principal coordinating structure for the National Machinery on Gender Equality. It is responsible for developing national action plans; advancing women's empowerment; and monitoring implementation and progress on gender policy. The OSW is also pivotal for liaison with civil society organisations.

- Gender Focal Points within National Departments: At the operational level, the main responsibility for ensuring the effective implementation of the National Gender Policy rests with individual government departments through the Gender Focal Points or Gender Units.

Within the Legislature, the machinery comprises three structures created in parliament to advance women's emancipation and gender equality.

- The Joint Monitoring Committee on the Improvement of Quality of Life and Status of Women: the Committee monitors the progress of government policy and assesses whether the implementation of national and international commitments on gender equality.

- The Parliamentary Women's Caucus: Established in 1994, this committee brings together women from all political parties. Its main objective is to bring women parliamentarians together to examine issues that affect them, and to create an enabling environment for women MPs.

- The Women's Empowerment Unit (WEU): The WEU is located in the Speaker's Forum, a structure that brings together speakers from national and provincial legislature. Its main focus is to identify areas that hinder women's full participation in the law-making process, and to focus on training and skills development for women lawmakers.

The Commission on Gender Equality (CGE) was established in 1997, and is an independent, statutory, advisory and research body. The key functions of the CGE include monitoring and evaluating polices and practices of state organs at any level; making recommendations about laws, policies and programmes to government; providing public education and information; resolving disputes through mediation and conciliation and ensuring the promotion and protection of gender equality.

A National Gender Policy has been developed in South Africa to recognise that majority of women are living below the poverty line. The document includes sections on context and vision, situational analysis, policy context, vision and principles for gender equity, a framework for implementation, guidelines for policy and monitoring and evaluation methods.

South Africa is ranked at 121 in the Gender-related Development Index (GDI) in the UNDP Human Development Report 2006.

Priority concerns for mainstreaming gender issues

Among the 12 critical areas of concern outlined in the 1995 *Beijing Platform for Action*, the Government of South Africa has identified the following for national action:

- Women and violence/human rights of women
- Women and poverty
- Women and health
- Women and education
- Women and the economy

- Institutional mechanisms for the advancement of women
- Women in power and decision-making.

Education

Public spending on education was 5.3% of GDP in 2002/03. There are nine years of compulsory education starting at age seven. Net enrolment ratios are 89% for primary education and 66% for secondary. The pupil–teacher ratio for primary education is 35:1 and for secondary 29:1. The school year starts in January.

About 15% of the relevant age group is enrolled in tertiary education (2002/03). Illiteracy among people aged 15–24 is 6.1% (6.5% for males and 5.7% for females, 1996 census).

Health

Durban Academic Hospital in KwaZulu-Natal, four new hospitals in Northern Province and many new health centres were built in the late 1990s. 87% of the population uses an improved drinking water source and 67% have adequate sanitation facilities (2002). Infant mortality was 54 per 1,000 live births in 2004 (89 in 1960).

AIDS is a dire problem; at the end of 2003, 21.5% of people aged 15–49 were HIV-positive. For many years the government appeared unable to accept the severity of the looming problem and failed to take measures to contain it. By 2000, when it became involved in controversy over its claim that AIDS was not caused by HIV, there were – by some international estimates – more HIV-positive cases in South Africa than any other country. By April 2002, however, the government had committed itself to lead the battle against HIV/AIDS, making antiretroviral drugs available through the health service.

Women and health

Women in South Africa, and single mothers in particular, are often economically disadvantaged, their access to health care is compromised. Clinics and schools are lacking in areas where poverty is rife, especially the rural areas. HIV is more easily transmitted in areas where general health is poor, and poor women have less access to information and resources that will help them make informed choices. 56% of all cases of HIV/AIDS affect women.

South Africa	Summary of gender profile				
Gender profile				1990	2000	2004
Population	Total population (000)			35,200	44,000	47,208
	Female population (% of total)			50	51	51
Labour force participation	Female labour force (% of total)			42	39	38
	Female unemployment (% of female labour force)			...	27.8	31.7
Education	Adult illiteracy rate (% of people aged 15+)		Female	19.8	...	19.1
			Male	17.7	...	15.9
	Net primary enrolment ratio (% of age group)		Female	91	91	89
			Male	88	90	88
	Net secondary enrolment ratio (% of age group)		Female	48	65	...
			Male	42	58	...
	Gross tertiary enrolment ratio (% of age group)		Female	11	16	17
			Male	13	13	14
Health	Life expectancy at birth (years)		Female	65	49	45
			Male	59	47	44
	Infant mortality rate (per 1,000 live births)			45	50	54
	Prevalence of HIV (% of people aged 15–24)		Female	...	34.3	...
			Male	...	15.8	...

Religion

Christians 68%; African independent churches predominate, although there are a number of other Christian denominations, and minorities of Muslims, Hindus and Jews. Traditional and Christian forms of worship are often blended.

Media

Among the many dailies in English are *The Cape Argus*, *Cape Times*, *The Citizen*, *Sowetan*, *The Star* (Johannesburg) and *This Day*. Leading Afrikaans-language dailies are *Beeld* (Johannesburg) and *Die Burger* (Cape Town). The most influential national weeklies are *Financial Mail*, *Mail and Guardian*, and *Sunday Times*. The *Sunday Independent* was launched in the latter 1990s.

South Africa has the largest and most sophisticated radio network in Africa. TV is available via cable and satellite as well as national terrestrial networks. There are 177 TV sets and 73 personal computers per 1,000 people, and 3.1 million internet users (2002).

Concerns for the future

South Africa's vision for the full realisation of gender equality is faced with many challenges and obstacles. To achieve a society free of racism and sexism the country must undergo a paradigm shift with regard to how resources are allocated and how people relate to each other. These challenges need to be translated into national priorities. All these priorities have compelling gender dimensions which need to be addressed if the country is to advance towards gender equality. One of the major challenges is poverty. This is a major problem for women in South Africa. The systematic and socially engineered location of women in rural areas, and the underdevelopment of infrastructure in these areas, has been directly responsible for the poor conditions under which the majority of South Africa's rural communities live. Other challenges faced include HIV/AIDS, access to employment opportunities, eradication of all forms of violence against women, and compliance with the policy and legislative framework.

Key contacts

- Chief Executive Office
  Office on the Status of Women
  Union Buildings
  Private Bag X1000
  West Wing,
  Union Buildings Pretoria 0001
  South Africa
  Tel: +27 12 300 5491/3/5
  Fax: +27 12 326 4176/323 2573

- Ms Joyce Seroke
  Chairperson
  Commission on Gender Equality
  Bramontein Centre
  10th Floor, 23 Jorrisen Street
  PO Box 32175
  Braamfontein 2017
  South Africa
  Tel: +27 11 403 7182
  Fax: +27 11 403 7188
  Email: cgeinfo@cge.org.za

Sri Lanka

KEY FACTS

Joined Commonwealth: 1948

Capital: Colombo

GDP growth (%): 3.3% p.a. 1990–2003

Official languages: Sinhala, Tamil

Time: GMT plus 6 hours

Currency: Sri Lanka rupee (SLRs)

Main telephone lines/1,000 people: 49

Mobile phones/1,000 people: 73

National Women's Machinery

Sri Lanka acceded to CEDAW in 1981 and to its Optional Protocol in 2003. Its National Women's Machinery is the Ministry of Child Development and Women's Empowerment. Its objectives are to formulate and implement policies, plans and programmes in respect of women's empowerment and for the advancement of quality of life for women; increase participation in national development policies and other spheres of life; and to implement the Women's Charter.

Sri Lanka is ranked at 93 in the Gender-related Development Index (GDI) in the *UNDP Human Development Report 2006*.

Priority concerns for mainstreaming gender issues

Among the 12 critical areas of concern outlined in the 1995 *Beijing Platform for Action*, the Government of Sri Lanka has identified the following, in order of priority, for national action:

1. Violence against women

2. Human rights of women

3. Institutional mechanisms for the advancement of women

4. Women and poverty

5. Women and health

Women in power and decision-making

Even though Sri Lankan women have held the highest posts in politics, and produced the first woman prime minister in the world, this has not significantly improved the status of Sri Lankan women. Sri Lanka is still a male-dominated society. Male supremacy is nurtured and enhanced in every possible way. Grassroots women are at the periphery of the decision-making process.

Violence against women

Violence has started to creep into the society at a fast rate. Gender-based violence has become a fact of life. Issues around women migrant workers have brought physical and mental damage to the entire family. Rape-related violence, emotional abuse, physical abuse, sexual harassment, domestic violence and violence related to spousal alcohol abuse are common. Socio-cultural practices such as dowry systems are not as prevalent as they used to be, but they still exist as a subtle cultural feature in the society.

Education

Public spending on education was 3.1% of GDP in 1998/99. There are nine years of compulsory education starting at age five. The pupil–teacher ratio for primary education is 23:1 and for secondary 20:1 (2003/04). The school year starts in January. Illiteracy among people aged 15–24 is 4.4% (4.9% for males and 4.0% for females, 2001 census).

Health

Both Western and Ayurvedic (traditional) medicine are practised, though most doctors practise Western medicine. A free health service is available, with hospitals and clinics countrywide, supplemented by several private hospitals and clinics in Colombo. 78% of the population uses an improved drinking water source and 91% have adequate sanitation facilities (2002). Infant mortality was 12 per 1,000 live births in 2004 (83 in 1960). Over 90% of children are born in hospital. Family planning is common, with about 68% of married women practising contraception. Polio has been eradicated, but malaria remains a problem.

Religion

Buddhists 70%, Hindus 15%, Christians 8% and Muslims 7%.

Media

Several daily newspapers in Sinhala, Tamil and English, including the state-owned *Daily News*, and independent *Daily Mirror* and *The Island*, and several weeklies, including *The Sunday Times* and state-owned *Sunday Observer*. There are 117 TV sets and 17 personal computers per 1,000 people, and 250,000 internet users (2002/2003).

Concerns for the future

Efforts towards mainstreaming gender into all aspects of national development requires greater and sustained policy, technical input and support. There is a need to put in place mechanisms to address violence against women, and to give women the right to participate equally in high-level decision-making positions.

Key contacts

- Mrs Indrani Sugathadasa
  Secretary
  Ministry of Child Development and Women Empowerment
  177 Nawala Road
  Narahenpita
  Colombo 5
  Sri Lanka
  Tel: +94 11 236 8373
  Fax: +94 11 236 9294
  Email: secycdwe@sltnet.lk

Sri Lanka | Summary of gender profile

Gender profile			1990	2000	2004
Population	Total population (000)		17,017	19,359	20,570
	Female population (% of total)		49	49	49
Labour force participation	Female labour force (% of total)		35	32	30
	Female unemployment (% of female labour force)		23.6	11.4	14.7
Education	Adult illiteracy rate (% of people aged 15+)	Female	15.3	11	...
		Male	7.1	5.6	...
	Net primary enrolment ratio (% of age group)	Female	...	...	98
		Male	...	...	99
	Net secondary enrolment ratio (% of age group)	Female	...	...	...
		Male	...	...	...
	Gross tertiary enrolment ratio (% of age group)	Female	3	...	...
		Male	6	...	...
Health	Life expectancy at birth (years)	Female	74	76	77
		Male	69	71	72
	Infant mortality rate (per 1,000 live births)		26	16	12
	Prevalence of HIV (% of people aged 15–24)	Female	...	0	...
		Male	...	0	...

Swaziland

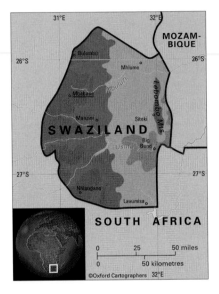

KEY FACTS

Joined Commonwealth: 1968

Capital: Mbabane

GDP growth (%): 0.2% p.a. 1990–2003

Official languages: siSwati, English

Time: GMT plus 2 hours

Currency: lilangeni, plural emalangeni (E)

Main telephone lines/1,000 people: 44

Mobile phones/1,000 people: 84

National Women's Machinery

Swaziland acceded to CEDAW in 2004. Its National Women's Machinery is the Gender Co-ordination Unit in the Ministry of Home Affairs. The objectives of the Unit are to mainstream issues of gender throughout all sectors of national development; to direct and coordinate all gender and development activities; to facilitate the development of gender-based analysis in policy development, planning and programming; to continuously monitor and evaluate the implementation of gender and development interventions and strategies nationally; and to foster development of gender networks locally and internationally for advocacy on all gender related issues.

Swaziland is sensitised to the importance of gender issues and has incorporated them as priority in the National Development Strategy (NDS) and the Economic and Social Reform Agenda (ESRA). At the level of ESRA, a task force has been established, and a position paper created which is presently being used as a guide for the formulation of the unit's activities.

In 1994, government launched the Swaziland Committee on Gender and Women's Affairs (SCOGWA) as the main technical coordinating body for the development of the gender programme. SCOGWA consists of relevant government ministries, NGOs, private sector, traditional groups, church groups and professional groups.

Swaziland is ranked at 146 in the Gender-related Development Index (GDI) in the *UNDP Human Development Report 2006*.

Priority concerns for mainstreaming gender issues

Among the 12 critical areas of concern outlined in the 1995 *Beijing Platform for Action*, the Government of Swaziland has identified the following, in order of priority, for national action:

1. Women in power and decision-making

2. Human rights of women

3. Violence against women

4. Women and poverty

5. Women and the economy

Women in power and decision-making

In Swaziland, women are generally under-represented in positions of power and decision-making. In the 2003 elections, only 10% of parliamentary positions were won by women. There is 30% female representation in the senate. The prevailing social and cultural practices still inhibit women's active participation in the political arena.

Violence against women

Gender violence is prevalent in Swaziland, in particular sexual and physical violence such as rape, incest and battery. Public awareness has been raised pertaining to issues of violence, and the reporting of cases is increasing. The government in collaboration with NGOs is engaged in public awareness, lobbying, advocacy, legal reform and structural measures, in the bid to eradicate gender-based violence in the country.

Education

Public spending on education was 7.1% of GDP in 2002/03. There are seven years of compulsory education starting at age six. Net enrolment ratios are 75% for primary and 32% for secondary. The pupil–teacher ratio for primary is 31:1 and for secondary 16:1. The school year starts in January.

About 5% of the relevant age group is enrolled in tertiary education (2002/03). Illiteracy among people age 15–24 is 11.9% (13.2% for males and 10.6% for females, 2000). There is a national library and a mobile library service to more remote parts of the country.

Health

Services are provided by the state, missions and some industrial organisations. 52% of the population uses an improved drinking water source and 52% adequate sanitation facilities (2002). Infant mortality was 108 per 1,000 live births in 2004, having risen sharply since the late 1990s due to AIDS (150 in 1960). At the end of 2003, 38.8% of people age 15 to 49 were HIV positive.

Women and health

Swaziland is a patriarchal society characterised by gender inequalities, which have hampered efforts to address the HIV/AIDS epidemic. Women and young girls are susceptible to sexual exploitation and abuse. Their economic dependency and lack of access to basic resources, such as land, have exacerbated their vulnerability to HIV/AIDS. 55% of all HIV/AIDS cases affect women.

Religion

Christians 77% and most of the rest hold traditional beliefs. Traditional beliefs often coexist with Christian beliefs.

Media

English-language dailies are *The Times of Swaziland/Sunday Times* and *The Swazi Observer/The Weekend Observer*. There are 34 TV sets and 29 personal computers per 1,000 people, and 27,000 internet users (2002/2003).

Concerns for the future

Efforts will continue to be focused on combating HIV/AIDS, implementing measures to address violence against women, and increasing the number of women in decision-making positions.

Key contacts

- Ms Jane Mkhomta
  Gender Analyst
  Ministry of Home Affairs
  PO Box 432
  Mbabane
  Swaziland
  Tel: +268 404 2941
  Fax: +268 404 4304
  Email: mattyjane22@yahoo.com

Swaziland | Summary of gender profile

Gender profile			1990	2000	2004
Population	Total population (000)		770	1,000	1,034
	Female population (% of total)		53	52	52
Labour force participation	Female labour force (% of total)		38	34	33
	Female unemployment (% of female labour force)		...	...	...
Education	Adult illiteracy rate (% of people aged 15+)	Female	30.1	21.4	...
		Male	26.3	19.2	...
	Net primary enrolment ratio (% of age group)	Female	76	76	77
		Male	73	76	76
	Net secondary enrolment ratio (% of age group)	Female	33	33	32
		Male	27	28	26
	Gross tertiary enrolment ratio (% of age group)	Female	3	4	5
		Male	4	5	4
Health	Life expectancy at birth (years)	Female	59	46	42
		Male	54	45	43
	Infant mortality rate (per 1,000 live births)		78	98	108
	Prevalence of HIV (% of people aged 15–24)	Female	...	39.5	...
		Male	...	15.2	...

Tonga

©Oxford Cartographers

KEY FACTS

Joined Commonwealth: 1970

Capital: Nuku'alofa

GDP growth (%): 2.0% p.a. 1990–2003

Official languages: Tongan, English

Time: GMT minus 11–10 hours

Currency: pa'anga or Tongan dollar (T$)

Main telephone lines/1,000 people: 113

Mobile phones/1,000 people: 34

National Women's Machinery

Tonga is not a signatory to CEDAW. Its National Women's Machinery is the Ministry of Education, Women's Affairs and Culture. Its mandate includes the co-ordination of women's activities and the management of the government's commitments to regional and international agreements and plans.

The Ministry is required to implement the 2001 National Policy on Gender and Development which aims to achieve gender equity by 2025. The Policy emphasises the role of the family in society, enhancing the status of the family to preserve traditions, recognising the social and cultural context of health needs, and equal participation of men and women in education.

Tonga is ranked at 55 in the Gender-related Development Index (GDI) in the *UNDP Human Development Report 2006*.

Priority concerns for mainstreaming gender issues

Among the 12 critical areas of concern outlined in the 1995 *Beijing Platform for Action*, the Government of Tonga has identified the following, in order of priority, for national action:

1. Institutional mechanism for the advancement of women

2. Women and the economy

3. Education and training of women

4. Women in power and decision-making

5. Women and health

Followed by: 6. Women and poverty; 7. Human rights of women; 8. Violence against women; 9. Women and the environment; 10. The girl-child; 11. Women in the media; 12. Women and armed conflict.

Action areas

Tonga will concentrate on the areas of violence against women, women in the economy, and women in power and decision-making, as part of its progress towards the eventual ratification of CEDAW.

Education

Public spending on education was 4.9% of GDP in 2002/03. There are nine years of compulsory education starting at age six. More than 90% of primary students attend state schools, while about 90% of secondary students attend church schools. The pupil–teacher ratio for primary is 22:1 and for secondary 15:1.

The school year starts in February. About 4% of the relevant age group is enrolled in tertiary education (2001/02).

Health

There are public hospitals on the islands of Tongatapu, Ha'apai and Vava'u, and dispensaries throughout the islands. The entire population uses an improved drinking water source and 97% adequate sanitation facilities (2002). The Tongan diet has, over time, moved away from traditional root crops to imported foods. Infant mortality was 20 per 1,000 live births in 2004.

Religion

Mainly Christians (Wesleyans, Roman Catholics, Mormons, Anglicans, Church of Tonga, Free Church of Tonga and Seventh Day Adventists).

Media

Newspapers include *Tonga Chronicle* (state-owned) and *Times of Tonga* and *Talaki* (both published in New Zealand). *Matangi Tonga* is a fortnightly news magazine. There are 20 personal computers per 1,000 people and 2,900 internet users (2002).

Key contacts

- Ms Polotu F Paunga
  Deputy Director & Head of Women's
  Affairs Programme
  Ministry of Education, Women's Affairs &
  Culture
  PO Box 851
  Nuku'alofa
  Tonga
  Tel: +676 23 227
  Fax: +676 28 892
  Email: polotu@gmail.com
          polotu@tesp.gov.to

Tonga	Summary of gender profile				
Gender profile			*1990*	*2000*	*2004*
Population	Total population (000)		94	100	102
	Female population (% of total)		49	49	49
Labour force participation	Female labour force (% of total)		33	33	38
	Female unemployment (% of female labour force)		...	...	...
Education	Adult illiteracy rate (% of people aged 15+)	Female	...	...	1
		Male	...	...	1.2
	Net primary enrolment ratio (% of age group)	Female	...	89	96
		Male	...	92	100
	Net secondary enrolment ratio (% of age group)	Female	...	76	...
		Male	...	69	...
	Gross tertiary enrolment ratio (% of age group)	Female	...	4	...
		Male	...	3	...
Health	Life expectancy at birth (years)	Female	71	73	74
		Male	69	71	71
	Infant mortality rate (per 1,000 live births)		27	22	20
	Prevalence of HIV (% of people aged 15–24)	Female	...	...	...
		Male	...	...	...

Trinidad and Tobago

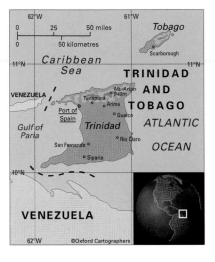

KEY FACTS

Joined Commonwealth: 1962

Capital: Port of Spain

GDP growth (%): 3.0% p.a. 1990–2003

Official language: English

Time: GMT minus 4 hours

Currency: Trinidad and Tobago dollar (TT$)

Main line telephones/1,000 people: 250

Mobile phones/1,000 people: 399

National Women's Machinery

Trinidad and Tobago acceded to CEDAW in 1990. Its National Women's Machinery is the Gender Affairs Division in the Ministry of Community Development, Culture and Gender. The Division is charged with protecting women's rights in all aspects of government and legislation. It has formulated the National Gender Policy, and designs and executes programmes for the socio-economic empowerment of women. Working alongside community groups, NGOs and other government agencies, the Division is also responsible for conducting gender training programmes.

The National Gender Policy and Action Plan were launched in 2002, with the purpose to advance the principles of gender equality and equity, and to identify strategies to mainstream the gender issues into the work of government and civil society.

Trinidad and Tobago is ranked at 57 in the Gender-related Development Index (GDI) in the *UNDP Human Development Report 2006*.

Priority concerns for mainstreaming gender issues

Among the 12 critical areas of concern outlined in the 1995 *Beijing Platform for Action*, the Government of Trinidad and Tobago has identified the following, in order of priority, for national action:

1. Women and poverty

2. Education and training of women

3. Violence against women

Violence against women

The Gender Affairs Division continues to design, implement and execute programmes via its Domestic Violence Unit to address the crucial problem of domestic violence in society. The Drop-in Centre programme offers counselling to victims of domestic violence including victims of rape and incest. The programme also provides information and referral services to people who require assistance to deal with other personal and family issues such as drug abuse, anger management, conflict management and teenage pregnancy. Outreach programmes are also conducted as a means of preventing violence and encouraging the establishment of support groups within the communities.

Women and the economy

The Non-Traditional Skills Training Programme provides an opportunity to urban and rural women between the ages of 18–50 to gain a marketable skill. It is a holistic programme which provides remedial literacy and numeracy, entrepreneurship and life skills training. The target group comprises single women who are the head of their household, have not attended or completed secondary school, and are either unemployed or in low paying jobs, and therefore find it difficult to manage their family affairs. The Women in Harmony Programme is designed to help increase employment opportunities for low-income women with limited or no skills, particularly single female head of households. Training is offered in two disciplines: Agricultural Production/Grow Box Technology/ Landscaping, and Elderly Care.

Education

Public spending on education was 4.3% of GDP in 2002/03. There are seven years of compulsory education starting at age five. Net enrolment ratios are 91% for primary and 72% for secondary. The pupil–teacher ratio for primary is 19:1 and for secondary 19:1. The school year starts in September.

About 9% of the relevant age group is enrolled in tertiary education (7% of males and 11% of females, 2002/03). Illiteracy among people age 15–24 is 0.2% (2002).

Health

Traditionally good services have suffered somewhat from reductions in public expenditure. 91% of the population uses an Improved drinking water source and 100% adequate sanitation facilities (2002). Infant mortality was 18 per 1,000 live births in 2004 (61 in 1960). At the end of 2003, 3.2% of people age 15 to 49 were HIV positive.

Religion

Mainly Christians (Protestants 30%, Roman Catholics 29%), Hindus 24% and Muslims 6%.

Media

English-language dailies include *Trinidad Guardian*, *Trinidad and Tobago Express* and *Newsday*; *The Bomb*, *The T'n'T Mirror*, *The Probe* and *Sunday Punch* are weeklies. There are 345 TV sets and 80 personal computers per 1,000 people, and 138,000 internet users (2002).

Concerns for the future

Efforts will continue to address the issue of gender-based violence, and look at ways to address the increase in HIV/AIDS infections through education and public awareness.

Key contacts

- Ms Monica Williams
  Director – Gender Affairs Division
  Ministry of Community Development,
  Culture and Gender Affairs
  Cnr Jerningham Avenue & Queen's Park East
  No. 8 Queen's Park East
  Port of Spain
  Trinidad and Tobago
  Tel: +1 868 623 7032 Ext: 165
          +1 868 625 3012
  Fax: +1 868 627 8303
  Email: monicstobago@yahoo.com

Trinidad and Tobago | Summary of gender profile

Gender profile			1990	2000	2004
Population	Total population (000)		94	100	102
	Female population (% of total)		49	49	49
Labour force participation	Female labour force (% of total)		33	33	38
	Female unemployment (% of female labour force)		...	...	...
Education	Adult illiteracy rate (% of people aged 15+)	Female	...	...	1
		Male	...	...	1.2
	Net primary enrolment ratio (% of age group)	Female	...	89	96
		Male	...	92	100
	Net secondary enrolment ratio (% of age group)	Female	...	76	...
		Male	...	69	...
	Gross tertiary enrolment ratio (% of age group)	Female	...	4	...
		Male	...	3	...
Health	Life expectancy at birth (years)	Female	71	73	74
		Male	69	71	71
	Infant mortality rate (per 1,000 live births)		27	22	20
	Prevalence of HIV (% of people aged 15–24)	Female	...	...	...
		Male	...	...	...

Tuvalu

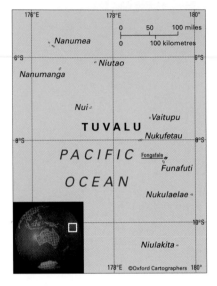

KEY FACTS

Joined Commonwealth: 1978

Capital: Funafuti

GDP growth (%): 5.1%p.a. (2000–04)

Official languages: Tuvaluan, English

Time: GMT plus 12 hours

Currency: Australian dollar

Main telephone lines/1,000 people: 65

Mobile phones/1,000 people: 0

National Women's Machinery

Tuvalu acceded to CEDAW in 1999. Its National Women's Machinery is the Department of Women in the Ministry of Home Affairs and Rural Development.

The National Women's Policy has been reformulated with focus on gender equality. The Policy is an integral part of the Tuvalu National Sustainable Development Strategies, Te Kakeenga.

Priority concerns for mainstreaming gender issues

Among the 12 critical areas of concern outlined in the 1995 *Beijing Platform for Action*, the Government of Tuvalu places priority on the following:

- Education and training of women
- Women and health
- Women and the economy.

Violence against women

Reports of violence against women are rare, but there is a lack of data. The police seek to address violence against women using traditional and customary methods of reconciliation rather than criminal prosecution. The law does not address domestic violence specifically, and acts of domestic violence are prosecuted under the assault provisions of the penal code. Domestic violence is not a source of broad societal debate. However, the Women's Department of the Ministry of Home Affairs sponsored a well-received national radio discussion on violence against women, in which the police encouraged women to report domestic violence. The police practise a 'no drop' policy under which they cannot drop charges in cases of domestic violence. There are currently no shelters or hot lines for abused women.

Women in power and decision-making

Participation by women in government and politics is limited, largely due to traditional perceptions of women's role in society. There are no female members of parliament or cabinet ministers. Two women ran for election to parliament in 2006 but both lost. Women normally hold a subordinate societal position, constrained both by law in some areas and by traditional customary practices. Nonetheless, women increasingly hold positions in the health and education sectors and were more active politically. In the wage economy, men hold most higher-paying positions, while women hold the clear majority of lower-paying clerical and retail positions.

Education

There are eight years of compulsory education starting at age seven. The pupil–teacher ratio for primary is 25:1 and for secondary 25:1 (2001/02). The school year starts in January. Adult illiteracy is less than 5%.

Health

There is a hospital on Funafuti and dispensaries on all the permanently inhabited islands. Health is generally good; there are occasional outbreaks of mosquito-borne dengue fever but no malaria. 93% of the population uses an improved drinking water source and 88% adequate sanitation facilities (2002). Infant mortality was 36 per 1,000 live births in 2004.

Religion

Mainly Christians, mostly of Church of Tuvalu (Ekalesia Tuvalu), autonomous since 1968 and derived from the Congregationalist foundation of the London

Missionary Society. There are small Roman Catholic communities on Nanumea and Nui and some Seventh Day Adventists and Baha'is.

Media

The government publishes *Tuvalu Echoes* fortnightly in English, and a news sheet, *Sikuleo o Tuvalu*, in Tuvaluan. Each island has a radio station and the Tuvalu Broadcasting Service transmits daily, but access to TV broadcasts is via satellite. There are 1,300 internet users (2002).

Concerns for the future

An issue of particular concern to Tuvalu is the uncertainty of Tuvalu's future because of climate change, as it compromises all efforts of gender development and the survival of people.

Key contacts

- Ms Saini T Simona
  Director of Women
  Ministry of Home Affairs and Rural Development
  Government New Building
  Private Mail Bag, Vaiaku
  Funafuti Island
  Tuvalu
  Tel: +688 20 328/9
  Fax: +688 20 821
  Email: iniona@hotmail.com
          miarud@tuvalu.tv

Tuvalu | Summary of gender profile

Gender profile			1990	2000	2004
Population	Total population (000)		...	11	10
	Female population (% of total)		...	52.5	...
Labour force participation	Female labour force (% of total)		...	...	...
	Female unemployment (% of female labour force)		...	...	...
Education	Adult illiteracy rate (% of people aged 15+)	Female	...	...	...
		Male	...	...	...
	Net primary enrolment ratio (% of age group)	Female	...	100	...
		Male	...	100	...
	Net secondary enrolment ratio (% of age group)	Female	...	73	...
		Male	...	83	...
	Gross tertiary enrolment ratio (% of age group)	Female	...	...	...
		Male	...	...	...
Health	Life expectancy at birth (years)	Female	...	69	...
		Male	...	65	...
	Infant mortality rate (per 1,000 live births)		43.5	34.9	36
	Prevalence of HIV (% of people aged 15–24)	Female	...	...	...
		Male	...	...	...

Uganda

KEY FACTS

Joined Commonwealth: 1962

Capital: Kampala

GDP growth (%): 3.6% p.a. 1990–2001

Official language: English

Capital: Kampala

Time: GMT plus 3 hours

Currency: new Uganda shilling (NUSh)

Main telephone lines/1,000 people: 2

Mobile phones/1,000 people: 30

National Women's Machinery

Uganda ratified CEDAW in 1985. Its National Women's Machinery is the Department of Gender, Culture and Community Development in the Ministry of Gender, Labour and Social Development. Its role is to create awareness on the need to address gender concerns, to ensure that initiatives, programmes, policies and laws address gender, culture and community development concerns, and to support the enhancement of the capacity of communities and stakeholders to deliver services effectively. The Department has adopted a participatory approach, where target beneficiaries participate in the planning, implementation, monitoring and evaluation of its programmes.

The National Women's Councils Statute 1993, established the Women's Council. It is a six-tier structure beginning at the village level, through district level, to national level. Through the councils, women are empowered to coordinate their activities and communicate their specific needs to the various levels of community planning.

The Directorate of Mass Mobilisation, Gender and Interest Groups in the Movement Secretariat were established in 1998. It is actively involved in political awareness, conscious-raising and sensitisation on gender related issues. The Directorate works through the structure of local councils and movement committees. The secretariat for women at the village, parish, sub-county and district level mobilises women and acts as their mouth-piece whenever necessary. There is at least one women's development group in every district.

The National Association of Women Organisations in Uganda (NAWOU) is the umbrella body for women organisations in Uganda. It was established in 1993, and is charged with the coordination of the activities of all women NGOs, groups and clubs.

The National Gender Policy was approved in 1997 by the government, as part of its policy of mainstreaming gender concerns in the national development process. The policy outlines strategies to achieve these objectives and the institutional framework, including roles and responsibilities of the line ministries and other stakeholders. The National Action Plan on Women was adopted in 1999, with the goal of achieving equal opportunities for women by empowering them to participate in and benefit from the social economic and political development.

Uganda is ranked at 145 in the Gender-related Development Index (GDI) in the *UNDP Human Development Report 2006*.

Priority concerns for mainstreaming gender issues

Among the 12 critical areas of concern outlined in the 1995 *Beijing Platform for Action*, the Government of Uganda, has identified the following, in order of priority, for national action:

1. Women in poverty / Women in the economy

2. Women and health

3. Human rights of women / Women in power and decision-making

4. The girl-child / Education and training of women

5. Violence against women

Women in poverty

Specific programmes have been established to address the problems of poverty. One such initiative is the Poverty Eradication Action Plan (PEAR) which establishes the policy framework for the eradication of poverty and prioritises public actions across sectors for the objective of poverty eradication through participatory approaches. A complementary but comprehensive plan on modernisation of agriculture has also been developed to contribute to the eradication of poverty. Other initiatives include programmes of micro finance to the deserving groups at concessional terms, and skill-development programmes which are organised to benefit specific groups. Non-governmental organisations and civil society have also played a complementary role in the fight against poverty.

Education

Public spending on education was 2.5% of GDP in 1999/2000. The primary net enrolment ratio is 16% (2002/03). The pupil–teacher ratio for primary is 53:1 and for secondary 18:1. The school year starts in February.

About 3% of the relevant age group is enrolled in tertiary education (2002/03). About 40% of all undergraduates are female (September 2003). Illiteracy among people age 15–24 is 19.8% (13.7% for males and 26.0% for females, 2002).

Health

Trained medical assistants (many of whom practise privately) make up to some extent for the lack of doctors. Formal health facilities, which are adequate everywhere except in the north of the country, are mostly provided by non-governmental organisations. 56% of the population uses an improved drinking water source and 41% adequate sanitation facilities (2002). Infant mortality was 80 per 1,000 live births in 2004 (133 in 1960). The chief causes of death among adults are AIDS-related illnesses, tuberculosis, malaria, and illnesses related to maternity; among children, malaria, pneumonia, diarrhoea. Uganda was the first African country openly to confront the menace of AIDS; the government runs a comprehensive information campaign directed at the general public. At the end of 2003, 4.1% of people age 15 to 49 were HIV positive.

Women and health

In the health sector, Uganda has prioritised healthcare services in the following areas; HIV/AIDS, tuberculosis, immunisation of children, child nutrition, reproductive and maternal healthcare. Emphasis is also placed on access to safe and clean water by the population. However access to treatment for those already living with HIV/AIDS is a national challenge and requires concerted efforts from the international community. Women make up 52% of those infected with the disease.

Religion

Christians 70% (mainly Roman Catholics and Protestants), Muslims 15%, and most of the rest holding traditional beliefs, which often coexist with other religions.

Media

English-language dailies include *New Vision* (state-owned) and *The Monitor*; and *The EastAfrican* is published weekly. Several private TV channels and radio stations were launched after liberalisation of the media in 1993. There are 18 TV sets and 4 personal computers per 1,000 people, and 125,000 internet users (2002/2003).

Concerns for the future

Uganda is working to implement the Social Development Sector Strategic Investment Plan 2003–2008, which defines

Uganda | Summary of gender profile

Gender profile			1990	2000	2004
Population	Total population (000)		17,758	24,309	27,821
	Female population (% of total)		50.3	50	50
Labour force participation	Female labour force (% of total)		47	48	48
	Female unemployment (% of female labour force)		1.3	...	3.9
Education	Adult illiteracy rate (% of people aged 15+)	Female	56.5	43.2	42.3
		Male	30.7	22.5	23.2
	Net primary enrolment ratio (% of age group)	Female	...	...	99
		Male	...	...	97
	Net secondary enrolment ratio (% of age group)	Female	...	12	14
		Male	...	14	16
	Gross tertiary enrolment ratio (% of age group)	Female	1	2	3
		Male	2	3	4
Health	Life expectancy at birth (years)	Female	48	45	49
		Male	44	45	48
	Infant mortality rate (per 1,000 live births)		93	85	80
	Prevalence of HIV (% of people aged 15–24)	Female	...	7.8	...
		Male	...	3.8	...

interventions for promotion of gender equality. There is focus on strengthening gender-planning capacity by increasing training and strengthening the legal framework and reforming laws where necessary.

Key contacts

- Mrs Jane S Mpagi
  Director, Gender and Social Development
  Ministry of Gender, Labour and Social Development
  PO Box 7136
  Kampala
  Uganda
  Tel: +256 41 251401/341034
  Fax: +256 41 256374/257869
  Email: mglsd@swiftuganda.com
             sanyumpagi2@yahoo.co.uk

- Mr Ralph William Ochan
  Permanent Secretary
  Ministry of Gender, Labour & Social Development
  2 Lumumba Avenue
  Simbamanyo Building
  PO Box 7136
  Kampala
  Uganda
  Tel: +256 41347 854/5/341034
  Fax: +256 41256 374
  Email: ps@mglsd.go.ug

United Kingdom

KEY FACTS

Capital: London

GDP growth (%): 2.5% p.a. 1990–2001

Official language: English

Time: GMT plus 0–1 hour

Currency: pound sterling (£)

Main telephone lines/1,000 people: 591

Mobile phones/1,000 people: 912

National Women's Machinery

The United Kingdom ratified CEDAW in 1986 and its Optional Protocol in 2004. Its National Women's Machinery is the Women and Equality Unit (WEU) in the Department of Communities and Local Government. The WEU works to reduce and remove barriers to social participation, improve legislative and institutional frameworks for equality, and support socio-economic opportunities for women. It is leading the development of a more integrated approach across government on equality, intervening when the normal processes of government would not deliver its gender equality objectives. The WEU leads legislation, monitors and evaluates the impact of policies, and measures improvements in gender equality against public service targets.

The Women's National Commission (WNC) is the official, independent, advisory body giving the views of women to the Government. It was established in 1969 and works alongside the WEU. It is an umbrella organisation representing women and women's organisations in England, Northern Ireland, Scotland and Wales to ensure that women's views are heard in public debate. It is the only organisation of this kind in the UK. The WNC is an advisory non-departmental public body therefore it is fully funded by government, but is able to freely comment on government policy.

Supported by the WEU, The Ministers for Women are responsible for promoting and ensuring that work on equality across government is coordinated effectively. The aim is to reduce and remove some of the barriers that currently face under-represented groups – in particular, the needs of black and minority ethnic women. It also works to improve the legislative and institutional frameworks for equality and support economic opportunities for women.

The Women and Work Commission (WWC) was set up by the Prime Minister in 2004 to investigate the causes of the gender pay gap, and to improve opportunities for women in the workplace. An Action Plan was produced in 2006, setting out a comprehensive package of measures across government to enable more women to realise their potential and to reduce the gender pay gap.

The Equality Act 2006 introduced Gender Duty from April 2007, requiring public authorities to eliminate unlawful discrimination and promote equality between women and men. The Equality Act also created the Commission for Equality and Human Rights (CEHR) which was given royal assent in 2006. The CEHR will take over the functions of the Equal Opportunities Commission, the Disability Rights Commission and the Commission for Racial Equality. It will also combat discrimination on the grounds of age, religion and sexual orientation.

The United Kingdom is ranked at 18 in the Gender-related Development Index (GDI) in the *UNDP Human Development Report 2006.*

Priority concerns for mainstreaming gender issues

Among the 12 critical areas of concern outlined in the 1995 *Beijing Platform for Action*, the Government of the United Kingdom has identified the following, in order of priority, for national action:

1. Women in the economy / Women in poverty

2. Violence against women

3. Human rights of women

4. Institutional mechanisms for the advancement of women

5. Women in power and decision-making

Followed by: 6. Women and health; 7. Women and armed conflict / Education and training of women; 8. Women in the media; 9. Women and the environment; 10. The girl-child.

Violence against women

Domestic violence affects millions of people. The government is determined to prevent domestic violence happening or recurring, to protect and support its victims, and to bring offenders to justice. The Home Office is working closely with other central government departments, regional government and local partnerships, particularly those responsible for crime and disorder, to ensure an effective, multi-agency response to domestic violence in the context of the Government's Strategic Framework, as set out in the consultation paper Safety and Justice and our Response to it. This approach led to the Domestic Violence, Crime & Victims Act 2004, which is the biggest overhaul of legislation on domestic violence in over 30 years.

Women in power and decision-making

The government does not believe that it would be right to make positive action

compulsory in order to increase the number of women elected. It is for political parties to decide for themselves whether they wish to increase the number of women candidates standing for election for their party and, if so, how to achieve this increase. What the government has done, however, is legislate so that parties can legally use positive measures for this purpose. An increase in the number of women elected would lead to a higher quality of decision-making, reflecting the greater diversity of experience of those making the decisions.

In addition, the UK faces a serious problem of lack of interest in the political system from the electorate. If politics looks old, white and male, it can seem irrelevant and dull to many people, and lead to lower participation rates and a reduction in democracy. Research published by the Electoral Commission suggests that having more women elected representatives actually encourages greater participation rates amongst women more generally. Representation also plays a symbolic role. It is important for decision-makers to be effective role models and to be truly representative of their electors. In the 2005 elections, 29.8% of MPs elected were women.

Women and the economy

The Women and Equality Unit is seeking to identify the barriers to women's economic participation and to address the barriers that act as a deterrent to equality of opportunity in the workplace. It is working to promote an effective work-life balance and to support the government in providing all children with the best start in life. Women who have taken time out of the workplace can find it hard to return to work. The government wants to help such women by removing the barriers which they face – both external, such as lack of childcare and flexible working opportunities, and personal, such as lack of workplace skills and confidence.

Education

Public spending on education was 5.3% of GDP in 2001/02. There are 12 years of compulsory education starting at age five. Net enrolment ratios are 100% for primary and 95% for secondary (2002/03). The pupil–teacher ratio for primary is 17:1 and for secondary 20:1. The school year starts in September.

About 64% of the relevant age group is enrolled in tertiary education (57% of males

United Kingdom	Summary of gender profile				
Gender profile			1990	2000	2004
Population	Total population (000)		57,561	58,900	59,479
	Female population (% of total)		52	51	51
Labour force participation	Female labour force (% of total)		44	46	46
	Female unemployment (% of female labour force)		6.5	4.8	4.2
Education	Adult illiteracy rate (% of people aged 15+)	Female	...	...	...
		Male	...	...	...
	Net primary enrolment ratio (% of age group)	Female	97	100	100
		Male	100	100	100
	Net secondary enrolment ratio (% of age group)	Female	81	95	97
		Male	82	94	94
	Gross tertiary enrolment ratio (% of age group)	Female	29	63	71
		Male	33	53	55
Health	Life expectancy at birth (years)	Female	79	80	81
		Male	73	75	76
	Infant mortality rate (per 1,000 live births)		8	6	5
	Prevalence of HIV (% of people aged 15–24)	Female	...	0	...
		Male	...	0.1	...

and 72% of females, 2002/03). There is virtually no illiteracy among people age 15–24.

Health

The National Health Service (NHS) provides free health care. It has a workforce of around 1 million people and is paid for mainly through general taxation. Cancer, heart disease and stroke are the major causes of death, while accidents are the commonest cause of death under 30. Up to end 1998, 16,028 cases of AIDS had been reported, and there were 33,764 recognised HIV infections. Cigarette smoking is the largest preventable cause of illness and death. About 27% of men and 13% of women drink alcohol to an extent that may put their health at risk. Infant mortality was 5 per 1,000 live births in 2004 (23 in 1960).

Religion

The majority of adherents to a religion are Christians (of a wide variety of denominations); independent churches and new religious movements increased in the late 20th century. There are substantial communities of Muslims, Hindus, Jews and Sikhs.

Media

There are about 120 daily and Sunday newspapers, of which some ten dailies and ten Sunday papers are national. 'Quality' newspapers include *Daily Telegraph* (established 1855), *Financial Times* (1888), *The Guardian* (1821), *The Independent* (1986), *The Scotsman* (1817 as a weekly, daily from 1855) and *The Times* (1785). There are 950 TV sets and 406 personal computers per 1,000 people, and 25 million internet users (2002).

Concerns for the future

There are continuing efforts being put into establishing a work-life balance for women. There are initiatives being affected to assist in this such as tax credits, flexible working hours and better access to childcare services. The government is also determined to prevent domestic violence happening or recurring, to protect and support its victims, and to bring offenders to justice.

Key contacts

- Ms Angela Mason
  Director
  Women's Equality Unit
  Department for Communities and Local Government
  Eland House
  Bressenden Place
  London
  SW1E 5DU
  United Kingdom
  Tel: +44 20 7944 4104
  Fax: +44 20 7944 6457
  Email: angela.mason@
         communities.gsi.gov.uk

United Republic of Tanzania

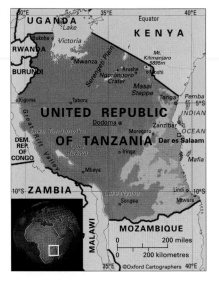

KEY FACTS

Joined Commonwealth: 1961

Capital: Dar es Salaam

GDP growth (%): 1.0 p.a.(1990–2003)

Official languages: Kiswahili, English

Time: GMT plus 3 hours

Currency: Tanzanian shilling (TSh)

Main telephone lines/1,000 people: 4

Mobile phones/1,000 people: 25

National Women's Machinery

The United Republic of Tanzania ratified CEDAW in 1985 and acceded to its Optional Protocol in 2006. Its National Women's Machinery is the Gender Development Division in the Ministry of Community Development, Gender and Children (MCDGC). It was established in 1985, and was raised to the status of Ministry in 1992. The MCDGC has the view of empowering people to recognise their own ability to understand themselves and their environment, and to change their attitudes positively, so that they can take a leading role geared at increased responsibility in improving and managing their living conditions effectively and efficiently.

The Ministry has developed three community development sector policies, which are being implemented and co-ordinated by experts at district, ward, village and sub-village levels. These policies are the Community Development Policy 1996, the Children Development Policy 1996, and the Women and Development Policy 2000.

In 2006, the President reassigned ministerial responsibilities, so that all gender related coordination and management which was formerly under the Vice-President's Office, moved under the control of the MCDGC.

NGOs are partners in development, and their function is to support the government efforts in gender mainstreaming. Their activities cut across different socio-economic sectors from national to grassroots level. The National NGOs Co-ordination Board was established to advise the Minister of NGOs issues.

The United Republic of Tanzania is ranked at 162 in the Gender-related Development Index (GDI) in the *UNDP Human Development Report 2006*.

Priority concerns for mainstreaming gender issues

Among the 12 critical areas of concern outlined in the 1995 *Beijing Platform for Action*, the Government of the United Republic of Tanzania has identified the following, in order of priority, for national action:

1. Human rights of women

2. Women and poverty / Women and the economy

3. Women in power and decision-making

4. Education and training of women

Women in power and decision-making

The Constitution has been amended to provide an increase in women's representation on the basis of proportional representation. There is a constitutional requirement that of the total number of Members of Parliament, women should occupy not less than 30%. In the 2005 elections, this figure was reached, with 30.4% female representation in parliament.

Violence against women

The government has put in place several measures to combat all forms of violence against women. Such measures include a National Plan of Action to combat violence against women and children, and provides for strategies and activities to be implemented by various stakeholders. There are also programmes run by NGOs to combat violence against women, which have resulted in the establishment of counselling centres for women to support victims of violence. Moreover, a campaign to combat the killing of old women suspected of being witches has reduced the killings, with communities now reporting such cases of violence.

Women and the economy

The National Micro-Finance Policy provides guidelines to achieve gender equity in accessing financial services in order to empower women economically.

It directs that special efforts be made to incorporate mechanisms that would make the services accessible to both women and men. The Policy also gives flexibility in regulating micro-finance institutions. Women in small and medium enterprises have been empowered economically by facilitating their access to financial facilities in the form of credit, training in entrepreneurship and business management, and accessing markets. Efforts are being made to assist women to acquire standards certification of their products and to access internal and external markets.

Women and poverty

In an effort to address the issue of feminisation of poverty the government has placed emphasis on formulation of policies, strategies and enactment of laws, which address women who form the majority of the population. In this regard, the Poverty Reduction Strategy (PRS) has allowed the channelling of additional resources to the social sectors, in addition to the economic and infrastructural ones. The social sectors include: education, water, health and cross cutting issues of HIV/AIDS, gender and environment where the feminisation of poverty occurs. Despite these achievements, the challenges which remain to be addressed include: articulation of poverty issues at the grassroots level; from a gender perspective capacity building interventions at the grassroots level to address various policy issues on poverty reduction and involvement of men and women in influencing policy and programme formulation processes to promote ownership and sustainability.

Education

There are seven years of compulsory education starting at age seven (2002/03). The primary net enrolment ratio is 82% (2004/05). The pupil–teacher ratio for primary is 58:1. The school year starts in January.

About 1% of the relevant age group is enrolled in tertiary education (2002/03). Illiteracy among people age 15–24 is 21.6% (19.1% for males and 23.8% for females, 2002 census).

Health

Muhimbili Medical Centre, Dar es Salaam, is the country's principal referral centre and teaching hospital. Other referral hospitals are at Moshi, Mwanza and Mbeya. 73% of the population uses an improved drinking water source and 46% adequate sanitation facilities (2002). Infant mortality was 78 per 1,000 live births in 2004 (142 in 1960). At the end of 2003, 8.8% of people age 15 to 49 were HIV positive.

Women and health

The government has addressed the issue of HIV/AIDS as one of the critical issues and established the Tanzania Council on HIV/AIDS (TACAIDS) which coordinate all AIDS control activities. They have also implemented the National HIV/AIDS policy, which gives guidelines in combating HIV/AIDS. 50% of HIV/AIDS infections are among women. The Strategic Framework for Community Based Protection of Women and Children against HIV/AIDS/STI's is expected to be a guiding tool for individuals, men and women, institutions, government and donor agencies and NGOs, in the struggle to protect women and children from HIV/AIDS infection, and includes measures for facilitating community participation

United Republic of Tanzania	Summary of gender profile					
Gender profile				1990	2000	2004
Population	Total population (000)			26,231	34,763	37,627
	Female population (% of total)			50.6	50.4	50
Labour force participation	Female labour force (% of total)			50	49	50
	Female unemployment (% of female labour force)			4.2	5.28	…
Education	Adult illiteracy rate (% of people aged 15+)	Female		49	…	37.8
		Male		24.5	…	22.5
	Net primary enrolment ratio (% of age group)	Female		50	52	85
		Male		49	51	87
	Net secondary enrolment ratio (% of age group)	Female		…	…	…
		Male		…	…	…
	Gross tertiary enrolment ratio (% of age group)	Female		0	0	1
		Male		1	1	2
Health	Life expectancy at birth (years)	Female		56	48	47
		Male		51	46	46
	Infant mortality rate (per 1,000 live births)			102	88	78
	Prevalence of HIV (% of people aged 15–24)	Female		…	8.1	…
		Male		…	4	…

Religion

On mainland: Muslims 35%, Christians 30%, and most of the rest holding traditional beliefs; (in Zanzibar) Muslims virtually 100%.

Media

The government-owned *Daily News* is published in English; *Uhuru*, owned by the ruling party, *CCM*, in Kiswahili. There are several independent newspapers including *The Guardian* and *Daily Mail*, and weeklies *Arusha Times*, *Business Times* and *The Express*. The first private television channel was launched in mainland Tanzania in 1994 and government-owned TV followed in 2001.

There are 45 TV sets and 6 personal computers per 1,000 people, and 250,000 internet users (2002/2003).

Concerns for the future

Focus will continue on efforts to combat the HIV/AIDS pandemic, and increasing education programmes for women. Programmes will emphasis women's economic empowerment and strengthening implementation of gender equality policies. There will also be continuing efforts focused on combating violence against women, and the human rights of women and the girl-child.

Key contacts

- Mrs Edine Mangesho
  Director of Gender Development
  Ministry for Community Development
  Gender and Children
  PO Box 3448, Dar-es-Salaam
  United Republic of Tanzania
  Tel:　+255 22 213 7677
  Fax:　+255 22 213 8527
  Email: edinemangesho2002@
  　　　yahoo.co.uk

Vanuatu

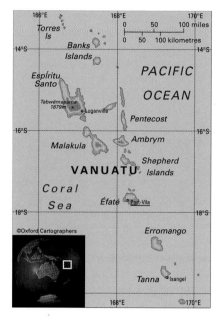

KEY FACTS

Joined Commonwealth: 1980

Capital: Port Vila

GDP growth (%): –0.3% p.a. 1990–2003

Official languages: Bislama, English, French

Time: GMT plus 11 hours

Currency: vatu (Vt)

Main telephone lines/1,000 people: 32

Mobile phones/1,000 people: 38

National Women's Machinery

Vanuatu acceded to CEDAW in 1995. Its National Women's Machinery is the Ministry for Women's Affairs. The Ministry has adopted the philosophy of 'Working in Partnership for Equality' to guide their practice and policy development and is mandated to implement, as well as monitor the implementation of gender-related programmes by other government agencies and NGOs.

The 2004–2007 Statement of Intent has identified health, literacy and the particular needs of rural women as a priority. Gender Focal Points have been established in all Ministries since 2001.

While the government does not as yet have a National Women's Advisory Committee, it established a new National CEDAW Committee in 2006 to oversee the recommendations from the 2004 CEDAW report, prepare for reporting in 2007 and plan for any recommendations emanating from the Concluding Comments from the UN CEDAW Committee.

Vanuatu is ranked at 119 in the Gender-related Development Index (GDI) in the *UNDP Human Development Report 2006*.

Priority concerns for mainstreaming gender issues

Among the 12 critical areas of concern outlined in the 1995 *Beijing Platform for Action*, the Government of the Vanuatu has identified the following, in order of priority, for national action:

1. Violence against women / Women in power and decision-making / Women in poverty / Institutional mechanisms for the advancement of women

2. Education and training of women / Women and health / Human rights of Women

3. The girl-child

4. Women and the economy

Violence against women

The Gender Equity Policy is very explicit in identifying violence against women and discriminatory laws as a hindrance to the advancement of women and developed policy and legislation on violence against women and children including rape, incest, domestic assault and sexual harassment. To move on this policy directive, the Family Protection Order Bill was drafted in 1997. After nearly ten years, it has still not been passed by parliament. The Vanuatu Women's Centre has been a staunch NGO struggling to raise violence against women as a national concern. Started in 1992 by a small group of women, this organisation is now the leading agency that provides counselling, legal aid and public awareness to halt all types of violence against women.

Women in power and decision-making

There are no legal barriers to the participation of women in any fields, but women remain very much in junior positions in both the public and private spheres. Barriers also exist in certain areas that have been seen as 'belonging to men' such that some religions prohibit women from holding certain and senior positions in the church or the Malvatumauri Council of Chiefs. In 2006 the Department of Women's Affairs begun to campaign for the introduction of a quota system as recommended by government at the National Women's Forum. In 2006, there were two women in parliament, one of whom holds a Ministerial portfolio and only the second Minister of State since 1980. The government is acutely aware of the low level of participation of women in decision-making positions, the Department of Women's Affairs has again placed this focus as a high priority area in its work plan.

Education

Public spending on education was 11% of GDP in 2002/03. Primary education, in French or English, is almost universal and provided at nominal charge. There are seven years of compulsory education starting at age six. Net enrolment ratios are 94% for primary and 28% for secondary. The pupil–teacher ratio for primary is 29:1 and for secondary 27:1. The school year starts in February. About 4% of the relevant age group is enrolled in tertiary education (2001/02).

Health

The major hospitals are in Port Vila and Luganville, with health centres and dispensaries throughout the country. 60% of the population uses an improved drinking water source and 50% adequate sanitation facilities (2002). Malaria is widespread. Infant mortality was 32 per 1,000 live births in 2004 (141 in 1960).

Women and health

The vision of the Ministry of Health is to protect and promote the health of all people living in Vanuatu. Since 1992, medical services to the public have been fully subsidised by the government. In other areas, all health expenses are free for those under the age of 18, over the age of 55, people with disabilities and those with certain diseases such as malaria, TB and STIs. Ante-natal and post-natal clinics provide their services free from charges. There are national policies on Primary Health Care, Food and Nutrition and Family Health and Planning. Attitudes of sexuality as a taboo subject need to be dispelled and in its stead, promotion of the heath rights of women and girls need to be escalated and entrenched in the minds of girls, boys, men and women. STIs are a major public health problem because of their impact on maternal and child health. For many women their position in society does not enable them to insist on fidelity, demand condom use, or refuse sex even when they suspect or know that their partner is already infected himself. Further, most women lack the economic power to remove themselves from relationships that carry major risks of infections. A number of factors that contribute to the increase of STIs relate to the prevailing cultural, social and economic norms existing in society which serve to further increase the vulnerability for women and girls to infections.

Religion

Mainly Christians (Presbyterians 37%, Roman Catholics 15%, Anglicans 15%, and Seventh Day Adventists 6%).

Media

Vanuatu Weekly is published by the government in Bislama, French and English. The independent *Vanuatu Trading Post* is twice weekly (Tuesday and Saturday), and *Nasara* weekly. Radio Vanuatu gives daily broadcasts in Bislama, French and English. A television station in Port Vila, opened in 1992, broadcasts in English and French. There are 15 personal computers per 1,000 people and 7,500 internet users (2002/2003).

Concerns for the future

The denial of the right to good health, to primary, secondary, vocational and tertiary education, to employment and training, to legal protection under the law, to enforcement of justice in instances of violation of fundamental rights are not being adequately addressed. More awareness and knowledge of and, use of human rights treaties, need to be conducted.

Vanuatu | Summary of gender profile

Gender profile			1990	2000	2004
Population	Total population (000)		149	191	207
	Female population (% of total)		48.5	48.7	49
Labour force participation	Female labour force (% of total)		46	47	47
	Female unemployment (% of female labour force)		…	…	…
Education	Adult illiteracy rate (% of people aged 15+)	Female	…	…	…
		Male	…	…	…
	Net primary enrolment ratio (% of age group)	Female	…	92	93
		Male	…	94	95
	Net secondary enrolment ratio (% of age group)	Female	16	27	36
		Male	19	31	42
	Gross tertiary enrolment ratio (% of age group)	Female	…	4	4
		Male	…	6	6
Health	Life expectancy at birth (years)	Female	65	70	71
		Male	62	66	67
	Infant mortality rate (per 1,000 live births)		48	38	32
	Prevalence of HIV (% of people aged 15–24)	Female	…	…	…
		Male	…	…	…

Key contacts

- Mrs Hilda Taleo
  Director
  Ministry of Women's Affairs
  Government of the Republic of Vanuatu
  Private Mail Bag 091
  Port Vila
  Vanuatu
  Tel: +678 25 099
  Fax: +678 26 353
  Email: mkaloran@vanuatu.gov.vu
         women@vanuatu.com.vu

initiatives to increase girls enrolment and retention need better coordination processes, identification of best practices and designing good advocacy programmes, especially among traditional and community leaders, is critical. Women's health is still a source of concern, especially HIV/AIDS incidence, sexually transmitted diseases, and maternal morbidity and mortality. Access to health care services also needs to be improved.

Key contacts

- Renee Nglazi
  Permanent Secretary (Ag)
  Gender in Development Division
  Office of the President
  PO Box 30208
  Lusaka
  Zambia
  Tel: +260 1 253 513
  Fax: +260 1 253 493
            +260 1 255 143
  Email: joe.kapembwa@cabinet.gov.zm

reference

Commonwealth map

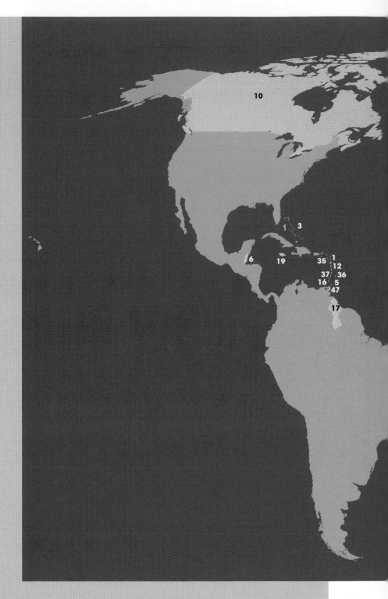

1   Antigua and Barbuda
2   Australia
3   The Bahamas
4   Bangladesh
5   Barbados
6   Belize
7   Botswana
8   Brunei Darussalam
9   Cameroon
10 Canada
11 Cyprus
12 Dominica
13 Fiji Islands (suspended from the councils
    of the Commonwealth in December 2006)
14 The Gambia
15 Ghana
16 Grenada
17 Guyana
18 India
19 Jamaica
20 Kenya
21 Kiribati
22 Lesotho
23 Malawi
24 Malaysia
25 Maldives
26 Malta
27 Mauritius
28 Mozambique
29 Namibia
30 Nauru (special member)
31 New Zealand
32 Nigeria
33 Pakistan
34 Papua New Guinea
35 St Kitts and Nevis
36 St Lucia
37 St Vincent and the Grenadines
38 Samoa
39 Seychelles
40 Sierra Leone
41 Singapore
42 Solomon Islands

43 South Africa
44 Sri Lanka
45 Swaziland
46 Tonga
47 Trinidad and Tobago
48 Tuvalu
49 Uganda
50 United Kingdom
51 United Republic of Tanzania
52 Vanuatu
53 Zambia

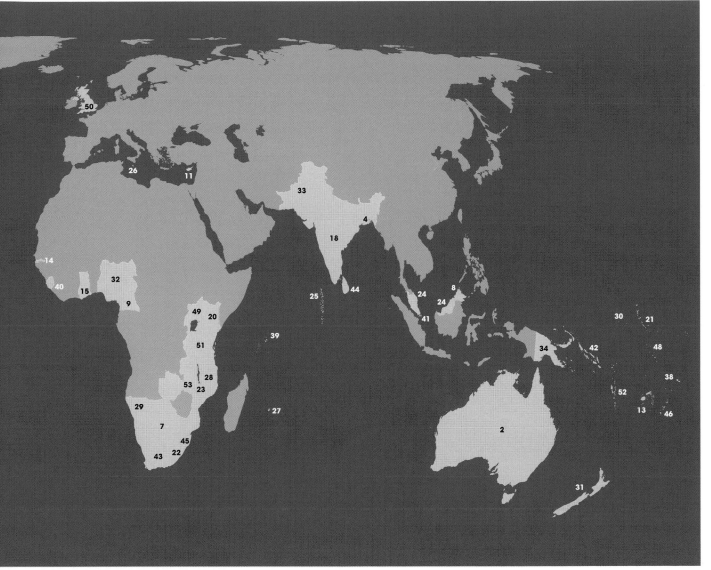

Map source: Commonwealth Secretariat/Maps-in-Minutes™

The designations and the presentation of material on this map, based on UN practice, do not imply the expression of any opinion whatsoever on the part of the Commonwealth Secretariat or the publishers concerning the legal status of any country, territory or area, or of its authorities, or concerning the delimitation of its frontiers or boundaries.

Acronyms

AAP	Africa Action Plan		DDRR	Disarmament, Demobilisation, Reintegration and Rehabilitation
AOA	Agreement on Agriculture		DHS	Demographic and Health Survey
ARROW	Asian-Pacific Resource and Research Centre for Women		DRC	Democratic Republic of Congo
ARVs	Antiretrovirals		EGI	Ethical Globalisation Initiative
AU	African Union		FEDUSA	Federation of Unions of South Africa
AWID	Association for Women's Rights in Development		FGM	Female Genital Mutilation
BEE	Black Economic Empowerment		FPTP	First Past The Post
CAP	Consolidated Appeals Process		GAP	Gender Action Plan
CARICOM	Caribbean Community and Common Market		GATS	General Agreement on Trade in Services
CAT	Committee Against Torture		GEM	Gender Entrepreneurship Markets
CBA	Cost Benefit Analysis		GEM	Girls Education Movement
CBO	Community-based organisation		GMS	Gender Management System
CBWN	Commonwealth Business Women's Network		GRB	Gender Responsive Budget
CEDAW	Convention on the Elimination of All Forms of Discrimination Against Women		HRU	Human Rights Unit
			HSRC	Human Sciences Research Council
CERD	Committee on the Elimination of Racial Discrimination		IANWGE	Inter-Agency Network on Women and Gender Equality
CERF	Central Emergency Response Fund		ICCPR	International Covenant of Civil and Political Rights
CFTC	Commonwealth Fund for Technical Cooperation		ICESCR	International Covenant of Economic, Social and Cultural Rights
CHOGM	Commonwealth Heads of Government Meeting			
COSATU	Congress of South African Trade Unions		ICPD	International Conference on Population and Development
CPA	Commonwealth Parliamentary Association			
CRC	Convention on the Rights of the Child		ICRW	International Center for Research on Women
CSA	Centre for the Study of AIDS		ICT	Information and Communications Technology
DAC	Development Assistance Committee		ICW	International Community of Women Living with HIV/AIDS
DAW	Division for the Advancement of Women			
DAWN	Development Alternatives with Women for a New Era		IDU	Intravenous Drug Users
			IFC	International Finance Corporation
DBS	Direct Budget Support		IGO	Intergovernmental Organisation

ILO	International Labour Organisation
IMF	International Monetary Fund
ITGN	International Gender and Trade Network
IWRAW	International Women's Rights Action Watch Asia Pacific
JAS	Joint Assistance Strategies
LACASSO	Latin American and Caribbean AIDS Support Service Organization
LGBT	Lesbian, Gay, Bisexual and Transgender
LRA	Lord's Resistance Army
LSSP	Land Sector Strategic Plan
MAP	Men as Partners
MDGs	Millennium Development Goals
MFI	Microfinance Institution
NABARD	National Bank for Agricultural and Rural Development (India)
NACTU	National Council of Trade Unions
NEPAD	New Partnership for Africa's Development
NGO	Non-Governmental Organisation
NHRIs	National Human Rights Institutions
NIAS	National Institute for Advanced Studies (India)
NWM	National Women's Machinery
ODA	Overseas Development Assistance
OECD	Organisation for Economic Cooperation and Development
PCF	Post-Conflict Fund
PEAP	Poverty Eradication Action Plan
PEP	Post Exposure Prophylaxis
PMTCT	Prevention of Mother to Child Transmission
PNG	Papua New Guinea
PPASA	Planned Parenthood Association of South Africa
PRODEM	Multi-Sectoral Demographic Project
PRSC	Poverty Reduction Support Credit

PRSP	Poverty Reduction Strategy Paper
PWH	Parliamentarians for Women's Health
REDLAC	Latin American and Caribbean Youth Network for Sexual and Reproductive Rights
RBI	Results-based initiatives
SADC	Southern African Development Community
SAHARA	Social Aspects of HIV/AIDS Research Alliance
SANGRAM	Sampada Grameen Mahila Sanstha
SEWA	Self-Employed Women's Association
SGJ	Sonke Gender Justice
SME	Small and Medium-sized Enterprises
SMME	Small Medium and Micro Enterprises
SRH	Sexual and Reproductive Health
SRHR	Sexual and Reproductive Health and Rights
STD	Sexually Transmitted Disease
STI	Sexually Transmitted Infection
SWAps	Sector-wide Approaches
TRC	Truth and Reconciliation Commission
TRIPS	Trade-Related Aspects of Intellectual Property Rights
UNECLAC	United Nations Commission for Latin America and the Caribbean
UNHCHR	United Nations High Commissioner for Human Rights
UNIFEM	United Nations Development Fund for Women
UNFPA	United Nations Population Fund
UNTAET	United Nations Transitional Administration in East Timor
VCT	Voluntary Counselling and Testing
WAMM	Women's Affairs Ministers Meeting
WBG	World Bank Group
WLUML	Women Living Under Muslim Laws
WTO	World Trade Organization

Commonwealth publications on gender

Mainstreaming Gender in Social Protection for the Informal Economy

Naila Kabeer

In this book Naila Kabeer explores the gendered dimension of risk, vulnerability and insecurity and hence the gendered need for social protection. Her emphasis is on the informal economy because that is where the majority of women, and indeed the poor, are to be found, but it is also where official efforts for social protection are limited.

The book enhances understanding of the constraints and barriers which confine women to more poorly remunerated, casual and insecure forms of waged and self-employment, and considers what this implies for women's ability to provide for their families and cope with insecurity. Kabeer assesses the different kinds of risks, vulnerabilities and insecurities associated with the pursuit of livelihoods in the informal economy and how these vary by gender. She considers different kinds of informal activities (entrepreneurs, home-based workers, petty traders and waged labour) with varying degrees of formality, and distinguishes between urban and rural locations.

Finally, Kabeer sets out policy guidelines for those interested in advancing the social protection agenda and ensuring that gender issues are appropriately addressed.

Dr Naila Kabeer is a Professorial Fellow at the Institute of Development Studies at the University of Sussex, UK.

New Gender Mainstreaming Series on Development Issues
August 2007, 272pp, GBP £20.00 ISBN: 978-0-85092-840-2

Gender and Trade Action Guide: A Training Resource

Catherine Atthill, Sarojini Ganju Thakur, Marilyn Carr and Mariama Williams

The links between gender, trade and development are increasingly being recognised. Developed out of a series of regional workshops, this *Action Guide* explores the different impacts of trade on women and men; provides practical tools on how to take advantage of the opportunities trade can offer to further development, alleviate poverty and promote gender equality; and suggests ways to get gender onto the international trade agenda.

The *Action Guide* is flexible and can be used by trainers or for self-study. It includes case studies, activities, training suggestions and recommended readings, and can be used as a basic introduction or as a resource to develop capacity building for others. It will enable people to take action and apply what is learned to their own context and requirements.

Aimed at a broad spectrum of people coming at the issues from many different angles of trade or gender – government officers in relevant trade sectors, gender specialists, NGOs, regional trade policy advisers and more – it is intended particularly for people who are responsible for capacity building and bringing about change, for example through training, briefing or lobbying.

June 2007, 200pp, GBP £15.00, ISBN: 978-0-85092-862-4

Boys' Underachievement in Education

Jyotsna Jha and Fatimah Kelleher

Gender disparity in education has usually been experienced as disadvantaging girls. Now a new phenomenon of boys' underachievement – both in terms of participation and performance – is appearing in a number of countries.

This book reviews the research on boys' underachievement and presents the arguments that have been put forward to understand its causes. The authors also present new studies from Australia, Jamaica, Lesotho and Samoa; and they use both the research and the evidence from the case studies to explore the causes and policy implications of this trend – the first time a truly cross-regional approach has been applied to the issue.

This book will interest all education policy-makers and analysts concerned to ensure gender equality in school education.

Co-published with the Commonwealth of Learning.

Jyotsna Jha is Advisor, Gender and Education, at the Commonwealth Secretariat, London.

Fatimah Kelleher is Education Programme Officer at the Commonwealth Secretariat, London.

December 2006; 60pp; GBP £20.00; ISBN 978-0-85092-845-7

Gender Mainstreaming in Conflict Transformation: Building Sustainable Peace

Commonwealth Secretariat

Issues of socio-economic development, democracy and peace are inextricably linked to gender equality. The main argument of *Gender Mainstreaming in Conflict Transformation: Building Sustainable Peace* is that gender equality needs to be placed on the policy and programme agenda of the entire spectrum of peace and conflict-related initiatives and activities in order to achieve conflict transformation. These include conflict prevention and early warning mechanisms; peace negotiations and agreements; peacekeeping, disarmament, demobilisation and reintegration; truth and reconciliation commissions; post-conflict reconstruction; and peace building and peace education.

Gender Mainstreaming in Conflict Transformation: Building Sustainable Peace grew out of a series of symposia and workshops held by the Commonwealth Secretariat in the post-Beijing decade in collaboration with other partners.

2005; 232pp, GBP £12.99; ISBN 978-0-85092-754-2

Mainstreaming Informal Employment and Gender in Poverty Reduction: A Handbook for Policy Makers and Other Stakeholders

Martha Alter Chen, Marilyn Carr and Joann Vanek

In this book, the authors highlight the lack of attention to employment, and especially informal employment, in poverty reduction strategies. They point to the links between being informally employed (as a woman or a man) and being poor. They do this within the context of major changes relating to economic restructuring and liberalisation and map out the impacts on different categories of informal producers and workers, both men and women.

The book draws widely on recent data and evidence of the global research policy network Women in Informal Employment: Globalising and Organising (WIEGO), as well as the knowledge and experience of the grassroots organisations in the network. Liberally illustrated with practical examples, it provides a convincing case for an increased emphasis on informal employment and gender in poverty reduction strategies, and sets out a strategic framework which offers guidelines for policy makers seeking to follow this approach.

New Gender Mainstreaming Series on Development Issues
2004; 248pp; GBP £12.99; ISBN 978-0-85092-797-9

Gender Mainstreaming in Poverty Eradication and the Millennium Development Goals: A Handbook for Policy Makers and Other Stakeholders

Naila Kabeer

Naila Kabeer brings together a set of arguments, findings and lessons from the development literature and the field of poverty eradication, which demonstrate that gender inequality is a critical factor in poverty and must be incorporated into poverty eradication strategies. She examines the relationship between gender equality and economic growth, and concludes that although there does appear to be a trade-off between gender inequality and economic growth in the short term in some economies, policies aimed at achieving gender equality are essential for long-term, sustainable and equitable development. The book illustrates the transformatory potential of increasing women's access to education and literacy; to paid work, particularly waged employment; and to political representation.

New Gender Mainstreaming Series on Development Issues
2003; 86pp; GBP £12.99; ISBN 978-0-85092-752-8

Gender Mainstreaming in HIV/AIDS: Taking a Multisectoral Approach

By December 2001, 24.8 million people had died from HIV/AIDS and 40 million people were living with the disease. Women, especially young women, had increasing infection rates and by 2002 the death rate among women was almost as high as that among men. This fed growing recognition that HIV/AIDS is not solely a health problem and that, to successfully address the pandemic, a gender perspective has to be mainstreamed into a broad-based and multi-sectoral response.

The Commonwealth approach to gender mainstreaming is the Gender Management System (GMS) a holistic, system-wide approach to bringing a gender perspective to bear in the mainstream of all government policies, plans and programmes. Efforts to contain the spread of HIV/AIDS challenge governments and communities to develop policies and programmes that are dynamic and react to the pandemic as it evolves. This calls for strong and creative leadership, including political will at the highest level and partnerships with all sectors of society.

Gender Mainstreaming in HIV/AIDS offers case studies from developing and developed countries. They illustrate how programmes promoting HIV prevention by addressing gender (and the social and economic factors that increase people's risk of infection) are most likely to succeed in changing behaviour. The book also contains an extensive list of on-line resources. It will be useful to development policy-makers, field staff and others addressing the HIV/AIDS pandemic from a gender-aware, multisectoral perspective.

New Gender Mainstreaming Series on Development Issues

Co-published with the Maritime Centre of Excellence for Women's Health (Dalhousie University and the IWK Health Centre).

2002; 164pp; GBP £8.99; ISBN 978-0-85092-655-2

Acknowledgements

The publishers hereby acknowledge the assistance of all the contributors who have helped in the production of this publication.

Rupert Jones-Parry, Editor

Ann Keeling, Commonwealth Secretariat

Sarojini Ganju Thakur, Commonwealth Secretariat

Auxilia Ponga, Commonwealth Secretariat

Meena Shivdas, Commonwealth Secretariat

Elsie-Bernadette Onubogu, Commonwealth Secretariat

Fatimah Kelleher, Commonwealth Secretariat

Mamusa Siyunyi, Commonwealth Secretariat

Christabel Gurney, Editorial

Samantha Masters, Design

Sandra Stafford, Editorial

Sara Austen, Nexus

Yvonne Gertenbach, Nexus

Simon Goodlad, Nexus

Marvin Kuzamba, Nexus

Thandi Meets, Nexus

Sources consulted for country profiles

Australian Government Office for Women

Cabinet Office, Gender in Development Division, Zambia

Council of Women of Brunei

Department of Communities and Local Government, United Kingdom

Department of Families, Community Services and Indigenous Affairs, Australia

Department of State for Women's Affairs, The Gambia

Federal Ministry of Women's Affairs, Nigeria

Ministry for the Advancement of Women and the Family, Cameroon

Ministry for the Family and Social Solidarity, Malta

Ministry of Child Development and Women's Empowerment, Sri Lanka

Ministry of Community Development and Gender Affairs, Women's Bureau, Dominica

Ministry of Community Development, Culture and Gender, Trinidad and Tobago

Ministry of Community Development, Gender and Children, Tanzania

Ministry of Community Development, Papua New Guinea

Ministry of Community Development, Youth and Sports, Women's Desk, Singapore

Ministry of Education, Women's Affairs and Culture, Tonga

Ministry of Gender and Family, Maldives

Ministry of Gender Equality and Child Welfare, Namibia

Ministry of Gender, Kenya

Ministry of Gender, Labour and Social Development, Uganda

Ministry of Gender, Lesotho

Ministry of Gender, Malawi

Ministry of Health, Human Services, Family Affairs and Gender Relations, Division of Gender Relations, St Lucia

Ministry of Home Affairs and Rural Development, Department of Women, Tuvalu

Ministry of Home Affairs, Gender Co-ordination Unit, Swaziland

Ministry of Human Development, Women's Department, Belize

Ministry of Human Services and Social Security, Women's Affairs Bureau, Guyana

Ministry of Justice and Public Order, Cyprus

Ministry of Labour and Home Affairs, Botswana

Ministry of Labour and Public Administration, Antigua and Barbuda

Ministry of National Mobilisation, Social Development, NGO Relations, Family, Gender Affairs, St Vincent and the Grenadines

Ministry of Social Affairs and Employment, Seychelles

Ministry of Social and Community Development, and Gender Affairs, St Kitts and Nevis

Ministry of Social Development, Grenada

Ministry of Social Transformation, Barbados

Ministry of Social Welfare, Gender and Children's Affairs, Sierra Leone

Ministry of Women and Child Development, India

Ministry of Women and Children's Affairs, Ghana

Ministry of Women Development, Pakistan

Ministry of Women, Community and Social Development, Samoa

Ministry of Women, Malaysia

Ministry of Women, Social Welfare and Training, Fiji Islands

Ministry of Women's Affairs, New Zealand

Ministry of Women's Affairs, Vanuatu

Ministry of Women's and Children's Affairs, Bangladesh

Ministry of Youth, Sports and Women's Affairs, Solomon Islands

Office of the Prime Minister, Bureau of Women's Affairs, Jamaica

Office of the Prime Minister, Grenada

Status of Women Canada

The Government of The Bahamas

Women and Equality Unit, United Kingdom

Statistics sourced from the World Bank Group Database of Gender Statistics.

Country data gathered from the Convention on the Elimination of All Forms of Discrimination Against Women (CEDAW) website.

Information on in-country contacts is current as at 30 April 2007.